Walter Blair
University of Chicago

Theodore Hornberger
University of Pennsylvania

Randall Stewart
Vanderbilt University

AMERICAN LITERATURE

a brief history

SCOTT, FORESMAN AND COMPANY

Chicago   Atlanta   Dallas   Palo Alto   Fair Lawn, N.J.

Acknowledgments

The authors are grateful to the publishers who have given permission to reprint excerpts from the following poems: "The Waste Land" and "The Lovesong of J. Alfred Prufrock" from *Collected Poems 1909-1962* by T. S. Eliot, copyright, 1936, © 1962, by Harcourt, Brace & World, Inc. "Night" and "Roan Stallion" by Robinson Jeffers, copyright, 1925, and renewed, 1953, by Robinson Jeffers. Reprinted by permission of Random House, Inc. "To the Stone-Cutters" by Robinson Jeffers, copyright 1924, and renewed, 1951, by Robinson Jeffers. Reprinted by permission of Random House, Inc. "Patterns" by Amy Lowell, copyright, 1915, by Houghton Mifflin Company. "An Ode in Time of Hesitation" from *Poems of William V. Moody* by William Vaughn Moody, copyright, 1901, by Houghton Mifflin Company. "Man Against the Sky" from *Collected Poems* by Edward Arlington Robinson, copyright, 1953, by The Macmillan Company.

Acknowledgment is also due for the original handwritten material appearing on the cover: "Route of Evanescence" by Emily Dickinson, courtesy of the Trustees of the Boston Public Library. "O Captain, My Captain" by Walt Whitman, courtesy of the Bettman Archives. Selections from the writings of John Greenleaf Whittier, courtesy of the Chicago Historical Society.

This volume presents a brief historical survey of American literature. The two parts of each of the six chapters offer (a) the intellectual background of American literature and (b) a survey of literary trends. Each chapter is followed by a chronological table of events significant to or in American literature. Brief biographies and evaluations of American writers are presented alphabetically in supplement to the historical material, and the index directs the student to further information in the text. Appended to each of the biographies is a bibliography of the major works of the author. The student can use these bibliographies as the starting point in developing a list of books that offer significant and enjoyable reading in American literature.

The teacher who is acquainted with the two-volume anthology *The Literature of the United States* will have no trouble recognizing that this historical survey is derived from the interchapter material. But this is not simply a reprinting; changes have been made throughout. The last chapter, particularly, has been extensively revised to bring it up to date.

This history is, therefore, more than an excerpt from a larger work and more than a supplemental textbook. Despite its brevity, the authors have endeavored to make it complete and independently intelligible. Many of the specific works in American literature referred to in this *Brief History* have been printed in a companion paperback, *The Literature of the United States, Short Edition*. Both books will, we believe, prove to be valuable tools for the student.

Walter Blair
Theodore Hornberger
Randall Stewart

CONTENTS

1

THE ENGLISH COLONIES
1588 - 1765

TO TREAD AND PLANT THAT GROUND

"Who can desire more content, that hath small meanes; or but only his merit to advance his fortunes, than to tread and plant that ground he hath purchased by the hazard of his life?"

JOHN SMITH

INTELLECTUAL CURRENTS

The Pattern of Colonial Culture

The story of the colonial period of the United States is, in its main outlines, familiar to all of us. It extends roughly from that first voyage of Columbus in 1492 to the Stamp Act in 1765, which brought to scattered and disunited English settlements the realization of their common interests and strength.

Columbus, seeking a new way of access to the riches of the Orient, found instead a New World and loosed upon it the expansive forces of the western European nations, already restlessly groping toward a new phase of their civilization. In the ensuing struggle for power, England was only gradually and belatedly involved. John and Sebastian Cabot had given her a claim to the northern continent of the new hemisphere, but it was nearly a century before men like Walter Raleigh sought to make good that claim by actual occupation. When it became clear that North America could offer little comparable to the easily won gold of Peru and the silver of Mexico, most Englishmen refused to grow excited over colonies, and many were openly scornful of such costly failures as that at Roanoke Island in 1585. Ultimately, however, their patriotism — a curious blend of nationalism and Protestantism — their renewed awareness of their role as a seafaring people, and their longing for wealth accounted for the tenuous successes of permanent settlements at Jamestown in Virginia in 1607 and at Plymouth in Massachusetts in 1620.

Thereafter the shape of things to come was perceptible to shrewd and well-informed men. From the Puritan Migration of 1628-1640, New England acquired a population of perhaps twenty-five thousand persons, enough to give her a long-enduring economic and cultural leadership in British America. Because it was difficult to administer a colony at a distance of three thousand miles, representative assemblies developed (the first of them in Virginia) which were comparable to the lower house of the English Parliament. From the absorption of the Dutch of New Amsterdam and the Swedes along the Delaware, the pattern of colonial life acquired variety and color. The religious motives of the Catholic Lord Baltimore and the Quaker William Penn lent distinction to the settlement of Maryland and Pennsylvania.

Up and down the Atlantic coastline, villages, farms, and plantations proliferated, and everywhere men sought to build that life which seemed to them desirable, compromising always with the hard facts of their environment and the often conflicting ambitions of their neighbors. By 1700 the colonists numbered more than a quarter of a million; by 1765, approximately a million and three quarters. They had been fortunate in being left pretty much to their own devices, or being interfered with only sporadically and unsystematically. For all their differences — and they had many — they agreed, in the mass, upon one thing: they wanted to control their own affairs. We know now, as Americans in 1765 could not know, that the road from such an agreement to Lexington and Bunker Hill and Independence Hall was inevitable, that the essential truth of their situation lay in Thomas Jefferson's epochal words: "When, in the course of human events, it becomes necessary for *one people*. . . ."

One people! Such the colonists in British America eventually became. Why and how they did so are still puzzling questions, despite the many words which have been written to explain the Revolution. The disintegrative forces of the colonial period were seemingly as powerful as those which operated for cohesion and unity. Intercolonial travel by land was difficult and uncommon. Personal and commercial connections between one colony and England were often closer than those between colony and colony. Marked religious differences prevailed, from Congregational New England to the Anglican establishments in Maryland, Virginia, and the Carolinas. Outside of New England there was little homogeneity of background, for by 1765 one out of every three

Pennsylvanians was German, every other North Carolinian was of Scotch-Irish ancestry, Negro slaves made up almost half the population of Virginia, and in South Carolina and Georgia the whites were actually outnumbered. Nevertheless, all were Americans, with characteristic political and social institutions and with a literature of their own which tells much of what they thought and argued and dreamed about.

Language, folklore, learning, the arts, literary tastes and types, legal, political, and educational institutions — everything except the land itself and a few skills acquired from the Indians — had been brought across the Atlantic Ocean. The process of transplantation had been by fits and starts and by devious routes; it had never been smoothly regular, almost never simple. Always involved in it had been change, adaptation, modification to meet the peculiar circumstances of the new environment. The old ways never worked quite perfectly under the new conditions. Men came who knew how to build houses, but they had to work with the building materials they found — lime for plaster, for example, was hard to come by — and they had to meet the exigencies of climates unlike those to which they had been accustomed. Physicians arrived, their minds stored with botanical medicine, only to discover that America had a flora of its own, whose medicinal use had to be discovered by experiment or learned from the natives. Traditions lingered, but necessity forced the quicker-witted to depend upon first-hand knowledge, and there was a sufficient variety of problems in the lands from Maine to Georgia to call forth all the ingenuity that experience could develop. Decade after decade the processes of transplantation and adaptation were repeated, with infinite minor variations. New men and women came from Europe, bringing new tools and talents and opinions and adapting them as best they could to what they found. Frontier succeeded frontier as immigrants pushed up the streams toward the mountains to find new farms and found new villages. In the growth of the colonies there were few breathing spaces; stability was short-lived, change incessant.

Nor was Europe static. In almost every field of human thought the period was tumultuous, full of conflict and revolutionary change. In economics, the feudal system was giving way to modern capitalism. In politics, the theory of the divine right of kings was dying under the blows of constitutional and contractual concepts. In religion, the schisms and sectarian rivalries which were the aftermath of the Protestant Reformation were hardly yet softened by the principle of toleration, which was eventually to bring a measure of amity. In science, revolution was continuous as Copernicus, Galileo, Bacon, Descartes, Boyle, Newton, and their associates and disciples changed both the world-view of western man and his method of advancing his exact knowledge of the world in which he lived. In literature and the arts, the creative outpouring of the Renaissance was succeeded by the more orderly but by no means barren reign of Neoclassicism.

The colonial era of the United States coincided, in short, with the germinal period of what we call the modern world. Europe, of necessity the chief constant factor to the people who settled in America, was itself becoming a new world. The more intelligent colonists, busy as they were with their own concerns, did not forget that they were participants in affairs of mighty moment, in the rebuilding of an old society as well as in the creating of a new one.

Colonial literature was consequently written as often for European readers as for American. It was produced out of necessity rather than leisure, by men and women who wrote because they had some immediate pressing purpose, economic, religious, or political, which could be furthered by writing.

The Economic Promise

The first and the greatest promise which the New World held out to Europeans was freedom from want. To landless men whose ancestors had been bound for centuries to the soil, America offered room to raise food and clothing, to attain the security of well-stocked barnyards and overflowing granaries. As Captain John Smith put it, "Who can desire more content, that hath small meanes; or but only his merit to advance his fortunes, than to tread and plant that ground he hath purchased by the hazard of his life?"

Colonial literature is therefore rich in accounts of the economic resources of the New World. The prospective immigrant wanted to know, in as much detail as possible, about his chances to earn a living. He did not always find accurate information, because the books about the colonies were often written by promoters whose evaluations were rosily optimistic rather than sober or cautious. From the explorers, travelers, and settlers, however, as well as from the promoters, there came in the course of time an enormous body of information on the topography, soils, plants, animals, and minerals of the various regions of British America. These writings told what would and would not grow. They paid particular attention to timber, because England needed ship supplies and her great forests were playing out. They commented in detail on game and fur-bearing animals, on fisheries, on the probabilities of mines.

The earliest English survey of what is now a part of the United States is Hariot's *Briefe and True Report of the New Found Land of Virginia* (1588). Thomas Hariot was Raleigh's friend and a member of the Roanoke expedition of 1585; his book is not merely the first but also one of the fullest and most accurate prognostications of the various ways in which a living might be earned in the New World. Many of John Smith's writings were of the same nature as Hariot's, and both his *Map of Virginia* (1612) and the *Description of New England* (1616) were read carefully by men who were considering emigration. No colony was launched without a similar "Map" or "True Report" of economic possibilities, followed by a local literature of promotion which was in turn succeeded by reports of progress. Of the many other books that might be named, the most important are Francis Higginson's *New England's Plantation* (1630), William Wood's *New England's Prospect* (1634), Thomas Morton's *New English Canaan* (1637), John Hammond's *Leah and Rachel; or, The Two Fruitful Sisters, Virginia and Mary-Land* (1656), George Alsop's *Character of the Province of Mary-Land* (1666), Daniel Denton's *Brief Description of New-York* (1670), William Penn's *Some Account of the Province of Pensilvania* (1681), Thomas Ashe's *Carolina* (1688), and Gabriel Thomas' *Historical and Geographical Account of the Province and Country of Pensilvania* (1698). These books made it clear that the fundamental needs of food, clothing, and shelter could be satisfied rather more easily in America than in Europe, and they suggested that industry and ingenuity could produce surplus and wealth beyond anything of which the common man in Europe dared to dream.

From the first discovery, indeed, the New World seemed to many a land of marvels, of limitless economic opportunity. The state of mind it created had been germinating over many centuries. The ancients had harbored traditions of wonderful western lands: the Elysian Fields, where happy souls went after death; the Islands of the Hesperides, where golden apples grew; Atlantis, that island continent swallowed up by earthquakes long before the time of Plato. In medieval times men had written of fabulously wealthy islands—Antillia and O'Brazil—somewhere in the western ocean, and the news had slowly circulated that the Norsemen had found a new, rich western continent called Vinland. These stories, combined with the ineradicable conviction that America was close to the legendary treasures of India, China, and the Spice Islands, had prepared the European mind for wonders, and it was duly delighted with the strange new plants and animals and humans of which the explorers wrote. Anything could happen in this New World.

There were only a few skeptics. Samuel Purchas, for example, in *Purchas His Pilgrimes* (1619), expressed the conviction that America was not so wonderful as some people seemed to think. "For what haue they," he wrote, "to oppose to our Elephants, Rhinocerotes, Camels, Horses, Kine, &c. Neither are the naturall fruits of America comparable to those of our World. Whence are their Spices, and best Fruits, but from hence, by transportation or transplantation? As for Arts, States, Literature, Diuine and Humane, multitudes of Cities, Lawes, and other Excellencies, our World enjoyeth still the priuiledge of the First-borne. America is a younger brother, and hath in these things almost no inheritance at all, till it bought somewhat hereof of the Spaniards, with the price of her Freedome." In the eighteenth century there were like-minded men, such as the Comte de Buffon and the Abbé Raynal, who were convinced that the American climate was so enervating that men and beasts degenerated there. Thomas Jefferson sought to refute such critics by compiling tables of the comparative weights of European and American animals and by assembling the skeleton of an American mastodon in his apartments in Paris.

Most Europeans, however, were more than willing to look to America with unbounded optimism, especially when, as often happened, they grew impatient with the state of things in their own civilization. The prevailing temper was that of the English philosopher George Berkeley, who pictured a Muse disgusted with Europe, waiting a better time

> In happy climes, where from the genial sun
>> And virgin earth such scenes ensue,
> The force of art by nature seems outdone,
>> And fancied beauties by the true.

Man was to be better treated by Nature in the western hemisphere. He was, in fact, to rise to new heights, far more impressive than mere economic abundance could attain.

> Westward the course of empire takes its way,
>> The four first Acts already past,
> The fifth shall close the Drama with the day;
>> Time's noblest offspring is the last.

Only the presence of a savage people stood in the way of New World greatness. The Indians, it is true, were not very numerous and, with some exceptions, not very dangerous. Some observers saw the hand of God in the plague which had decimated the New England tribes just prior to the English settlement in that region; others argued that a few heathens should not be allowed to stand in the way of living-room for good, civilized Christians. The prospective settler wanted, of course, to know about the Indians. They were an economic fact to be reckoned with—a possible source of wealth, through trade or conquest, and a probable source of danger, if they resented, as they easily might, the invasion of their hunting grounds by land-hungry Europeans. The Indians, therefore, have a large place in almost every book which surveyed New World resources. Hariot devoted one fourth of his book to their description. Smith was always anxious to estimate their military strength. It cannot be said that the English always dealt justly with the aborigines; Roger Williams and William Penn were exceptional in their concern about obtaining land by purchase and treaty. Most of the settlers proceeded upon the expedient conviction that the Indians who stood in their path were treacherous and inferior animals to be eliminated with as little compunction as the rattlesnakes, the wolves, and the bears. The story of the gradual dispossession of the Indians is one of the blackest chapters in colonial annals.

Other than economic considerations appear in the literature about the Indians. Their novelty, the unsettled problem of their origin (were they, for instance, descendants of the lost Ten Tribes of Israel?), their uncanny skill in woodcraft, their strange social and political organization, their stoic endurance of pain and their sadistic pleasure in torture, their heathen faith—all created an interest which amounted to fascination. The Pocahontas legend, whether or not Smith invented it out of whole cloth, is a good example of the tendency to create a "noble savage." There developed in connection with the Indians the attitude known as primitivism, the glorification of the unspoiled simplicity of the "uncivilized." Primitivism was in the main based upon objection to the complexities and maladjustments of European life. In the colonial period it is more common in the books of Europeans than in those written by persons who had actually been in contact with the savages, although Thomas Morton's *New English Canaan* is a notable exception. Later, in the eighteenth century, primitivism appeared in the poems of Philip Freneau, the essays of Michel Guillaume St. Jean de Crèvecoeur, and the *Travels* of William Bartram. It continued well into the nineteenth century and is an essential part of the philosophical background of James Fenimore Cooper's Leather-Stocking tales and Henry Wadsworth Longfellow's *Hiawatha* (1855).

Colonial literature also mentions occasionally the slow growth of manufacturing, although the full development of industrialization was to come much later. In the "currency tracts" (see *Colonial Currency Reprints*, ed. Andrew McFarland Davis, 4 vols., 1910) one can find a picture of the extent of self-sufficiency provided by age-old home industries such as weaving, and in William Byrd's "A Progress to the Mines" (1732) a brief sketch of colonial ironmaking.

Most of us will agree that the New World fulfilled its economic promise. Like the man in the folk tale whose three wishes were fulfilled, but never quite as he expected them to be, the first Americans did not attain freedom from want as effortlessly as some of them had expected. They had to learn patience and thrift and the most efficient use of their vast new environment, and they had to adjust themselves to other than merely local circumstances. But attain it they did, and colonial literature reveals both the nature and the realization of their desires.

The Religious Life

Next to getting a living, the chief concern of great numbers of the colonists was religion. Some of them, indeed, regarded the saving of souls — their own and those of other people — as the most pressing matter of existence. To understand the men and women who established the pattern of American life we need to know in some detail their religious and theological background and its reflection in literature.

The first thing to remember is that most of the colonists, whatever their church, were keenly aware of the Reformation. The Bible had been in the hands of Englishmen, in their own language, only since 1535, and to most of them it was a fresh and inexhaustible revelation of the will of God. The persecutions of the reign of Queen Mary, the fear of a Spanish invasion (which it was believed would have been swiftly followed by an Inquisition in England), the memory of the Gunpowder Plot of Guy Fawkes, the vexed problem of the royal succession, and the endless series of debates about church government and ritual—all were as close to the English in the early seventeenth century as the events of the period since 1865 are to present-day Americans.

The earliest attempts to colonize reflect the rivalry between Catholics and Protestants. Both Hariot and Smith emphasized the heathenism of the Indians, implying that it was the sacred duty of the English to convert them to the true faith, that is, to Anglicanism, before they could be led astray by the Catholic Spaniards or French. Although the settlers who came to America with any such altruistic intentions were obviously few and far between, six English colonies—Plymouth, Massachusetts Bay, Maryland, Rhode Island, New Haven, and Pennsylvania—were nonetheless founded by religious groups or leaders to whom economic considerations were clearly secondary. Why this was the case can be understood only by reference to the peculiar circumstances of the Reformation in England.

Between Henry VIII's break with the Pope and the end of the reign of Queen Elizabeth, the Church of England had arrived at a *status quo* justly described as moderate Protestantism. The break with Rome was complete. The ruler was the acknowledged head of the English Church; monastic orders had been abolished, and most of the lands accumulated over the centuries by the Church had been nationalized; church services were held in English rather than in Latin; and the people had been provided with the English Bible and the English *Book of Common Prayer*. On the other hand, much that seemed "papist" to the more extreme Protestants remained—the hierarchy of parish priests, bishops, and archbishops, intimately connected with the structure of the civil state; richly ornamented churches and vestments; and set forms of prayer and worship.

English dissent consisted of innumerable groups and individuals who believed that the Reformation had not gone far enough. Some wanted to remove all vestiges of Catholic practices and rituals, placing more emphasis upon the sermon and the Bible as the chief means of bringing souls to Christ—these were ordinarily called Puritans. Others desired to substitute a measure of lay control for the system of benefices, bishops, and archbishops—they were the Presbyterians. Still others wished each congregation to decide for themselves what form of worship they were to follow—these were the Separatists, Independents, or Congregationalists, also sometimes called Brownists, after their first spokesman, Robert Browne (1550?-1633?). In addition, there were many shades of opinion regarding the proper forms of worship and the most desirable form of church government. With the passage of time, differences of opinion about these matters multiplied rather than diminished.

The Anglican leaders sought continuously to enforce conformity to the *status quo*. As early as 1604, James I, speaking of the Puritans, announced, "I shall make them conform themselves or I will harry them out of the land, or else do worse." With the accession of Charles I in 1625, the more militant bishops had the support of a king with absolutist leanings, and unremitting efforts to insure conformity began. Under William Laud, Bishop of London from 1628 until 1633, and thereafter Archbishop of Canterbury, Primate of England, until his execution in 1645, clergymen who failed to follow the prescribed forms of worship were brought into church courts, tried, and punished, most often (as in the case of Thomas Shepard) by being forbidden to exercise any clerical functions. Among them were many of the men who became the leaders of the New England colonies.

The Pilgrims who came to Plymouth were Separatists. Some of them emigrated to Holland, found the atmosphere there too "foreign" for their taste, and determined to settle in America. They were poor and would not have been able to make the voyage in the *Mayflower* had not the necessary capital been provided by a group of "merchant adventurers" of London. William Bradford was the mainstay of the settlement and church which they founded in Massachusetts. In 1692 Plymouth became a part of the Province of Massachusetts Bay.

The Puritans of the Massachusetts Bay Company came to New England only when it became clear that further reform within the English Church was impossible. They took care to bring their charter with them, and they intended to establish a state in which the kind of church they wanted might thrive. In contrast to the Pilgrims, they were wealthy and well educated, many of them being substantial property owners or professional men, university-trained as was their governor, John Winthrop. Furthermore, they were numerous; between 1628 and 1640 there was a constant stream of immigrants. Not all of them were as earnest in their religion as Winthrop and the ministers, but Bay Colony leadership was shrewd. Social, political, and educational institutions were so securely established that no study of the genesis of American life can ignore the Puritan tradition. Before the Puritans had been long in New England, they agreed upon a form of church government which was partly Congregational, partly Presbyterian—the *Cambridge Platform* of 1649. By that time the Westminster Assembly had effected changes not wholly dissimilar within the Church of England, although they were to be largely annulled by the Restoration in 1660.

Puritanism, however, was more than an attitude toward forms of worship and church government. It was then, as it is now, a word used to describe a strait-laced way of life, a concern with moral conduct so great as to lead some individuals to attempt what we now think of as unwarranted control of the personal lives of their neighbors, a rigid repression of acts and fashions that today are no longer considered evil. Such was Puritanism at its worst. At its best it provided men with a sense of social responsibility, an earnestness about life which had in it both intellectual conviction and intense, sometimes even mystic, piety.

Underlying Puritan earnestness was Calvinism, a stern and legalistic theology constructed by the Genevan reformer, John Calvin (1509-1564). Calvinism portrayed God as a sovereign whom man, in the person of Adam, had disobeyed, thereby breaking an inexpressibly sacred and solemn covenant. Upon Adam and all his race, retribution had justly fallen. Through Christ, however, man had been given a second chance, although that chance was extended only to those men whom God had "elected" to be saved. Most men were predestined to damnation, as they deserved. Although one could never be wholly sure of being among the fortunate few for whom salvation was foreordained, life was to be lived in a search for the divine will, as it might be expressed in one's own struggle for serenity, through one's spiritual growth, or as it might be interpreted from events in the external world. To walk uprightly in the sight of God, and to seek to follow His will—these were the aims of the Calvinist and the origin, as has often been remarked, of the "New England conscience."

Calvinism was the dominant theology of the entire colonial period, and it survives to some extent in the formal creeds of most Protestant churches other than the Lutheran. Non-Calvinists have always found it "harsh," chiefly because of its humiliating picture of human nature as utterly corrupt, regenerable only by the grace of God. In its defense two things may be said: it is not difficult for anyone except the blindest optimist to observe unpalatable depths of "cussedness" in human beings, and it is evident that to some individuals (see, for example, Jonathan Edwards in his "Personal Narrative," 1740) the Calvinistic glorification of God gave an exhilaration and a direction to life which few faiths rival.

From the first, Calvinism had its opponents. Of the many that might be described, four are so important to the student of literature that their description is a necessity. These four—Antinomianism, Arminianism, Quakerism, and Deism—had one thing in common: they granted human nature a more dignified place than the Calvinists were willing to grant it. Otherwise, they were most dissimilar. Antinomianism and Arminianism were merely theological positions, not necessarily connected with a particular church any more than was Calvinism itself. Quakerism was and is the doctrine of a religious society, the Friends, theologically not very far removed from Calvinism. Deism was neither theology nor a church, but a philosophical position, a state of mind.

Antinomianism has approximately the place in religion that anarchy has in politics; that is to say, it is the denial of any authority beyond the individual. The Antinomian controversy which shook the Bay Colony to its foundations in 1636 and 1637 ended with the banishment of Anne Hutchinson for spreading, among other heresies, the doctrine that God revealed Himself directly to individuals, so that one could know whether or not one was of the "elect." Such thinking challenged both the Calvinistic concept of the Bible as God's final revelation and the social control which was basic in the thought of such leaders as Winthrop.

Arminianism takes its name from the Dutch theologian, Jacobus Arminius (1560-1609), who held that one could achieve salvation in part through "good works," that is to say, through living a moral and upright life. It was regarded by the Calvinists as derogatory to the sovereignty of God and was one of the "errors" which Edwards was most anxious to refute in his *Freedom of the Will* (1754). When the evangelical preachers of the eighteenth century took religion to the people, "good works" formed a more concrete appeal than abstruse theology, and the Methodist movement particularly became tinged with Arminian thought.

Quakerism is the only one of the many radical Protestant opinions of the seventeenth century which has continued in its original form to be influential to the present day. The people who first called themselves "Children of Light" and, later, the Society of Friends, organized under the leadership of George Fox (1624-1691) in the late 1640's. Their popular name was given them in jest, after Fox had asserted that even magistrates would come to "tremble before the word of the Lord." The Friends believed that the duty of man is to follow the Bible and the "Inner Light," that "pure wisdom" which comes from above. With a quietistic listening for the "openings" from God, they combined the social control of "speaking out" in meeting, by which the promptings of the Inner Light were communicated to and passed upon by other Friends—a control which preserved them from the Antinomian lawlessness. They believed that all men are brethren, that all violence (and especially war) is evil, that worldly distinctions of class and dress are meaningless, that the taking of oaths is blasphemous. They had no professional clergy, and they tended to distrust higher learning. Bitterly persecuted in New England as late as 1677, they established themselves in New Jersey and Pennsylvania, where they became a powerful force for the abolition of slavery and for social reform of many varieties. They produced relatively few writers, but their equalitarianism and humanitarianism have always been influential in American life. John Woolman (1720-1772) was their greatest writer, and Whittier their chief spokesman in nineteenth-century American literature, but the Quaker influence may easily be discerned in the work of Walt Whitman and many lesser figures.

Deism is ordinarily dated from the writings of the English philosopher Lord Herbert of Cherbury (1583-1648). Herbert approached the problem of religion from a purely rational point of view, similar to what we would now call the comparative method. He found that in all ages and in all times, whether pagan or Christian, men had agreed on five axioms: (1) that there is a God; (2) that He ought to be worshiped; (3) that piety and virtue are the essentials of worship; (4) that man ought to repent his sins; and (5) that there are rewards and punishments in a future life. Veneration of the Bible as the revelation of God is wholly absent from this rational analysis, and it is the rejection of revelation which is the distinguishing mark of Deistic thought. In the latter part of the seventeenth century, rationalism spread rapidly, in part as a result of the scientific advance, and there was widespread acceptance of the Deistic view that one could arrive at religious truth by the use of reason. Although the Deistic controversy was primarily an English affair, Increase and Cotton Mather were attacking the Deists before the end of the century, and Edwards' *Divine and Supernatural Light* (1734) would scarcely have been written had it not seemed important to refute the Deistic emphasis upon the place of reason in religion. The best-known Deistic work by a colonial American is Benjamin Franklin's *Dissertation on Liberty and Necessity, Pleasure and Pain* (1725), which its author later accounted an "erratum," or mistake. No reader of Franklin's writings will be long in doubt, however, of his fundamental agreement with Lord Herbert of Cherbury. The Deistic principles of many of the leaders of the Revolution, including Washington, Jefferson, Hamilton, and Ethan Allen, lend credibility to the picture of an American "cult of reason" in the late eighteenth century, but that, together with the mare's nest stirred up by Thomas Paine's *Age of Reason* (1794-1796), must await discussion in another chapter.

Toleration and revivalism, perhaps the most characteristic features of American religious life, also have their origins in the colonial period. Both are still, after all these years, matters for the thoughtful concern of every American.

Roger Williams founded Rhode Island in 1636 as a tiny island of refuge for "heretics" like Anne Hutchinson and the Quakers. He was far ahead of his time, for not until the chartering of Pennsylvania in 1681 was there a second colony ready to receive all victims of religious persecution. Maryland, to be sure, passed a Toleration Act in 1649 as a protection for the Roman Catholics, but Jews and Unitarians were not desired. The American colonies, some of them none too willingly, bowed to the provisions of the Toleration Act passed by Parliament in 1689, and thereafter the principle of religious freedom was given at least lip service. Nonconformists to the dominant pattern of religious life were by no means safe, however, although in later years intolerance to one group or another was often a result of economic competition as much as of religious conviction.

Revivalism, while not wholly native, has probably never flourished elsewhere so consistently as in America. Its origins are to be sought in the religious situation of colonies founded by earnest and pious folk who saw their children slipping away from the faith as life became easier and more secular. This situation developed in New England shortly after 1650 and is signalized by the adoption of the Half-Way Covenant of 1662, which admitted the children of church members to church membership (although not to communion) without the previously required confession of "religious experience." For most of the sixty years thereafter, New England clergymen seized upon every possible opportunity to expound the decadence of religion, the necessity of a return to the ways of the founders, the dangers of apostasy, and the innumerable evidences of divine disfavor in comets, witchcrafts, earthquakes, fires, and storms. Signs of laxity were viewed with alarm in innumerable writings by the Mathers. Cotton Mather's *Magnalia Christi Americana* (1702) is the best-known complaint of the decline of religion and the diminishing influence of the clergy, but sermons to the same effect are so numerous that Perry Miller has described them as a distinct type—the jeremiad.

After 1720, religion was reinvigorated by what is known as the "Great Awakening," which was characterized by widespread revivals which reached the younger folk and the lower classes in all the colonies. Through the Awakening, religion found new leaders and a somewhat broader base; it became perceptibly less intellectual and more emotional. The revivals are believed to have begun with certain Dutch Reformed churches of New Jersey in the 1720's; they soon afterwards appeared in the Scotch-Irish Presbyterian churches of Pennsylvania; by the 1730's they had arrived in New England, where Edwards was soon absorbed in their strange phenomena. Six times between 1729 and 1770 the colonies felt the impulse of the preaching of George Whitefield (1714-1770), an English evangelist who had been associated with the Wesleys in the development of Methodism. Whitefield, who had the advantage of Calvinistic convictions, preached to vast crowds, often out-of-doors, and invariably aroused great enthusiasm. The Baptists and the Methodists also extended their ranks through highly successful revivals, particularly in the southern colonies, in the decades just before the Revolution.

The literature relating to revivalism is enormous; one scholar estimates that there are more than thirty-five thousand separate pieces which refer to the Awakening. Best known, probably, are Edwards' *Some Thoughts Concerning the Present Revival of Religion in New England* (1742) and Charles Chauncy's answer in *Seasonable Thoughts* (1743).

The effect of revivalism was to make religion more the personal concern of the common man than it had been before, and it is not an accident that its development coincided with the spread of a humanitarian concern for the poor and the unfortunate. It has remained characteristic of American Protestantism, although often frowned upon by settled clergymen and the higher economic levels of society. In spite of the fact that it has tended to divide churches and has lent itself to the self-seeking of some unscrupulous evangelists, revivalism has kept its appeal through recognition of the importance of emotional release.

Commonwealth-Building

A third great concern of the colonists and a theme of colonial literature, intimately connected with the economic and the religious, was the political hope which the New World offered. Americans were thinking, from the first, of the possibility of a new kind of state.

John Smith was not alone in observing that there was a parallel between Europe in his time and the declining years of the Roman empire. Although England had become a great and strong nation under Queen Elizabeth, there seemed to be more distressing poverty, more selfish wealth, more injustice and social unrest than there had ever been before. We can now see that feudalism was disintegrating slowly, that hereditary and class privileges had survived longer than serfdom, and that capitalism had not provided men with sufficient social responsibility. Smith is clear enough in his conviction that "rich men for the most part are growne to that dotage, through their pride in their wealth, as though there were no accident could end it, or their life." In America, a land of greater plenty, he believed that merit and industry might find their fair rewards and that all men might work together for the common weal.

Smith's frequent use of the word "commonwealth" is significant, for to his generation a commonwealth was a state in which all citizens — not merely a few — had an interest in the government. This is not to say that Smith was a democrat, for he was not. He vaguely expressed the general dissatisfaction of his time with the political *status quo*. The Renaissance was the age in which American political philosophy was born. Men were dreaming of an ideal commonwealth as they had not been dreaming since Plato in the fourth century B.C.

The political climate of opinion of the age of geographical discovery is suggested by More's *Utopia* (1515-1516) and Bacon's *New Atlantis* (*c.* 1617). Such dreams of a new society were paralleled by the nostalgia of the primitivists, who looked back to a Golden Age in which men lived in amity, untroubled by such bickerings as those produced by the Reformation and the new national rivalries. Talk of a "brave new world" was in the air, and it was not silenced by American experience. So many were thinking of a better state that Shakespeare, in *The Tempest* (*c.* 1610), created an "honest old counsellor," Gonzalo, whose satirical remarks are worth recalling:

I' th' commonwealth I would by contraries
    Execute all things; for no kind of traffic
Would I admit; no name of magistrate;
    Letters should not be known; riches, poverty,
And use of service, none; . . .

All things in common nature should produce
Without sweat or endeavour; treason, felony,
    Sword, pike, knife, gun, or need of any engine,
Would I not have, all foison, all abundance,
    To feed my innocent people. . . .
I would with such perfection govern, sir,
    T' excel the golden age.

At least eight American colonies—Plymouth, Massachusetts Bay, Maryland, Rhode Island, New Haven, Carolina, Pennsylvania, and Georgia—show traces of their founders' thinking in terms of an ideal commonwealth. In most of them religious and economic motives were also involved, but these, too, have their place in the history of political experimentation. The communistic beginnings of the Pilgrims, the theocracy of Massachusetts Bay and New Haven, the toleration principles of Rhode Island, Maryland, and Pennsylvania, John Locke's "ideal" constitution for Carolina, and James Oglethorpe's notion of a refuge for debtors in Georgia—all had political implications. The most discussed experiment is that of Massachusetts Bay.

The full story of the transformation of the dream of an ideal commonwealth into the workaday institutions of British America, not ideal but on the whole far less aristocratic than those of Europe, is highly involved. We should remember, however, that colonial literature reflects at least three processes or developments: (1) the familiar pattern of transplantation and adaptation, in this case of English political and legal institutions; (2) the relative freedom from interference which was the result of unsettled problems of political authority in the mother country; and (3) the growth of democracy and local control, usually attributed to the influence of Separatism, which trained the humble to share in church government.

All are well illustrated in Winthrop's *The History of New England* which describes the conflict between aristocracy and democracy in the Bay Colony. The aim of Winthrop and his companions was to found a theocracy, a state of which the head should be God, the fundamental law His word, the Bible. They wished a Bible commonwealth in which civil authority should contribute in every possible way to the welfare of the Puritan church. As John Eliot said in *The Christian Commonwealth* (1659), "there is undoubtedly a form of Civil Government, instituted by God himself in the holy Scriptures." This conviction, rather than any statutory provision, accounts for the leadership of the clergy in the seventeenth century. The magistrates consulted the "elders," that is, the ministers, in every important debate on policy. But Winthrop had too much of the lawyer's respect for statute and for precedent to throw overboard the common law and the example of England, and it was not long before Massachusetts had a bicameral legislature and a legal code drawn from experience, not from the Bible. Because the Bay Company founders had the foresight to bring their charter with them, their government survived the chaotic conditions of the Civil War in England. The independent attitude of the town of Hingham, described by Winthrop, shows the strength of the ideal of local autonomy in an era which had adopted a modified form of Separatism.

Bradford and Williams reveal in their writings much the same background. From Plymouth, the original Separatist community, we have the *Mayflower Compact* (1620), earliest of American written constitutions and, like Winthrop's speech on liberty, a reflection of the development of Calvinism which is called "Covenant" or "Federal" theology. In it the Pilgrims agreed to "solemnly and mutually in the presence of God, and one of another, covenant and combine our selves togeather into a civill body politick, . . . and by vertue hearof to enacte . . . such just and equall lawes . . . as shall be thought most meete and convenient for the generall good of the Colonie, unto which we promise all due submission and obedience." The *Compact* has a well-deserved distinction. It was Separatism, too, which led Williams to assert his doctrine that the power of the civil state must not serve the purposes of a single church. Other colonies copied the idea of a social compact, and other colonies came gradually to recognize the value of toleration.

The conflict between the ideal of government by the few and the ideal of government by the many runs throughout American literature. In the colonial time it is to be seen in a vast body of writings relating to the theocracy in Massachusetts and the various attempts of men like Cotton Mather to return to the "New England Way." The belief of the ruling classes that things were not going well may be felt in Sewall's *Diary* and Mrs. Knight's *Journal* — the common people were often rowdy and obstreperous. Occasionally the common man found defenders, of whom the most notable was John Wise. His two works, *The Churches Quarrel Espoused* (1710) and *A Vindication of the Government of New-England Churches* (1717), had important political implications and were reprinted in 1772, in the midst of the Revolutionary crisis.

The colonies did not achieve the ideal commonwealth, but they present a consistent picture of an effort to serve the common interest of all, according to the lights of the men who led them. "Their Cheif Red Letter day," Mrs. Knight said truly of the inhabitants of Connecticut, "is St. Election, which is annually Observed according to Charter, to choose their Governor; a blessing they can never be thankfull enough for, as they will find, if ever it be their hard fortune to loose it."

Superstition and Science

The reader of colonial literature cannot fail to notice that most writing of the era is punctuated with "It pleased God" and "a special providence of God appeared"—recognitions of the immediate concern of the Deity for His universe and His people. Although most conspicuous in the historical works and diaries of the Puritans, these expressions may readily be found in the reports of such hard-bitten gentlemen of fortune as John Smith.

In Bradford, Winthrop, Sewall, and Mather, however, such references are often accounted superstitious by latter-day readers, who live in a world wherein the uninterrupted order of nature is taken for granted and a scientific world-view prevails. We need to reflect briefly, therefore, upon the place of science in the thought of colonial Americans, especially when we encounter Sewall's comment on Mather's pulpit exposition of the Copernican hypothesis: "I think it inconvenient to assert such Problems."

The age unquestionably accepted the providential order of nature, a world in which the Lord intervened not merely to mark the sparrow's fall but to reward and punish in accordance with His inscrutable ends. We must not conclude too easily, however, that the seventeenth and eighteenth centuries were deliberately unscientific. On the contrary, they were the age of Bacon, Boyle, Descartes, Newton, Laplace, and many other first-rank scientists, whose search for truth was emulated, although not of course with such brilliant success, on this side of the Atlantic. Benjamin Franklin was not the first American, although he remains the most famous early experimenter, to study natural phenomena.

Colonial literature shows both a persistent scientific curiosity and the universal economic motive for the investigation of nature. Hariot impressed the Indians with mathematical instruments, the lodestone, and spring clocks, and Smith fascinated Opechancanouh with his sign-language exposition of astronomy and geography. Both men, moreover, classified and described natural phenomena in accordance with the best methods at their command, as did their innumerable successors among the travel writers and promoters. Bartram was a skilled botanist. Bradford, as likely as anyone to see the hand of God in all events, found room to "leave it to naturallists to judge" the value of his hypothesis of the results of earthquakes, and did not find his view of providence inconsistent with the search for natural causes of the immoralities present in 1642. Byrd's journals abound in medicinal, botanical, and zoölogical observations; both he and Cotton Mather were members of the Royal Society of London and contributed to its *Philosophical Transactions*, the foremost scientific periodical of the age.

There is abundant evidence, in short, that the sense of the nearness of God and the operation of His providence did not outlaw the study of nature. Sewall's "inconvenient" in response to Mather was probably not the expression of opposition to scientific knowledge, but the more common feeling that science and religion ought not to be mixed. Despite the dominance of theology, actual distrust of science is rarely encountered in the colonial era.

The Fine Arts

Painting, sculpture, music, and architecture, which now lend much to the richness of life and literature, were of relatively little interest to the colonists and are mentioned only seldom in their writings. We need not review the details of their beginning, but we should remember that they existed and that they manifested both the invariable pattern of transplantation and adaptation and the dominance of religion in the daily life of the people.

Painting was devoted almost exclusively to the portraiture of much-loved clergymen or the members of well-to-do families. There were portraits painted in New England as early as 1641; one of the best known is that of Samuel Sewall made by a native amateur sometime before 1730. The first portrait engraving known to have been made in the British colonies was a woodcut of Richard Mather dating from 1670; the first line engraving on copper, a portrait of Increase Mather made about 1701; the first mezzotint for framing, a portrait of Cotton Mather made in 1727.

Sculpture was confined, prior to the nineteenth century, to the carving of angels, death's-heads, and other symbols upon tombstones, and to carving in wood. Yet the stroller in colonial graveyards often comes away with a clearer notion of our ancestors' surprising fearlessness of death, and the visitors to museums containing ships' figureheads and other woodcarvings can gain a fresh impression of the imagination of a seafaring, hand-skilled folk.

Music at first consisted of the singing of psalms, in which the Puritans took great pains. The first book published in America was the famous *Bay Psalm Book* (1640). The historians of music also make much of the instrumental performance of religious compositions among the early German settlers in Pennsylvania. Secular music was rare before the Revolution, even in the South.

Of all the arts, architecture is most closely related to the life of the people, and, together with such crafts as weaving, dyeing, silver-working, and cabinetmaking, it is most interesting to the student of colonial civilization. Houses and their furnishings were made by craftsmen without the guidance of architects and decorators, and ordinarily with native materials. The styles of the Old World were carried over and adapted to the new materials and climates with such variety as might be expected in a people drawn from all the corners of Europe. In architecture, to take a single example, such eclecticism was produced as may be observed by a half-hour's stroll through any modern subdivision. Here may be found the architectural legacies of the half-timbered gables of Renaissance England, the multiple-flued chimneys of the Jacobean era, the small, slanting dormer windows of Dutch New Amsterdam, the stuccoed walls of Spanish St. Augustine, and innumerable other importations. But it is the steepled church, perhaps, which is the most characteristic production of colonial America, where men admired or remembered the many London churches built by Sir Christopher Wren after the Great Fire of 1666.

The Circumstances of Literary Production

In addition to a knowledge of the intellectual and social backgrounds of colonial times, we need to have some conception of the circumstances of literary production in the years before 1765, for the state of printing and the book trade often determine the status of literature. Among the factors which merit examination are the extent of literary connection with Europe, the spread and quantity of printing, the place of periodicals, and the nature of the reading public.

As we should expect, the greatest number of important books written by or relating to the colonists were published in Europe. Most of the significant books written in America in the seventeenth century were printed abroad as were many of those written later (Cotton Mather's *Magnalia*, for example). Mather's *Wonders of the Invisible World* and Edwards' works were reprinted quickly in Great Britain. The colonial author wrote not merely for his neighbors but for the larger world. In many cases he found a more sympathetic audience abroad than at home.

For a time it would have been impossible for books to be published in the colonies, and it was always difficult. Printing was established in Massachusetts in 1639, in Maryland and Pennsylvania in 1685, in New York in 1693, and in all of the other original colonies before 1763. It was based usually upon the necessity for copies of the laws and other public papers. Almanacs, school textbooks, legal and business manuals, newspapers, and other useful but scarcely literary productions accounted for the bulk of the work. Lengthy books were expensive to manufacture, and very few of them were printed in the colonies. Sermons, pamphlets, and small volumes of poems were fairly common. One very common practice for those who admired a particular sermon was to subsidize its printing and then distribute copies to appreciative friends, as Samuel Sewall liked to do. Such distribution of a funeral sermon was evidently regarded as a suitable memorial to departed relatives. Much of the material was reprinted from English editions. There is reasonably good evidence that the quantity of theological literature was greatest in New England, that of belles-lettres and political literature greatest in the middle colonies, and that of legal literature greatest in the South. In general, the production of the colonial printers was strongly utilitarian. Statutes, almanacs, and in the course of time newspapers were the staples of the colonial press. Many sermons were printed, often at the expense of a man of wealth who liked the preacher or wished to memorialize a deceased relative. To print a big book, such as Samuel Willard's

Compleat Body of Divinity (1726), required the cooperation and the type of several printers. It was not easy for colonial authors to rush into print.

The book-buying public was relatively small; the average edition of books and pamphlets in the early part of the eighteenth century was probably between three and five hundred copies. As a matter of fact, much of what we now read as colonial literature, including the works here mentioned from the pens of Bradford, Winthrop, Sewall, Mrs. Knight, Byrd, and Edward Taylor, was not even in print before 1765.

Newspapers, although they were unknown for a large part of the period, constituted the staple work of colonial printers by 1750. *Publick Occurences*, which appeared at Boston in 1690, was suppressed after a single issue, so that the *Boston News-Letter*, established in 1704, is usually regarded as the first American newspaper. Other important early newspapers include the *American Weekly Mercury* of Philadelphia (founded 1719), the *New-England Courant* of Boston (1721), the *New York Gazette* (1725), the *Maryland Gazette* of Baltimore (1727), the *Pennsylvania Gazette*—Franklin's paper and the best of colonial newspapers—(1730), the *South Carolina Gazette* of Charleston (1732), and the *Virginia Gazette* of Williamsburg (1736). Most of these papers were of very modest size at first, and it was many years before there was much space for literary material. Sometimes, as in the case of James Franklin's *New-England Courant*, a printing-shop became the center of an informal club of literary-minded gentlemen, and Benjamin Franklin used the *Pennsylvania Gazette* to promote the cooperative and political ends which he had in mind.

Gradually newspapers began to find room for letters, political articles, discussions of science and technology, even essays and poems. Although most of this material was ephemeral, there were such exceptions as Franklin's "Silence Dogood Papers." Magazines as a rule came out later than newspapers. The first two, imitative of London periodicals, were printed at Philadelphia in 1741, by Franklin and his rival, Andrew Bradford. Neither lasted a year.

The colonial printer was often postmaster and bookseller as well. Many books were imported, and as time went on their distribution was accomplished by peddlers and auctions as well as by bookshop sales. A few of the more ambitious books were sold by subscriptions obtained before they were actually printed. All in all, it seems certain that in the colonies most readers, like most serious authors, looked abroad for their literary life.

American traditions about censorship and control of the press had their beginnings in this time. There are incidents during the period in which governors or councils brought action against printers, but it seems probable that the colonial press was as free or even freer than that of England. As early as 1696 a Massachusetts jury refused to convict a printer for publishing a work which had offended the officials and the clergy, and in 1735 the famous trial of Peter Zenger in New York enhanced the precedent that libel laws were not to be readily used to suppress freedom of speech and freedom of the press. By the beginning of the Revolutionary period the colonial press was in a position to play what from some points of view may be regarded as a decisive part in the drama of political action.

T. H.

LITERARY TRENDS

Moses Coit Tyler, in his *History of American Literature, 1607-1765* (1878), classified colonial books in two groups: those written for English readers and those composed for the Americans themselves. In the former group he perceived six types of material: (1) books whose purpose was to' send home tidings of "welfare or ill fare"; (2) those written to appeal legal or financial matters to superior tribunals in the homeland; (3) apologetics, designed to defend the colonies against injurious aspersions by their enemies; (4) those writings particularly devoted to the Indians; (5) "descriptions of nature in America"; and (6) accounts of gradual innovations in politics, laws, creeds, and religious and domestic usages. Among the writings composed for the colonists themselves he found four types of material: (1) sermons and other religious treatises; (2) histories; (3) poems; and (4) prose with miscellaneous purposes.

Tyler's classification is still useful, but its fundamental distinction conflicts with a belief of later scholars that the colonists seldom wrote merely for themselves. As we turn now to the problems of literary forms and excellence, we can describe the bulk of colonial writings under seven classes. The principle of division is still that of content, but we shall consider particularly the structural problems which faced colonial writers, and their solutions in: (1) accounts of voyages; (2) promotion tracts; (3) sermons; (4) polemical tracts and treatises; (5) histories and biographies; (6) diaries and autobiographies; and (7) poems. The absence of plays and novels in colonial America also requires brief explanation.

Accounts of Voyages

The simplest in structure of the literary types common in the colonies was the account of a voyage, from which developed the later literature of travel. This was at first a plain narrative, usually written by a plain man with few literary talents. Its organization was chronological; and the writer merely amplified, from memory, notes, or a journal, the events he had experienced, expanding whenever his own interests or those of his prospective readers seemed to demand it. The letter in which Columbus reported his first voyage of discovery is a good example; another is John Brereton's *Briefe and True Relation of the Discouerie of the North Part of Virginia* (1602), the earliest English account of the New England coast. The type prevails in the great collections of voyages which were edited by Richard Hakluyt, Samuel Purchas, and John Harris *(Collection of Voyages and Travels,* 1705). Although written to provide information, the account of a voyage was seldom impersonal and sometimes achieved a sharpness of effect and a charm scarcely excelled by polished literary art.

Mrs. Knight's *Journal* adapts the type quite naturally to a land journey, as does Byrd's "Progress to the Mines." Byrd's two versions of the *History of the Dividing Line* show how readily miscellaneous information could be inserted in the loose framework of a travel narrative. Travel literature forms one of the largest classes of American writing. It is closely related to the economic motive in colonization, but it still lends itself readily to comment on social life and customs, on personalities, and even to sheer entertainment.

Promotion Tracts

The writer of the promotion tract almost invariably had to struggle with a topical arrangement. He had to make some division of his material so that he could generalize attractively about the resources of the region he was describing. He was not always familiar with his material; he could make only limited use of narrative; and he needed to appear judicious and relatively impersonal. Promotion tracts therefore vary somewhat in structure, according to the different solutions of the problems.

Hariot wisely followed his main interest — economic resources — in his account of Virginia. First he described commodities already found or raised in Virginia in quantities sufficient to be marketable: useful plants, minerals, and furs. He then listed commodities known to be sufficient in quantity to sustain life: grains, vegetables, fruits, game animals, fowl, and fish. A third section listed miscellaneous commodities and included his account of the Indians.

John Smith's *Description of New England* and his *Map of Virginia* employed a far more common structure. They began with the general geographical features and then described the climate, winds, soils, rivers, settled places, plants, animals, birds, fish, minerals, and Indians. The *Map* was more systematically organized; in his *Description* Smith himself realized that his enthusiasm had carried him away, and at one point asks his readers to return a little with him, adding that he is not "sufficiently yet acquainted in those parts, to write fully the estate of the Sea, the Ayre, the Land, the Fruites, the Rocks, the People, the Government, Religion, Territories and Limitations, Friends and Foes: but as I gathered from the niggardly relations in a broken language to my understanding, during the time I ranged those Countries." It will be noted that Smith had a list of topics, arranged in an order proceeding from the general to the particular. This systematic approach he probably derived from the geographical literature of the day, which in turn is a reflection of the almost invariable approach of the medieval schoolmen to the study of the external world.

When the works of Aristotle were the highest authority in science, they were studied according to a settled system. One began with the *Organon* and the *Physica*, which deal with logic and the general properties of natural bodies; next came the *De Caelo*, a description of the heavens; next the *De Generatione et Corruptione*, which treats the four elements — fire, water, earth, and air — and their various combinations and interactions; next the *Meteorologica*, which describes the various processes of change in the elements; next various discussions of "perfectly mixed" bodies and "imperfectly mixed" ones, inanimate (stones, metals, and minerals); and finally the *De Anima* and the *Historia Animalium*, descriptions of animate bodies (plants and animals). After that came the study of man.

Many promotion tracts besides Smith's were based ultimately upon this tradition, for it was the topical arrangement most familiar to educated men. Francis Higginson's *New England's Plantation* begins with the following statement: "And because the life and wel-fare of euerie Creature here below, and the commodiousnesse of the Countrey whereas such Creatures liue, doth by the most wise ordering of Gods prouidence, depend next vnto himselfe, vpon the temperature and disposition of the foure Elements, Earth, Water, Aire, and Fire. . . . Therefore I will indeauour to shew you what *New-England* is by the considerations of these apart, and truly endeauour by Gods helpe to report nothing but the naked truth." Wood's *New England's Prospect* proceeds from the general to the particular, but Morton's *New English Canaan* varies that order slightly.

Although the careful reader will discover many minor variations, the general outline of the promotion tracts is remarkably consistent. They comprise a large part of colonial literature. Closely related to these tracts are the "progress reports" sent back to those at home by actual settlers. They have a larger proportion of narrative but are not greatly different.

Sermons

The sermon was the most highly developed literary type in colonial literature, and a collection of the sermons available in print and in manuscript would run quickly into the thousands. Men and women listened to sermons on every Sunday; often they went to lecture sermons during the week; they heard sermons on such public occasions as elections, Thanksgiving and fast days, military trainings, and funerals. The more serious of them kept, in their diaries or notebooks, records of the sermon texts and even the main heads of the discourses to which they gave their attention. In an age wherein the pulpit was the center of intellectual life, it is not surprising that much of the best writing was in sermons.

Only a few of the many sermons by the American Puritans have been reprinted. They are most readily available in a microcard series prepared by the American Antiquarian Society. A few early sermons have been reprinted in the collected editions or in facsimile, and the interested student can find samples of the preaching of John Cotton, Roger Williams, Thomas Hooker, and Thomas Shepard. Not until we reach the early eighteenth century, however, do we find, in Jonathan Edwards, a preacher whose works are easily located.

The Puritan sermon was most often organized according to a set pattern. A Scriptural text is chosen, doctrines are derived from it, reasons given for these doctrines, and uses of the doctrines suggested. Within this framework numerous variations were possible, such as questions and answers, homely illustrations, eloquent passages, and the frequent citation of parallel texts.

Today's reader may be amused by the "firstlys," "secondlys," etc., but he should remember that earnest churchgoers wanted to know where they were, so that during the week they could discuss within the family the soundness of their minister's third "use." From Cotton to Edwards the pattern varied little in its larger outlines.

There are a number of intricate problems in the sermon structure which reward study—the extent of influence of the logic of Petrus Ramus, for example, and the conflict between the "plain" and the more ornate styles. For us, however, the important consideration is to understand the purpose of the sermon. It was designed then, as now, to persuade men to consider honestly the state of their souls. The minister was to preach the gospel of Jesus Christ, to awaken his hearers to the supreme importance of faith and regeneration, to the urgent necessity of assuming an active part in the eternal warfare within man's soul between good and evil, the spirit and the flesh, God and the Devil. The sermon was the essence of Protestantism, more important, in actuality, than any single theological dogma. With the Calvinists, for example, the sermon was the chief means of preserving believers from fatalistic acceptance of their lot. That most men were foreordained to sin and damnation and that there was nothing the individual could do about it, are doctrines which might easily have led to despair and passive indifference. The sermons, however, were based on the even more powerful doctrines that divine grace did come to some men, and that to those who received it, grace was a constant growth, an increasing understanding of perfection, an endless enlarging of one's capacity to deal with doubt and sin and temptation. Hence the soul-searching of the Puritans, the esteem and affection for "soul-ravishing" clergymen like Shepard, the vast respect for the sublime certainty with which Edwards testified to the "spiritual Light" which is "the dawning of the Light of Glory in the Heart." Men and women found sermons thrilling because sermons indicated the innumerable ways of analyzing and strengthening the inner life.

The sermon, in short, was both an appeal to man's imperfect reason and a stirring of his emotions, both an intellectual experience and a glimpse of the magnificent poetic vistas of God's promise to the regenerate soul. It provides the real key to the religious life of the colonial age. Remote as some of the sermons may seem to the modern reader, the sermon literature of colonial America can stand comparison with that of any people. It called forth the finest literary talents of the time.

Beginning of Controversial Writing

Theological and political discussion also produced a large literature of controversy. Decisions had to be made about church government, institutional organization, governmental policy, and theological positions, and there were often wide divergences of opinion. The numerous tracts and treatises which grew out of these controversial issues varied widely in their structure. Sometimes they were constructed as a series of queries to which the author gave his well-considered answers. The fiction of addressing a "letter" to a friend was often used. John Cotton and Roger Williams, for example, debated the question of religious toleration in a long series of pamphlets published between 1643 and 1652. The best known is William's *The Bloudy Tenent* (1644), which deals with an earlier argument in "A Letter of Mr. Cotton to Mr. Williams" (1643) through a dialog between Truth and Peace. Topical arrangement which often took the form of a point-by-point refutation of a preceding pamphlet or treatise was also a common method of organization.

We cannot generalize readily about the literary form of the literature of controversy. Its most striking difference from similar material of today is perhaps the fact that so little of it appeared in magazines; their development as a forum for literary debate came in a later period.

The volume and variety of tracts and treatises can best be suggested by listing a few of the more important titles, in addition to those by Williams, Eliot, Cotton Mather, Wise, Edwards, and Franklin which have already been mentioned. Among the books of enduring significance are the following: Richard Mather's *Church Government and Church Covenant* (1643); John Cotton's *Way of the Churches of Christ in New England* (1645); Nathaniel Ward's *Simple Cobler of Aggawam in America* (1647); Thomas Hooker's *Survey of the Summe of Church Discipline* (1648); Increase Mather's *Cases of Conscience concerning Evil Spirits Personating Men* (1693); Samuel Sewall's *Selling of Joseph* (1700); Cotton Mather's *Essays to Do Good* (as *Bonifacius*, 1710) and *Christian Philosopher* (1721); Franklin's *Modest Inquiry into the Nature and Necessity of a Paper Currency* (1729) and *Proposals relating to the Education of Youth in Pensilvania* (1749); Jared Eliot's *Essay on Field Husbandry in New England* (Part I, 1748); John Woolman's *Some Considerations on the Keeping of Negroes* (Part I, 1753); James Otis' *Vindication of the Conduct of the House of Representatives of Massachusetts Bay* (1762) and *Rights of the British Colonies Asserted and Proved* (1764). Religion, fashions, social reform, science, agriculture, politics — all are represented, and the list might easily be extended. This type of literature had its models in the imprints of Europe, but its content is invariably and peculiarly American. It is the basis of the tradition of free discussion and a free press and is perhaps, to the intellectual historian, the most significant part of colonial writing.

Histories and Biographies

Historical and biographical writing formed a large part of colonial literature because it seemed important, for various reasons, to preserve a record of what happened in the New World. In its simplest form this writing was annalistic, a simple statement of historical and biographical fact. The histories of Bradford and Winthrop and Nathaniel Morton's *New-England's Memoriall* (1669) follow the natural chronological order and set down the main events of each year. The colonial historian was not satisfied with factual annals, however; he conceived it his duty to interpret events. Not much of the work was objective, by present-day standards of historical inquiry, but it reveals awareness of the many possible uses of history.

Mixed motives can be perceived in most colonial histories and biographies. Smith's *The Generall Historie of Virginia* (1624) was both a justification of himself as a principal actor in the affairs described and a defense of colonization in general. Smith also had a distinctly modern conception of the close connection between history and geography. Bradford's *The History of Plymouth Plantation* (1620-1647) was written by a great leader who feared that the children of the founders would fail to cherish the achievement of a pious little group of heroes whose hard work had won, so Bradford believed, the special favor of God. Winthrop's *The History of New England* (1630-1649) is strongly flavored with the same providential theory of history as Bradford's book, the same defensiveness, and a lawyer's respect for exact knowledge of precedents and experiments in institutional organization. Cotton Mather's sixty-odd biographies in *Magnalia Christi Americana* exemplify a tendency to defend the "New England Way," as well as to emulate the didactic purpose of Bradford. Byrd's two works (1728), *The Secret History* and *The History of the Dividing Line*, and Samuel Peters' *General History of Connecticut* (1781) had axes to grind as well as information to tell.

Much colonial historical writing was tinged with the belief in a providential order of nature, and hence took on a distinctly theological quality. If events were to be interpreted as the working out of the divine plan, which man could never know in its entirety, a monstrous birth might be quite as significant to a reflective mind as a victory in battle or a great political or religious compromise. To the modern reader, Winthrop seems to jump readily from affairs of great moment to the most trivial events. This attitude tended to make history discontinuous except to the reader fascinated by the search for moral meanings in events. It is characteristic of most seventeenth-century writing, appearing most vividly in Edward Johnson's *History of New England* (1654) and reaching its culmination in Cotton Mather's *Magnalia Christi Americana* (1702). For the providential theory the colonists had the example of the Book of Kings, the Roman historian Livy, and many ecclesiastical annalists from the time of St. Augustine.

More rationalistic tendencies may also be observed in colonial historiography. William Bradford suggested natural causes, not only Providence, for the outbreak of immorality in New England. Judicious and objective methods were foreshadowed in Thomas Prince's *Chronological History of New England*, the first volume of which appeared in 1730, in William Stith's *History of the First Discovery of Virginia* (1747), and most notably in Thomas Hutchinson's *History of the Province of Massachusetts Bay*, of which the first volume was published in 1764. These works likewise had European models, although Hutchinson's was the only one to show traces of the regard for institutional development which made Voltaire's *Age of Louis XIV* (1751) a landmark.

Diaries and Autobiographies

An amazing number of colonists kept diaries or wrote autobiographies. Their purpose was sometimes practical—the desire to have a record of the weather, the planting and harvesting of crops, business transactions, and personal affairs. More often, perhaps, and almost always in the case of the autobiographies, the aim was fundamentally theological. Earnest Calvinists wished to study the state of their souls, and one of the best possible methods was to preserve a day-by-day or systematic account of temptations, struggles, and meditations, from which might be drawn some indication of their state of grace.

The best colonial example of a religious autobiography is probably Jonathan Edwards' "Personal Narrative." In its constant concern with the all-absorbing problem of man's relation to God it is typical of numerous Puritan self-searchings. Other examples almost as well known are the autobiography and "Meditations and Spiritual Experiences" of Thomas Shepard, and the voluminous diary of Cotton Mather.

Those diaries which are most treasured by later generations, however, are the ones in which soul-searching is leavened by concern with temporal affairs. Winthrop's journal, Samuel Sewall's diary, the travel journal of Mrs. Knight, and the shorthand diaries from which William Byrd "wrote up" his histories of the Dividing Line and his "Progress to the Mines" are important because they preserve for us the customs, manners, and personalities of relatively worldly people. We learn from them of the food, the drink, the social life, the household appointments, the gardens, the crimes, the births, marriages, and deaths—the external life, in short, of seventeenth- and eighteenth-century Americans.

Sewall's *Diary* is perhaps the best. It does not compare with the great English diaries written at approximately the same period by John Evelyn and Samuel Pepys, for Sewall's world was more circumscribed than theirs. Like all great diarists, however, Sewall has the virtue of revealing himself as a human being, beset by frailties and inadequacies and little vanities.

It is worth remembering that two of the greatest of the early American books—Benjamin Franklin's *Autobiography* (1759) as well as John Woolman's *Journal* (1774)—are in the direct line of descent from one of the most popular types of colonial literature. Of them we shall have more to say in Chapter 2.

Poems

American poetry prior to 1765 was, when compared to that of England in the same period, small in quantity and, with very few exceptions, vastly inferior in quality. No colonial poet reached the level of Herbert, Herrick, Cowley, Butler, Prior, Young, or Thomson, to say nothing of the front-rank poets, Donne, Milton, Dryden, and Pope. Moreover, the colonial versifiers displayed a deplorable tendency to imitate the poetic diction and verse forms of their trans-Atlantic betters.

Early American verse can, nevertheless, add to our knowledge of the pattern of culture and the place of the arts in colonial life. Some of it has a respectable originality in thought or subject matter, and some of it, notably that which expressed the religious faith of the most sensitive individuals, has genuine poetic merit.

The most utilitarian use of rhyme and meter is mnemonic; maxims and stories in verse are easier to remember verbatim than those in prose. Not a little colonial verse is based upon this fact, from the rhymed accounts of English Protestant history by the Rev. John Wilson (see *Handkerchiefs from Paul*, ed. K. B. Murdock, 1927) down to the Rev. Michael Wigglesworth's famous summary of Calvinistic theology, *The Day of Doom* (1662). Even the compilers of the *Bay Psalm Book* (1640), although their main purpose was to translate the Hebrew with the greatest possible exactness, chose to put the psalms to be sung in the New England churches in English meter, which is to say in the ballad stanza of folk poetry:

> The Lord to mee a shepheard is,
>   want therefore shall not I.
> Hee in the folds of tender-grasse,
>   doth cause mee downe to lie.

> To waters calme me gently leads
> Restore my soule doth hee:
> he doth in paths of righteousnes:
> for his names sake leade mee.

The use of the ballad stanza reveals the strength of popular tradition in the face of novel conditions — in this instance the Puritan respect for the Hebrew text of the Scriptures. Poetry as art suffered severely, but its basic elements survived.

Vaguely related to the mnemonic purpose, although essentially didactic in the same way as colonial historical writing, are the numerous historical poems of the colonial period. Bradford himself tried his hand at this type of writing, but the best-known examples are Benjamin Tompson's narratives of King Philip's War: *New Englands Crisis* (1676) and *New-Englands Tears for Her Present Miseries* (1676). Both display the providential theory of history in an elaborate form. Related to biographical writing, moreover, are the numerous funeral elegies, at which many New England clergymen tried their hands. Most modern readers will be satisfied to know Benjamin Franklin's recipe for such an elegy without reading many of the originals on which he based his conclusions:

> For the subject of your Elegy, Take one of your Neighbors who has lately departed this Life; it is no great matter of what Age the Party dy'd, but it will be best if he went away suddenly, being *Kill'd, Drown'd*, or *Frose to Death*.
>
> Having chose the Person, take all his Virtues, Excellencies, &c. and if he have not enough, you may borrow some to make up a sufficient Quantity: To these add his last Words, dying Expressions, &c. if they are to be had; mix all these together, and be sure you strain them well. Then season all with a Handful or two of Melancholly Expressions, such as, *Dreadful, Deadly, cruel cold Death, unhappy Fate, weeping Eyes,* &c. . . . let them Ferment for the Space of a Fortnight, and by that Time they will be incorporated into a Body, which take out, and having prepared a sufficient Quantity of double Rhimes, such as *Power, Flower; Quiver, Shiver; Grieve us, Leave us; tell you, excel you; Expeditions, Physicians; Fatigue him, Intrigue him;* &c. you must spread all upon Paper, and if you can procure a Scrap of Latin to put at the End, it will garnish it mightily; then having affixed your Name at the Bottom, with a *Moestus Composuit*, you will have an Excellent Elegy.

The more sophisticated poetry of the colonial era was likely to have a classical flavor, understandable in an age and place where higher education gave a central place to the learned languages. Not a few colonists composed Latin verses, and translations and paraphrases constituted a common exercise. The height of "highbrow" verse-making was *Pietas et Gratulatio*, published at Boston in 1761. A tribute to the new king, George III, it contained three poems in Greek, sixteen in Latin, and twelve in English, most of them by recent graduates or faculty members of Harvard College. Individuals trained in the classics were also interested in the work of the English Neoclassical school, and there were many colonial poems in the manner of the satires of Dryden and Pope, the mock-heroics of Butler, and the philosophical pieces of Thomson, Young, and Pomfret. These are often interesting for their content, although it is disconcerting to find colonial poets expressing boredom with court and city life when, as someone has said, five minutes' walking would have taken any one of them into a cow pasture. We may safely leave the works of Mather Byles, John Adams (the clergyman, not the statesman), George Webb, William Livingston, the younger Thomas Godfrey, Nathaniel Evans, Joseph Green, and other would-be "wits" to the specialist, re-membering, however, that these gentlemen were the literati of their day and, whatever their deficiencies, cherished the tradition of belles-lettres in a world frequently too busy for art.

The religious poetry of the period, perhaps best represented by the works of Anne Bradstreet and Edward Taylor, was another matter. Although these writers imitated French and English religious poets— Du Bartas, the English Spenserians, Donne, Herbert, Quarles, and Crashaw—they had the true poet's gift of conveying intensity of indi-vidual experience. Their poems are probably the finest literary expression of the inner life of American Puritanism and have the same interest as the best of the diaries and spiritual autobiographies.

Plays and Novels

Fiction and drama, which bulk large in later American literature, were almost nonexistent in the colonial period. Both were distrusted by serious-minded persons, in England as well as in America, although it is not just to ascribe their absence entirely to Puritan influence. A theater requires considerable capital and a public in the habit of play-going, neither of which is often to be found except in the largest centers of population. As a class, moreover, actors were long mistrusted by civic authorities, as the history of the London theater shows. These factors alone would be enough to account for the antagonism to stage plays which appears in colonial laws forbidding their public performance. Virginia was one of the few colonies without such legislation, but the earliest mention of a play acted in the colonies suggests some prejudice even there. In 1665 three citizens of Accomac County were called upon to appear in costume and tell what they said in *Ye Bare and Ye Cubb*. They were discharged and their accuser forced to pay the court charges.

The Puritans, however, unquestionably delayed the development of an American drama. Their influence had closed the theaters in England for eighteen years, and many colonists shared the resentment of English Puritans for the ridicule of Puritanism in Elizabethan drama. Remembered also was the association of the theater with the immoralities of king and court and the vigorous attack on the theater by the church fathers of the latter days of the Roman empire. To the famous English attacks on the theater by Stubbs (1583), Prynne (1632), and Collier (1698) there was at least one American parallel: Increase Mather's *Testimony against Several Prophane and Superstitious Customs, Now Practised by Some in New England* (1687).

There was no effort to keep printed plays out of the college libraries, and as time went on there seems to have been sporadic interest in them in academic halls. There is some evidence that students at Harvard were thinking of histrionic things in the 1690's — a doubtful tradition that Benjamin Colman, later a prominent liberal clergyman, wrote a Latin play entitled *Gustavus Vasa* in 1690, and an allusion to examining "several of the Scholars about the Comedy" in Increase Mather's diary for 1698. The students at William and Mary offered a "pastoral colloquy" before the governor in 1702, and later in the eighteenth century undergraduates at Philadelphia, Princeton, New Haven, and Cambridge were frequently experimenting with dialogs and dramatic exercises. *The Prince of Parthia*, by the younger Thomas Godfrey, one of the literary group centering in the College of Philadelphia, was written in 1759, published in 1765, and actually produced on a professional stage in 1767. Imitative of the English heroic drama, it was a natural outgrowth of the discovery of belles-lettres by undergraduates and their friends.

New tastes and attitudes were accepted by the general public only gradually, despite the efforts of entranced amateurs, the visits of professional actors, and the changing tone of English drama. The first play to be printed was *Antroboros* (1714), a political satire published anonymously by Robert Hunter, governor of New York. Williamsburg built a theater in 1716, but there is no evidence that it was used until twenty years later. New York probably was entertained by a group of professional actors in 1732, and Charleston had a brief "season" in 1735. A company which performed Addison's *Cato* in Philadelphia in 1742 was arrested and forbidden to appear again. Going to New York, it performed *Richard III*, *The Beggar's Opera*, and other plays in 1750. An amateur performance scandalized conservative Boston in that same year, although George Lillo's bourgeois tragedy, *George Barnwell* (1731), had been reprinted in *The New-England Weekly Journal* within a year after its appearance in London. American theatrical history is usually said to have begun in 1752, with the arrival of Lewis Hallam's "American Company," which had a continuous history in repertoire until 1774, when the Continental Congress forbade theatrical performances "for the duration." The American Company played at Williamsburg, New York, Philadelphia,

Annapolis, Newport, Providence, Charleston, and several towns in Virginia, and succeeded (sometimes by such stratagems as offering *Othello* as a series of "Moral Dialogues") in familiarizing the more venturesome colonists with the plays of Shakespeare, Marlowe, Dryden, Congreve, Farquhar, Addison, Steele, Cibber, Ambrose Philips, and others. But there was no native drama.

Nor did colonial Americans produce either novels or novel-like narratives comparable to those of Bunyan, Defoe, and Swift. This is less surprising than that there should have been no drama, for the novel as a form had by no means reached its full maturity. The seriousness of the reading public left little time for long romances, although a good many of them appear on colonial booklists, and the pleasure in swift-moving narrative was partly provided for by the accounts of voyages and travels, the somewhat lurid accounts of captivity among the Indians, and the other factual material such as reports of the experiences and final hours of pirates and murderers and the descriptions of remarkable providences and witchcrafts. Many works of fiction which supposedly portrayed life must have seemed dull in comparison to more direct reporting. Quite probably the prevalent attitude toward fiction was not far from that in one passage of Cotton Mather's *Manuductio ad Ministerium*, where he advises divinity students to enjoy the recreation of poetry but not to be so set upon it

> as to be always poring on the *Passionate* and *Measured* Pages. Let not what should be *Sauce* rather than Food for you, Engross all your Application. . . . Indeed, not merely for the *Impurities* which they convey, but also on some other Accounts, the *Powers of Darkness* have a *Library* among us, whereof the *Poets* have been the most *Numerous* as well as the most *Venemous* Authors. Most of the modern *Plays*, as well as the *Romances* and *Novels*, and *Fictions*, which are a sort of *Poems*, do belong to the Catalogue of this cursed Library.

> T.H.

***Chronological Table of*
LITERATURE AND HISTORY**

1492	Columbus, discovering islands in the western ocean, believed he had reached part of Asia
1497	Cabot touched the North American coast, laying the foundation for English territorial claims in the New World
1507	■ Martin Waldseemüller's *Cosmographiae Introductio*, German treatise

on geography, wherein the newly discovered western hemisphere was named "America" in honor of Amerigo Vespucci, Italian navigator

1535   ■ The Bible first fully translated into English, by Miles Coverdale

1536   ■ Calvin's *Institutes of the Christian Religion*

1539   De Soto landed in Florida and marched west toward Mexico; before his death in 1542 he had reached the Mississippi and explored as far north, perhaps, as what is now Kentucky

1540   Coronado began an expedition into what is now New Mexico, Arizona, and the Great Plains

1549   ■ First *Book of Common Prayer* (revisions in 1552, 1559, 1604, 1662), criticized by those who wished to rid the English Church of "popish" ritual

Uniform church service prescribed in England

1562   John Hawkins made the first of three privateering voyages to the West Indies, bringing England into direct conflict with Spain for New World riches

1572   St. Bartholomew's Day Massacre of about 10,000 Huguenots strengthened anti-Catholic feeling in England

1577   Francis Drake began a voyage taking him through the Straits of Magellan, along the western coast of the Americas (where he took possession of New Albion—present-day California and Oregon—in the name of Queen Elizabeth), and back to England (1580) by way of Java and the Cape of Good Hope

1578   Charter for exclusive colonization in North America granted by the Queen to Sir Humphrey Gilbert and associates, among them Gilbert's half brother, Walter Raleigh

1582   ■ Richard Hakluyt's *Divers Voyages*

1584   Charter granted to Raleigh (Gilbert's ventures having failed) guaranteeing to colonists in North America the political rights of Englishmen

1585   Raleigh sent seven ships to America, landing 107 men on Roanoke Island

1586   Raleigh's colony returned to England by Drake's ships when needed supplies failed to arrive on schedule · Decision that Chesapeake Bay area would be better for colonization than Roanoke, where the Indians were hostile

1587	120 persons left on Roanoke through the treachery of a ship captain; when a supply expedition finally arrived in 1590, this "lost colony" had vanished, leaving no trace except the word "Croatan" carved on a tree
1588	■ Hariot's *Briefe and True Report of the New Found Land of Virginia*
	Destruction of the Spanish Armada in the English Channel, marking emergence of England as the chief sea power in the world
1602	The first of a series of expeditions (made during the years 1602-1605 under Captains Gosnold, Pring, and Waymouth) to the coast between present-day Maine and Martha's Vineyard; these explorations revived English interest in North America
1603	■ Shakespeare's *Hamlet* printed
	Death of Elizabeth (reigned 1558-1603); accession of James I · Champlain made his first voyage to New France, exploring the St. Lawrence River
1606	Charters granted to two colonizing groups, the London and Plymouth Companies, who divided the territory of Virginia between them
1607	Jamestown, first permanent English settlement in North America, founded by the London Company
1608	■ John Smith's *True Relation*
	Quebec founded by Champlain · Migration of the Scrooby congregation of Separatists to Holland, the starting-point of William Bradford's *History of Plymouth Plantation*
1609	Henry Hudson discovered the river now bearing his name
1611	■ The *King James Version* of the Bible
1612	■ Smith's *Map of Virginia*
1614	Northern part of Virginia explored by Smith for the Plymouth Company and named by him "New England" · Colony established by the Dutch at the mouth of the Hudson
1616	■ Smith's *Description of New England*
1619	First representative assembly convened in Virginia · Negro slaves first imported
1620	■ *Mayflower Compact* signed in Cape Cod Bay, 11 November
	Charter granted by the London or Virginia Company to English capitalists, on behalf of the Separatists in Holland, for a settlement somewhere

south of the Hudson · The *Mayflower*, driven off her course by storms, landed the Pilgrims on the shore of Massachusetts Bay

1621   Patent for the Pilgrims' settlement obtained from the Council for New England, successor to the Plymouth Company

1622   ■ *Mourt's Relation*, by William Bradford and Edward Winslow, first authentic description of the Pilgrim settlement at Plymouth

1624   ■ Smith's *Generall Historie* · Winslow's *Good News from New England*

Annulment of the Virginia charter, making that settlement the first royal colony

1627   Charter granted to the Massachusetts Bay Company · Thomas Morton arrested and deported by the authorities of the Plymouth Colony

1630   ■ Smith's *True Travels* · Francis Higginson's *New England's Plantation*

"Great Migration" of the Puritans of the Massachusetts Bay Company, led by Governor John Winthrop, which by 1640 brought more than 20,000 persons to New England

1634   ■ William Wood's *New England's Prospect*

Maryland settled

1636   Roger Williams founded Providence in Rhode Island · Harvard College founded (classes begun in 1638)

1637   ■ Thomas Morton's *New English Canaan*

1640   ■ *Whole Booke of Psalmes*, better known as the *Bay Psalm Book*

1641   ■ Thomas Shepard's *Sincere Convert* · Massachusetts *Body of Liberties*

1642   Civil War in England precipitated by attempt of Charles I to impeach and imprison five members of the House of Commons

1644   ■ Williams' *Bloudy Tenent of Persecution for the Cause of Conscience*

1649   Charles I tried and executed (reigned 1625-1649); Charles II crowned in exile in 1651 · England declared a commonwealth and the House of Lords abolished

1650   ■ Anne Bradstreet's *Tenth Muse Lately Sprung Up in America*

1651   Parliament passed the first Navigation Act, designed to undermine the commercial supremacy of the Dutch; it provided that no goods should be imported from Asia, Africa, or America, except in English vessels; with supplementary acts in 1660 and 1663 it became one of the chief sources of friction between the American colonies and the British ministry

1660	The Restoration brought Charles II to the English throne
1662	■ Michael Wigglesworth's *Day of Doom*
	Act of Uniformity purged the Church of England of dissenting clergymen and sent another wave of ministers to America · Half-Way Covenant adopted by the New England churches, admitting to membership the children of church members, without requiring a public relation of previous religious experience
1664	New Netherlands taken by the English
1667	Treaty of Breda, after the Second Anglo-Dutch War, gave all Dutch colonies in America to England and Acadia (later Nova Scotia) to France
1668	William Penn became a Quaker · Joliet explored the Great Lakes · La Salle explored the Ohio country, perhaps reaching the Mississippi
1674	■ Samuel Sewall's *Diary* begun
1675	Beginning of King Philip's War (1675-1676), marked by numerous massacres and the burning of frontier villages
1676	■ Benjamin Tompson's *New Englands Crisis*, a series of poems on the providential delivery of New England from the threat of King Philip · Increase Mather's *Brief History of the Warr with the Indians*
	Bacon's Rebellion, an early instance of conflict between a royal governor (William Berkeley of Virginia) and those whom he governed
1678	"Popish Plot" to oust Charles II and place James, Duke of York, an avowed Catholic, on the throne; some thirty-five persons executed before it was discovered that the evidence was fabricated
1681	■ Penn's *Some Account of the Province of Pensilvania in America*
	Charter obtained by William Penn for a new colony on the Delaware · Massachusetts called upon to surrender its charter
1685	Death of Charles II (reigned 1660-1685); accession of James II
1688	Connecticut and Rhode Island charters revoked · James II permitted to escape to France — the so-called "Glorious Revolution"
1689	■ Cotton Mather's *Memorable Providences relating to Witchcrafts and Possessions* · John Locke's *Treatise of Civil Government*, setting forth the contract theory of government which was to influence American political philosophy
	Deposition of James II (reigned 1685-1689); accession to the throne of Mary (daughter of James II) and her husband, William of Orange

1690	Sir William Phips conquered Acadia but failed in an expedition against Quebec,—the chief American actions in the War of the League of Augsburg (1689-1697), King William's War in America; under the Treaty of Ryswick, France recognized William as king and Anne as his successor
1691	New Massachusetts charter made property the basis of suffrage and destroyed the vestiges of direct church control in the government
1692	Phips made royal governor of Massachusetts · Special court appointed to investigate the witchcraft outbreak at the village of Salem
1693	Cotton Mather's *Wonders of the Invisible World*
	William and Mary College chartered (classes begun about 1710)
1701	Yale College founded · Death of James II in exile in France; his son James Francis Edward Stuart (1688-1766), "the Old Pretender," recognized as James III by Louis XIV of France
1702	■ Cotton Mather's *Magnalia Christi Americana*
	Death of William III (reigned 1689-1702; Mary died in 1694); accession of Anne · Beginning of the War of the Spanish Succession (1702-1713), Queen Anne's War in America
1704	■ Sarah Kemble Knight's *Journal* begun
1707	Formal union of England and Scotland under the name of Great Britain, with a single Parliament
1710	■ Cotton Mather's *Bonifacius* or *Essays to Do Good*
1713	Treaty of Utrecht, ending the War of the Spanish Succession, gave to Great Britain all French claims to Acadia, Newfoundland, and the Hudson Bay Settlement; France retained Canada
1714	Death of Anne (reigned 1702-1714); accession of George I, Elector of Hanover
1717	Compagnie d'Occident formed in Paris to colonize on the banks of the Mississippi; rumors of gold and silver mines led to furious stock speculation known as the "Mississippi Bubble," which collapsed in 1720
1718	New Orleans founded
1721	■ *New-England Courant* (1721-1726) established; contained Benjamin Franklin's first characteristic writing, the "Dogood Papers" · Cotton Mather's *Christian Philosopher*
1726	■ Cotton Mather's *Manuductio ad Ministerium*

1727	Death of George I (reigned 1714-1727); accession of George II
1728	■ William Byrd helped run the boundary line between Virginia and North Carolina, keeping the diary which he later elaborated into his *History of the Dividing Line* and *Secret History of the Line*
1732	■ First issue of *Poor Richard's Almanac*
1733	Sugar Act, passed to protect British interests in the West Indies, threatened colonial trade
1734	■ Jonathan Edwards' *Divine and Supernatural Light*
1738	George Whitefield made the first of five evangelical tours of the American colonies · First spinning machines patented in Great Britain
1740	Charity school founded in Philadelphia, from which developed the College of Philadelphia and, eventually, the University of Pennsylvania
1741	■ Edwards' *Sinners in the Hands of an Angry God* · Bradford's *American Magazine* and Franklin's *General Magazine* established at Philadelphia
1742	■ Edwards' *Some Thoughts Concerning the Present Revival of Religion in New England*
1743	■ Charles Chauncy's *Seasonable Thoughts on the State of Religion in New England*
1744	Beginning of the War of the Austrian Succession (1744-1748), King George's War in America
1748	■ Montesquieu's *Esprit des lois*, French political treatise largely responsible for the separation of powers under the American Constitution
	Treaty of Aix-la-Chapelle, ending the .War of the Austrian Succession, restored Louisbourg on Cape Breton Island to the French and left control of the Ohio country undetermined
1749	■ Franklin's *Proposals relating to the Education of Youth in Pensilvania*
	British grant of more than a half-million acres to the Ohio Company roused French fears that there were plans to separate Canada from Louisiana
1750	■ Jonathan Mayhew's *Discourse Concerning Unlimited Submission and Non-Resistance to the Higher Powers* asserted the right of revolution under conditions such as those of 1642 and 1688
1751	■ Franklin's *Experiments & Observations on Electricity*

1752	First regular theatrical company visited the colonies · Change of calendar from the Julian (Old Style) to the Gregorian (New Style)
1753	■ John Woolman's *Some Considerations on the Keeping of Negroes*, Part I
	French seized the Ohio country, taking prisoner British traders in the region; George Washington, aged twenty-one, sent by Governor Dinwiddie of Virginia to protest
1754	■ Edwards' *Freedom of the Will* · Franklin presented his *Plan of Union* to the Albany Conference
	Washington led two companies of Virginia militia against the French and, after initial successes, was forced to surrender on terms which permitted him to return with his men to Virginia · State of undeclared war recognized by call for delegates from all the colonies to meet at Albany, New York, June: two plans for intercolonial organization proposed: (1) that by Governor William Shirley of Massachusetts, which would give the colonial governors the power to organize for defense, with the expenses to be met by a tax levied by Parliament — a plan vigorously opposed by Franklin on the ground that it was taxation without representation; (2) Franklin's plan, providing for a president-general appointed by the king and a grand council or intercolonial legislature of forty, elected by the colonial assemblies · King's College (later Columbia University) founded
1755	British and American troops under General Braddock, advancing on Fort Duquesne, were totally defeated · Franklin active in getting supplies to Braddock's troops and in supervising the construction of forts to protect Pennsylvania from invasion · Acadians deported en masse from Nova Scotia
1756	■ John Woolman's *Journal* begun
1757	Fort William Henry captured by the French · Franklin sent to London by the Pennsylvania assembly, which desired full control of the expenditure of public funds · Seven Years' War (1756-1763) formally declared (French and Indian War in America)
1758	■ Franklin's *Way to Wealth*, in *Poor Richard Improved*
	Tide of the French and Indian War turned toward the British, with the conquest of Louisbourg by forces under Jeffrey Amherst and the occupation of Fort Duquesne, now renamed Pittsburgh · House of Commons resolved that "the claim of right in a colonial Assembly to raise and apply public money, by its own act alone, is derogatory to the crown. and to the rights of the people of Great Britain"
1759	Ticonderoga, Niagara, and Quebec taken by the British and Americans

1760 ■ Franklin's *Interest of Great Britain Considered with Regard to Her Colonies*, a plea for the annexation of Canada and a united Anglo-American empire

Death of George II (reigned 1727-1760); accession of George III

1761 Colonial administration reflected a general "tightening up" to help ease the financial strain of the war, which had concluded in America but not in other parts of the world · Attempt to give "writs of assistance" in the execution of general search warrants to Massachusetts customs officials called forth the anger of James Otis, who in a famous speech developed the classic colonial theory of inalienable rights to life, liberty, and property security

1762 ■ Otis' *Vindication of the Conduct of the House of Representatives of the Province of Massachusetts Bay*, first public statement of the "no taxation without representation" argument

Spain secretly acquired from France all of Louisiana west of the Mississippi · Although the British controlled Canada, they were faced with much Indian hostility, as was evident by the Conspiracy of Pontiac (1762-1763)

1763 By the Treaty of Paris, ending the Seven Years' War, Great Britain received all of Canada from France, Florida from Spain · Rumors circulated that Parliament intended to tax the colonies for part of the cost of the war, and perhaps enforce the long-forgotten Navigation Acts (see 1651)

1764 ■ Otis' *Rights of the British Colonies Asserted and Proved* asked for colonial representation in Parliament if that body was to levy taxes on America

Parliament modified the Sugar Act, with obvious intentions of taxing the colonies   .

1765 ■ Stephen Hopkins' *Rights of Colonies Examined*, a pamphlet similar to those by Otis · Martin Howard's *Letter from a Gentleman at Halifax to His Friend in Rhode Island*, first important Tory answer to Otis and Hopkins, arguing that the colonies were legally corporations, with privileges stated in their charters, and that the colonists were "virtually" represented in Parliament, which was not organized on a territorial principle · Daniel Dulany's *Considerations on the Propriety of Imposing Taxes in the British Colonies for the Purpose of Raising a Revenue by Act of Parliament* objected to Howard's argument

Stamp Act, March · Americans reacted to news of the Stamp Act with a pamphlet war, riots, and the mobbing of prominent Tories · Stamp Act Congress convened in New York, October; drew up a declaration of rights and grievances, petitioned the king, and sent memorials to both houses of Parliament

2

THE NEW REPUBLIC
1765 - 1829

TO SECURE THE BLESSINGS OF LIBERTY

"We, the people of the United States, in order to form a more
perfect union, establish justice, insure domestic tranquillity,
provide for the common defense, promote the general welfare, and
secure the blessings of liberty for ourselves and our posterity, do or-
dain and establish this constitution for the United States of America."

UNITED STATES CONSTITUTION

INTELLECTUAL CURRENTS

A New and a Proud Nation

The most distinctive aspects of the second great stage of American development were the stabilization of independent political institutions and the corresponding cultural nationalism which pervaded almost every phase of American thought. This stage is often called the early national period. Although various other dates might be given, it is justifiably described as beginning with the Stamp Act Congress of 1765, wherein the united political power of Americans was first demonstrated, and as ending in 1829 with the inauguration of Andrew Jackson as seventh President of the United States, an event which was a triumph for the common man.

These sixty-four years present a picture of world-shaking change. This was the age of the American Revolution, the ratification of the

Constitution, and the development of the two-party system of government. It was the age of George Washington and John Paul Jones, of Shays' Rebellion and the Whiskey Insurrection, of the Louisiana Purchase and the Lewis and Clark Expedition, of the War of 1812, of Henry Clay and Daniel Webster and John C. Calhoun, of the Missouri Compromise and the Monroe Doctrine. In Europe it was the age of the French Revolution and of the rise and fall of Napoleon, of the romantic revival and the industrial revolution in England.

Like all periods of rapid change this one was inexpressibly complex, but it was marked by the general collapse of anachronistic institutions and philosophies. The "haves" were ranged against the "have nots," the proponents of centralized control against those who wished more local autonomy, absolutists and authoritarians against all colors of individualists and democrats. It should be remembered, of course, that the familiar clashes of the era—Mercantilism *vs.* Free Trade, Imperialism *vs.* Home Rule, Tory *vs.* Whig, and Federalist *vs.* Republican—existed in some form long before 1765 and, under other names, still exist, for in the realm of human affairs few basic differences are ever decisively and finally settled. But western civilization during this period painfully sought new compromises in these perennial conflicts, and those it arrived at, while not wholly satisfactory and far from the last full measure of democracy, were considerably more democratic than the world had known before.

Because the most magnificent promise of the American way of life is the fullest possible development of the individual within a society providing equal and exact justice for all, the literature of the early national period has extraordinary interest. The problems faced by the generations who lived between 1765 and 1829 are essentially today's problems. No American, instructed by recent decades in the painful complexity of political events—however remote they may at first seem—can afford to be ignorant of the ideas of George Washington, Alexander Hamilton, Thomas Jefferson, Thomas Paine, John Adams, Andrew Jackson, and their associates. The writings of these men, together with the Declaration of Independence and the Constitution, form a body of political literature which for richness, variety, and importance to the present day is second to none in the world. Even the belles-lettres of the period, slight in comparison to the work of the English romanticists, take on new meaning when read in terms of the political matrix in which they had their origin.

American nationalism was based upon both the geographical isolation of the English colonies and the political, economic, and social controversies which resulted in revolution. The debate over the Stamp Act divided the colonists into two parties: conservatives and radicals, or, to give them the names more common at the time, Tories and Whigs, Loyalists and Patriots. The lines of cleavage varied from colony to colony, but the radical leaders came mainly from the middle classes, whose distrust of British control was often mingled with antipathy to the ruling aristocracy. Anti-British feeling was combined from the first with a glorification of the common man and his place in the world. The victorious party consisted of those Americans least aware and least desirous of commercial, social, religious, and cultural ties with Great Britain. Aggressive and self-confident, they had nevertheless a self-conscious anxiety to show themselves "just as good" as the Tories they had so effectually chased out. Crèvecoeur's "The American Belisarius" (1780) vividly suggests the emotional basis of their position.

Self-consciousness was indeed characteristic of the entire period. The idea of inferiority, and particularly of inferiority to Britain, was unendurable, and Americans were extraordinarily sensitive to criticism. Patriotism often silenced intelligent objectivity; the person who expressed much skepticism regarding American character, institutions, or destiny found himself exceedingly unpopular.

The train of events, moreover, was propitious for the growth of nationalism. Of the elements contributing to unity, such diverse factors as the Revolution itself, the conservative reaction to the upheaval in France, the Napoleonic wars, and Westward expansion deserve recalling.

Many democratic tendencies were accentuated or set in motion by the Revolution. Large estates were confiscated and divided; small business and manufacturing were stimulated; church establishments were attacked; slavery, imprisonment for debt, and humiliating punishments were regarded with growing disfavor; the idea of universal education at state expense was voiced. Americans were far from being of one mind about these matters, but they recognized that such tendencies differentiated the United States from the nations of the Old World. They agreed, moreover, in insisting that they were now ready to arrange their own affairs, and in being sublimely confident that they could arrange them better than the English had arranged theirs. The Americans were a "new" people, as Crèvecoeur put it. They were ready to teach the rest of the world; they were weary of being taught.

The assertion of the rights of man by the revolutionists in France seemed at first a gratifying justification of the American example. European convulsions soon brought, however, a strong conservative reaction among Americans, already doubtful that they had wholly solved their political problems. The Federalists, who under the leadership of Hamilton controlled the government from the adoption of the Constitution until 1801, were perhaps not lovers of the common man, but they were still fervent nationalists. They planned and worked to create a strong federal union that would be able to withstand possible attack from abroad and to suppress internal disorder. Events proved that they were both wise and patriotic.

The Napoleonic wars, which disrupted commercial and diplomatic accord with Europe, made American isolation much more complete than it had been before. When the United States was finally drawn into a second war with England—the War of 1812—the nation achieved that economic self-sufficiency which had long been talked about but had never quite been a reality. Textile and iron industries grew up quickly, and Americans faced the occupation of the West with full assurance that they had the means to fulfill their dreams of greatness.

The West, despite its individualism, was even more nationalistic than the older seaboard states. It looked to the central government for its lands and the means of access to them, and its local ties were new and weak. It was the West which was least respectful of Europe, most certain that the United States, if necessary, could lick the entire Old World.

From the perspective of the twentieth century it is clear that the bonds of Europe were not cut sharply, that the old pattern of transplantation and adaptation continued as immigrants like Albert Gallatin and P. S. Dupont de Nemours brought their talents to the service of American life. Nationalism, however, was peculiarly significant to literature, for it led Americans to attempt the impossible—the creation, overnight, of a tradition of belles-lettres. To the nationalist the possession of a first-rate literature of politics and a highly reputable literature of religion was not enough; if poetry, fiction, and the drama were the marks of a great culture, America must have them. If, as Aristotle had asserted, epic poetry was the height of literary art, the United States must have epic poems comparable in grandeur to the North American continent and the superior political institutions of the Republic.

Such was the attitude which lay behind the work of Philip Freneau, Royall Tyler, the Connecticut Wits, William Cullen Bryant, Washington Irving, and James Fenimore Cooper. In Commencement and Fourth of July orations, in newly founded magazines with "United States" or "Columbian" or a state or city name conspicuous in their titles, in anthologies, and in books, Americans hammered at the theme of intellectual independence, the creation of a literary culture better than anything which had yet appeared or which was likely to appear in monarchical Europe. However, they did not succeed in creating such a culture before 1829.

National pride led to many pleas for more generous support of American writers and to many elaborate defenses of America against the criticism of British editors and travelers. This material, most voluminous after the War of 1812, has been labeled the "Paper War" and is not of general interest, although both Cooper and Irving contributed to it. It had, however, one very important effect—it focused the attention of American writers more sharply than ever before upon the native scene. What, they asked themselves, was unique in American life? In their attempt to answer that question they became deeply concerned with native types, dialects, manners, scenery, and institutions. Despite their frequent failure to solve the problem of finding fresh or appropriate forms in which to clothe their new literary materials, they left a body of writing notable both for its variety and for its interpretation of American life.

Political Thought

This period's extensive literature of politics and political philosophy may best be summarized as it centers around four stages of American history: (1) the debate about self-government which extended from the Stamp Act to the Declaration of Independence; (2) the Revolution itself; (3) the struggle for stability and an acceptable balance of the opposing political philosophies of Hamilton and Jefferson; and (4) the continuing battle of the common man for his share of the responsibilities and rewards of political office.

(1) The philosophy and the events which lay behind the Revolution are readily gathered from John Dickinson's "Liberty Song" (1768), Benjamin Franklin's "Edict by the King of Prussia" (1773) and "Rules by Which a Great Empire May be Reduced to a Small One" (1773), John Adams' *Novanglus* (1775), Jonathan Boucher's *View of the Causes and Consequences of the American Revolution* (1797), Thomas Paine's *Common Sense* (1776), and the Declaration of Independence itself (1776). Franklin provides a good description of most of the economic and political irritations enumerated also in the Declaration; the others give an impression of the emotions of the period, deeply rooted as they were in social and religious differences. Boucher deserves particular study, because the Tory position is often ignored or neglected.

These writings are only a small part of the literary debate of 1765-1776. Pamphlets, speeches, sermons, and state papers appeared in profusion. Outstanding among the Whig pamphlets are those by Samuel Adams, James Otis, Daniel Dulany, and John Dickinson, together with the first works of Hamilton and Jefferson. The Tory position was maintained by such writers as Martin Howard, Daniel Leonard, and Samuel Seabury. Patrick Henry's "Give me liberty or give me death" speech of March 1775 is a part of the full picture, as is Francis Hopkinson's political allegory, *A Pretty Story* (1774). In a little more than a decade a large body of polemical prose appeared, presenting arguments based both upon specific legal or constitutional positions and upon abstract philosophies of government. Both types of argument are observable in the Declaration.

The legal position of the Patriots—denial of the authority of Parliament to levy "internal taxes" on the colonies, assertion of the doctrine of "no taxation without representation," and demands that the colonial legislatures be recognized as the only just means of obtaining "consent of the governed"—proved in the end less defensible than direct appeal to the right of revolution. For that and other "natural rights" specifically named in the Declaration, the Patriots had the precedents of the revolutions which had driven Charles I and James II from the English throne. They knew their history and their political philosophy; their writings show close study of the theories of Thomas Hobbes, Sir Robert Filmer, John Locke, and many other English and European thinkers. They had behind them, moreover, a solid tradition of theological disputation. It is impossible to read their presentations of the colonial case without gaining an increasing respect for the caliber of their minds and the clarity of their exposition.

(2) The "clash of resounding arms" at Lexington ended the constitutional debate and brought to the fore more emotional and persuasive writers — propagandists they would now be called. Their task was to unite and hold in line a Revolutionary party which was never perhaps more than a two-thirds majority of the population; their method was to appeal to the interests and the prejudices of as many different groups as they could. Master of them all was Paine, whose *Crisis* series (1776-1783) ranks with the best propaganda ever written. Newspapers and magazines carried much similar material, including numerous poems such as Freneau's "Memorable Victory" (1781), Hopkinson's "Battle of the Kegs" (1778), and Dwight's "Columbia, Columbia, to Glory Arise" (1793). Popular songs, ballads, and hymns, with ever-changing lyrics, also had their place in the literary war. Too, there were extensive verse satires, of which the most famous was John Trumbull's *M'Fingal* (Part I, 1775) — an imitation of Samuel Butler's *Hudibras* (1663-1678), an English satire. The Loyalists, too, had their propagandists, of whom the best known were Joseph Stansbury and Jonathan Odell. They show clearly the social cleavage of the Revolution, for they almost invariably assumed a snobbish tone toward the "rabble." Few printing presses were available to the Loyalists, however, and their opinions must be sought in letters, diaries, parodies of Patriot songs, and such accounts of affairs as Boucher's *View*, published later in England. Neither party was averse to name-calling or scurrility, and it is perhaps no accident that the most good-natured of Revolutionary songs, the spirited "Yankee Doodle," is the only one which has remained on the lips of Americans. As Crèvecoeur's "The American Belisarius" reveals, it was not a time of tolerance or generosity toward one's enemies.

(3) In the literature of the years between the end of the war and the stabilization of the new government, a rational and deliberate tone is again uppermost, although undertones of emotion are not lacking. Its great monument, outside of the Constitution itself, is *The Federalist*, in the main the work of Hamilton. Washington's *Farewell Address* (1796), the inaugural speeches of Jefferson (1801, 1805), and the political content of such pieces as Tyler's *The Contrast* (1787), H. H. Brackenridge's *Modern Chivalry* (1792), and Freneau's "Stanzas to an Alien" (1799) round out the picture of the political issues of the era. Fuller representation would include *The Anarchiad* (1786-1787) and numerous other works by the Connecticut Wits, most of whom were strongly Federalist in their convictions. Joel Barlow, author of *Advice to the Privileged Orders* (1791) and *The Conspiracy of Kings* (1792), was a notable exception to the Federalist trend in writing.

Especially interesting here is the repetition, with variations, of the age-old conflicts. Centralized control and local autonomy, government by the few and government by the many—these were again among the alternatives. Woodrow Wilson and others have suggested that the Constitution was based upon a political philosophy derived ultimately from Newtonian physics, to the effect that opposing political forces can be balanced one against another, and the state, though constantly moving, preserved in equilibrium. John Adams was probably the chief American exponent of this philosophy, with his distrust of unlimited democracy and his theory that executive, aristocratic, and democratic elements must be preserved in any stable government by elaborate checks and balances. The French political philosopher Montesquieu, widely read in America, had much the same idea. Whatever its precise sources, the Constitution unquestionably reflects a conservative reaction to Revolutionary doctrines. It has proved flexible enough, however, to protect both majorities and minorities with reasonable success for over 150 years.

(4) The Federalists, however right they may have been, were not astute politicians. They did not disguise their belief that the masses counted for little, the *aristoi* for much, and they ignored local loyalties and conditions which they would have done well to study. The common people demanded respect throughout the period, and toward the end of it they received from most successful politicians the flattery which has ever since been theirs. They wanted their leaders "folksy," and they did not care whether or not words were meticulously pronounced and diplomatic protocol rigorously observed. They did not, in short, accept the notion of Captain Farrago (in Brackenridge's *Modern Chivalry*) that those who handle the affairs of state should be informed on fundamental principles and skilled in public speaking. In 1828, the common people came into their own and elected Andrew Jackson. They did not, of course, find thereby an immediate solution to the unending problems of democratic government.

Irving's satirical portrait of Jefferson in the *Knickerbocker History* (1809) gives some indication of the political temper of the last phase of the early national period, but the citizenry in Cooper's *The Pioneers* (1823) is even better evidence. Special privileges had to go, even though it might mean economic waste, ignorance enshrined in public office, and general irresponsibility. Cooper's own attitude, expressed far more irascibly elsewhere, was precisely that of the orderly man who surveys the litter in a public park on the morning after the Labor Day weekend. He doubted that the common people were yet prepared to take care of their heritage. The political spirit of the period was best expressed by Andrew Jackson himself in the peroration to his *Farewell Address* (1837). Pride in the national accomplishment and assurance that there was no longer danger from abroad were combined with the recognition that "It is from within, among yourselves, from cupidity, from corruption, from disappointed ambition, and inordinate thirst for power, that factions will be formed and liberty endangered. It is against such designs, whatever disguise the actors may assume, that you have especially to guard yourselves."

Economic Development

The problem of earning a living was not so frequently or so fully the concern of literature after 1765 as it had been before. Nevertheless, the later writing can be better understood with some knowledge of the economic thought and conflicts which distinguished American life in the early national period. Fundamental, of course, was the desire of individuals to "get on" in the world. Simple living, thrift, and industry, the ideals preached in *Poor Richard's Almanac*, were the ideals of most men. They were praised by writers as diverse as Crèvecoeur, Washington, Jefferson, Dwight, and Barlow. Such easygoing, shiftless characters as those portrayed by Washington Irving in "Rip Van Winkle" were decidedly not the heroes of the era. Americans were on their way to full acceptance of the gospel proclaimed in 1838 in Longfellow's "A Psalm of Life":

> Let us, then, be up and doing
>   With a heart for any fate;
> Still achieving, still pursuing,
>   Learn to labor and to wait.

Most Americans probably felt that money was the chief thing to be up and doing about, and they did not question the validity of that end for work. John Woolman was not of that sentiment; like Thoreau in a later generation he wished to know the result of the pursuit of wealth. Far more averse to luxuries and pomp than many who cried out against them from higher places in the world, he reached a thought-provoking conclusion: "Wealth desired for its own sake Obstructs the increase of Virtue, and large possessions in the hands of selfish men have a bad tendency, for by their means too small a number of people are employed in things usefull, and therefore some of them are necessitated to labour too hard." A few other observers — Crèvecoeur and Dwight, for example — expressed a similar concern lest moneygetting end in too wide a discrepancy between the very rich and the very poor, but Poor Richard's disciples would scarcely have admitted the possibility that men could labor too hard.

What were the main features of the American economy? In 1765 Americans were primarily an agricultural people, and they were still so in 1829, but in the interval the economy of the nation underwent great changes which had their due effect upon literature. Three such changes may be mentioned: (1) the shift from a colonial to a national economy, although with continuing conflicts between those who wanted a centralized control of commerce, manufactures, finance, and transportation and those who wanted a large measure of local control; (2) the far-reaching development of industry and the factory system; and (3) the creation, through expansion to the West, of an enormous domestic market.

The colonies in 1766 were dependencies of a nation which, in so far as it had a colonial policy, had accepted the Mercantilist doctrine that overseas possessions should supply the home country with raw materials and serve as a market for manufactured products. The trade regulations based upon this theory caused much hard feeling, as may readily be seen in Franklin's "Edict" and "Rules"; they were, of course, one of the principal causes of the Revolution. Mercantilism was also partially responsible for the British desire to limit expansion to the West, where the control of markets would be more difficult. That attitude aroused as much antagonism, probably, as either the trade regulations or the taxation which was sought to help pay for the French and Indian War; the Virginians were particularly unwilling to give up the West to the Indians. As Paine's *Common Sense* shows, the Americans had arrived at the point where they thought in "continental" terms, and they were determined to control not merely their internal affairs but their economic life as well.

The success of the Revolution permitted the development of home manufactures and the West. The federal government gradually acquired title to the Western lands, and with the Constitution, internal tariff barriers were removed. Washington's *Farewell Address* provides a good view of the hope that the natural economic rivalries of the various sections might be minimized, a hope later echoed by Jefferson and Jackson. Americans did not agree, however, on the extent to which the central government should aid the states in internal improvements or "protect" infant industries or control the financial structure of the nation. They never have agreed on these matters, but their disagreements were especially sharp in the age of Hamilton's *Report on Manufactures*, of the clamor of the West for roads and canals, and of Jackson's titanic struggle against the Second Bank of the United States.

Industrialization was forced upon the United States by the situation in Europe, where France and Great Britain were at war almost continuously from 1793 until 1815. The unprecedented development of American foreign trade involved the nation in its first attempt to make good its right to trade as a neutral with belligerent nations, in the face of Napoleon's Berlin and Milan Decrees and the British Orders in Council. The Embargo Act of 1807 and the War of 1812 are usually credited with effecting a large measure of self-sufficiency in manufactures, although the full effect of the factory system was not to be felt until several decades later. Irving's Knickerbocker satire on governing by proclamation suggests the Federalist attitude toward Jefferson's theory of economic isolation to avoid embroilment in war. Bryant's "A Meditation on Rhode Island Coal" (1826) reflects the development of industrialization.

The occupation of the West began almost immediately after the Revolution, but it was enormously accelerated by the introduction of new means of transportation. The steamboat reached the Ohio River in 1811, only four years after Robert Fulton's first successful demonstration on the Hudson. Roads and canals followed swiftly; the Cumberland or National Road had reached Zanesville, Ohio, by 1825, the year in which the Erie Canal was completed. The railroad era was soon to come, for construction of the Baltimore and Ohio began in 1828. The West soon had its own literature, reflecting the turbulence of the period, as may be seen in the writings of Morgan Neville and Peter Cartwright (1785-1872). Its development is also suggested by Cooper's *The Pioneers* (1823), despite a slightly earlier setting, and by Bryant's "The Prairies" (1833). From the time of the *Western Review* (1819-1821), published in Lexington, Kentucky, this western section had periodicals of its own and a local literature.

Religion

Religion remained vastly important to Americans, but it did not occupy quite so central a position in the national life as it had previously. The disruption and damage of the Revolution perceptibly weakened the position of many churches; Congress was forbidden by the Constitution to make any laws leading to the establishment of a state church; and the Bill of Rights asserted the principle of complete religious freedom. Disestablishment in those states which had supported particular churches followed, and the period as a whole displays that wide variety of religious thought to which Americans are now accustomed. Nationalistic tendencies may be discerned in various denominations and in the continued dominance of Protestantism, but they are of minor significance.

This is not to say that religious fervor lessened, or that sectarianism disappeared. The masses wanted churches; denominational rivalries were no less intense; and the literature of religion was still enormous. Calvinism remained a powerful force through the influence of such followers of Edwards as Dwight, and it may be observed in a watered-down form in certain lines of Bryant's "Inscription for the Entrance to a Wood" (1821) and "To a Waterfowl" (1818). Revivalism flourished at intervals throughout the period, especially in the West, as Cartwright's autobiography suggests. Quakerism, no longer noisily militant, found its finest American exponent in Woolman.

From the standpoint of literary history, however, the distinctive feature of the age is the emergence of the rationalistic and humanitarian doctrines of Deism and Unitarianism. Neither was new; neither was widely popular. The virulence with which they were both attacked gives us some hint of their effect upon the age, and from this distance it is clear that their common confidence in the powers of the human mind and their common tendency to present a man-centered rather than a God-centered world expressed something basic in the times.

Deism (see p. 12), which denied the revelation of God in the Bible, preferring to seek religious truth through human reason, regarded religious duties as primarily humanitarian. Franklin arrived at Deistic beliefs early in life and he seems never to have deserted them. After his *Dissertation on Liberty and Necessity* (1725), however, he never expounded them openly, evidently having reached the conclusion that the orthodox Christian churches operated as a desirable social control, doing more good than harm. Somewhat similar attitudes are to be seen in Crèvecoeur, Freneau, Jefferson, and even Washington. With the French Revolution, however, Deism became momentarily a proselyting faith, spread in Deistic newspapers, magazines, and societies, as well as in more or less formal treatises. Three of the last are worth mention: Ethan Allen's *Reason the Only Oracle of God* (1784), for which the Revolutionary hero of Vermont was largely indebted to a Dr. Thomas Young; Paine's *The Age of Reason* (1795); and Elihu Palmer's *Principles of Nature* (1802). These works were the object of almost unbelievably violent attacks by such orthodox Christians as Dwight, who regarded Deism not only as the worst form of infidelity and materialism but also as the handmaid of political radicalism. Deism was effectually destroyed, for the masses were not willing to give up the authority of the Bible, whatever they thought of social and political controls.

Unitarianism, the denial of the doctrine of the Trinity and the divinity of Jesus Christ, is fully explained in William Ellery Channing's "Unitarian Christianity" (1819). It had been common among the upper and more rationalistic classes in Boston and other large New England towns since the 1780's and became a matter for violent debate only after 1805, when a Unitarian was appointed to the professorship of divinity in Harvard College. Differing from Deism in its acceptance of revelation, it is chiefly significant for its similar emphasis upon human nature and reason and for its humanitarianism. The genesis of the succeeding age of reform, in so far as that reform was stimulated by Transcendentalism (see p. 75), has often been found in Unitarianism. Closely related to it is Universalism, organized as a formal sect in 1794 with the central doctrine that, since God is all-good, He could never have intended other than that all men shall be saved—a position which had been anticipated some years earlier by Charles Chauncy. These doctrines, although not widely popular, challenged the dominance of Calvinism throughout the nation.

Science and Education

When Benjamin Silliman founded the *American Journal of Science and Arts* in 1818 with the express purpose of raising science to "the elevation of our national character," he added one more link to the chain of nationalistic ambitions. The period abounded in new scientific associations, museums, libraries, and colleges. This aspect of the age is seldom apparent in literature because of the advance of specialization, but it is worth recalling to the reader of Franklin, Freneau, the Connecticut Wits, and even Cooper. Scientific rationalism was spreading rapidly, and it was finding institutional support. Irving's satire on Jefferson's fondness for gadgets suggests that the advance of science was not universally appreciated; on the other hand, the absence of persistent appeals to a providential order of nature will be observed by every reader, and the scientific world-view may be regarded as generally accepted.

Neither the common schools nor the universities found much genuine state support before 1829; the democratization of education was to come somewhat later. The principle that the state should educate its citizens and exert itself for the diffusion of knowledge was, however, clearly enunciated by Washington and Jefferson and other of the founding fathers. The setting aside of public lands in the West for the maintenance of school systems had not succeeded, but the foundation had been laid. Dwight's prophecy of "new-born Oxfords" in the West (in *Greenfield Hill*, 1794) and Cooper's account of the grandiose educational dreams of Templeton in *The Pioneers* show that Americans were thinking of education.

The Fine Arts

The fine arts, relatively unimportant in the colonial period, were especially susceptible to the later urgings of nationalism. Their connection with literature, moreover, was much more intimate than it had been before. While it cannot be said that they attained genuine distinction before 1829, their development was extraordinary and well worth attention.

The piety which had supported portraiture in the earlier age now became patriotic, and the founders of the Republic were given generously such immortality as paint could provide. The numerous portraits of Washington by Gilbert Stuart (1755-1828) are the best-known example of a demand which gave a livelihood to a dozen or more painters in the period. Most of them were trained abroad, many under Benjamin West (1738-1820), an expatriate from Pennsylvania who was President of the Royal Academy from 1792 until his death. Large historical paintings of incidents of the Revolution were also popular, although the most familiar, Emanuel Leutze's "Washington Crossing the Delaware," was painted somewhat later. Most interesting to students of literature, however, because it paralleled the literary search for new material, was the beginning of a landscape school with such painters as Thomas Cole (1801-1848), to whom Bryant addressed his sonnet, "To Cole, the Painter Departing for Europe" (1829). Numerous galleries, art schools, and associations were founded, of which the most important was the National Academy of the Arts of Design, founded in 1826 and still in existence.

Sculpture was to develop later, although by 1825 a few Americans were settling in Italy to learn that art. They were soon to return to fill the halls of the Capitol at Washington with nationalistic statuary. The carving of ship figureheads still was a folk form of sculpture which later generations have much admired; the observant reader will notice Freneau's reference to the "girl at the head" in his "Lines by H. Salem" (1791).

Music became somewhat more popular in the period, with the organization of choral societies in the larger towns, even as far west as Cincinnati. There was much music in the cities, and in the 1820's opera was introduced. Immigrants continued to provide the most genuine music-lovers, and except for a few songs such as Samuel Woodworth's "The Old Oaken Bucket" (1818), not even lyrics were American. Dwight's "Columbia, Columbia, to Glory Arise" is an example of the patriotic songs which found places in the popular books of music. Francis Scott Key's "The Star-Spangled Banner" is the major contribution of the era, although its melody is not native.

Perhaps the most fascinating survival of the cultural nationalism of this period is the classical revival in architecture, with which Cooper had so much fun in *The Pioneers*. Sponsored by Jefferson, who fell in love with the Roman remains at Nîmes in southern France (and with the Maison Carré in particular), classical forms dominated both public and domestic architecture from shortly after the Revolution until the 1840's. They were closely connected with the conviction that American tastes should be exemplary and republican; they disregarded, as Cooper so neatly demonstrated, the American climate and the American way of life. Colonial and Georgian styles survived, especially in the seaboard towns, and the great architect of the period was Charles Bulfinch (1763-1844), designer of the State House at Boston. The period is memorable, moreover, for the first architectural competition for designs for the national capitol.

T.H.

LITERARY TRENDS

The Circumstances of Literary Publication

The literate American between 1765 and 1829 had great advantages over his colonial ancestors. He was the heir of an enormous expansion of printing, of the establishment of a periodical press scarcely equalled in vigor elsewhere in the world, and of the acceptance to a degree before unknown of the protection of literary property by copyright. None of these developments had reached its height by 1829, but their collective importance to literature can scarcely be overemphasized.

Many of the books of the period were printed in America for American readers. Some of the exceptions—certain pieces by Franklin, Crève-coeur's *Letters*, Boucher's *View*, and Paine's *Age of Reason*—are those whose circumstances of publication were peculiar. Irving and Cooper were among the few authors who had audiences on both sides of the Atlantic, and they developed the custom of arranging for nearly simultaneous editions in London and New York.

The spread of printing can be suggested by statistics. In 1810 the census found 202 paper mills in the United States. Charles Evans, who sought in his *American Bibliography* to list all American imprints before 1820 (and did not complete the task), found 35,854 items before 1800, of which 25,634 were printed between 1766 and 1799 inclusive, as against 10,220 items between 1639 and 1765. He listed 329 imprints for 1765 and 784 for 1799. Nor was this steady increase centralized; it was, indeed, less so than would be the case today. The chief center of printing until the Revolution was Boston; Philadelphia then held the lead until the 1820's when it went to New York. But there were presses in all the larger towns, including those in the West, and many of them published books as well as newspapers and magazines. All printing was still by hand, on flat-bed presses, but improvements and industrialization were in the offing. The Columbian Iron Press, developed about 1807, substituted the principle of the fulcrum for that of the screw. Steam and revolving cylinder presses were soon to be adopted, and one American, William Church (1778-1853), had patented in London in 1827 a typecasting and composing machine.

The stimulation to printing was primarily political, for this was the age of party journalism. Much of the political writing by Franklin, Adams, Paine, Jefferson, Hamilton, and Freneau first appeared in newspapers, which, despite paper shortages and military occupations, played a highly important role in the Revolution. The war over, newspapers multiplied; it is said that about two hundred were published simultaneously by 1801. Dailies appeared at Philadelphia and New York in 1783 and 1785, when those cities numbered about 25,000 persons. In the Hamilton-Jefferson period, party journalism swiftly came to maturity with the help of Freneau, who was an energetic propagandist for Jeffersonian Republicanism. Newspapers survived the Alien and Sedition Acts (see Freneau's "Stanzas to an Alien"); their place in political controversy is vividly revealed by Jefferson's attention to them in his *Second Inaugural*. Bryant, it will be remembered, made his fortune as editor and part owner of the New York *Evening Post*, founded by Hamilton in 1801. In short, throughout the period newspapers increased rapidly in numbers (by 1829 there were probably more than a thousand of them), in size, and in influence.

Magazines developed more slowly. F. L. Mott has estimated that about seventy-five were begun between 1783 and 1801, several hundred more during the first third of the nineteenth century. Most of them were short-lived but they played a large part in the rise of belles-lettres. Some of those which contained material of lasting literary interest were the *United States Magazine* (Philadelphia, 1779, edited by H. H. Brackenridge), the *New-York Magazine* (1790-1797), and the *North American Review* (Boston, 1815-1939). Other important literary outlets included the *Farmer's*

Weekly Museum (Walpole, N. H., 1793-1810, edited chiefly by Joseph Dennie), the *Columbian Magazine* (Philadelphia, 1786-1792), the *American Museum* (Philadelphia, 1787-1792), the *Massachusetts Magazine* (Boston, 1789-1796), and the *Port Folio* (Philadelphia, 1801-1827, edited by Dennie). These periodicals, and others like them all over the nation, provided a market for poems, essays, fiction, and literary criticism such as had never before been available. They were the background for the magazine world which supported Edgar Allan Poe in the next decade.

The American author, moreover, was favored after 1790 by a national copyright law protecting him from the unauthorized use of his work within the United States (but not, it will be noted, abroad) for a period of fourteen years, with the possibility of an extension for another fourteen. This law, based upon the similar law passed in Great Britain in 1710, and upon legislation in Connecticut in 1783, was a great boon, although it did not protect American writers from the competition of pirated English books. International copyright was not achieved until 1891.

The book trade developed rapidly after the Revolution, and before the end of the period publishing, as now understood, was replacing older methods of bridging the gap between author and reader. Bookstores and printing establishments transformed themselves into publishers, and some of the familiar names of present-day publishing appeared. The firm of Wiley was founded by Charles Wiley in 1807, that of Harper by J. and J. Harper, printers, in 1817, that of Appleton by Daniel Appleton in 1825. Americans, nevertheless, were still largely dependent upon Great Britain; it has been estimated that American presses supplied only twenty per cent of current books in 1820, only thirty per cent in 1830.

Nationalism and Romanticism

The content of American literature between 1765 and 1829 was largely determined by the peculiar circumstances of American life and shows in large measure the dominant nationalistic pattern of thought of the period. When we turn, however, to problems of literary form, we are at once impressed by a quite dissimilar and even a conflicting factor—the continuing influence of European and especially English literary tradition. Our early national literature was written at approximately the same time as the so-called romantic revival in England occurred, and its connections with that movement are so numerous that some scholars have preferred to describe it as American romanticism.

Some of the major American romanticists (it must be remembered that numerous later writers, such as Poe, might be grouped with them) are Freneau, Bryant, Irving, and Cooper. These writers, like their English contemporaries—Wordsworth, Coleridge, Scott, Byron, Shelley, and Keats, to name the most important—represent something new. Their similarity may be readily demonstrated by a brief consideration of the five elements which are sometimes said to be the identifying marks of romanticism:

(1) The revolt against the literary forms and ideas of Classicism and Neoclassicism, which is evident in varying ways in the work of Wordsworth, Byron, and Shelley, has some parallel in the relatively new forms of fiction developed by Irving and Cooper (and later Poe), and in the political poetry of Freneau and Bryant.

(2) The new emphasis upon the imaginative and emotional qualities of literature, apparent in all the English romanticists, is likewise observable in all the Americans. It includes a liking for the picturesque, the exotic, the sensuous, the sensational, and the supernatural.

(3) The strong tendency to exalt the individual and the common man, characteristic especially of Wordsworth, was in America almost a national religion, as we have seen.

(4) The fresh interest in external nature, for which Wordsworth is again most famous, may be felt in the poetry of Freneau and Bryant and in the novels of Cooper.

(5) The literary use of the more colorful aspects of the past, common in the work of Coleridge, Scott, and Keats, is also to be found in Freneau's use of the "ruins of empire" theme, in Bryant's fascination by the Mound Builders, in Irving's effort to exploit the legends of the Hudson River region, and in Cooper's long series of historical tales.

It is not surprising, then, that the Americans have often been compared with the English romanticists. Doubtless they were deeply influenced by the literary fashions of Great Britain and instances may be shown of direct imitation. Yet we must not too hastily dismiss all of their work as imitative, nor ignore their very great differences from the English. Americans contributed to romanticism as much, perhaps, as they derived from it. The interplay of forms and ideas was simply the continuation of a cultural bond with Europe which no degree of national pride could wholly sever. Always the American writers were drawn in two directions, on the one hand to their own land, which usually furnished them with the content for their writings, and on the other hand to that cosmopolitan tradition which ordinarily furnished them with the forms in which they shaped their ideas.

Types of Diminishing Importance

A distinctive feature of the period is the rise to greater importance than ever before of poetry, the essay, drama, and fiction — those forms in which the ideas of the writer are shaped within a fairly well defined aesthetic pattern. It cannot be said that Americans uniformly displayed, within these forms, that cultural independence which they thought so desirable. The rise of belles-lettres nevertheless indicates the appearance of a class of men who thought of themselves as literary artists, and of a reading public ready for literature other than the merely informational or utilitarian.

With the advent of more polished and more self-consciously literary writers, the distinctive ideas of the age were much more likely to find expression in belles-lettres than had previously been the case. Accounts of voyages, promotion tracts, sermons, histories, and biographies continued to be written, but their characteristics changed somewhat and they no longer held a central place.

Pieces closely related to but not truly accounts of voyages or promotion tracts are Crèvecoeur's *Letters* (1782) and Bartram's *Travels* (1791). The former is really a series of essays, and Bartram's book, too, has an essay-like quality, if one skips judiciously. Other examples of this type may be found in such works as Jonathan Carver's *Travels* (1778), Jefferson's *Notes on the State of Virginia* (written about 1782), Flint's *Geography and History of the Mississippi Valley* (1827), and the travel books of Bryant, Cooper, and Irving.

Sermons similarly became freer and more polished under the influence of ideals of composition like those expressed by Channing. They were still innumerable, but they began to be overshadowed by other literary types. Dwight's sermons are probably more typical of the time than Channing's, but they and the hundreds of others published during the period are now seldom read. The methods of oral discourse developed in the pulpit had their influence upon political oratory, which, as we shall see, now came into favor.

As we should expect, the nationalistic temper of the period had an immediate effect upon history and biography. The events of the Revolution were recorded, its heroes immortalized by such works as John Marshall's *Life of Washington* (1804-1807), and there was a flood of local histories, headed by Jeremy Belknap's *History of New Hampshire* (1784-1792). Little of this work was objective, and Irving's burlesque of antiquarianism and local pedantry in his *Knickerbocker History of New York* was doubtless needed. History was to be popularized in several decades by Prescott, Motley, and Parkman. Cooper's history of the United States Navy and Irving's many biographies, however, should not be forgotten. Such writings were thoroughly characteristic of the period in which these men matured.

Polemical Tracts and Treatises

The literature of persuasion was, of course, outstanding in an age of constant political discussion. It had a conspicuous place from the first, as we have seen; now it reached a very high level indeed in such examples as Franklin's "Edict" and "Rules," Adams' *Novanglus*, Paine's *Common Sense, American Crisis,* and *Age of Reason,* Barlow's *Advice to the Privileged Orders,* and *The Federalist.* Many other works might be named from the period, for the great bulk of political writings belongs to this class, as do many theological treatises. Closely related to the tract and treatise on the one hand, and to the sermon on the other, are the innumerable political addresses and orations, the best known of which are the Farewell Address of Washington and Jefferson's inaugurals.

As was the case in the colonial period, the structure of this material defies generalization. Certain new tendencies are, however, evident. The development of newspapers and magazines made place for short pieces like Franklin's, and for lengthy series of essays and letters such as those by Adams, Paine (in the *Crisis*), and Hamilton. The latter were quite evidently influenced by the rise to prominence of the English periodical essay.

Topical arrangement continued to dominate, with the nature of the controversy determining the pattern. Of especial interest is the meticulous planning of *The Federalist,* described in the first number of that series, and the variety which was achieved by Paine, both in *Common Sense* and in the *Crisis* series. The addresses and orations will be found to have remarkably similar structure, except that to the topical arrangement the speaker's invariable exordium (introduction) and peroration (conclusion) are added. The modest beginning and the highly dignified conclusion, often embodying an appeal to divine guidance, which characterize most of the speeches of the era, are still a part of the pattern of discourse expected of our national leaders.

The rhetorical height of the period was unquestionably the Declaration of Independence, which combines the topical structure of the tract with the tones and methods of oratory. The rhetorical standards of the time are revealed by a comparison of the simplified final form with Jefferson's rough draft. The careful balance of emotion and reason makes the Declaration a model of its kind, and it is not surprising that its phrases have never lost their vividness. Paine's writings have a similar oratorical ring, as do Hamilton's (although less frequently); it is unfortunate that we have no authentic text of the speeches with which Patrick Henry and James Otis electrified their audiences, for they too were doubtless masterpieces of persuasion.

Diaries and Autobiographies

Franklin's *Autobiography* and Woolman's *Journal* would be found on any list of the great books of the period. They form a remarkable contrast, although both are related to the tradition of self-examination which goes back to the recitals of religious experiences which both the Puritans and the Quakers once required. These recitals, usually chronological in structure and didactic in purpose, depended on the attractiveness of the self-revealed personality for their relative success. Franklin, therefore, sought to explain his rise in the world despite a few mistakes, while Woolman told of his struggles to isolate himself from participation in the inhumanity of man to man. The one was a worldly, shrewd, and understandably self-satisfied man, the other a saint-like radical. Both have their place in the formation of the American character.

Poems

Poetry, which had been cultivated from the first in America, now began to bulk much larger. The work of two poets, Freneau and Bryant, would be included in any complete collection of the poems of major American verse-makers. Also of significance are the poets of the Revolution; the Connecticut Wits—Dwight and Barlow; and the sentimentalists—Wilde and Woodworth.

The singers of the Revolution were more concerned with propaganda than with artistic finish, but the relative sophistication of their forms as compared with those of the *Bay Psalm Book* and *The Day of Doom* is immediately evident. Popular ballad meters were retained, together with such ballad devices as repetition and refrain, but both "Yankee Doodle" and "The Battle of the Kegs" consistently use feminine rhymes and "Nathan Hale," probably the finest of the anonymous ballads, has a subjectivity unusual in the type.

The Revolutionary songs are, in fact, somewhat more free and fresh in their forms than most of the poems of the Connecticut Wits, who regarded themselves as the "highbrows" of their time. The Wits had studied English literature and accepted the "rules" of classicism, including that respect for established types which is sometimes described as the "tyranny of the genres." Dwight thought so highly of Denham, Pope, Thomson, and Goldsmith that he incorporated whole lines of theirs in *Greenfield Hill* and deliberately imitated their forms and diction even though he was dealing with American themes and problems. Barlow, least conservative of the Wits, felt most at home in the mock-heroic and the iambic pentameter couplet perfected by the predecessors and contemporaries of Pope. Nor are the examples here the most flagrant instances of the way in which a reverence for classical forms vitiated the sometimes original ideas of the Connecticut Wits. Their efforts at the epic— Dwight's *Conquest of Canaan* (1785) and Barlow's *Columbiad* (1807) —are the most familiar evidences of misguided nationalistic endeavor.

We may leave sentimentalism for definition in connection with fiction, remembering, however, that such pieces as "The Lament of the Captive" and "The Old Oaken Bucket" merely foreshadow the reign of tears and self-pity in the holiday gift-books of the 1830's and 1840's. These poems reflect the romantic tradition quite as obviously as those of the Connecticut Wits reflect the Neoclassical, but they are much less pretentious and appealed to a public only casually concerned with literary art.

Freneau and Bryant, taken together, show the steady progress of romanticism in America. Freneau's admiration for the classics, Milton, and Ossian identifies him as a precursor of the romantic revival as was the English poet Thomas Gray, whom he much resembles. Bryant, with his many similarities to Wordsworth, had deep roots in the English poetic theory of the eighteenth century; his concept of the imagination and his emphasis upon the moral quality of beauty sometimes were in conflict with his more romantic glorification of emotion. There is evident a similar progress in forms, marked by the change from established patterns to great variety and flexibility. Freneau's regular verse forms give way to Bryant's experiments with anapestic substitutions in iambic meter.

Examination of the minor poetry written between 1765 and 1829 will corroborate this description of the trend, and may be conveniently accomplished by looking through some of the anthologies of the age. Elihu Hubbard Smith's *American Poems, Selected and Original* (1793), *The Columbian Muse* (1794), and Samuel Kettell's *Specimens of American Poetry* (1829) are particularly valuable. The transition was by no means over by 1829.

Essays

Newspapers and magazines played their part in the increase of poetic production, but they were most fundamental, perhaps, to the American development of the literary essay. The essay form had firmly established itself in England with *The Spectator* (begun 1711) of Addison and Steele, and its prestige was much enhanced by Samuel Johnson, Oliver Goldsmith, and other later authors. Its brevity and variety, together with the ease with which it could be adapted to didactic purposes, made it very attractive to Americans, who had had nothing quite like it before except the squibs in the almanacs, Thomas' *The Farmer's Almanack*, Franklin's *Poor Richard's Almanac*, and his *Way to Wealth* (1774). As early as 1722 Franklin was imitating *The Spectator* in his brother's newspaper, over the signature of "Silence Dogood." Thereafter the newspaper or magazine which lacked its "Tomo Cheeki" (Freneau) or "Jonathan Oldstyle" (Irving) or "Oliver Oldschool" (Joseph Dennie) was a rarity. The attempt to maintain a dignified anonymity gave a sameness to these productions in a type which depends for its success upon the personality, even the idiosyncrasy, of the author. In Irving's *Sketch Book*, however, the essay achieved genuine distinction. Crèvecoeur, moreover, has some claim to being regarded as one of the earliest of nature essayists.

Newspaper and magazine requirements were likewise responsible for the beginnings of American literary criticism in reviews and leading articles. Bryant's lectures on poetry, although prepared for oral delivery, might easily have taken the review form, as much of his other criticism did. The earliest American reviewers learned their trade from the British quarterlies, much as they deplored the strictures of those journals on American politics and culture.

Plays

Imitation and adaptation of European models, combined with the all-pervading nationalism, appeared also in the drama. Royall Tyler's *The Contrast*, produced in 1787, is an admirable illustration of the trend.

Important changes in the theatrical situation must first be noted. The repertoire company system which had grown up during the colonial period survived the closing of most of the principal theaters in the decade after 1774, but before 1829 it was giving way to the "star" system, which throughout the nineteenth century brought famous English actors to tour the chief American cities. Prejudice against the theater lessened, as is evident from the opening of an undisguised theater in Boston in 1794, and the repeal in 1789 of a long-ignored Pennsylvania law against stage plays. Neither public support nor international copyright laws, however, yet favored a native drama. All that can be said is that the theater became firmly established, with an ever-increasing number of native-born actors, managers, and playwrights.

Some native plays, now lost, may have been produced in the years just before the Revolution. During the conflict itself some political use was made of dramatic dialogs and satires, but few of them were actually produced; H. H. Brackenridge's *Battle of Bunkers-Hill* (1776) is typical. Beginning with Tyler, however, American playwrights began to see their work on the professional stage. Many of them were amateurs like Tyler and James Nelson Barker (1784-1858) of Philadelphia. Two—William Dunlap (1766-1839) and John Howard Payne (1791-1852)—made the theater their profession, so that a brief description of their work will provide an impression of theatrical affairs and of the difficulties which lay in the way of native drama. Their plays were traditional in structure; it is only in experimental theaters that attempts are made to extend the limits of dramatic form.

Dunlap, born in New Jersey, was a boy in New York City during the Revolution. Between 1784 and 1787 he was in London, studying painting under Benjamin West and attending many plays. He began writing soon after his return to New York and in 1789 had his first production. Before his death he wrote at least twenty-nine original plays, adapted and translated twenty-one more from the German and the French, and published, in 1832, the first history of the American theater. As manager of the Park Theater in New York in 1796-1805, he turned largely to foreign themes and fashions, but his most famous tragedy, *André* (acted in 1798), was based upon a well-known spy story of the Revolution and exemplifies the tendency to use nationalistic material.

Payne's chief distinction rests upon the fact that he was first of all an actor, trained in the American theaters. Like Washington Irving, he did most of his writing for the English audience and was inclined to be critical of the failure of his countrymen to support native authors. He went to England in 1813 and did not return for nineteen years. More than sixty plays have been attributed to Payne, the best known of which are the tragedy *Brutus* (1818), which became one of the widely popular plays of the century; *Clari or the Maid of Milan* (1823), an adaptation from the French into which was inserted Payne's most famous composition, "Home, Sweet Home"; and *Charles the Second* (1826), a comedy in which Washington Irving was his collaborator. As the titles indicate, Payne looked abroad for his themes and models.

At home, however, Tyler had numerous successors in the attempt to glorify the Revolutionary struggle and native American types. Not many of them had sufficient theatrical sense to succeed, and it may be added in their defense that the drama everywhere was in one of its not infrequent doldrums.

Novels and Short Stories

The prejudice against fiction which had marked the colonial period did not disappear in America until well after 1800. Jefferson, Dwight, and Noah Webster must be counted among the many who expressed belief that stories gave wholly false notions of life to impressionable youth. Nevertheless, fiction grew steadily more popular. In the late eighteenth century circulating libraries specializing in fiction prospered at the expense of the young ladies who demanded romance, and the new magazines, although expressing a suitable editorial concern about the possible moral effect of fiction, could not afford to bar it from their pages. By the 1780's American authors were ready to help supply the market with native productions, often meeting the anticipated criticism by protestations that their tales were drawn from "real life," or pointing out that they invariably portrayed the awful consequences of sin and the fair rewards of virtue. That sin was made attractive was purely coincidental.

The prevailing nationalism was evident in the quest for American setting and characters, but the American novel in its first stages was nevertheless heavily indebted to English models. Three distinct trends may be discerned, in an order which is roughly chronological. (1) The earliest American novels were adaptations of the fiction of sentiment and sensibility which had made the reputations of Samuel Richardson and Laurence Sterne; Mrs. Hannah Webster Foster's *The Coquette* (1797) is generally regarded as the best example of the type. (2) Americans next imitated the sensationalism of the so-called Gothic romance, as practiced in its later stages by Mrs. Ann Radcliffe, and the mystery-laden propaganda novel of which William Godwin's *Caleb Williams* (1794) is typical; this trend is illustrated by the work of Charles Brockden Brown (1771-1810) and, so far as propaganda is concerned, by H. H. Brackenridge's *Modern Chivalry*. (3) Finally, the society or domestic novel, for which Fanny Burney and Jane Austen were famous, and the historical romance as developed by Sir Walter Scott became naturalized in the United States; in these forms James Fenimore Cooper led the way, achieving the first really striking success.

Sentiment and sensibility—alike in their release of the "tender" emotions but differing in that sentimentalism was didactic and moral, sensibility deliberately throat-filling and tear-jerking—can scarcely be separated in *The Power of Sympathy; or, The Triumph of Nature* (1789), written "to expose the dangerous Consequences of Seduction and to set forth the advantages of female Education." Usually accepted as the first American novel, it was long attributed to Mrs. Sarah Wentworth Morton, but is now claimed for William Hill Brown. Mrs. Susanna Haswell Rowson's *Charlotte Temple, a Tale of Truth* (1791) was more popular. Many other sentimental novels might be named, and seduction and suicide and floods of tears filled many pages of fiction far into the nineteenth century. For most readers, however, *The Coquette* will be sufficient introduction to the type. Its form—a series of letters—was derived from Richardson's *Pamela* and *Clarissa Harlowe* and, while not universal, was characteristic. The contemporary reaction against such fiction may be accurately gauged by Tyler's *Contrast*, in which sentimentalism is vigorously attacked.

Charles Brockden Brown made use of the epistolary form in *Jane Talbot* (1801) and *Clara Howard* (1801), but he is better known for his "thrillers": *Wieland* (1798), *Ormond* (1799), *Arthur Mervyn* (1799-1800), and *Edgar Huntley* (1799). These are remarkable for their use of such mysteries as ventriloquism and sleepwalking, as well as for wonder-working heroes and deep-dyed villains. Brown's imitation of the Gothic romance and of Godwin is unmistakable but not slavish. His work shows traces also of social purpose, although that theme was best used by Brackenridge, whose models were *Don Quixote* and Henry Fielding. *Modern Chivalry* is a rambling book, partly a satirical tract on the times (for which it is now usually read) and partly a picaresque romance, with Teague O'Regan as its rogue hero.

The work of Cooper, weak as it is in some respects, was a clear improvement over earlier attempts in the form. His first effort, *Precaution* (1820), was an imitation of the Jane Austen type of English domestic fiction, and foreshadowed a lifelong concern with social distinctions. *The Spy* (1821) was doubtless suggested by the success of the then unidentified author of *Waverley* and *Ivanhoe* in combining history and fiction. Nationalism helped to make Cooper's work popular, but he must be credited with great skill in obtaining suspense in those parts of his novels in which physical action dominates, as well as with advances in the use of setting and characterization. The escape-pursuit pattern, evident at intervals throughout *The Pioneers*, is the structure in which he excelled; unfortunately he often combined it with overelaborate mysteries such as that of the Effinghams. Unquestionably, however, Cooper made the American novel respectable, and his excursions into new types were paralleled by the novels of Lydia Maria Child (1802-1880), Catherine Maria Sedgwick (1769-1867), and James Kirke Paulding (1778-1860).

Unlike the novel, the short story was largely dependent upon the magazines, and therefore had a relatively even start in international competition. Its beginnings are closely connected with those of the essay and with "characters," delineations of unusual or typical personalities. Franklin came close to the short story in "The Way to Wealth" and "The Ephemera," while Crèvecoeur's "The American Belisarius" is half-essay, half-story. The English magazines, although full of Oriental and moral tales, widely imitated in America, had not perfected the short story by 1815, nor had the German and French storytellers. The Americans had, therefore, a relatively new field, in which the contributions of Irving were outstanding. The story sketches of Irving retained many of the characteristics of the essay: a sense of the author's presence and manipulation, leisurely movement, a fullness of detail that is sometimes almost digression, and the achievement of atmosphere rather than suspense and sharp climax. Although few of his contemporaries rivalled him, it is not unreasonable to argue that with the short story Americans first took a place in the mainstream of world literature.

T.H.

Chronological Table of
LITERATURE AND HISTORY

1766 ■ Numerous pamphlets printed relating to the Stamp Act and the right of Parliament to tax the colonies

Benjamin Franklin examined before the House of Commons, 28 January · Declaratory Act, 7 March, affirmed the right of Parliament to legislate for the colonies "in all cases whatsoever" · Stamp Act repealed, 18 March

1767 ■ John Dickinson's *Letters from a Farmer in Pennsylvania* argued that British regulation of colonial trade had been unfair

Townshend Acts, effective 20 November, imposed duties on paper, tea, glass, and painter's lead · The Earl of Hillsborough became secretary of state responsible for American affairs

1768 ■ *Circular Letter*, drafted by Samuel Adams for the Massachusetts House of Representatives, urged all colonial assemblies to resist the policies of the British ministry

Massachusetts House dissolved after defying Hillsborough's order that it rescind the *Circular Letter* · British troops moved to Boston from Halifax to impress the Whig "extremists"

1769 ■ Samuel Adams and others, *An Appeal to the World, or a Vindication of the Town of Boston*

Nonimportation agreements adopted throughout the colonies caused British merchants to press for the repeal of the Townshend Acts

1770 Boston Massacre, 5 March · Townshend Acts repealed, with the exception of the duty on tea · Population (estimated) about 2,000,000

1771 ■ Franklin wrote first part of his *Autobiography*

First spinning-mill established by Samuel Arkwright in Derbyshire, England

1772 ■ Philip Freneau and H. H. Brackenridge, *Rising Glory of America*

Local committee of correspondence formed in Boston by Samuel Adams · The *Gaspee*, a revenue cutter, burned by Rhode Island citizens

1773 ■ Franklin's "Edict by the King of Prussia" and "Rules by Which a Great Empire May be Reduced to a Small One"

Hutchinson Letters, sent to Boston by Franklin, undermined the little remaining colonial confidence in the British ministry · Intercolonial committees of correspondence established · Boston Tea Party, 16 December

1774 ■ John Woolman's *Journal* · John Adams' "Novanglus" letters in the Boston *Gazette* · Thomas Jefferson's *Summary View of the Rights of British America* · Alexander Hamilton's *Vindication of the Measures of Congress* · Francis Hopkinson's *Pretty Story* · Edmund Burke's *Speech on American Taxation*, best example of the British Whig support for American complaints

Five "Intolerable Acts" passed by Parliament as a result of Boston Tea Party · First Continental Congress met in Philadelphia, 5 September, demanded the repeal of the "Intolerable Acts," and formed a "Continental Association" for administering nonimportation and nonexportation agreements · Sharp division of Americans on the question of resistance to British policy

1775 ■ Samuel Seabury's *Westchester Farmer* pamphlets, most important exposition of the Loyalists position · Hamilton's *The Farmer Refuted* · John Trumbull's *M'Fingal*, first part · Burke's *Speech on Conciliation with America*

General Gage marched from Boston to seize military supplies at Concord, 18 April, his intention being announced by Paul Revere · Skirmishes at Lexington and Concord, 19 April · Second Continental Congress convened at Philadelphia, 10 May · Battle of Bunker Hill, 17 June · Washington assumed command of the Continental army besieging Boston, 3 July · Americans captured Montreal, November, but were eventually forced to withdraw from Canada

1776   ■ Thomas Paine's *Common Sense* · *The Declaration of Independence*

Boston evacuated by the British, 17 March · Sentiment for independence culminated in the *Declaration*, signed 4 July and 2 August · British army landed on Long Island, 22 August, and soon occupied Manhattan Island · Nathan Hale executed, 22 September · Washington and his troops forced to retreat across New Jersey · Americans heartened by victory at Trenton, 26 December · Various naval actions, in which John Paul Jones emerged as a skillful leader · Organization of state governments begun

1777   ■ Hopkinson's *Political Catechism*

First supplies received from France · British occupied Philadelphia, September · General Burgoyne, after marching from Canada, surrendered to the Americans under General Gates at Saratoga, 17 October · Articles of Confederation, legalizing the Continental Congress, submitted to the states for ratification; adopted in 1781 · "Conway Cabal" to displace Washington as commander-in-chief failed · Winter quarters at Valley Forge

1778   American independence recognized by France and a military alliance effected · Unofficial aid received from Spain · Philadelphia evacuated by the British, 18 June

1779   ■ Hopkinson's *Battle of the Kegs*

Spain declared war on Great Britain, 16 June · The *Serapis* captured by the *Bon Homme Richard*, commanded by John Paul Jones, 23 September

1780   British captured Charleston · Spaniards took Mobile · Benedict Arnold's treason discovered, 26 September · Major John André executed, 2 October · Various military actions in North Carolina and Virginia, hereafter the chief battle area · Population (estimated) about 2,800,000

1781   ■ Philip Freneau's *British Prison-Ship* · Samuel Peters' *General History of Connecticut*

Action at Eutaw Springs, South Carolina, 8 September · British campaign in the South ended with surrender of Cornwallis and his troops at Yorktown, Virginia, 19 October

1782   ■ Crèvecoeur's *Letters from an American Farmer*

Provisional peace treaty signed at Paris, 30 November

1783   End of the war proclaimed by Washington, 19 April · Treaty of Paris, 3 September, recognized American independence, restored Florida to Spain · New York evacuated by the British, 25 November

1784   Ordinance providing for the survey and sale of public lands in the West, later supplemented by the Ordinance of 1785 and the famous Northwest Ordinance of 1787

1785   ■ Timothy Dwight's *Conquest of Canaan*

John Adams appointed minister to Great Britain, with instructions to negotiate commercial agreements and settlement of Western land question, the British being still garrisoned in the forts at Detroit, Niagara, and elsewhere

1786   ■ The Connecticut Wits' *Anarchiad* · Freneau's *Poems*

Shays' Rebellion in Massachusetts, first Populist uprising · Annapolis Convention, September, dominated by Hamilton, issued call for a convention to consider amending the Articles of Confederation

1787   ■ Royall Tyler's *Contrast* acted · John Adams' *Defence of the Constitutions of Government of the United States*

Constitutional Convention held at Philadelphia, 14 May-17 September · Constitution submitted for state ratification, nine votes being sufficient

1788   ■ Alexander Hamilton, James Madison, and John Jay, *The Federalist* · Freneau's *Miscellaneous Works*

Constitution ratified by the ninth state, New Hampshire, 6 April

1789   ■ Washington's *First Inaugural* · John Adams' *Discourses on Davila* begun

Constitution in effect, 4 March · Washington and Adams chosen President and Vice-President, 6 April · Washington inaugurated in New York City, 30 April · Fall of the Bastille, Paris, 14 July · Declaration of the Rights of Man, 4 August

1790   ■ Susanna Haswell Rowson's *Charlotte Temple*

First United States census: population approximately 4,000,000

1791 ■ William Bartram's *Travels* · Joel Barlow's *Advice to the Privileged Orders* · Paine's *Rights of Man*, first part · Hamilton's *Report on Manufactures* · *National Gazette* founded, with Freneau as editor

First ten amendments to the Constitution (Bill of Rights) · First Bank of the United States chartered · Vermont admitted as the fourteenth state

1792 ■ H. H. Brackenridge's *Modern Chivalry*, first part · Barlow's *Conspiracy of Kings*

Kentucky admitted as the fifteenth state · Paine imprisoned in Paris · Capitol at Washington begun · Washington reëlected President

1793 Louis XVI executed · France declared war on Great Britain, Holland, and Spain, being already at war with Austria and Prussia · "Citizen" Genêt landed in the United States · United States proclaimed neutrality despite the alliance of 1778 with France · Reign of Terror in France · Cotton gin invented by Eli Whitney

1794 ■ Dwight's *Greenfield Hill* · Paine's *Age of Reason*, First part

Whiskey Insurrection in western Pennsylvania

1795 Treaty of San Lorenzo permitted American navigation of the Mississippi and the deposit of export goods at New Orleans duty free

1796 ■ Barlow's *Hasty-Pudding* · Washington's *Farewell Address*

Tennessee admitted as the sixteenth state · John Adams elected second President, with Jefferson as Vice-President · British troops finally withdrawn from the Western forts

1797 ■ Tyler's *Algerine Captive*

Anti-French feeling increased by the attempt of Talleyrand, foreign minister for the Directory, to bribe American emissaries — "X.Y.Z. Affair"

1798 ■ Charles Brockden Brown's *Wieland* · William Wordsworth and Samuel Taylor Coleridge, *Lyrical Ballads*, a landmark in the development of the English Romantic Movement

Alien and Sedition Laws, an expression of the Federalist fear of "French principles" · The Virginia and Kentucky Resolutions, set forth the states' rights position of the Jeffersonian Republicans

1800 Jefferson elected third President · United States census: population nearly 5,500,000

1801 Numerous Federalist judges appointed under the "lame duck" Judiciary Act · John Marshall became Chief Justice of the Supreme Court

	· Jefferson inaugurated in the new capital city, Washington · Tripoli declared war on the United States
1802	Ohio admitted as seventeenth state
1803	Expedition under Meriwether Lewis sent to the Northwest, under authorization made by Congress · Louisiana purchased from Napoleon for $15,000,000 · John Marshall established doctrine of "judicial review" in the case of *Marbury vs. Madison*
1804	Death of Hamilton · Jefferson reëlected President
1807	■ Washington Irving and others, *Salmagundi* · Barlow's *Columbiad*
	Anti-British feeling aroused in the United States by the *Chesapeake* affair, June, in which seamen were taken off an American man-of-war · Jefferson, by proclamation, forbade the entrance of British warships into American harbors · Embargo Act, 21 December, prohibited all ships from leaving American ports
1808	■ William Cullen Bryant's *Embargo*
	Importation of slaves into the United States forbidden · Jefferson became highly unpopular as a result of the economic distress caused by the Embargo Act · James Madison elected fourth President
1809	■ Irving's *Knickerbocker History of New York*
	Embargo Act repealed · Non-Intercourse Act passed, permitting American shipping to destinations other than French and English ports
1810	United States census: population of approximately 7,240,000
1811	Charter of the First Bank of the United States lapsed without renewal · United States broke off diplomatic relations with Great Britain, after failing to obtain agreement on the rights of neutrals
1812	Louisiana admitted as the eighteenth state · United States declared war on Great Britain · Madison reëlected President
1813	Blockade of American ports established by the British, after a number of naval victories by the Americans · American fleet under Perry victorious at Put-in-Bay, on Lake Erie, 10 September
1814	Washington captured by the British, 24 August · Hartford Convention assembled, 15 December, to express New England disapproval of the war; although there was talk of secession, the convention contented itself with recommending amendments to the Constitution · Treaty of Ghent, 24 December, ended the War of 1812 but failed to settle any of the major differences
1815	■ *North American Review* established · Freneau's *Poems on American Affairs*

British defeated in the Battle of New Orleans, 8 January · Napoleon returned from Elba, 1 March, was defeated at Waterloo, 18 June, and banished to St. Helena, 8 August

1816 Indiana admitted as the nineteenth state · James Monroe elected fifth President

1817 ■ Bryant's "Thanatopsis," in the *North American Review*

Mississippi admitted as the twentieth state

1818 Illinois admitted as the twenty-first state · Boundary between the United States and Canada defined

1819 ■ Irving's *Sketch Book*

Alabama admitted as the twenty-second state · Tallmadge amendment to the bill for the admission of Missouri brought the slavery question to the forefront in national affairs · Florida acquired from Spain

1820 ■ James Fenimore Cooper's *Precaution*

Missouri Compromise adopted · Maine admitted as the twenty-third state · United States census: population of more than 9,500,000 · Monroe reëlected President

1821 ■ Bryant's *Poems* · Cooper's *Spy*

Missouri admitted as the twenty-fourth state

1822 ■ Irving's *Bracebridge Hall*

1823 ■ Cooper's *Pilot, Pioneers*

1824 ■ Irving's *Tales of a Traveller*

John Quincy Adams elected sixth President

1826 ■ Cooper's *Last of the Mohicans*

1827 ■ Cooper's *Prairie* · Edgar Allan Poe's *Tamerlane and Other Poems*, published anonymously

1828 ■ Nathaniel Hawthorne's *Fanshawe* · Irving's *Life and Voyages of Christopher Columbus* · Noah Webster's *American Dictionary of the English Language*

"Tariff of Abominations," high protective tariff unacceptable to the South · Doctrine of nullification stated by John C. Calhoun in the "South Carolina Exposition," adopted by the legislature of that state · Andrew Jackson elected seventh President

3

THE AMERICAN RENAISSANCE
1829 - 1860

WE WILL SPEAK OUR OWN MINDS

"We will walk on our own feet; we will work with our own hands; we will speak our own minds."

EMERSON

INTELLECTUAL CURRENTS

Between the triumph of the frontier in Jackson's election and the days of the Civil War, the United States emerged a flourishing nation — a nation for the common man, a nation with a culture, a nation of promises.

This was the period of renaissance, the period of awakening and development, when Americans were at last to begin speaking their own minds. The writers of the era considered in this chapter belong mostly to New England; and indeed the New England writers loom large in any history of American literature during the years from 1829 to 1860. Two great writers of the period were outside the New England orbit: Edgar Allan Poe and Herman Melville. Yet neither was unmindful of New England, for Poe was sharply critical of Transcendentalists and abolitionists, and Melville was profoundly affected by one of New England's chief writers, Nathaniel Hawthorne.

New England in Its Golden Day

The period of 1829-1860 in New England has had applied to it a variety of happy designations: Barrett Wendell called it "The Renaissance of New England," Lewis Mumford, "The Golden Day." But by whatever name it is known, it was the greatest literary period in the history of New England. This was a rich period, and in their writings the men of Boston and Cambridge, Concord and Salem set forth their all-embracing ideas and attitudes on religion and the conception of human nature, democracy and the common man, industry and the expanding frontier, slavery and the Civil War, science and human progress.

Changing concepts of God and man. The most important factor in the religious thought of New England in this period was the break with Calvinism. Boston clergymen had become increasingly liberal in the eighteenth century (as shown in the opposition between Chauncy and Edwards), but it was not until the beginning of the nineteenth century that Unitarianism was strongly established. The appointment in 1805 of an avowed Unitarian to the chair of Divinity at Harvard, hitherto occupied by staunch Calvinists, may be taken as marking the transition. And yet the change from Calvinism to Unitarianism was perhaps not so complete, even in eastern Massachusetts, as some have supposed. That William Ellery Channing, the most influential of the early Unitarians, should have delivered his famous "Moral Argument Against Calvinism" as late as 1820 would seem to suggest the tenacity of the old orthodox beliefs. Preaching from his Unitarian pulpit in 1831, Emerson designated the Calvinistic and Unitarian groups as the "rigid" and the "liberal" parties, respectively, and urged his hearers to "borrow something of eternal truth from both of these opinions."

The chief points of difference between Calvinism and Unitarianism as expounded by Channing and his successors can be summarized briefly: (1) The two beliefs differed in their conceptions of the Deity. Calvinism emphasized God's inexorable justice; Unitarianism stressed His benevolence. The Unitarians questioned the justice of the doctrine of election: a God who says (according to Wigglesworth) "I do save none but mine own elect" seemed arbitrary and capricious. (2) The two beliefs differed in their conceptions of Christ. According to Calvinism, Christ is literally the Son of God, the second member of the Holy Trinity. According to Unitarianism, Christ is divine only in the sense in which all men are divine or have an element, however small, of divinity in their nature. The difference between Christ and ordinary mortals becomes one of degree, not of kind. (3) The two beliefs differed in their conceptions of man. Calvinism asserted the innate depravity of man, his predestination, and the necessity of his salvation through the atoning death of Christ. Unitarianism insisted upon man's innate goodness and his spiritual freedom. The Atonement became unnecessary to Unitarians, who preferred to point to Christ's life as an example to be emulated by men already potentially good.

As a young man Channing lived for two years in Virginia, where he presumably absorbed French romantic philosophy. From Rousseau and writers of his school, Channing probably derived, and imported into the Boston of the early 1800's, the ideas of the excellence of human nature and its infinite perfectibility. The inscription on the base of Channing's statue in Boston aptly summarizes his contribution to the religious thought of New England: "He breathed into theology a humane spirit and proclaimed anew the divinity of man." In his *The Flowering of New England* Van Wyck Brooks justly declares, "By raising the general estimate of human nature, which the old religion had despised, Channing gave a prodigious impulse to the creative life."

By 1820 Channing could say, "Calvinism is giving place to better views. We think the decline of Calvinism one of the most encouraging facts in our passing history." Unitarianism became the religion particularly of the fashionable and the well-to-do in and around Boston. "Whoever clung to the older faith," remarks Barrett Wendell, "did so at his social peril." Unitarianism, however, did not conquer the whole of New England. There were scattered Unitarian outposts, such as the parish of Sylvester Judd in Augusta, Maine, but the older faith continued dominant in the regions west and north of Boston.

Apart from both Calvinists and Unitarians, the Quakers were a comparatively small but important group. In early New England, Quakers were apt to be obstreperously fanatical (witness the seventeenth-century Quakeress in Hawthorne's "Gentle Boy"), but by the time of John Woolman (1720-1772) their fanaticism had diminished, and in nineteenth-century New England they were, in the words of one historian, "inconspicuous and inoffensive."

Like the Calvinists, the Quakers believed in the divinity of Christ and in the Bible as the inspired word of God. Like the Calvinists, too, they insisted upon the essential sinfulness of man: "Too dark ye cannot paint the sin," said Whittier, their chief representative in literature, in "The Eternal Goodness," his best poetical statement of the Quaker belief. But Whittier in the poem objects to the "iron creeds" of the Calvinists and to their emphasis upon God's wrath; he prefers to think of "our Lord's beatitudes." The Quakers emphasized the "Inner Light," which God, they believed, gave to all human beings and which afforded an infallible guide to a righteous life. Quakerism was more benevolent and humanitarian than Calvinism, and more pietistic than Unitarianism. A mere layman might experience some difficulty in distinguishing between the doctrine of the inner light and the Emersonian doctrine of intuition.

Emerson, after less than three years in the Unitarian ministry, resigned his pulpit in 1832 because of a growing dissatisfaction with the official role of the clergyman and the formalities of the church. Unitarianism, he felt, was good as far as it went; but it did not go far enough toward the rehabilitation of the individual. The new doctrine of which Emerson became the chief interpreter is known as Transcendentalism. Emerson's *Nature*, published in 1836, was the bible of the early Transcendentalists, and the "Transcendental Club" was, from 1836 until about 1844, their center of activity. Another focus was a quarterly magazine, *The Dial* (edited by Margaret Fuller, 1840-1842, and by Emerson, 1842-1844), which published many contributions by Transcendentalists during its brief existence. The group as a whole was greatly influenced by the idealistic philosophies of other lands and ages: by Plato and the Neo-Platonists, by the Oriental Scriptures, by Kant and other German idealists — particularly as interpreted by Coleridge and Carlyle.

Transcendentalism has been defined philosophically as "the recognition in man of the capacity of knowing truth intuitively, or of attaining knowledge transcending the reach of the senses." It has been described historically as having been "produced by the importing of German idealism into American Unitarianism." The last definition indicates an important relation between Transcendentalism and Unitarianism and requires a consideration of the similarities and differences between the two.

Unitarianism prepared the way for Transcendentalism by insisting that man is essentially good and may trust his own perceptions of religious truth. Channing spoke of "the confidence which is due to our rational and moral faculties in religion" and said that "the ultimate reliance of a human being is and must be on his own mind." But it is important to observe two points of difference: (1) Channing, the Unitarian, expressed confidence in "our *rational* faculties." Emerson, the Transcendentalist, drew a sharp distinction between the "Understanding," by which he meant the rational faculty, and the "Reason," by which he meant the suprarational or intuitive faculty; and he regarded the "Reason" as much more authoritative in spiritual matters than the "Understanding." (2) The Transcendentalists carried this reliance upon the intuitive perceptions of the individual much further than conventional Unitarianism would warrant — carried it so far as to set aside even the authority of the Christian Bible. "Make your own Bible," said Emerson. "Select and collect all the words and sentences that in all your reading have been to you like the blast of a trumpet, out of Shakespeare, Seneca, Moses, John, and Paul." Emerson would renounce all authority, all standards and laws externally imposed: "Nothing is at last sacred but the integrity of your own mind." He proclaimed this glorification of intuition and the repudiation of all external religious authority to a Unitarian audience at Harvard in 1838: "Thank God for these good men [meaning the Saints and the Prophets] but say 'I also am a man.' " The result was a storm of protest. Emerson's Transcendentalism had gone far beyond the bounds even of liberal Unitarianism.

Transcendental thought in the abstract can be best studied in

Emerson. His disciples, of whom there were many, were usually interested more in practice than in theory and attempted to apply Emerson's individualistic doctrines in various practical ways. George Ripley, for example, organized the famous utopian community at Brook Farm; Theodore Parker militantly espoused reforms in church and state; Margaret Fuller advocated the emancipation of women; Henry Thoreau made a famous experiment in living at Walden Pond.

Many passages in Thoreau seem echoes of Emerson, though Thoreau's expression of the thought is always more concrete than Emerson's. "The fact is," Thoreau wrote in his journal in 1853, "I am a mystic, a transcendentalist, and a natural philosopher to boot"—meaning by "natural philosopher" a scientific student of nature. The emphasis in the statement is significant. Mystical, transcendental passages abound in Thoreau, especially in his earlier writings, as they abound everywhere in Emerson. But as Thoreau grew older, his interest in the observation and description of the world of nature became more and more absorbing. He became—as his journals of the 1850's attest—more of the natural philosopher and somewhat less of the Transcendentalist.

Transcendental ideas scarcely touched the writers of Boston and Cambridge. Influenced by his medical studies, Dr. Holmes approached religious problems from the scientific point of view. He objected to the Calvinistic condemnation of sinners because he believed that wrongdoing is often the result of an unfortunate heredity; bad men, he thought, should be treated as if they were insane. On the positive side, he had no transcendental ardor, but rather a rationalistic belief in the ability of the soul, in favorable circumstances, to "build more stately mansions." Longfellow's religious thought—such as it was—was mildly Unitarian, pleasantly optimistic about life and death. And Lowell, although he could write appreciatively of the stimulating effect of Emerson (". . . he made us conscious of the supreme and everlasting originality of whatever bit of soul might be in any of us"), was not a disciple; nor was he in sympathy with Transcendental ideas. "The word 'transcendental,' " he declared in the unsympathetic essay on Thoreau, "was the maid of all work for those who could not think." The men of Boston and Cambridge found the Concord air too rarefied for their mundane needs.

The chief spokesman of the opposition to Transcendentalism, however, was Hawthorne, who returned, in part at least, to the Calvinist position. He satirized utopian reforms on the ground that superficial reform measures avail nothing so long as the human heart, which is innately sinful, remains unregenerated. "Purify that inward sphere," he advised in "Earth's Holocaust," "and the many shapes of evil that haunt the outward will vanish of their own accord." He satirized Unitarianism and Transcendentalism in "The Celestial Railroad" (1843); Bunyan's arduous pilgrimage seemed to him still the best way of reaching the Celestial City. In stories and novels he showed that evil is an everpresent reality, not an illusion to be brushed aside, and that self-reliant individualism alone does not save man from disaster. Hawthorne is a striking example of the persistence of the Puritan point of view in an age of liberalism and progressivism.

But it would be a mistake to suppose that the Puritan inheritance affected Hawthorne alone. It was everywhere present, giving native roots and indigenous strength to New England's flowering. The religious emphasis was a Puritan trait, as was the emphasis on books and reading. The Transcendental pursuit of perfection was the old Puritan pursuit of perfection in a new guise and on different terms. The diaries of Emerson, Thoreau, and Hawthorne continued an old Puritan practice; and the soul searchings in Emerson and Thoreau recall passages in Cotton Mather and Jonathan Edwards. When Emerson said that the poet "must drink water out of a wooden bowl," he was quoting the austerest of English Puritans, John Milton. The austerity of Emerson and Thoreau, and of Hawthorne, too, was of the essence of Puritanism. If this Puritan essence was considerably diluted in the other writers of the period, it nevertheless made itself felt. It came out in the ethical earnestness of Longfellow and Lowell and in their native attachments. In sum, the great period of New England literature would have been impossible without the two centuries of Puritan inheritance. It is hardly an accident that the three New England writers of the period whose works seem most likely to endure—Emerson, Thoreau, and Hawthorne—are the writers whose roots were deepest in New England's Puritan past.

Democracy, Industrialism, Expansion

From 1829 to 1860 the two major political parties in the United States were the Whigs and the Democrats. Conservative men of property in New England were likely to be Whigs; liberals and men of little or no property were likely to be Democrats.

The election of Andrew Jackson of Tennessee by the Democrats in 1828 is one of the great landmarks in the evolution of American democracy. The common man, whether backwoodsman, farmer, or small merchant, regarded Jackson, the conqueror of the Creek Indians and the hero of New Orleans, as a popular champion. Jackson's Whig opponent, the "aristocratic" John Quincy Adams, carried only New England and the North Atlantic states; the South and West went solidly for "Old Hickory." During the Jacksonian period, government in America became more democratic. The movement toward democracy, which had begun with the War of Independence and which had been arrested somewhat in the 1790's owing to a certain apprehension caused by the excesses of the French Revolution, now resumed its onward course. State constitutions were liberalized. Religious tests and property qualifications for holding office were at last removed, and manhood suffrage was adopted generally.

New England looks at the new democracy. To many New Englanders Jackson and his supporters seemed the dregs of democracy. Emerson wrote to Carlyle, "A most unfit person in the Presidency has been doing the worst things; and the worse he grew, the more popular." But it would not be fair to Emerson to suppose that this snobbish statement represents his real attitude. Like most educated men, he doubted at times the wisdom of the uneducated masses. "The mass," he wrote in a skeptical moment, "are animal, in state of pupilage, and nearer the chimpanzee." But despite moments of skepticism, he held firmly to his faith in the ultimate wisdom of the people. The belief that "God is in every man" was to him "the highest revelation." And he said in another passage on the subject, "The great mass understand what's what." It should be remembered that Emerson took sharp issue with his friend Carlyle on the subject of democracy: when Carlyle advocated what we today should call a fascist doctrine, Emerson vigorously dissented. He could think of many benefits that might come from even the "rank rabble party, the Jacksonism of the country." For one thing, this new democracy of the West might cure America of its slavish dependence upon Old World literature and Old World traditions, might "root out the hollow dilettantism of our cultivation." And he came ultimately to an admiration of Jackson himself. Writing in 1862 of the truly memorable things which he associated with the national capital, he mentioned along with the eloquence of Webster and the "sublime behaviour" of John Quincy Adams, the "fine military energy of Jackson in his presidency."

Jackson's fine military energy appealed also to James Russell Lowell, who wrote in his "Latest Views of Mr. Biglow":

> Ole Hick'ry wouldn't ha' stood see-saw
>   'Bout doin' things till they wuz done with,—
> H'd smashed the tables o' the Law
>   In time o' need to load his gun with;
> He couldn't see but jest one side,—
>   Ef his, 'twuz God's, an' thet wuz plenty;
> An' so his *'Forrards'* multiplied
>   An army's fightin' weight by twenty.

It must have required a great adjustment for the New England mind to appreciate a man like Andrew Jackson. Emerson and Lowell were capable of making the necessary accommodation, and Nathaniel Hawthorne, alone among the major New England writers, was a loyal member of the Democratic party and a staunch supporter of Jackson. Late in life he recorded in his journal the considered judgment, "Surely Jackson was a great man." But despite the personal challenge of Jackson himself, Emerson spoke for the generality of educated New Englanders when he said that the Whig Party had the "best men"; the Democratic Party, he added, had the "best cause."

The "best cause" became more and more pervasive in the literature of the period. An earlier democratic impetus had been supplied by the English Romantic Movement. When Emerson, in *The American Scholar* (1837), hailed as one of the "auspicious signs" the exploring and poetizing of "the near, the low, the common," he was thinking particularly of the English Romantic poets. And when Longfellow celebrated the village blacksmith, and Whittier, the barefoot boy, the inspiration was at least partly derived from Burns and Wordsworth. Thus initiated, the democratic movement in literature was broadened and deepened and made more American by the fresh impetus of Jacksonian Democracy. Lowell affords a good illustration, for with him the democratic attitude evolved from the romantic and literary to the realistic and American. His celebration of Lincoln in 1865 as "New birth of our new soil, the first American" is a landmark in the democratic evolution of the New England mind. His full development in this direction is seen in his famous address on "Democracy" (1884), in which he said:

> I recollect hearing a sagacious old gentleman say in 1840 that the doing away with the property qualification for suffrage twenty years before had been the ruin of the State of Massachusetts. . . . I lived to see that Commonwealth twenty odd years later paying the interest on her bonds in gold. . . . To the door of every generation there comes a knocking, and unless the household, like the Thane of Cawdor and his wife, have been doing some deed without a name, they need not shudder. It turns out at worst to be a poor relation who wishes to come in out of the cold.

Thus Lowell, the Brahmin, spoke for democracy and the forgotten man.

Another Brahmin, Oliver Wendell Holmes, was not visibly touched by the evolution of democratic thought in America. In the *Autocrat of the Breakfast-Table* (1858), he clung tenaciously to his aristocratic bias: "Self-made men? — Well, yes. Of course everybody likes and respects self-made men. It is a great deal better to be made in that way than not to be made at all. . . . But *other things being equal*, in most relations of life I prefer a man of family." His favorite subjects in poetry were aristocratic types ("Dorothy Q," 1871; "The Last Leaf," 1831) and aristocratic heirlooms ("On Lending a Punch-Bowl" 1848). It is not without significance in this connection that many of the writings of Dr. Holmes seem less vital and less important today than those of his more democratic contemporaries.

The machine vs. self-reliance. The Jacksonian revolution affected the entire country; the industrial revolution was confined largely to the Northern states, and its effects became especially important in New England. After the War of 1812, business capital and initiative in New England were diverted from commerce to manufacturing, and the abundance of water power and skilled labor guaranteed the success of the factory system. The most striking new feature of the New England landscape about 1820 was the factory village, built near some waterfall and consisting of mills and houses for the "operatives." Conditions were much more agreeable in the new factory villages of New England than in the older manufacturing centers of England. Workers in the New England factories were mostly farmers' daughters from the surrounding country. Hawthorne in one of his rambles about the countryside remarked on the bright, cheerful faces looking out through the factory windows. A notable instance was Lowell, Massachusetts (founded in 1822), where the factory girls dressed neatly, were properly chaperoned, and published a literary weekly. By 1840 there were some 1200 cotton factories in the United States, two thirds of which were in New England.

One result of the industrial revolution in New England was the accumulation of wealth, a good deal of which was used for cultural purposes. Many New Englanders studied in Europe. The colleges of New England grew in resources and prestige. Almost every town had its free public library and its Lyceum, where an instructive course of lectures was given during the winter. Emerson, and even Thoreau, lectured on many Lyceum platforms. In the cities, mechanics' institutes offered vocational training. The Lowell family might be cited as illustrating the happy marriage of wealth and culture: one uncle of James Russell Lowell founded the manufacturing city which bears his name; another uncle established the famous Lowell Institute in Boston, where lectures have been given for more than a century by distinguished scientists, scholars, and men of letters.

To most New England writers of the period the industrial revolution no doubt seemed more beneficent than otherwise. One major writer, however—Henry David Thoreau—spoke out loud and bold against the mechanization of American life. Thoreau's objection was based upon the fundamental principle, Emerson's principle, of self-reliance. A man ought to do for himself the things which more and more were being done by machines: he ought to walk instead of riding on the train; he ought to build his own house, make his own clothes, bake his own bread. The machine brought on the division of labor which reduced men from integers to fractions. "Where is this division of labor to end?" Thoreau cried in *Walden*; and he added a statement the force of which is only today becoming apparent: "No doubt another *may* also think for me; but it is not therefore desirable that he should do so to the exclusion of my thinking for myself."

Compared with Thoreau's, the comments of other writers on the advancing machine age seem less decisive. Emerson entered a mild demurrer in *Self-Reliance* (1841), warning that "the harm of the improved machinery may compensate its good"; but, in the long run, he was willing to accept the machine as part of the "beneficent tendency." Hawthorne seems to have been apprehensive of evil results; to him, apparently, the machine was a malevolent monster. One finds in his journal the following note for a story: "A steam engine in a factory to be supposed to possess a malignant spirit; it catches one man's arm and pulls it off; seizes another by the coat-tails, and almost grapples him bodily; catches a girl by the hair, and scalps her; and finally draws a man and crushes him to death." Here was a conception out of which Hawthorne might easily have developed a tale of Gothic horror, and perhaps also of social prophecy.

A conspicuous and characteristic product of the industrial revolution in America was the man of big business, the captain of industry. The subject received scant attention in the literature of the period. One passage, however, is of particular interest — a passage in Emerson's *Journals* which expresses the writer's great admiration of John M. Forbes, a builder of railroads in the West in the 1860's:

> Forbes is an American to be proud of. Never was such force, good meaning, good sense, good action, combined with such domestic lovely behaviour. . . . Wherever he moves, he is the benefactor. It is of course that he should shoot well, ride well, sail well, administer railroads well, carve well, keep house well, but he was the best talker also in the company. . . .

The type has suffered at the hands of later writers. Perhaps Emerson was naïve; or possibly the type deteriorated in the post-Civil War period; or, quite likely, the American businessman was given less than justice by the satirists and "debunkers" of the 1920's.

New England looks west with mixed feelings. Thinking in New England along political, economic, and social lines was conditioned not only by Jacksonian Democracy and the industrial revolution; it was conditioned also by the Westward movement.

In the early years of the century New Englanders had settled in western New York and Ohio; by the 1840's they not only had occupied Indiana, Illinois, and southern Michigan, but had ventured as far as Wisconsin, Minnesota, and Iowa. A popular song summed up the invitation to the West:

> Come all ye Yankee farmers who wish
> to change your lot,
> Who've spunk enough to travel beyond
> your native spot. . . .

Despite the ties between New England and the West, conservative New Englanders were inclined to deprecate the Westward migration. There were economic reasons for this attitude: the draining off of energetic young people tended to keep high the price of factory labor, and the revenue from the sale of public lands in the West furnished an argument to Southerners for lowering the tariff. There were moral reasons also. The appeal to "spunk" to leave "your native spot" in the song quoted above was reversible since one might argue that more spunk was required to succeed in one's native place, particularly if that place was a New England farm. "The wise man stays at home," said Emerson. And possibly Whittier was thinking of those who were tempted by the West when he emphasized the noble austerity of life in New England:

> Then ask not why to these bleak hills
> I cling, as clings the tufted moss. . .
> Better with naked nerve to bear
> The needles of this goading air,
> Than, in the lap of sensual ease, forego
> The godlike power to do, the godlike aim to know.

Migration to the West was regarded by many high-minded New Englanders as a decline to a lower level. Some reformers, on the other hand, made the point that Westward migration might be checked if certain improvements were made at home. Sylvester Judd said of his fictional utopia, described in *Margaret: A Tale of the Real and Ideal* (1845), that "the mania for removing to the West, which prevails all over New England, has here subsided."

The Western theme does not bulk very large in the writings and memoirs of the authors of New England's Renaissance, but a few details may be of interest to suggest their views and attitudes. Hawthorne was interested in the West, although his knowledge of the subject was not great. In the 1830's he traveled by stagecoach and canal boat as far as Niagara Falls and recorded his observations in a few slight but revealing sketches. While American consul at Liverpool, he met more Westerners than he had ever seen in Salem or Concord, some of whom he viewed with disapproval. A Mr. Lilley from Ohio, for example, he described in his notebooks as "a very unfavorable specimen of American manners — an outrageous tobacco chewer and atrocious spitter on carpets." But some years later in Concord he met young William Dean Howells, an Ohioan, whose manners were irreproachable. Hawthorne was (as Howells recorded) "curious about the West, which he seemed to fancy much more purely American, and said he would like to see some part of the country on which the damned shadow of Europe had not fallen."

To Lowell, as to Hawthorne, the West seemed more purely American because it was freer from European influences. (The same point was to be made at the end of the century by the historian Frederick Jackson Turner.) When "Nature" made Lincoln, Lowell said in his "Commemoration Ode" (1865),

> For him her Old-World moulds aside she threw,
>> And choosing sweet clay from the breast
>> Of the unexhausted West,
> With stuff untainted shaped a hero new . . .
>> Nothing of Europe here. . . .

The great Americans in the early history of the Republic — Franklin, Washington, Jefferson, and the rest — possessed a culture which was largely European; but the culture of Lincoln was "untainted" by the Old World. Lowell's appreciation of this fact is all the more remarkable because, as a lifelong student of the Romance languages and literatures, he himself was an embodiment of European culture. Such an insight into the significance of the West was beyond the reach of another devotee of European literature, Longfellow, whose conception of the subject, as revealed in *Hiawatha* and *Evangeline*, was literary and romantic.

Unlike Longfellow, Thoreau was a tough, realistic writer who was qualified by temperament and personal habits to appreciate the values of the Western frontier. From Thoreau's point of view, life in New England had become too sophisticated; he spoke repeatedly of "these degenerate days." "We need the tonic of wildness," he declared in *Walden* (1854); and in "Walking" (1862), he said, "The West is but another name for the Wild." He praised the sturdy self-reliance of the pioneer. If the race is to retain its vigor, men must live "a primitive and frontier life." Such a life had been lived by the settlers of New England, and Thoreau liked to quote from the colonial historians, particularly from Edward Johnson, who told how the first inhabitants of Concord were forced to live in a cave and "cut their bread very thin." Such a Spartan existence was enjoyed also, he supposed, by the Western frontiersman. "Adam in Paradise," he declared, "was not so favorably situated on the whole as is the backwoodsman in America." The backwoodsman whom Thoreau envisaged, we may be sure, was not of the lawless or mercenary sort; rather he was the sober New Englander dedicated to plain living and high thinking on a farm in Michigan or Illinois. The gold rush to California was quite another matter. The greed and the gambling instinct therein displayed, he thought, were a "disgrace on mankind." The California spectacle of 1849, he said, made of God "a moneyed gentleman who scatters a handful of pennies in order to see mankind scramble for them."

If Thoreau praised the West for its primitive qualities, Emerson praised it for its astonishingly rapid acquisition of culture. He lectured many times throughout the Middle West in the 1850's, going as far as Beloit, Wisconsin, where on January 9, 1856, he found an interested audience despite a temperature of thirty degrees below zero. The spread of culture on the frontier was to him indeed remarkable. Having heard piano music on one of his Western travels, he wrote:

Witness the mute all hail
The joyful traveller gives, when on the verge
Of craggy Indian wilderness he hears
From a log cabin stream Beethoven's notes
On the piano, played with master's hand.

The college in Evanston blew down one night (Emerson recorded in his journal in 1857), but so great were the energy and progressivism of the founders of Northwestern that "they raised it again the next day, or built another." To Emerson, the West seemed the country of the future. He warned his Eastern readers that some day the sturdy Westerner would "gather all their laurels in his strong hands." Emerson's treatment of the West (which one finds chiefly in his *Journals*) emphasizes his identification not only with New England but with all America as well.

Slavery and Civil War. Still another influence on New England thought about political, economic, and social problems was the growing controversy over Negro slavery in the South and the tragic climax of the Civil War. The details of the antislavery movement and the role of Whittier as New England's chief abolitionist in literature are reserved for a later chapter, where the two sides — Northern and Southern — may more conveniently be brought together. Here we are concerned with the movement as a stimulus to thought and with the reactions of the major New England writers, Whittier excepted, to that stimulus.

Longfellow, as we might expect, was only mildly responsive. His sentiments were broadly and sincerely humanitarian; he believed that slavery was a great evil. But he was not active in reform, for he disliked controversy and preferred to write his poems on other subjects. Longfellow did, however, compose a few poems on slavery, of which "The Slave's Dream" (1842) may be regarded as typical of his attitude and method of treatment. The slave in the poem falls asleep in a rice field and dreams of his former life in Africa, where he had been a king and had ridden a spirited horse bridled with golden reins. The description would be more applicable to a knight of medieval romance, and it reflects Longfellow's preoccupation with European romantic literature. When the Union was threatened by the sectional dispute, he wrote the noble and justly famous poem "The Building of the Ship" (1850), which was a poetical plea — matching Webster's plea in prose — for the preservation of the Union:

Thou, too, sail on, O Ship of State!
Sail on, O Union, strong and great!

Lowell was much more vocal than his fellow Cantabrigian. He had well-defined political convictions, and he enjoyed being in the thick of the fray. In the first series of *The Biglow Papers* (1848), he vigorously opposed the Mexican War, which Northern abolitionists unanimously regarded as having been precipitated by Southern strategists with the aim of extending slave territory in the Southwest:

> They jest want this Californy
> So's to lug new slave states in. . . .

He declared himself opposed to all war, "Ez fer war, I call it murder. . . ," and preferred the separation of the North and South to slavery:

> Ef I'd my way I hed ruther
> We should go to work an' part. . . .

In the second series of *The Biglow Papers*, written in 1862 when the Army of the Potomac had met with ill success, he abandoned his early pacifism and argued for a more vigorous prosecution of the War by the North:

> Oh for three weeks o'Cromwle an' the Lord!
> Up, Isr'el to your tents an' grind the sword!

After the Civil War, however, Lowell directed his best poetical efforts toward reunion. Writing in 1875 in commemoration of the one hundredth anniversary of Washington's taking command of the colonial army, he extended the hand of reconciliation from Massachusetts to Virginia:

> Virginia gave us this imperial man . . .
> She gave us this unblemished gentleman.
> What shall we give her back but love and praise
> As in the dear old unestranged days. . . .

Ever responsive to changing conditions, Lowell's attitudes show, it seems fair to say, his flexibility, adaptability, and capacity for growth in his thinking on political questions.

It so happened that Lowell was usually on the side of the majority; Thoreau had a predilection for the side of the minority, often a minority of one. He had the rare personal courage to carry his convictions to their logical conclusion, even if that conclusion meant the defiance of civil law. He refused to pay taxes to a government which allowed slavery, and as a consequence spent a night in the Concord jail. The record of this episode is given in "Civil Disobedience" (1849). He records in his journal that, contrary to the Fugitive Slave Law, on at least one occasion he helped a slave escape into Canada. While John Brown was in prison awaiting execution, Thoreau made a speech in Brown's behalf at Concord, and again at Boston and at Worcester, to unsympathetic audiences. In his famous

"Plea for Captain John Brown" he said, "It was his peculiar doctrine that a man has a perfect right to interfere by force with the slaveholder, in order to rescue the slave. I agree with him." Thoreau is the best example in American literature of the extremely individualistic position: that a man must do what he believes to be right with utter disregard for the conventions of society and the laws of the state.

Emerson was as individualistic in theory, though in practice a good deal more amenable to laws and conventions. Nor did he have the crusading spirit of Thoreau. He was nevertheless an active opponent of slavery after 1850, and, like Thoreau, he spoke publicly in defense of John Brown. The high point in his participation in public affairs came on January 1, 1863, when he read the "Boston Hymn" at a meeting to celebrate the Emancipation Proclamation and was interrupted by the cheering crowd at the famous lines:

> Who is the owner? The slave is owner,
> And ever was. Pay *him*.

Alone among the great New England writers, Hawthorne did not give his approval to the antislavery movement. Possibly, from the Calvinistic point of view, chattel slavery seemed not the greatest of evils: all mankind were victims of a worse bondage — the bondage of sin. He was distrustful of reforms and reformers: reformers were likely to be impractical fanatics; reforms were superficial and as often as not proposed remedies which were worse than the disease. After the manner of the old Puritans, he believed that an inscrutable Providence would bring about the needed reform "at some brighter period, when the world should have grown ripe for it." Furthermore, as a loyal member of the Democratic party of James K. Polk and Franklin Pierce, Hawthorne subscribed to the conventional party arguments that (1) slavery was entitled to recognition and protection under the Constitution; (2) the Union was threatened with disruption by the activities of the abolitionists; and (3) the welfare and happiness of the Negro himself would be jeopardized by his emancipation. During the Civil War he found his position as a Northern Democrat embarrassing; he was looked at askance by friends and neighbors. He did not, however, join those Northern Democrats, known as Copperheads, who opposed the prosecution of the War and advocated a return to the *status quo ante bellum*. "I always thought that the War should have been avoided," he wrote in 1863, "although since it has broken out, I have longed for military success as much as any man or woman of the North." Devoted as he was to the older Union established by the founding fathers, he felt in 1863 that the permanent separation of North and South was inevitable, and persuaded himself "to be content with half the soil that was once our broad inheritance." He did not live to see the end of the War.

Science and Human Progress

Natural science advanced with remarkable rapidity in the nineteenth century, and its effects became more and more pervasive. In England—to mention only two of many notable publications in the scientific field—Sir Charles Lyell's *Principles of Geology* (1830-1833, 3 vols.) established the antiquity of the earth and the gradual evolution of its surface, and Charles Darwin's *Origin of Species* (1859) presented the theory of the evolution of man through a process of natural selection. In New England, and elsewhere in America, scientific activity in all of the fields kept pace with developments in the Old World. Benjamin Silliman at Yale published his *Elements of Chemistry* in 1830; Asa Gray at Harvard brought out a notable *Manual of the Botany of the Northern United States* in 1848; Louis Agassiz of Switzerland began in 1846 a distinguished career at Harvard in the field of comparative zoölogy. The Harvard Astronomical Observatory in 1846 was equipped with the world's largest telescope; and in 1847 the American Association for the Advancement of Science was organized in Boston in order "to promote intercourse between American scientists, to give a strong and more systematic impulse to research, and to procure for the labors of scientific men increased facilities and wider usefulness." New England writers were aware of these scientific developments, and their writings reflect, in various ways and degrees, the influence of the new facts and the new theories of experimental science.

Emerson greeted the scientific movement with enthusiasm. "One of the distinctions of our century," he wrote, "has been the devotion of cultivated men to natural science; the benefits thence derived to the arts and to civilization are signal and immense." Late in life he declared, "If absolute leisure were offered me, I should run to the college or the scientific school which offered the best lectures on Geology, Chemistry, Minerals, and Botany." Although one cannot be sure that Emerson read all of the scientists to whom he refers in his writings, his scientific reading was remarkably wide and certainly included, among other things, the works of Newton, Linnæus, Buffon, Lamarck, Lyell, Gray, Agassiz, and Darwin. But Emerson was not himself a scientist, nor was he interested in science for its own sake. Science was of value to him for the moral and spiritual implications which scientific fact and theory suggested to his mind—a quite unscientific reason. He liked to draw illustrations of spiritual truth from physical phenomena and his pages abound in analogies between natural and spiritual laws. He was delighted, furthermore, by the doctrine of evolution, particularly by the earlier evolutionary theory of Lamarck, which seemed to him to confirm his optimistic hope for mankind. Paraphrasing Lamarck, he wrote as a motto for *Nature*:

> And striving to be man, the worm
> Mounts through all the spires of form.

If the worm might become man, if the caterpillar might evolve into a philosopher, then the future of the constantly evolving human race became glorious to contemplate.

Thoreau's relation to science was much more intimate than Emerson's. Thoreau was interested in nature for its own sake quite as much as for its Transcendental meanings. A student of botany and zoölogy, he liked to use the Latin names of plants and animals when he wrote about them. He sent to Agassiz for identification specimens of fishes and turtles, some of which were unknown to the Harvard professor. Thoreau did not have, however, either the equipment or the temperament of the genuine scientist. He did not go beyond description of behavior and classification. He would not murder to dissect. A hawk could be best studied, he maintained, not as a "dead specimen," but free and soaring above the fields. In short, Thoreau was, to use the phrase of his friend Ellery Channing (a nephew of William Ellery Channing), "the *poet*-naturalist."

Among the Brahmins, Longfellow and Lowell gave little attention to science, though Longfellow shared the general faith in the contributions of science to human progress. Lowell, on one occasion, twitted the Darwinians upon their arrogant assumption that evolution had supplanted God in the modern world (see his "Credidimus Jovem Regnare"). A third Brahmin, however, achieved a real distinction in science. Oliver Wendell Holmes studied medicine in Paris and from 1847 to 1882 was professor of anatomy and physiology in the Harvard Medical School. His most famous contribution to medical science was his essay on "The Contagiousness of Puerperal Fever" (1842), which materially aided the efforts of the medical profession to reduce the mortality of women in childbirth. Holmes' medical training gave him a scientific approach to his literary subjects. He became particularly interested in the problem of the bearing of heredity upon moral responsibility, which is the subject of his novel *Elsie Venner* (1861) and of other writings. He stated the problem as follows in the Preface to the novel:

> Was Elsie Venner, poisoned by the venom of a crotalus [rattlesnake] before she was born, morally responsible for the 'volitional' aberrations, which translated into acts become what is known as sin, and, it may be, what is punished as crime? If, on presentation of the evidence, she becomes by the verdict of the human conscience a proper object of divine pity and not of divine wrath, as a subject of moral poisoning, wherein lies the difference between her position at the bar of judgment, human or divine, and that of the unfortunate victim who received a moral poison from a remote ancestor before he drew his first breath?

Holmes anticipated by at least a generation the approach of modern neurology. He was the author of many volumes of popular novels, essays, and verse, but he nevertheless considered his article on childbed fever his best title to fame.

Hawthorne, once again, is found perversely at odds with this self-confident, progressive, optimistic age. He discovered a danger in the new emphasis upon experimental science. In "Rappaccini's Daughter" (1844), "Ethan Brand" (1851), and elsewhere, he examined the scientist and discovered that the scientist had been dehumanized. Of Dr. Rappaccini, "as true a man of science as ever distilled his own heart in an alembic," Hawthorne wrote: "His patients are interesting to him only as subjects for some new experiment. He would sacrifice human life, his own among the rest, or whatever else was dearest to him, for the sake of adding so much as a grain of mustard seed to the great heap of his accumulated knowledge." Likewise, Ethan Brand, a scientist in the field of experimental psychology, became "a cold observer, looking on mankind as the subject of his experiment"; he "lost his hold of the magnetic chain of humanity"; he became "a fiend." Hawthorne seemed to think that the exclusive cultivation of the scientific faculty produces atrophy of soul, and creates and lets loose in the world an agent which is "fiendish" because utterly unmoral. The mid-nineteenth century did not take the warning seriously. Now, a hundred years later, Hawthorne's point becomes more plainly perceptible.

Herman Melville: Explorer of the World and Enigmas

After a boyhood in New York City and Albany, a voyage to Liverpool, three years in the South Seas, a brief second residence in New York City, and a journey to London and Paris, the much-traveled Herman Melville settled in 1850, at the age of thirty-one, at "Arrowhead" near Pittsfield, Massachusetts. Obviously he was not a product of Massachusetts or a part of the literary movement of New England, but his Massachusetts residence — which lasted, with interruptions for other travels, for more than twenty years — brought him within the sphere of influence of the New England Renaissance. He met in the Berkshires many of the New England writers and struck up a stimulating and sympathetic friendship with Hawthorne, who in 1850-1851 resided at nearby Lenox. It is significant that Melville wrote his greatest book, *Moby Dick*, during the months of his close association with Hawthorne and that he dedicated the book to Hawthorne.

Like Hawthorne, Melville was concerned with the darker side of human fate. Both insisted upon the reality of evil in the world; both were skeptical of the optimism of Emerson and his benevolent theory of the Universe; both presented the tragedies of the mind and soul. Hawthorne agreed with Bunyan's *Pilgrim's Progress*, where man is represented as going through life weighed down by a burden of sin. Melville called Ecclesiastes "the truest of all books . . . the fine hammered steel of woe."

Melville dwelt much upon the evil in the world. He had seen at first hand the brutality of ship captains, the depravity of Old World cities, the vices brought to the South Sea islanders by "civilized" invaders. More than that, evil appeared triumphant (as in *Pierre*), even when man's motives were virtuous. Why, Melville asked, did a good God — if indeed He is good — permit evil in His world? Melville could not accept the Universe with as much resignation as his friend Hawthorne. He persisted in challenging the sphinx riddle, courageously, defiantly.

In *Moby Dick*, which is a compendium of Melville's metaphysical speculation, Captain Ahab relentlessly pursues the White Whale only to be destroyed in the end. The allegory is susceptible of many interpretations. To Ahab "all evil was visibly personified and made practically assailable in Moby Dick." Ahab, however, is not the embodiment of unmixed good: his conduct is irrational and foolhardy; it is contrary to the well-being of others; it is motivated by revenge. Elsewhere, Ahab (and perhaps Melville) saw in Moby Dick "outrageous strength with an inscrutable malice sinewing it," and he hated chiefly the *inscrutability* of the whale. The story perhaps represents man's hopeless but heroic attempt to search out the inscrutable, to know the unknowable; the tragedy of man becomes the tragedy of his limited comprehension. But whatever the interpretation — and each reader must make his own, for the allegory with its countless ramifications is too complex to admit of a simple, categorical definition — Melville's Ahab, like Ethan Brand and other characters of Hawthorne, becomes completely obsessed with this one pursuit and sacrifices everything else to it. If the tragedy of man is his inability to possess complete knowledge of himself and his destiny, Ahab's tragedy is his monomania, the narrow range of his interests.

Melville's chief concern was with the profound enigmas — the nature of God and man, the mystery of "Providence, Foreknowledge, Will and Fate" — and like Milton's philosophers he "found no end, in wandering mazes lost." He was not, however, indifferent to the more mundane problems of modern society, and scattered through his works one finds abundant evidence of his awareness of contemporary social questions.

His own observation of tyranny on shipboard and the exploitation of the native population on the Pacific islands had awakened in him a flaming passion for social justice in a truly democratic society. This passion expressed itself angrily in *White-Jacket*, where he condemned the naval practice of flogging, and philosophically and satirically in *Mardi* (1849), where he surveyed the governments, beliefs, and manners of much of the nineteenth-century world.

The latter book is of special importance for the student of Melville's social ideas with reference to his own country. He was critical of America's faults. "Vivenza [the United States] was a braggadocio": boastfulness was getting to be a national habit; after all, God should be given some credit for our mountains and rivers. The existence of slavery nullified our noble

Declaration of Independence. The war against Mexico was foisted upon the nation by the imperialistic action of the President. The California of the gold rush was a "golden Hell." And speaking more radically, Melville pointed out the imcompleteness of our freedom: political freedom alone was not enough, for "freedom is more social than political." But despite these and many other imperfections, the young American democracy inspired in Melville an ardent faith. The West was a source of fresh hope — Westerners "were a fine young tribe; like strong new wine they worked violently in becoming clear." "In its better aspect," he declared, "Vivenza was a noble land": "Like a young tropic tree she stood, laden down with greenness, myriad blossoms, and the ripened fruit thick-hanging from one bough. She was promising as the morning. Or Vivenza might be likened to St. John, feeding on locusts and wild honey, and with prophetic voice, crying to the nations from the wilderness. Or, childlike, standing among the old robed kings and emperors of the Archipelago, Vivenza seemed a young Messiah, to whose discourse the bearded Rabbis bowed." Like Hawthorne, Melville was a philosophical pessimist and a political optimist. It was possible to believe in original sin and still be a democrat.

Edgar Allan Poe: Southerner

The greatest writer of the ante-bellum South, Edgar Allan Poe, has usually been thought of as completely aloof from the intellectual currents of his time. V. L. Parrington confirmed this view in his famous pronouncement, "The problem of Poe, fascinating as it is, lies quite outside the main current of American thought. . . ." It is true that Poe was not a philosopher, like Emerson, or a political propagandist, like Lowell, or a critic of society, like Thoreau. But it does not follow that he was without ideas and attitudes which are relevant both to his own work and to the history of American thought.

The late Professor Margaret Alterton summed up Poe's social and political attitudes as follows:

> Poe rejected democracy, social reform, and the doctrine of progress. . . . He had no faith in democratic institutions and no belief in human perfectibility or natural goodness. He despised the mob. . . . He endorsed and defended the institution of slavery, and regarded the abolition movement with horror as an envious attack on the rights of property.

Poe, in short, went to the aristocratic extreme.

One reason for Poe's attitudes, no doubt, was his proud, fastidious temperament; another, his desire to identify himself with, and be accepted by, the aristocracy of his adopted region, the South. His repeated attacks on New Englanders seem to have been motivated, in part, by regional prejudice—the following attack on Lowell, for example: "Mr. Lowell is one of the most rabid of the abolition fanatics, and no Southerner who does not wish to be insulted . . . should ever touch a volume of this author."

If Poe's aristocratic sentiments seem a little artificial and stagey, they nevertheless colored his view of life and conditioned the kind of fiction he wrote. "The House of Usher" is a typical Poe symbol of an aristocracy decadent but beautiful. The decay of the Usher line contained no seeds of a democratic birth. The attitude is, at bottom, perhaps the Gothic-aristocratic admiration of a noble and picturesque ruin.

Poe was so completely the artist that any discussion of his ideas and attitudes is likely to impinge upon the discussion of his literary achievements, for his ideas and attitudes can hardly be treated apart from their embodiment in his poetry and fiction. Two aspects of his thought, however, may be mentioned. These aspects are separable, and yet in the ultimate reaches of Poe's thought they seem to unite in a mystic union.

One is a scientific rationalism, which is best illustrated in *Eureka*. In this quasi-philosophical work, Poe attempted an analysis of the universe based upon Newtonian principles. He was concerned with such philosophical pairs as repulsion-attraction, diffusion-gravitation, variety-unity. The universe, Poe believed, had a mathematical beauty and precision in which one might catch a glimpse of the divine. He said: "The plots of God are perfect. The Universe is a plot of God." Poe may have thought that in his own plot structures he was embodying a divine principle.

Another aspect of Poe's thought might be called imaginative idealism. It would be interesting and instructive to compare the idealisms of Poe and Emerson. Though both owed something to Coleridge, Poe's idealism was essentially different from Emerson's. "Beauty," Emerson said with staid Puritan accent, "is the mark God sets upon virtue." Poe, on the other hand, spoke of "the human aspiration for Supernal Beauty," in the contemplation of which one experiences "an elevating excitement of the soul." Poetry could give, Poe thought, a vision of this supernal beauty: in the reading of poetry, he said, "we are often made to feel, with a shivering delight, that from an earthly harp are stricken notes which cannot have been unfamiliar to the angels." Although it may not be true that he was confusing an excitement of the nerves with a true vision of the Ideal, it seems fair enough to say that whereas Emerson's idealism was profoundly moral, Poe's was narrowly, possibly morbidly, aesthetic.

Poe, then, was not divorced from his age, but reflected important facets of the American mind. His social and political conservatism was buttressed by the scientific analogy of a perfect and stable universe. His aestheticism was, on its negative side, a protest against the Puritan over-emphasis on the moralistic in literature. His concept of the Idea was a union of mathematics and music—a "supernal beauty" pure and unearthly. And Poe himself became our chief symbol of the American artist who is at odds with the crass world about him.

Religion and Politics among the Southern Gentry

Religious questions were not nearly so vital in Southern literature as in the literature of New England and in the writings of Melville. Southern writers, in general, did not concern themselves with spiritual laws, like Emerson; or with the remorse for sin, like Hawthorne; or with metaphysical speculation, like Melville. Indeed, in religious matters the cultivated Southerner was likely to be tolerant to the point of indifference. John Pendleton Kennedy's account of Frank Meriwether in *Swallow Barn* (1832) may be regarded as fairly typical of the gentry of the Old South:

> If my worthy cousin be somewhat over-argumentative as a politician, he restores the equilibrium of his character by a considerate coolness in religious matters. He piques himself upon being a high-churchman, but is not the most diligent frequenter of places of worship, and very seldom permits himself to get into a dispute upon points of faith. If Mr. Chub, the Presbyterian tutor in the family, ever succeeds in drawing him into this field, as he occasionally has the address to do, Meriwether is sure to fly the course; he gets puzzled with scripture names, and makes some odd mistakes between Peter and Paul, and then generally turns the parson over to his wife, who, he says, has an astonishing memory.

Good form, however, required a decent respect for the outward observances of religion. Among the aristocracy, the Episcopal Church was the best form; the Presbyterian, though less good, was socially acceptable. Meanwhile, it should be noted, the revivalistic evangelism of the Methodists and Baptists flourished on the frontiers west of Charleston and Richmond, and by the time of the Civil War had enlisted such a large following as to change materially the religious complexion of the South.

By the conservative Southerner, the Puritan, as in *The Yemassee*, was likely to be thought a disagreeable fellow—crabbed in temperament, morbid in the pursuit of virtue. William Gilmore Simms preferred the Cavalier type. If religious ideas became articulate in the Charleston of Simms or the Baltimore of Kennedy, they were likely to take on a rationalistic, eighteenth-century flavor. The following statement by Kennedy, written on his sixty-fifth birthday, might have come from Franklin or Jefferson: "I endeavor to avoid the uncharitableness of sectarian opinion, and maintain an equal mind toward the various forms in which an earnest piety shapes the divisions of the world of believers—tolerating honest differences as the right of all sincere thinkers, and looking only to the kindly nature of Christian principle as it influences the personal lives and conduct of men, as the substantial and true test of a sound religion."

Politics, however, were quite another matter. The Old South had a genius for politics, and nothing delighted the Charleston lawyer or the

Virginia planter more than a political discussion. The hero of *Swallow Barn* was a Jeffersonian Democrat who supported the rights of the states against "the ambitious designs of the general government" and preferred the agrarianism of the South to the mercantilism and industrialism of the North. In early life Kennedy doubtless agreed with his hero; but he later opposed the new Jacksonian Democracy, satirizing it vigorously ·in *Quodlibet*. As a result of his connections with the business interests of Baltimore, he abandoned his early Jeffersonian principles, became a Whig advocate of the protective tariff for manufacturers, and ended a staunch Unionist and Republican.

Simms' ·political course was the reverse of Kennedy's. Whereas the latter began as a states' rights man and became a Unionist, Simms began as a Unionist and became an ardent champion of states' rights. New occasions teach new duties, Simms might have said. When he opposed nullification in South Carolina in 1832, he was supporting Old Hickory and the issue was the tariff. When he advocated nullification in South Carolina twenty years later, he was supporting Calhoun and the issue was slavery.

Although Simms was more democratic in his sympathies than Kennedy — possibly because of his youthful experiences on the Southwestern frontier, the Jackson country — the two men were agreed in the belief that the business of government belonged in the abler hands of the ruling class, which was ordinarily the planter aristocracy. Considerations of wisdom, prudence, and efficiency seemed to them to dictate such a view. As to the subject races — the Indian and the Negro — writers like Kennedy and Simms believed that their state of subjection argued their intrinsic inferiority to the whites and that the white superiors of the blacks should maintain them in humane tutelage until some distant time when emancipation might prove feasible. Kennedy no doubt agreed with his Virginia Planter who said in the 1820's, "The question of emancipation is exclusively our own, and every intermeddling with it from abroad will but mar its chance of success." He painted a disarming picture of the master-slave relationship at Swallow Barn, where he found "an air of contentment and good humor and kind family attachment." He looked forward to gradual emancipation and the possible success of colonizing experiments. Simms' view was substantially the same in 1835, as his treatment of the subject in *The Yemassee* suggests. His later violent championship of slavery as "a wisely devised institution of heaven" can be understood only in the light of the sectional controversy of the 1850's, the literature of which is deferred until the next chapter.

Despite democratic sympathies discoverable in the works of Emerson, Hawthorne, Melville, Simms, and other writers of the period, the complete champion of the common man, irrespective of race, does not appear in American literature before Whitman.

R.S.

Foreign and Domestic Impulses

The period of 1829-1860 was rich not only in ideas but also in artistic expression. Although New England produced more than its share of great artists, other sections also nurtured authors of whom they might well have been proud. The South was represented by two fiction writers, Kennedy and Simms; the Southwest (as we shall see in Chapter 5) by a great group of humorists. Both the South and the East were the background for Edgar Allan Poe. New York was represented by Herman Melville, whose best fiction ranks with the finest our country has produced, and also by a preëminent poet, Walt Whitman. The consideration of Whitman, whose notable career began near the end of this period, in 1855, and extended until 1892, we postpone until later.

In designating this period the American Renaissance, critics have had in mind, doubtless, certain similarities it had to the English Renaissance. The English period, which preceded the American by about two and a half centuries, had produced a host of great writers and literary masterpieces. In the literary productions, whether they were created by giants such as Marlowe, Spenser, and Shakespeare or by lesser men, two impulses had been operative, one foreign and the other native. The exciting discovery of foreign literary works, both old and new, had accounted in part for such works as Shakespeare's *Julius Caesar*, based upon the *Lives* by the Greek biographer-historian Plutarch (translated by North in 1579), and his *Othello*, derived from an Italian *novella* by Cinthio which had first appeared during Shakespeare's lifetime. The patriotic enthusiasm of the day, which had soared during the reign of Queen Elizabeth, found expression in Shakespeare's historical plays such as *Henry IV* and *Henry V* as well as in many of his dramas with foreign settings.

Similarly, during the American Renaissance both foreign and domestic influences, old and new, were notable. Respectful study of ancient and contemporary foreign works and travel abroad, which acquainted authors with European culture, left their marks upon not only the stuff but also the form of our literature. At the same time, proud of their unique democratic system and of the vast nation whose beauty and strength they were coming to know, many authors recounted the history of their land and attempted to depict accurately native scenes and characters.

The Essay—a Standard Form Takes on New Qualities

In this period, as in the preceding one, the essay was an important literary form; but a combination of old and new influences, as well as the personal predilections of each author, gave the type distinctive qualities.

Poe: critic and journalist. Poe's essays and articles show kinship in two ways with writings of authors across the seas. For one thing, he was in the tradition of European authors who alternated between the roles of critics and creators. Such German predecessors as Goethe (1749-1832), Schlegel (1767-1845), Tieck (1773-1853), and Schelling (1775-1854) were critics and philosophers as well as poets. And so were several British authors known by Poe: Coleridge, who wrote his literary autobiography and several fine lyrics; Wordsworth, who theorized about his poems in critical prefaces; Shelley, who wrote a *Defence of Poesy* and lyrics of great excellence; Byron, who wrote *English Bards and Scotch Reviewers* and who also wrote lyrics which Poe admired greatly. Poe, similarly, philosophized about literature and criticized it, justifying poetry in general and his own poetry in particular—in works such as "The Philosophy of Composition" (1846), "The Poetic Principle" (1850), and in numerous published reviews.

Poe worked frequently in the tradition of important Britons and Scots who were reviewers for influential periodicals such as *The London Magazine, The Examiner, Blackwood's Magazine, The Quarterly Review,* and *The Edinburgh Review.* Such men as Francis Jeffrey (1773-1850), William Hazlitt (1778-1830), Leigh Hunt (1784-1859), John Wilson (1785-1854), Thomas De Quincey (1785-1859), and J. G. Lockhart (1794-1854) were journalists whose work for magazines enhanced their literary reputations. Poe's reviews of current books, such as "Review of *Twice-Told Tales,*" were journalistic contributions resembling overseas reviews both in their procedure and their tone. At times they were as ferocious as any in the notoriously stern British reviews, but generally they were intelligent estimates which augmented Poe's fame as a critic.

Lowell: critical, reminiscent. Of the famous Massachusetts men, perhaps the nearest to traditional essayists was James Russell Lowell. Yet the patterns he followed obviously were not those of abstract, relatively impersonal essays such as some British authors had written in the eighteenth century. What he wrote was, as a rule, quite personal. A large share of his prose, that which dealt with issues of the day—candidacies, governmental policies, political theories—might have appeared in newspapers and did appear in magazines which took stands on current affairs.

Such prose served its purpose well in its time and has interest now both historical and literary. Examples of the former are "Democracy" (1884) and "On a Certain Condescension in Foreigners" (1869). The prose by Lowell most important as literature is critical or reminiscent—"Keats" (1854), "Chaucer" (1870), "Shakespeare Once More" (1868), "Emerson the Lecturer" (1861), or "A Good Word for Winter," and "Cambridge Thirty Years Ago." In both critical and reminiscent essays an important factor is the revelation of Lowell's personality—his wit, his learning, his enthusiasm, his sensitivity, his novel way of putting things. One of his volumes bore a title which might have been used for many — "Fireside Travels." He wrote as if he were putting down on paper the sort of talk an informed professor, blessed with a good sense of humor, might deliver to an intelligent college student who had dropped in for an evening chat by the library fire in Elmwood. Lowell poured out enthusiasms, drove home points by unctuously quoting now and then from old books pulled down from towering tiers of shelves, frolicked with classical allusions or Latin quotations, rolled felicitous phrases over his tongue. In particular, Lowell was a master of the epigram — a condensation of his observation and judgment into witty or striking phrases and sentences. Despite some unevenness in his achievements, Lowell's work in the field of the personal essay was outstanding.

Holmes: conversational, neoclassical. Holmes, like Lowell, wrote much prose of a frankly utilitarian kind — in his case, prose which made use of the doctor's scientific interests and training, as in "Mechanism in Thought and Morals" (1870). Whatever such writing contributed to the thought of the period — and many believe that it contributed a great deal — the work in prose which showed Holmes at his inimitable best was more like the informal talk of a New England drawing room or boarding house than like a lecture delivered in the medical school. Such work took the unique form employed in the *Breakfast-Table* series, written over a period of thirty-three years (1858-1891).

The literature which Holmes knew as a boy did its part to shape his essays. He was fond of remarking how much it had meant to him to have been born and reared "among books and those who knew what was in books," to have had a chance, as a youngster, to page through first editions of eighteenth-century classics in the large library which his forbears had collected. "All men are afraid of books," he claimed, "who have not handled them from infancy." The form of his essays had its parallels with those written in the period with which he felt a spiritual kinship — the eighteenth century. This had been the period of his boyhood idols, Addison and Steele, authors of *The Spectator*, which as *The New Yorker* of its day, reviewed, laughed at, or philosophized about people and events of eighteenth-century London.

The Autocrat, the Professor, and the Poet of Holmes' series were Spectators commenting upon contemporary manners; and boarding-house society, like the club to which the Spectator had belonged, was "very luckily composed of such persons as were engaged in different ways of life, and deputed as it were out of the most conspicuous classes of mankind." Sketches introduced characters in such a way as to catch *Spectator*-like types — the landlady's daughter, for instance: "(Aet. 19+. Tender-eyed blonde. Long ringlets. Cameo pin. Gold pencil-case on a chain. Locket. Bracelet. Album. Autograph book. Accordeon. Reads Byron, Tupper, and Sylvanus Cobb, Junior, while her mother makes the puddings. Says 'Yes?' when you tell her anything.)" Essays in the form of conversation—dialogs—had been used frequently in the eighteenth century: by Shaftesbury to comment upon ethics; by Berkeley, on philosophy; by Hume, on natural religion; and by Franklin, on a variety of subjects —e.g., "Dialogue Between Franklin and the Gout" (1780). In a similar manner the *Autocrat* papers record many conversations of the boarding-house members. James Boswell (1740-1795) had reported the sparkling talk and what Holmes called the "bow-wow manner" of autocratic Samuel Johnson; and Holmes acknowledged indebtedness to this model in the subtitle of the *Autocrat*—"Every Man His Own Boswell." In *Tristram Shandy* (1760) Laurence Sterne had recorded meandering talk interspersed with personal essays and punctuated with dashes in a manner foreshadowing Holmes' eccentric punctuation.

Nineteenth-century publications, too, probably suggested several devices which gave the *Autocrat* papers novelty. Possibly the magazine or the annual (which first achieved remarkable popularity in this period), with its alternation of story, essay, and poems, suggested a similar intermingling of types. The dramatic interplay in personalities common to fiction may have suggested the author's habit of giving his conversations a dramatic quality and of running a plot (like one in a magazine serial story) through his papers. Like Lowell, Holmes no doubt followed the example of nineteenth-century English essayists—such as Lamb and Hazlitt—in talking intimately of his life, his personal prejudices, his feelings. The Autocrat is, in effect, Holmes airing many of his own views to fellow boarders. "He was a well-behaved gentleman at table," testified the Autocrat's landlady, "only talked a good deal, and pretty loud sometimes, and had a way of turnin' up his nose when he didn't like what folks said . . . Many's the time I've seen that gentleman keepin' two or three of the boarders settin' round the breakfast table after the rest had swallered their meal, and things was cleared off . . . and there the little man would set . . . a-talkin' and a-talkin',—and sometimes he would laugh, and sometimes the tears would come into his eyes . . . He was a master hand to talk when he got a-goin'."

Thoreau and Emerson: philosophical, transcendental. A kind of discourse distantly related to informal talk left its imprint upon Thoreau's prose works, whether short pieces, such as "Walking" (1862), or longer ones in which numerous essays were linked, such as *Walden* (1854). For Thoreau kept a detailed journal in which, from day to day, he set down his experiences, observations, and thoughts, and from this he drew materials relevant to his essays, as needed. These diaries were written with artistic care, the passages in them were carefully integrated with other parts of essays in which they were used, and the sentences were scrupulously polished, so that in the end there was less improvisation than there perhaps appeared to be. In learning to shape sentences to his needs—by studying the metaphysical poets, by translating Greek dramas and passages from Greek poets, by aping English prose masters—Thoreau became indebted to earlier authors. "Every sentence," he wrote, with these models in mind, "is the result of long probation, and should be read as if its author, had he held a plough instead of a pen, could have drawn a furrow deep and straight to the end."

Since the conveying of rich personal experience and meaning by straight furrow expressions was, in Thoreau's opinion, the chief task of the writer, what shaped his prose style more than anything else was his philosophy. To see what Thoreau was trying to do, the reader must understand that, despite all his accumulations of scientific data in his journal, Thoreau's way of thinking led him to care little for strictly scientific writing. He attempted, instead, in his finished works, to write in the role of a philosopher. The scientist, according to Transcendental beliefs, recorded the workings of the mere intellect—the "Understanding." The great writer, the man of vision, by contrast, recorded the discoveries of a faculty above mind and more important—the "Imagination" or the "Reason," which intuitively perceived in natural objects the truth of which they were symbols. Said Thoreau:

> It is the subject of the vision, the truth alone, that concerns me. The philosopher for whom rainbows, etc., can be explained never saw them. With regard to such objects, I find that it is not they themselves (with which men of science deal) that concern me; the point of interest is somewhere *between* me and them (i.e., the objects). . . .

Seeing the inner meanings of natural phenomena, the great writer employed those phenomena, Thoreau believed, to communicate those meanings. "My thought," he explained, "is a part of the meaning of the world, and hence I use a part of the world to express my thought."

When he filled his pages with vivid details, he attempted to present them so as to make them illuminating in the Transcendental sense: he wanted to see and set down particular instances of the universal law so that readers might find his own sense of "reality"—the higher kind—in them. His stay at Walden was a search for basic truths, "for the essential facts of life," and his circumstantial record of the stay (or more precisely of an ideal stay based upon sixteen years of records in his journal) was an attempt to convey his insights in meaningful symbols. And elsewhere than in *Walden* his constant practice was to show the eternally true in terms of the particular. "There was an excellent wisdom in him, proper to a rare class of men, which showed him the material world as a means and a symbol," wrote Emerson. "To him there was no such thing as size. The pond was a small ocean; the Atlantic, a large Walden Pond." Thus certain that the small stood for the large, Thoreau expounded higher meanings here and there in his writings by using paradoxes or philosophical generalizations, but for the most part he trusted minutely recorded concrete details on page after page to convey his meaning.

Emerson, though extraordinarily concrete for a philosopher, was more abstract than Thoreau. "In reading Thoreau," he said, "I find the same thought, the same spirit that is in me, but he takes a step beyond and illustrates by excellent images that which I should have conveyed in a sleepy generality." Trained in the composition of sermons and lectures, Emerson, in speeches such as "The Divinity School Address" (1838) and in essays often largely derived from his lectures, had the interest that preachers and lecturers frequently have in generalizing, in following lines of reasoning. Perhaps it is not inaccurate to say that while Thoreau's emphasis was particularly upon concrete things, Emerson's emphasis was upon philosophical relationships.

Emerson set forth what he conceived to be the task of the philosopher in his study of his idol Plato: it was to follow the natural course of the mind as it related the One which was the Oversoul to the Many, or as it related the Many to the One.

> The mind [he wrote] is urged to ask for one cause of many effects; then for the cause of that; and again the cause . . . self-assured that it will arrive at an absolute and sufficient one,—a one that shall be all. . . . Urged by an opposite necessity, the mind returns from the one to that which is not one, but . . . many; from cause to effect; and affirms the necessary existence of variety, the self-existence of both, as each is involved in the other. These strictly-blended elements it is the problem of thought to separate and reconcile.

Such was the idea Emerson had of the method of his essays, and a reader who has a great deal of patience and some skill in dialectic can, indeed, see that the essays are constructed according to this pattern.* Most readers, however, will not care to follow the involvements of his peculiar Transcendental structure. They will find that, though some of Emerson's essays have organizations such as they have seen in other compositions, most appear to lack coherence and unity. These readers will agree with Carlyle's remarks to Emerson in a letter about the *First Series of Essays:*

> The sentences . . . did not . . . always entirely cohere for me. Pure genuine Saxon; strong and simple; of a clearness, of a beauty —But they did not, sometimes, rightly stick to their foregoers and their followers: the paragraph not as a beaten *ingot*, but as a beautiful square *bag of duckshot* held together by canvas!

*For some analyses of Emerson's essays according to this principle see W. T. Harris, "Ralph Waldo Emerson," *Atlantic*, 1882, CL, 238-252; and Walter Blair and Clarence Faust, "Emerson's Literary Method," *Modern Philology*, 1944, XLII, 79-95.

For them, the virtue of the essays will be found chiefly in individual sentences — sentences excellent for their extraordinary proverbial quality, for their compact expression of profound thoughts. Even such small units as sentences, however, show that Emerson, like other essayists of his day, combined old materials and methods with newly discovered ones which particularly appealed to him, thereby making his purposeful writing seem a new thing.

American Fiction Comes into Its Own

When authors of the prewar period wrote fiction, they were inclined to consider carefully whether the setting of their narratives should be remote or near at hand in both time and space. Both kinds of settings were popular in the literature which was generally admired. German and British Gothic romances — or tales of terror — utilizing exotic backgrounds were extremely popular; so were Sir Walter Scott's historical novels, the last of which appeared in 1832. Across the ocean, in addition, flourished fiction which portrayed the manners and talk of common folk. This fiction had a large audience in the United States: Sir Walter Scott, Maria Edgeworth (1767-1849), and Charles Dickens (1812-1870), who wrote about common folk, were perhaps the most popular authors in this country — native authors included — during this period. When our authors told stories, they adapted both types of settings and characterizations to their own purposes.

Poe: skilled craftsman. Early in his career as a fictionist, Poe wrote a letter to T. W. White, owner of the *Southern Literary Messenger*, explaining how he had happened to write one of his weird stories. He had, Poe indicated, been reading successful magazines, foreign and American, and had found that a certain kind of story evidently was in demand. He mentioned "The Spectre in the Log Hut" (*Dublin University Review*), "The Last Man" (*Blackwood's*), "The Suicide" and "The Dance of Death" (*Godey's*), and "The Spectre Fire Ship" (*Knickerbocker*). All these were in the tradition of the Gothic tale of terror, which had flourished since the mid-eighteenth century. The most popular tales, Poe said, represented "the ludicrous heightened into the grotesque; the fearful colored into the horrible; the witty exaggerated into the burlesque; and the singular heightened into the strange and mystical." Poe could turn out stories with any of these effects, but he was at his best in creating the second and fourth of them. Such spine-tingling tales as "Ligeia" (1838), "The Fall of the House of Usher" (1839), "The Masque of the Red Death" (1842), and "The Cask of Amontillado" (1846) owe much to the Gothic romances.

They also owe much to Poe's self-conscious craftsmanship. Thinking in terms of the faculty psychology and of the "science" of phrenology, widely accepted during his day, Poe devised a theory about writing tales which, fortunately, retained some of its validity after these "sciences" had lost theirs. Poe conceived of two elements in a tale—incident and tone—as stimuli to a response by the reader. The skillful artist, therefore, was one who carefully formulated exactly the effect he wished to achieve, then invented and combined events and told of them in words chosen to establish the preconceived effect. A tale so wrought, he felt, could not fail to "leave in the mind of him who contemplated it with a kindred art, a sense of the fullest satisfaction." The process, some have thought, was a somewhat mechanical one; but Poe's skill in both invention and execution, when he followed his formula, made possible achievements which, in particular genres, have not been surpassed.

Hawthorne: romance and allegory. Subordinating everything in the tale to the effect, Poe skillfully utilized characteristic backgrounds, characters, and incidents of Gothic romance. But Poe believed that the most soul-stirring effect could be achieved by blurred rather than precise details. Here, of course, he differed from Hawthorne, whom he greatly admired and at times rather badly misread—differed, as a matter of fact, from most New Englanders. In this period, one who saw a Yankee village from a distance noticed first of all the tidy white-spired churches which were an important and recurrent motif in the quiet green landscape—a motif which stood for a great force in the life of the section. Founded by zealots, New England for decades had produced moralizing literature, and it continued to produce it even when its authors wrote fiction. For Hawthorne, preëminent among New England fictionists, the theme of the tale was tremendously important. Although the Gothic influence was almost as pronounced with Hawthorne as it was with Poe, and though sentimental fiction and allegorical narrative were important in shaping his fiction, these devices were subordinated to Hawthorne's own New England purpose.

As has frequently been noticed, paraphernalia of the tale of terror—animated ancestral portraits, fiendlike villains, men who sold their souls to the devil, witches, unnatural portents—figured notably in this author's tales and novels. The influence of sentimental fiction, too, is clear—even in such a masterpiece as *The Scarlet Letter* (1850). The penalty of seduction, a chief stock-in-trade of the sentimentalists of the day, is the chief substance of this great romance. A typical character of the fiction of sensibility—a child bringing sunshine into the home and gently leading parents to virtue—is little Pearl, an important character in the work. The misled feminist and the ministering angel popular in fourth-rate novels are combined in the portrayal of Hester. Calvinistic villainy common in sentimental fiction was bestowed upon Chillingworth. The sensibility of the minister and his dying glimpses of heavenly glory are hackneyed motifs in the sentimental pattern. And in the tales, too, one familiar with the fiction of feeling will see its stuff used by Hawthorne.

Hawthorne was further influenced by a type of fiction not of his own time so much as of the distant past—the allegorical narrative, which, from childhood, he had read with much pleasure. When in 1843 he listed the authors he considered most notable, it is significant that along with such conventional choices as Homer, Cervantes, Shakespeare, and Milton he named masters of fable and allegory: Aesop, Ariosto, Spenser, and "Bunyan, moulded of homeliest clay, but instinct with celestial fire." Other influences in addition to his liking for these authors encouraged him to borrow from them. Like Emerson, he had philosophical ideas about the artist's duty to give meaning to natural objects when he depicts them. The artist, he felt, cannot exactly reproduce the grandeur of nature which itself suggested truth. His "only resource," he decided, was to substitute something "that may stand instead of and suggest the truth." His Preface to *The House of the Seven Gables* (1851) suggested that a great advantage of a Romance was that it "has fairly a right to present . . . truth under circumstances, to a great extent, of the author's own choosing or creation." This truth, moreover, might be the unifying element. "In all my stories, I think," he remarked, "there is one idea running through them like an iron rod, and to which all other ideas are referred and subordinate . . . " Lowell's comment noted the same sort of ideational unity: "It is commonly true of Hawthorne's romances," he said, "that the interest centres in one strongly defined protagonist,—perhaps we should rather say a ruling Idea, of which all the characters are fragmentary embodiments."

Subtly adapted devices of allegorical fiction—for the portrayal of background, the depiction of character, and the selection of incidents— made possible Hawthorne's amalgamation of Gothic and sentimental elements in truly impressive fiction. Reminiscent of Spenser's Forest of Error or Bower of Bliss, in which many details of background are made to stand for the author's concepts, are Hawthorne's descriptions of the Pearson cottage in "The Gentle Boy" (1832) or the exotic garden in "Rappaccini's Daughter." Characters, too, are made embodiments of ideas according to allegorical formulas. Sometimes older allegorists, for instance, associated significant articles or details of dress with a character: in *Pilgrim's Progress* Christian always labors under his heavy burden; in *The Faerie Queene* the knight has his "bloudie crosse." In "The Minister's Black Veil" (1836) Hooper wears his puzzling but meaningful bit of crepe. Again, older allegorists at times showed physical deformities which betokened spiritual deformities, as in the cases of Bunyan's Giant Despair and Spenser's Malbecco. Similarly, Hawthorne made the boy who alone could not yield to the "gentle boy's" influence a twisted cripple. Hawthorne ingeniously conceived many other symbolic attributes of characters to signify their import: the gleaming smile of Minister Hooper and the perfume of Beatrice, to cite only two examples.

"The Artist of the Beautiful" (1844) both embodies and expounds Hawthorne's critical theory. The story treats, as its author says, "the troubled life of those who strive to create the beautiful," and the opening paragraph establishes a contrast—between the artist, working in bright light, and the thwarters of the artist, standing in darkness—which is important throughout the tale. Warland, who is given the attributes of the eternal artist, is the creator of a butterfly in the beauty of which is "represented the intellect, the sensibility, the soul" of such a creator. Each of the other characters is, in one way or another, a thwarter of the artist, and each is so presented as to signify one of the hostile forces which work against art. All the details, images, and happenings in the tale are richly fused with the meaning, in a manner which is highly typical of the unique art which Hawthorne discovered for himself.

Melville: symbol and actuality. In 1850 Hawthorne and Melville, living a few miles apart but not yet personally acquainted, read one another's writings and found them good. What each author said about the other indicates likenesses and differences. Melville admired Hawthorne for confronting the darker aspects of life. (See "Hawthorne and His Mosses," 1850.) Hawthorne wrote:

> I have read Melville's works with progressive appreciation of the author. No writer ever put reality before the reader more unflinchingly than he does in *Redburn* and *White-Jacket*. *Mardi* is a rich book, with depths here and there that compel a man to swim for his life. It is so good that one scarcely pardons the writer for not having brooded long over it, so as to make it a good deal better.

Clearly there was a kinship between Melville and Hawthorne in artistry as well as in philosophy. Both thought that the theme of a fictional work—that which is more than surface meaning—was very important. Both thought that an author should manipulate imagery, characterization, and plot to convey his ideas. But Hawthorne indicated a difference when he complained that his neighbor had not "brooded" enough over his material. Melville's fiction, if we may employ Hawthorne's terms, did not subdue "the Actual." "He felt instinctively," as William Ellery Sedgwick asserts in *Herman Melville*, "that the effective use of a fact as symbol, having both inward and outward reference, depended on the preservation of its outward reality." Melville's aim—comparable with the way of writing which Hawthorne contrasted with his own achievement in the Preface to *The Scarlet Letter*—was "to diffuse thought and imagination through the opaque substance of today, and thus to make it a bright transparency . . . to seek, resolutely, the true and indestructible value that lay hidden in the petty and wearisome incidents, and ordinary characters. . . ." Though Hawthorne could not write thus, could not thus simultaneously convey meaning and a sense of actuality, he could admire others who were able to, since he recognized that writing of this type achieved a similar object in a contrasting fashion.

Mardi (1849) is not the best illustration of Melville's typical procedure. Despite Hawthorne's criticism, this work is closer to the mode of what he called "a Romance" than anything else Melville wrote. Romance though it is, it includes more earthy details (for example, a satirical description of Congress) than Hawthorne would have been likely to insert into his own writings. In Melville's more typical works, he presents many particular and vivid details based on facts and experiences which are found in the everyday lives of seamen. It is in this respect that the contrast between Hawthorne and Melville is clearly shown. Melville's selection and presentation of such "actual" facts made them seem near at hand and at the same time meaningful. "Benito Cereno" (1855)—one of Melville's typical stories and one of his best—is a good example. Based on a first-hand account of Delano's real experience, it loses little of its factuality when it is transformed into fiction. The changes in details, and the structure make possible the development of a significant theme. *Moby Dick* (1851), Melville's masterpiece, is full of numerous detailed notations about general practices concerning whaling and about the whaling voyage in pursuit of the white whale in particular. At the same time, however, numerous meaningful allegorical and symbolic touches are embodied in the descriptive material and the plot.

Kennedy and Simms: romance and reality. The portrayal of real life without much philosophizing was the purpose of several fictionists contemporary with Melville. Some of them clearly patterned their work after Washington Irving and his school—notably Caroline Kirkland in the sprightly *A New Home—Who'll Follow?* (1839), and John Pendleton Kennedy of Baltimore, in *Swallow Barn* (1832). Something like Irving's romantic picture of England entered, however, into Kennedy's depiction of the ante-bellum plantation. As F. P. Gaines asserts in *The Southern Plantation:*

> He threw the glamour of romantic coloring over all: over the century old brick mansion with its ornate approaches, its wings, its doors, its great hall, its spacious rooms, its antique furniture; over the characters, their dress, conversations, points of view; over the meals . . .; over the Negro quarters . . .; over the whole conduct of life. . . .

William Gilmore Simms, too, according to his own avowal, tried to adhere to "real life" in presenting "man in all his phases." Influenced by Cooper and Scott, however, in many of his novels he turned his attention to the past. Furthermore he unfortunately followed the example of his models in creating a number of colorless heroines and stuffy heroes. Nevertheless, in presenting the comic Porgy of *The Forayers* (1855) and sundry poor whites, and in describing Southern scenes, he managed to infuse a good deal of reality into his pages.

Horse Sense and Humor

Still it remained for the humorists of the day, both Northern and Southwestern, to get the largest amount of common life into their depictions. Their technique for showing scenes of ordinary life was, in important ways, the freshest of the period. The humor of the Southwest moved so far in the direction of realism, in fact, that it has been placed in Chapter 5 where its value in preparing for postwar realism may be clearly shown.

The ancestry of the New England humorists of the day, a notable group, is to be traced less directly to the eighteenth-century wits who inspired Holmes than to the portrayers of American character in almanacs, tales, and travel books of the nineteenth century. Scott's fiction, too, with its representation of low characters by the depiction of manners, dress, and speech, had some value as a model for these limners of folk indigenous to a particular part of the country.

Preachments figured in the writings of almost all the most notable Northern humorists. Seba Smith led the group to see the great possibilities of humorous writing with a purpose when, in 1830, he launched his creation, Jack Downing, upon a career destined to last (with some interruptions) until the eve of the Civil War. In letters which he wrote to the homefolk or to newspaper editors, Smith's character Jack told of his adventures in politics, and now and then one of the family would write Jack news of how things were going back in Downingville. Since Jack purportedly spent a great deal of time with leading public men in Washington, on the battle front during the Mexican War, and in the European capitals, many interesting things about current controversies turned up in the letters.

So wide a following did Jack gain that C. A. Davis, a commercial man in New York, deliberately stole the character (simply renaming him J. Downing) and used him to help Financier Nicholas Biddle in the fight against Andrew Jackson's United States Bank policy. Davis' J. Downing had a brief career and fought a losing battle, but Biddle was sure that Downing had been a good fighter. And when, in the days of the Mexican War, James Russell Lowell was looking around for a way of preaching his views to a wide public, he, like Smith and Davis, hit upon the idea of letting one Hosea Biglow speak for him. The result was that this scion of a Brahmin family wrote some of the most memorable examples of this kind of humor.

Written to appeal chiefly to the relatively uneducated Yankee farmers and mechanics, humorous pieces had to dramatize the way of thinking prevalent in that class. According to that way of thinking the best person to point out the path to what was true and what was right was one with sound common sense — a person who had been born with a sound head, who had had experiences in the world of men rather than of books, and who arrived at his solutions of current problems on the basis of those experiences.

This philosophy, given new prestige by its triumphs in Jacksonian politics, determined the nature of the characters which were to appear in these papers—either horse-sense characters such as Jack Downing and Hosea Biglow, or fool characters such as Birdofredum Sawin, or both. The characters blessed with common sense offered sound solutions to current problems; the chump characters urged actions which were patently muddleheaded. Since the earmarks of either kind of character would be his background, his way of thinking, his way of talking, it was necessary to show something about his environment and to let him talk a good deal. But since the pieces had to appear in the columns of the rather skimpy newspapers of the day, they had also to be short.

These factors largely determined the nature of the Yankee humorous writings of Smith, Davis, Lowell, and dozens of others such as George E. Foxcraft, Tobias H. Miller, Matthew F. Whittier, and Thomas Chandler Haliburton. The characters divided sharply on the basis of their being either common-sensible or the opposite, and various devices were used to make clear to which class they belonged. Their talk was that of the uneducated—the native dialect which more and more, as time passed, was to shape the style of American literature. The talk showed, in brief snatches, what kind of minds they had, what their background and experience had been, what they had figured out on the basis of their experience. Often, if they were strong on common sense, they uttered aphorisms of the sort favored by ordinary men in America ever since the days of Poor Richard. (Examples are Jack Downing's "Sometimes rum gets folks so they can't see at all—so do the newspapers"; or Hosea Biglow's "The moral question's always plain enough; it's jes' the human-natur' side thet's tough.") Often, too, if their creators knew well the background and characteristics appropriate for them, these salty characters were portrayed with an abundance of authentic detail—and the matter as well as the manner of the fiction about them was both native and novel.

Poetry: A Combination of the Old and the New

The nearest approach in this period to such humor in poetry—by authors other than Lowell, of course—is offered by the ballads and folk songs of the singers of the West. These were in the tradition of ancient and modern balladry—composed by the people (or by an artist who felt and thought as they did), for the people, and kept alive by the people. At this time, little attention was paid to such crude poems, but in a later period many serious poets learned much about art and life from these earthy and vigorous songs.

For the most part, the poetry of this prewar period had more of the elegance and remoteness characteristic of Poe than of the simplicity and immediacy of the author of any folk ballad. The background of the cultured New England poets led them to think of poetry as the height of elegance.

Among the books which Holmes listed as obligatory reading for a boy of a good Boston or Cambridge family was "Pope, original edition, 15 volumes, London, 1717." Not only Holmes but others as well who had learned to like literature as youngsters in ancestral libraries had a natural tendency to worship somewhat old-fashioned literary gods. Bowdoin and Harvard were likely to encourage this tendency with their classical curriculums and their courses in writing based upon Blair's old-fashioned, square-toed *Rhetoric*. When Emerson was in Latin school, his favorite declamation was from the "Pleasures of Hope," a typical eighteenth-century philosophizing poem written by Campbell in heroic couplets. When he versified an old nursery story for his brother, Emerson wrote:

> So erst two brethren climb'd the cloud capp'd hill,
> Ill-fated Jack and long-lamented Jill,
> Snatched from the crystal font its lucid store,
> And in full pails the precious treasure bore.
> But ah! by dull forgetfulness oppress'd
> (Forgive me, Edward), I've forgot the rest.

Many gems of expression in these lines might have been by polished Alexander Pope. The superstition that this same Pope was "the greatest poet that ever lived" was, Lowell confessed, inculcated in him by childhood teachers; and, similarly, the other famous New England authors from babyhood to manhood listened to encomiums of the older poets.

But the tradition of culture, though it fostered approval of old ideas and models, also fostered the discovery and development of new ones. The new forces it put to work made certain that the prominent authors would modify, in various fashions, the ways of looking at things and the ways of voicing attitudes. Poe, who lived in England briefly during his youth, avidly read books and magazines from overseas. Literary men of Massachusetts might be sketchily informed about the nation to the West and to the South, but in this period they were likely to widen their horizons by traveling extensively in the Old World. As Parrington has noticed, the New England Renaissance "involved three major strands: the social Utopianism that came from revolutionary France; the idealistic metaphysics that emerged from revolutionary Germany; and the new culture that spread with the development of literary romanticism . . . these strands . . . are but different, new world phases of a comprehensive European movement. . . ." The widespread revolutionary spirit invaded not only the quiet Cambridge libraries but also the woods by Walden Pond.

From the old and new books which they discovered abroad and at home, American authors took hints about poetic techniques. They learned procedures in writing from modern writers such as Goethe, Wordsworth, Coleridge, Byron, Shelley, and Keats and from those of other times, such as the writers of Norse epic poems, the authors of ancient Oriental works, and Plato and the Neo-Platonists. In much of the poetry of the section, as a result, there was a combination of the old and the new — and every author's individual conception of poetry determined the nature of the combinations which he produced.

Poe: poet of unearthly beauty. Poe, as Professor Killis Campbell observed,

> began his career as a poet by imitating Byron and Moore; he came a little later under the spell of Shelley; and both in his theorizing as to poetry and in the application of those theories to his own art he proclaimed himself the ardent disciple of Coleridge. In . . . 'The Raven,' 'The Haunted Palace,' and 'Annabel Lee' he followed, even though afar off, in the footsteps of the balladists; . . . and there is an unmistakable Gothic strain both in his earlier and some of his later verses.

Thus Poe was indebted not only to many of his immediate predecessors, but he was indebted, also, to some of his contemporaries, notably Mrs. Browning and an American poet now pretty well forgotten, Thomas Holley Chivers.

Despite such relationships to others, Poe wrote poetry which was, in some ways, unique. This was partly because of his ability to imagine and portray scenes of unearthly beauty — dreamlands, fairylands, cities in the sea, ghoul-haunted woodlands, and the like. It was partly because he wrote in accordance with rather precise theories — theories about the "single effect" of poetry, about the handling of meter and sound, and about the indirect ways "meaning" or "truth" should be hinted, though not articulated, in poetry.

Holmes: "florist in verse." Much of Holmes' poetry had a periwig-and-velvet-breeches quality about it. In such verse there were so many similarities in form and substance to that of Goldsmith, Pope, Gray, Campbell, Gay, and others of their century that Holmes appeared, in the words of one critic, to be "less a revival of the eighteenth century than its latest survival."

Holmes' kinship with the coffee-house gentry was in part the result of his paying them the tribute of imitation, in part the consequence of his seeing poetry, as they often had, as a graceful social accomplishment. "I'm a florist in verse," he sang, "and what would people say, if I came to a banquet without my bouquet?" So successful was he at writing "by request of friends" that around Boston, almost invariably, first-class celebrations, anniversaries, banquets, receptions, and professional meetings were likely to list on the program an appearance of Dr. Holmes, poem in hand. Again, he wrote verse appropriate for reading at somewhat more informal gatherings, "at the breakfast table," perhaps, or "over the teacups."

All this meant a good deal about his poems. For *vers de société* or *vers d'occasion*, he saw as well as had the Neoclassicists, had to have certain qualities of tone and form. In it deep emotion was as much out of place as it would be in a social group; the tone had to be light — wit and pathos were better than deep feeling. Much depended upon exactly the right phrasing — polished but conversational, graceful, witty, condensed. With these points in mind, Holmes wrote some of the finest familiar verse this country has produced.

Yet Holmes himself in the end considered his most typical poems evidences of his talent rather than of his genius. Eventually he came to feel that his earliest conception of poetry, that of a young man "trained after the schools of classical English verse," had represented "simple and partial views," since it had dealt too exclusively with "the constructive side of the poet's function." "I should rather say," he continued, "if I were called upon now to define that which makes a poet, it is the power of transfiguring the experience and shows of life into an aspect which comes from his imagination and kindles that of others." His occasional poems, he told Lowell, were "for the most part to poetry as the beating of a drum or tinkling of a triangle is to the harmony of a band." True poetry, he believed, was inspired: its thought and to some extent its form came to a poet in an intuitive flash. Only once during his career did he feel sure that he had written such poetry — in "The Chambered Nautilus" (1858).

This romantic concept of the inspired poet was shared by all the famous New England literary men, both those of Cambridge and those of Concord. These men differed only in their ideas about the extent to which a poem was inspired as compared with the extent to which it was consciously contrived. The Brahmins rather tended, with Holmes, to see careful artistry playing an important part. They also joined him in allowing the older conception of poet as teacher to shape their writings.

Longfellow: master of words and accents. Longfellow in particular has been praised by recent scholars for his technique and scolded for his didacticism. His prosodic skill was developed most definitely, perhaps, by his achievement of the exacting task of changing over to English, without signs of painful effort, the *chansons* of French troubadours, the *lieder* of German lyricists, the *terza rima* and sonnets of Italians, the eclogues of Latin poets, the sagas of Finnish bards. However he acquired his skills, as Professor Shepard says, "Together with his thought, he had at the same moment a clear notion of the form in which it could be expressed most effectively . . . and it is for this reason that in his better work the thought seems to fill the form without crowding or inflation."

Longfellow's art concealed art largely because of its simple natural-ness. Unlike most poets, he managed to get both rhyme and rhythm without using many unusual words and, as a rule, without changing the normal order of phrases and sentences. What Professor Allen, in his *American Prosody*, says about the hackneyed poem "The Village Blacksmith" hints at similar compliments which might be paid to more important achievements: "Its severe simplicity of diction and regularity of rhythm is likely to make us underestimate the technical achievements. . . . There are only two inversions in the whole piece: 'a mighty man is he' and 'onward through life he goes.' The natural speech and syntax . . . was practically unique in American versification in 1839." The poems of Longfellow employ diction that is simple and a grammatical arrangement that is natural. He can use without ostentation or evident difficulty each of the ordinary meters (iambic, anapestic, dactylic, and trochaic), some of them in unusual ways, and can combine them with several metrical devices which are quite extraordinary. (Note the refrain of "My Lost Youth," 1855; and the spacing of accented syllables in "The Skeleton in Armor," 1841; "Jugurtha," 1880; and "The Tide Rises," 1880.)

This master of words and accents could, at times, make each word, each line do its job. The plots of his best narratives he developed in excellent order. His best lyrics — whatever might be said against their preachments — at least have the unity which development of a single thought or sentiment gives them. The unity of thought in such poems as "The Rainy Day," "The Arrow and the Song," and "Jugurtha," cannot be surpassed; in each the first part offers some image, and the second part suggests, usually with the aid of incremental repetition, the spiritual connotation in a detailed parallel. Similarly, "The Bridge" starts with a description of a scene, then passes to the meaning of the scene to the poet, and ends by applying the meaning to all men. In such simple structures, there is integration of the sort important in sonnets, a form particularly well handled by Longfellow.

Despite such prosodic skill and such unity and coherence of thought, Longfellow often failed to please for three reasons. The thought which held together a lyric of his was too often platitudinous. Secondly, more even than Holmes or Lowell, he was a bookish, library poet. One sees why Whitman complained of Longfellow's poetry being "reminiscent, polish'd, elegant, with the air of finest conventional library, picture-gallery or parlor, with ladies and gentlemen in them. . . ." Finally, although his poems were logically constructed, they were likely to be badly put together emotionally — or connotatively. That similes and metaphors should be more than handsome ornaments — that they should be as organic to the poem as the thought — he apparently did not conceive. Hence in many of his poems he used imagery which modern readers find incongruous, and in only a few did he avoid jarring connotations.

Lowell: pioneer in freedom of verse form. Professor Howard Mumford Jones has noticed that "readers do not turn to Lowell as they do to Longfellow, for a body of verse; and though certain lyrics are individual favorites, they are such as two or three other poets might have written. 'To the Dandelion' is Keatsian; many readers confuse 'The First Snowfall' with Bryant's poem on the same theme, and 'The Present Crisis' inevitably suggests Whittier." This comparison can be carried further: *A Fable for Critics*, with its Pope-like critiques, suggests Holmes; and "Auspex" might well have been written by Longfellow. Lowell perhaps busied himself too much with other matters to develop a poetic style all his own.

Yet in some of Lowell's work there are merits not discoverable in Holmes or Longfellow. His *Biglow Papers* are the most effective political satire in verse yet written in America, and *A Fable for Critics* combines sharply phrased wit with shrewd literary judgments as no other poetry in this country has. In his famous "Commemoration Ode" he showed ability in shaping a long contemplative poem beyond the skill of his fellow Brahmins. He had exactly the perception of the emotional relationship that Longfellow lacked. "My notion of a true lyric," he said, "is that the meaning should float steadfast in the centre of every stanza, while the vapory emotions . . . float up to it and over it, and wreathe it with an opal halo which seems their own, but is truly its own work. The shades of emotion over, there floats the meaning, clear and sole and sharp-cut in its luminous integrity. . . ." Lowell wrote some poems in which the figurative language thus related the emotion it connoted to the meaning as a whole: "To the Dandelion," "The Courtin'," and "Auspex" are instances. Finally, Lowell did make the sort of technical contribution to American versification best suggested by his irregular "Ode Recited at the Harvard Commemoration." In Professor Allen's words, this poet's prosody "introduced into American poetry the freedom which we find in the first two or three decades of nineteenth-century English poetry. . . . This freedom includes a more varied placing of accents and the combination of different kinds of feet to produce a suggestiveness of tone and cadence. . . . Yet . . . Lowell's versification is more important for the lessons it teaches than for the poetic beauty it achieved."

Emerson and Thoreau: rebels against nineteenth-century forms. Some free verse lines of the Transcendentalist, Ralph Waldo Emerson, serve to set off his aims in poetry from those of the Brahmins who have just been considered:

> I will not read a pretty tale
> To pretty people in a nice saloon
> Borrowed from their expectation,
> But I will sing aloud and free
> From the heart of the world.

Thoreau, another Transcendentalist, also stated a view of writing at variance with that of the genteel Cambridge men when he wrote: "Enough has been said in these days of the charm of fluent writing. . . . The surliness with which the woodchopper speaks of his woods, handling them as indifferently as his axe, is better than the mealy-mouthed enthusiasm of the lover of nature. Better that the primrose by the river's brim be a yellow primrose, and nothing more, than that it be something less." In some ways, so far as form and substance were concerned, the most radical of the ante-bellum New England versifiers were the Transcendentalists, Emerson in a few great poems and Thoreau in even fewer.

"The form [of Transcendental poetry]," Cooke notes, "is often rugged, the verse is halting and defective. The metres stumble, and . . . rhymes are not correct. The poems are . . . metaphysical, subtle, and complicated in their thought. . . ." Unlike Longfellow, who acquired his free and easy ways with verse by echoing foreign metrical schemes, or Lowell, who came late enough to learn lessons from Shelley, the Transcendentalists found their chief models in a seventeenth-century school of unorthodox versifiers. From the metaphysical poets — Marvell, Crashaw, Donne, and others — who had rebelled against the dulcet melodiousness of Elizabethan lyricists, these rebels against the nineteenth-century saccharinity learned something about the forcefulness which results from breaking up regular patterns. It may be true, as some critics claim, that the very infrequency of the Concord men's excursions into verse had something to do with the harshness of their songs. But the most important cause for their radicalism, probably, was that the nature of Transcendental poetry, like that of Transcendental prose, was influenced strongly by the philosophy of its creators.

According to this philosophy the matter and the expression of a poem, one and inseparable, were both spontaneously inspired. Theoretically, this would lead a Transcendentalist, trusting his "instinct," to set down his songs without change; actually, it did cause them to tinker with initial expressions less than other poets did. And the intuitive expression, in their opinion, would carry to others the message the poets themselves had been vouchsafed. It would do this because the poets would pass on to readers the same symbols which originally had suggested eternal verities to the poets. "Things," said Emerson, "admit of being used as symbols, because nature is a symbol, in the whole, and in every part." The whole theory of Emerson and his group has been admirably summarized by Miss Gorely (in "Emerson's Theory of Poetry," *Poetry Review*, July-August 1931, XXII, 272-273):

> Emerson . . . believed that poetry . . . comes into being as the result of inspiration. In that moment the poet sees the very essence of things. . . . The poet makes the unseen visible by means of language. But he is not the conscious creator. Vision,

also, shows him the symbols and the thought takes its own form in language that is rhythmical. Because of this, there is a certain indwelling beauty of poetry . . . poetry is spiritual and forms a link between the visible and invisible worlds.

Thus the symbols were important, and the ideas of deep perceptions for which the symbols stood were even more important — so significant that, as in earlier metaphysical poetry, they controlled everything else in a poem. The sentiment often cultivated by the Brahmin poets was practically crowded out by the thought. Since only imagery which developed such a thought was relevant, merely ornamental imagery was avoided. And the concept being expressed determined the general structure of the poem. "It is not metres, but metre-making argument," said Emerson, "that makes a poem, — a thought so passionate and alive, that, like the spirit of a plant or an animal, it has an architecture of its own and adorns nature with a new thing." This theory suggested the four chief methods for ordering material used by Emerson and Thoreau: (1) as in "The Snow-Storm" (1841) or "Though All the Fates" (1849), the poet might give a description of an object or scene which embodied and implied meaning; (2) as in "Brahma" (1857) or "The Summer Rain" (1842), the poet might list a number of parallel phenomena; (3) as in "Each and All" (1839) or "Inspiration" (1849), the poet might record the process by which he arrived at a great truth; (4) as in "Rumors from an Æolian Harp" (1842), the poet might record a state of inspiration.

Logically, the meter in such poems should be appropriate for the emphasis of both the symbols and the truths for which the symbols stand. "There is a soberness," wrote Thoreau, "in a rough aspect, as of unhewn granite, which addresses a depth in us, but a polished surface hits only the ball of the eye." And Emerson, in "Merlin," pointed out that:

> The kingly bard
> Must strike the chords rudely and hard,
> As with hammer or with mace;
> That they may render back
> Artful thunder, which conveys
> Secrets of the solar track. . . .

In these ways, the Transcendental poetry of Emerson and Thoreau looked backward to seventeenth-century metaphysical poetry, forward to the type of poetry admired most in the middle decades of the present century.

Thus in the essay, in fiction, and in poetry, the authors of the period 1829-1860 combined old and new materials and techniques. As a result, these writers gave memorable expression to the ideas about which our countrymen were excited during the American Renaissance, one of the richest periods in our literary history.

W.B.

1829 ■ Poe's *Al Aaraaf, Tamerlane, and Minor Poems* · Irving's *Conquest of Granada*

Andrew Jackson inaugurated seventh President

1830 ■ Holmes' "Old Ironsides"

The settled frontier reached Independence, Missouri

1831 ■ Poe's *Poems* (second edition) · Whittier's *Legends of New England* · W. L. Garrison established the *Liberator*, an antislavery journal, at Boston

Nat Turner's slave insurrection in Virginia, in which over fifty whites were killed, and for which the *Liberator* was blamed by slaveholders

1832 ■ Bryant's *Poems* · Irving's *Alhambra* · Kennedy's *Swallow Barn*

Jackson reëlected President · Oberlin became the first coeducational college

1833 ■ Poe's "A MS Found in a Bottle" · Seba Smith's *Life and Writings of Major Jack Downing*

Cyrus H. McCormick's reaper · Abolition of slavery in the British colonies · The English Factory Act, which improved working conditions in English factories

1834 ■ *Narrative of the Life of David Crockett of West Tennessee*

1835 ■ Irving's *Tour on the Prairies* · Poe began his contributions to the *Southern Literary Messenger* in Richmond · Kennedy's *Horse-Shoe Robinson* · Simms' *Yemassee* and *Partisan* · Longstreet's *Georgia Scenes*

1836 ■ Irving's *Astoria* · Emerson's *Nature*

Fall of the Alamo · Arkansas, the twenty-fifth state, admitted with slavery · Martin Van Buren elected eighth President

1837 ■ Irving's *Adventures of Captain Bonneville, U.S.A.* · Emerson's *The American Scholar* · Hawthorne's *Twice-Told Tales*

Financial panic · Republic of Texas, with Sam Houston as president, recognized by the United States · Michigan admitted as the twenty-sixth state

1838 ■ Kennedy's *Rob of the Bowl* · Emerson's "Divinity School Address" · Cooper's *American Democrat*

Atlantic crossing by steamships

1839 ■ Longfellow's *Voices of the Night*

1840 ■ Poe's *Tales of the Grotesque and Arabesque* · Cooper's *The Pathfinder* · Dana's *Two Years Before the Mast*

1200 cotton factories in the United States, two thirds being in New England · United States census: population 17,000,000, including 400,000 free Negroes and 2,500,000 slaves · William Henry Harrison elected ninth President

1841 ■ Cooper's *The Deerslayer* · Emerson's *Essays* (First Series) · Longfellow's *Ballads and Other Poems* · Thorpe's "Big Bear of Arkansas"

Death of Harrison; succeeded by John Tyler as tenth President · Act for preëmption of public lands: settlers could preëmpt 160 acres at $1.25 per acre

1842 ■ Hawthorne's *Twice-Told Tales* (second edition) · Longfellow's *Poems on Slavery* · Holmes' "The Contagiousness of Puerperal Fever"

1843 ■ Thompson's *Major Jones's Courtship*

1844 ■ Emerson's *Essays* (Second Series) · Lowell's *Poems*

Morse's telegraph used between Washington and Baltimore · James W. Polk elected eleventh President

1845 ■ Poe's "The Raven"

Florida and Texas, the twenty-seventh and twenty-eighth states, annexed to the Union with slavery, making fifteen slave states to thirteen free · The *Rainbow*, first of the clipper ships which became famous in the following decade, built in New York

1846 ■ Poe's *Literati*, profiles of New York writers · Hawthorne's *Mosses from an Old Manse* · Whittier's *Voices of Freedom* · Melville's *Typee*

Great famine in Ireland, after which Irish immigration to the United States reached a new high · Treaty with Great Britain determined the Oregon boundary line · War with Mexico, "by act of Mexico" · Wilmot Proviso, prohibiting slavery in any territory to be acquired from Mexico, passed the House but defeated in the Senate · Iowa, the twenty-ninth state, admitted as a free state

1847 ■ Poe's "Ulalume" · Emerson's *Poems* · Longfellow's *Evangeline*

1848 ■ Poe's *Eureka* · Lowell's *Fable for Critics; The Biglow Papers, First Series;* and *Vision of Sir Launfal*

Mexican cession of what is now California, Nevada, Utah, and Arizona · Gold discovered in California, resulting in the famous "rush" · Wisconsin, the thirtieth state, admitted as a free state, restoring the balance of free and slave states · Zachary Taylor elected twelfth President · Widespread revolutions in Europe.

1849 ■ Thoreau's *A Week on the Concord and Merrimack Rivers* and "Civil Disobedience" · Melville's *Mardi* and *Redburn* · Parkman's *Oregon Trail*

1850 ■ Emerson's *Representative Men* · Hawthorne's *The Scarlet Letter* · Whittier's *Songs of Labor and Other Poems* · Melville's *White Jacket* · John C. Calhoun's *Speech on the Slavery Question* · Daniel Webster's *Seventh of March Speech*

Death of President Taylor; succeeded by Millard Fillmore as thirteenth President · Compromise of 1850: admission of California, the thirty-first state, as a free state · A drastic Fugitive Slave Law · First act of Congress making land grants to aid in construction of railroads—in this case, the Illinois Central · United States census: population 23,000,000

1851 ■ Hawthorne's *The House of the Seven Gables* · Melville's *Moby Dick*

1852 ■ Hawthorne's *The Blithedale Romance* and *Life of Franklin Pierce* · Melville's *Pierre* · Mrs. Stowe's *Uncle Tom's Cabin*, greatest literary stimulus to the antislavery movement

Franklin Pierce elected fourteenth President

1853 ■ Joseph G. Baldwin's *Flush Times of Alabama and Mississippi*

1854 ■ Thoreau's *Walden*

Kansas-Nebraska Act establishing "squatter sovereignty" in those territories; bloody conflicts between free-state and slave-state settlers; emergence of John Brown · Republican Party first organized as protest against the Kansas-Nebraska Act

1855 ■ Longfellow's *Hiawatha* · Simms' *Forayers* · Whittier's "Barefoot Boy" · Whitman's *Leaves of Grass* · Melville's *Benito Cereno*

1856 ■ Emerson's *English Traits* · Simms' *Eutaw* · Whitman's *Leaves of Grass* (second edition, containing Emerson's letter)

James Buchanan elected fifteenth President

1857 ■ Founding of the *Atlantic Monthly* in Boston, with Lowell as editor ·

Founding of *Russell's Magazine* (1857-1861) in Charleston, with Paul Hamilton Hayne as editor

Chief Justice Taney's Dred Scott decision: a Negro was not a citizen and therefore had no right to bring suit in a Federal court · Financial panic

1858 ■ Longfellow's *The Courtship of Miles Standish* · Holmes' *The Autocrat of the Breakfast-Table*

The Lincoln-Douglas debates in Illinois on questions arising from the slavery issue · Minnesota admitted as thirty-second state

1859 ■ Irving's *Life of Washington*, 5 vols.

Oregon admitted as thirty-third state · Silver discovered in the Comstock lode, Nevada · First oil well, Oil Creek, Pennsylvania · John Brown's raid on Harper's Ferry

1860 ■ Emerson's *The Conduct of Life* · Hawthorne's *Marble Faun* · Thoreau's "Plea for John Brown" · Whitman's *Leaves of Grass* (third edition) · Howells' campaign biography of Lincoln

United States census: population 31,500,000, including 450,000 free Negroes and 4,000,000 slaves · South Carolina seceded from the Union · Abraham Lincoln elected sixteenth President

1861 ■ Timrod's "Ethnogenesis" and "The Cotton Boll" · Holmes' *Elsie Venner*

Telegraphic communication opened across the continent · Kansas, the thirty-fourth state, admitted as a free state · Mississippi, Florida, Alabama, Georgia, Louisiana, and Texas seceded from the Union · Confederate States of America organized at Montgomery with Jefferson Davis as president · The Civil War began when the Confederates fired on Fort Sumter, 12 April · Virginia, Arkansas, Tennessee, and North Carolina joined the Confederacy · Great Britain and France recognized the belligerency of the Confederate States · The First Battle of Bull Run

1862 ■ Holmes' *Songs in Many Keys* · Browne's *Artemus Ward: His Book*

Merrimac-Monitor engagement in Hampton Roads, first battle of ironclads · The Battles of Shiloh, Seven Days, Second Bull Run, Antietam, Murfreesboro

1863 ■ Hawthorne's *Our Old Home* · Longfellow's *Tales of a Wayside Inn* · Whittier's "Barbara Frietchie" · Lincoln's "Emancipation Proclamation" and *Gettysburg Address*

West Virginia admitted as thirty-fifth state; formed by secession from

Virginia · Death of Stonewall Jackson at Battle of Chancellorsville · Battle of Gettysburg (1-3 July) and surrender of Vicksburg (4 July), the turning point of the War

1864 ■ William Cullen Bryant's *Thirty Poems*

Battles of the Wilderness, Spottsylvania Courthouse, Cold Harbor · Grant versus Lee in Virginia · Farragut at Mobile Bay · Sherman's March to the Sea · Nevada admitted as thirty-sixth state · Lincoln reëlected President

1865 ■ Lincoln's *Second Inaugural* · Lowell's "Commemoration Ode" · Whitman's *Drum-Taps* · Mark Twain's "Celebrated Jumping Frog of Calaveras County"

Surrender of Lee to Grant at Appomattox, 9 April · Assassination of Lincoln, 14 April; Andrew Johnson succeeded him as seventeenth President

1866 ■ Whittier's *Snow-Bound*

4

THE CIVIL WAR
1850 – 1865

"Over the carnage rose prophetic a voice,
Be not dishearten'd, affection shall solve the problems of freedom yet,
Those who love each other shall become invincible,
They shall yet make Columbia victorious."

WHITMAN

INTELLECTUAL CURRENTS

The Irrepressible Conflict

The Civil War was the bloodiest conflict which the world had seen up to that time, and it struck a blow which was almost fatal to the American Union. The issues were complex and confused. On the Northern side, the primary objective of the abolitionists was the destruction of slavery as an institution, while the aim of the nationalists was the preservation of the Union. On the Southern side, many fought to defend slavery—an institution whose rights had been guaranteed by the Constitution—while others believed that the basic issue was the vindication of the sovereignty of the individual state. Beneath these immediate issues lay the conflict between two radically different forms of society: the democratic, industrial economy of the North and the aristocratic, agrarian economy of the South. Although the causes of conflict were deeply imbedded in the American past, a series of dramatic events in the 1850's precipitated the outbreak of war in 1861.

The Fugitive Slave Law of 1850, which compelled the return of runaway slaves to their owners, fanned the fires of abolitionism. Emerson declared that he would not obey it; Thoreau actually helped at least one fugitive slave to escape into Canada; and the gentle-souled Whitman implied in one of his poems that he would aid all such fugitives with his "firelock" if the occasion should arise. A decisive incident occurred in Boston in 1854, when an infuriated mob attempted to rescue Anthony Burns, a fugitive slave, from the police, and United States troops intervened to enforce the law.

The rival efforts of Northerners and Southerners to control Kansas, where the issue of slavery was to be decided by popular vote, resulted in bloody strife in that territory in 1855. In a speech called "The Crime Against Kansas," Senator Charles Sumner of Massachusetts spoke too harshly of Senator Butler of South Carolina; whereupon Butler's young kinsman, Preston Brooks, assaulted Sumner on the floor of the Senate and inflicted an injury from which Sumner never fully recovered. The controversy over Kansas hastened the organization, in 1856, of the Republican Party, with a platform opposing the extension of slavery.

Sectional bitterness was increased still further in 1857 by the Dred Scott decision of Chief Justice Taney. Having been taken by his owner into a free state and then brought back into a slave state, Dred sued for his freedom. The Supreme Court denied his petition, declaring that since a Negro was not a citizen, he did not have access to the courts. The decision was attacked by Lincoln in his famous debates with Stephen A. Douglas. Still more dramatic and more far-reaching in its effects was the attempt of John Brown, a fanatical abolitionist, to foment an insurrection of slaves in Virginia. After having captured the federal arsenal at Harper's Ferry in October 1859, he was arrested by a company of marines under Colonel Robert E. Lee, and was later tried and executed. Emerson and Thoreau spoke out in Brown's defense, while Southerners were horrified by the threat of a black uprising. The "martyrdom" of Brown contributed enormously to the rise of sectional feeling. He became the subject of a stirring battle song in 1861 which Northern soldiers were to sing during the war: "John Brown's body lies a-moldering in the grave,/His soul is marching on!"

The election to the Presidency in 1860 of the Republican nominee, Abraham Lincoln, precipitated the secession movement in the South. The new party was exclusively the party of the North; political lines were more completely sectional than ever before. Since Lincoln had declared that "this government cannot endure permanently half slave and half free," and the Republican Party vigorously opposed the extension of slavery, Southern extremists believed that they were forced to choose between abolition and secession. South Carolina seceded from the Union in December 1860, and by February 1861, Georgia, Alabama, Florida, Mississippi, Louisiana, and Texas had followed her example. Shortly thereafter, the Confederate States of America was organized in Montgomery, Alabama, with Jefferson Davis as president. On April 12, 1861, the Confederate batteries in Charleston harbor fired on the federal garrison in Fort Sumter, which surrendered the next day. Soon after this decisive event marking the opening of the war, Virginia, Arkansas, Tennessee, and North Carolina joined the Confederacy.

The choice between state and nation was a difficult one for many Southerners to make. The old constitutional argument that the states were older than the Union (true of course of only the original thirteen) and that the Union consequently derived its authority from the states was no doubt intellectually convincing to some. But loyalty is based in the emotions rather than in the intellect. The most distinguished officer of the Confederate army, Robert E. Lee, resigned his commission in the United States Army when Virginia seceded because, as he put it, "I have been unable to make up my mind to raise my hand against my native state, my relatives, my children, and my home." A New England writer, Hawthorne, expressed sympathy with Lee's view when he said, with a touch of irony: "If a man loves his own State and is content to be ruined with her, let us shoot him if we can, but allow him an honorable burial in the soil he fights for."

At the outset of the war, the South believed that cotton alone was a guarantee of victory; that if deprived of cotton, the textile industry — and therefore the entire economy — of the North and of England would collapse. The Southern expectation was not realized. England, though on the point of doing so in 1862, never recognized the Confederacy. The issue was to be decided by arms alone, and the overwhelming superiority of the North in population and resources permitted little doubt of the eventual outcome. It is hardly necessary here to recount the shifting tides of battle during the four years of war. The turning point came in July 1863, when Lee was defeated at Gettysburg and Vicksburg capitulated after a long siege. The surrender of Lee to Grant at Appomattox on April 9, 1865, in effect terminated the war. The assassination of Lincoln five days later plunged the nation into the turmoil of reconstruction, which for the South proved to be more trying in many ways than the war itself.

Attackers and Defenders of Slavery

From the foregoing brief survey it is clear that slavery was the great issue before the American people, and it is not surprising that slavery was the subject of much of the literature, both Northern and Southern, during the decade which preceded the Civil War.

In the North, the two chief representatives of antislavery literature were John Greenleaf Whittier and Mrs. Harriet Beecher Stowe. Both writers were motivated by a sincere devotion to the cause of human freedom. Whittier's poems were characterized by a fiery intensity rarely equalled even in polemical verse. His "Ichabod" (1850) was a scorching condemnation of Webster for his support of the Fugitive Slave Law:

> Let not the land once proud of him
>> Insult him now,
> Nor brand with deeper shame his dim,
>> Dishonored brow.

A better, though equally partisan, poem was his "Massachusetts to Virginia" (1843), with its swinging rhythm and its impressive roll call of the Massachusetts counties. If the author's zeal caused him to forget that New Englanders had once been actively engaged in the slave trade—as when he said to Virginia,

> But that one dark loathsome burden ye must stagger
>> with alone,
> And reap the bitter harvest which ye yourselves have
>> sown!—

the poem was none the less effective both as an indictment of the South and as a summons to action at home. Mrs. Stowe's *Uncle Tom's Cabin*, which was published in 1852, reached a larger number of readers than did all of Whittier's poems combined; indeed, the novel immediately became, and remained for many years, a best seller. It was dramatized and was long successful on the stage. Mrs. Stowe's appeal was more sentimental than Whittier's; her book emphasized the pathos of the traffic in Christian souls.

Among the early defenders of slavery was John Pendleton Kennedy, the Baltimore novelist. Although he has already been considered as a creator of romantic fiction, it should be recalled here that in *Swallow Barn*, published in 1832, he presented a reassuring picture of the friendly relations which existed between master and slaves on a Virginia plantation.

The abolitionist attacks of the 1840's and 1850's called forth a more elaborate and more vigorous defense. Calhoun pointed out that slavery was a necessary part of the Southern economy and that its abolition would destroy the South:

> The Southern States are an aggregate, in fact, of communities, not of individuals. Every plantation is a little community, with the master at its head, who concentrates in himself the united interests of capital and labor, of which he is the common representative. These small communities aggregated make the State in all, whose action, labor, and capital is equally represented and perfectly

harmonized. Hence the harmony, the union, the stability of that section.

With the rising tide of sectional feeling, Southern apologists carried the argument to still greater extremes. William Gilmore Simms doubtless spoke for a substantial body of Southern opinion when he declared in 1852 that "slavery is a wisely devised institution of heaven devised for the benefit, improvement, and safety, morally, socially, and physically, of a barbarous and inferior race, who would otherwise perish by famine or by filth, by the sword, by disease, by waste, and destinies forever gnawing, consuming, and finally destroying."

The final step in the Southern defense carried the war to the enemy. The condition of the slaves on Southern plantations, it was argued, was infinitely better than that of the workers, or wage-slaves, in Northern factories and mines. William J. Grayson's *The Hireling and the Slave*, which was published in 1854, pointed out the contrast in Pope-like couplets: in Northern industrial communities,

> Gaunt Famine prowls around his pauper prey,
> And daily sweeps his ghastly hosts away;
> Unburied corpses taint the summer air,
> And crime and outrage revel with despair . . .

while on the Southern plantation,

> Warm social joys surround the Negro's cot,
> The evening dance its merriment imparts,
> Love, with its rapture, fills their youthful hearts,
> And placid age, the task of labor done,
> Enjoys the summer shade, the winter sun.

A middle position between the extremes of Northern abolitionism and Southern eulogy was taken by Webster and Lincoln. Throughout the controversy the aim of both men was not to destroy slavery but to preserve the Union, and both incurred the ill will of the abolitionists. Although they believed that slavery was an evil and opposed its extension, they were willing to respect its constitutional rights in the slave states if thereby the Union might be saved. Webster's desire for his country was best expressed in the noble peroration, "Liberty and Union, one and inseparable, now and forever." Lincoln's attitude as late as August 1862 was expressed in the famous letter to editor Horace Greeley: "My paramount object in this struggle is to save the Union, and is not either to save or to destroy slavery. . . . What I do about slavery and the colored race, I do because I believe it helps to save the Union." The Emancipation Proclamation, announced on January 1, 1863, was a shrewd political weapon as well as a great humanitarian document. It united the cause of the Negro with that of the Union and gave to the Civil War in the eyes of the world the dignity of a crusade for human liberty.

The Literature of the War Years

Much of our best literature dealing with the Civil War was not written until many years later — Stephen Crane's *The Red Badge of Courage* in 1895, for example, and Stephen Vincent Benét's *John Brown's Body* in 1928. During the war itself, the memorable literature on the subject of the war was small in amount: a few poems by Whittier and Timrod, several popular songs, the speeches of Lincoln, and Whitman's collection of poems, *Drum-Taps*.

Since Whittier's work as propagandist had been largely accomplished before the outbreak of the war, he was content during its course to write an occasional poem. In "Barbara Frietchie" (1863) he celebrated an instance of loyalty to "the old flag" in the border state of Maryland, though it was a loyalty which he and other abolitionists had done much to undermine. In "Laus Deo" (1865) he rejoiced at the passage of the constitutional amendment abolishing slavery. The amendment marked the final triumph of the cause for which he had labored, with energy and self-sacrifice, for thirty years.

While Whittier did his best work before and after the war, actual hostilities had the magical effect on Henry Timrod, the Southern poet, of calling forth poems far superior to anything else he ever wrote. "Ethnogenesis" (1861) and "The Cotton Boll" (1861) are compositions which entitle Timrod to a higher rank among our poets than he has yet been accorded. In these poems he reiterated many of the traditional Southern arguments: the Constitution recognized slavery, and the Bible did not prohibit it; the bond slave of the South was treated more humanely than the wage-slave of the North; Southern cotton was necessary to the prosperity and happiness of the world. In eloquent, moving verse he described his conception of the South's mission and of the Southern character. The exportation of cotton under a system of free trade, he thought, would bind the nations together in lasting peace. The Southern character and its influence on the rest of the world were typified for him in the Gulf Stream, which ". . . through the cold, untempered ocean pours its genial streams."

The war also called forth Lincoln's finest utterances. In the *First Inaugural* (1861) he faced the difficult situation already created by the secession of seven Southern states. Lincoln asserted that the Union was indisoluble, and promised that no force other than that necessary to hold federal property and collect federal duties would be used against the erring states. He concluded with an appeal "to the better angels of our nature."

The Gettysburg Address (1863), second only to the Declaration of Independence, is our most classic expression of the American democratic ideal; it was so phrased as to be always applicable. America was "conceived in liberty and dedicated to the proposition that all men are created equal." Americans should "highly resolve . . . that this nation, under God, shall have a new birth of freedom; and that government of the people, by the people, and for the people, shall not perish from the earth." Delivered a little more than a month before Lee's surrender and the author's death, the *Second Inaugural* (1865) regarded the war as the righteous judgment of God on both North and South for the sin of slavery. The task before us, he said, was to proceed "with malice toward none, with charity for all . . . to bind up the nation's wounds . . . to do all which may achieve and cherish a just and lasting peace among ourselves, and with all nations." Lincoln's humane and wise view of postwar policy made his death a tragic loss to the South.

Before the war began Walt Whitman had brought out the first three of the many editions of *Leaves of Grass* and had laid down his basic principles in those early volumes. He espoused Emerson's doctrine of the divinity of man, and, prompted by his larger and warmer sympathies, applied it literally and concretely to all men. He espoused, too, Emerson's belief in a transcendental intuition, which fused perhaps indistinguishably in his mind with an inherited Quaker belief in the Inner Light. His Quaker inheritance (which possibly was fully as important as the Emersonian influence) contributed also to his independence, his sense of brotherhood with all men, and his love of peace. His mysticism, which became more emphasized in his later life, seems a blend of Emerson, the Quakers, and the Orient. His celebration of the body, however, was derived from none of these sources: it shocked Emerson particularly and drove him to opposition.

Whitman was a great equalitarian—his very catalogs were symbols of the equalizing power of his democracy. The "Myself" of his longest poem was Everyman. The experiences related in his poems were partly actual and partly imaginary. So great was his faculty of empathy that he could project himself into the personalities of others in a very real sense and thus become "the hounded slave" or "the mashed fireman." He took his stand for absolute equality; he desired nothing for himself which others could not have in the same measure. It was natural that such a complete democrat should oppose slavery, and equally natural that such a sensitive sympathizer with all men should not bear arms against the slave owner. The war wrought no change in Whitman's basic ideas and attitudes. He was still "the caresser of life," still "a Southerner soon as a Northerner." His war poems reveal no partisan rage like Whittier's or Timrod's, nor were they concerned with the issues of the war. He felt a profound compassion for all soldiers and the mothers of soldiers, whether Yankee or Rebel.

Aside from polemics and sectional rancor, with which he was not at all concerned, Whitman's *Drum-Taps* (1865) affords the richest account of the war to be found in our poetry. One group of poems conveys the excitement of the early enlistments—the scholar is torn from his school; the bridegroom, from his bride. Another group pictures military scenes as sharply as a camera, and more suggestively—the cavalrymen slumping in their saddles while the horses drink from a stream, the shadowy forms of men and horses around the campfire on a mountainside. Other poems describe hospital scenes with modern realism or reveal the poignant suffering of a mother just notified of her son's death.

Though the war contributed nothing to Whitman's ideas, and changed not at all his fundamental attitudes, it stimulated the poet and clarified and spiritualized his poetry. He was never again to sing so lustily (and as some thought, sensually) of the "jolly bodily phase." His poetry became more mystical. His greatest poem, "When Lilacs Last in the Door-yard Bloom'd" (1865), reflects these changes. In this poem, written as an elegy on the death of Lincoln, due emphasis is given to the grief of the poet, memorialized by "lilac and star and bird"; due emphasis is given also to the sorrow of the nation, the funeral procession, and the tolling of bells. But these details are the background of the poet's mystical exaltation in the hymn to death. In the poem's burning core, America and the war and Lincoln are forgotten.

Except in such moments of mystical release, Whitman never forgot America. "Thou Mother with Thy Equal Brood" (1872) celebrated the restoration of the Union and the new solidarity of "these states." *Democratic Vistas* (1871) revealed an acute concern for the evils, more and more apparent, in our rapidly developing industrialism. But in the poems after the Civil War, Whitman recurred with an increasing frequency and a growing intensity to the mood of the Lincoln poem in his ultimate quest of a "passage to more than India."

R.S.

LITERARY TRENDS

Varied though they were, the writings of this period were alike in being works intended to persuade. The appeals made during the bitter controversy about slavery and kindred matters, and during the consequent war, urged moderation or fierce opposition. And the poems of Walt Whitman, though they did not deal with slavery, eloquently preached the poet's doctrines about the individual and society. It was only natural that all such writings, since they were meant to influence opinions and beliefs, not only conformed to ways of thinking and feeling then current, but also took forms particularly likely to appeal to the tastes of the day. Some of the authors, nevertheless, created literature which was to have other than historical interest long after the controversy had ended.

Works dealing with the slavery controversy, naturally, were quite likely to reflect the spirit of the times by being intemperate. Objective historians have made it clear that neither side was blameless — that neither North nor South had a monopoly upon virtue. As was all too human, however, a majority of people on each side felt that they were wholly right and their opponents wholly wrong. "Both [parties]," Lincoln observed in his *Second Inaugural*, "read the same Bible, and pray to the same God; and each invokes his aid against the other." Each party asked such aid with superb confidence that God and right were on its side and the forces of evil on the other. This belief often found expression in literary productions strongly tinged with elements of melodrama — one group of characters was pictured as too villainous, another group too innocent, to remain quite believable to readers of later, less impassioned times. The acrimony and the anger which then seemed inevitable were to appear extreme to readers far in time from the contest.

Modern readers are likely, also, to perceive a rather quaint quality in the two extremes of literary style which the taste of the day obviously approved. One extreme sort was literary, learned, allusive, and usually solemn, often highly ornate and figurative. Such a style is represented in the passage in William J. Grayson's *The Hireling and the Slave* which portrays child laborers in the North:

> There, unconcerned, the philanthropic eye
> Beholds each phase of human misery;
> Sees the worn child compelled in mines to slave
> Through narrow seams of coal, a living grave,
> Driven from the breezy hill, the sunny glade,
> By ruthless hearts, the drudge of labor made,
> Unknown the boyish sport, the hours of play,
> Stripped of the common boon, the light of day,
> Harnessed like brutes, like brutes to tug, and strain,
> And drag, on hands and knees, the loaded wain . . . .

Such ink-stained phrases as "the philanthropic eye," "the breezy hill, the sunny glade," "unknown the boyish sport," "the common boon," and "the loaded wain" give the verse a tone which would be disastrous to a poem written to sway readers today. At the other extreme was a vernacular style, unlearned, earthy, humorous, homely in any figures of speech which it happened to employ. This style is represented by a passage expressing ideas somewhat similar to those of Grayson — the comment of W. T. Thompson's homespun character, Major Jones, in 1847 upon the sad plight of the charwomen of Philadelphia:

The servant galls was scrubbin the doresteps of the houses and washin off the pavements in front of 'em. I looked at 'em as I rode along in the hack, and I couldn't help feelin sorry to see such butiful, rosy-cheeked white galls, down in the dirt and slop in the streets, doin work that is only fit for niggers. They say here they aint nothing but slewers—but I seed sum that I would tuck for respectable white galls if I had seed 'em in Georgia.

Here, in a style which was the Southern counterpart of Hosea Biglow's Yankee versifying, the author used ungrammatical phrases, misspellings, and words which, if they were found in argumentative writings today, would prejudice many against the author. Modern readers tend to prefer writings which, like those of Emerson and Thoreau—or of Lincoln—avoided both extremes.

Whether moderns like the two styles or not, they should have little trouble understanding the attitudes to which the two ways of writing appealed—attitudes which have coexisted for a long time. One attitude was that bookish learning provided the best clues to truth and virtue, the other that experience and common sense taught men best what was true and virtuous. As far back as the 1720's and 1730's, two kinds of appeal had been illustrated by Cotton Mather and Benjamin Franklin. The ideal author, Mather said, "could not have writ as he does if he had not read very much in his time." "And his composures," Mather went on, "are not only a cloth of gold but stuck with as many jewels as the gown of a Russian ambassador." Franklin's Widow Silence Dogood and Poor Richard, by contrast, depended upon the teachings of experience rather than the teachings of books and used the simple language of farm folk and mechanics. Later, the Jeffersonian aristocrat and the Jacksonian common man provided a similar contrast. In recent times, the opposing attitudes have again been exemplified—on the one hand by "brain trusters" and theorists in government, and on the other by "practical" men who have been chiefly schooled by experience. Thus, these contrasting styles dramatically represent two continuing American attitudes.

Oratory

The chief instrument for dispute in the period, by general agreement at the time, was oratory. Rightly or wrongly, it was still assumed that nothing so swayed public opinion as speeches. The function now jointly performed by books, the newspapers, moving pictures, television, and the radio was then chiefly performed by speakers addressing public meetings or legislative bodies.

To be sure, all oratory is likely to lose much of its force when, instead of being spoken, it is translated into print. The excitement of the occasion and the reactions of the audience are lost, as are any impressions made by the physical appearance of the speaker and by the sound of his voice. Those who saw massive, dark-browed Daniel Webster and heard his thunderous voice always were tremendously impressed (there was a saying that no human being was ever really so great as Webster appeared to be), and all who wrote of him in retrospect were sure that his great presence had much to do with his forensic power. Similarly, speeches delivered by even lesser men lost much of their power when they became printed instead of uttered words.

But modern readers find that there are barriers above and beyond the usual ones to appreciation of the oratory of the midcentury. The most formidable barrier is the style—or styles—of spoken discourse. In this field of literature, as in others, there were at the time two extremes. One was discoverable in the talks of local politicians delivered to neighbors and, at times, in the speeches of national figures. This extreme was parodied in an unsigned skit which went the rounds of the newspapers in the 1840's; it purported to be a speech of Candidate Earth, who wanted his backwoods neighbors to elect him sheriff. Said he:

> Now, gentlemen, don't you think they ought to make me sheriff? I say, if Bob Black has floated farther on a log, killed more Injuns, or stayed longer under water than I have, elect him; if not, I say what has he done to qualify him for the office of sheriff? Did any of you ever know him to call for a quart? I never did; I have known him to call for several half-pints in the course of a day, but I never did know him to step forward manfully and say, "Give us a quart of your best." Then I say again, what has Bob Black done to qualify him for sheriff?

In similar (though probably even less literate) language, Davy Crockett and other backwoods candidates regularly appealed for votes. And the very simplicity of the diction, its very freedom from adornment, recommended the speakers to constituents who believed they prized horse sense above "book larnin'." The other extreme was represented not only in the orations of men still remembered for this eloquence—Daniel Webster, Wendell Phillips, Henry Clay—but also of a number who today have been pretty well forgotten: John Randolph, George McDuffie, Seargent S. Prentiss, William C. Preston, Thomas Corwin, and others. Often the style used by these men was to the style of Candidate Earth as the style of Grayson was to that of Major Jones.

At the time, even when their words were not heard but read, these orators were extraordinarily effective. Time after time, they moved audiences to scornful laughter, to tears, to cheers, and constantly they molded public opinion both in the centers of learning and in the backwoods territory of Candidate Earth. (Whether they admitted it or not, backwoods folk were awed by learning.) The usually calm Professor

George Ticknor of Harvard supplied an instance when, the evening after he had heard a speech by Webster, he wrote an account of his reactions in a letter: "Three or four times I thought my temples would burst with the gush of blood . . . . When I came out I was almost afraid to come near him [Webster]. It seemed to me as if he was like the mount that might not be touched and that burned with fire. I was beside myself, and am so still." The implication was that Webster was inspired as he spoke, and the scholar was, therefore, awed by the almost superhuman result. As one reads other comments upon orations of the period, one sees that this picture of the transported speaker and awe-struck listeners is quite common.

Eloquence, many believed, was essentially like poetry. Irresistibly it mastered the speaker. "True eloquence," said Webster in 1826, in his speech on Adams and Jefferson, "comes, if it come at all, like the out-breaking of a fountain from the earth, or the bursting forth of volcanic fires, with spontaneous, original, native force." And the inspiration which so mastered the speaker communicated itself to the audience. "By eloquence," said Bryant in his *Lectures on Poetry*—also in 1826, "I understand those appeals to our moral perceptions that produce emotion as soon as they are uttered. It is in these that the orator is himself affected with the feelings he would communicate, that his eyes glisten, and his frame seems to dilate, and his voice acquires an unwonted melody, and his sentences arrange themselves into a sort of measure and harmony, and the listener is chained in involuntary and breathless attention."

Some of the most admired passages in the oratory of the day, in consequence, were remarkably figurative and rhythmic. Particularly admired, for instance, was the conclusion of Webster's most celebrated speech in the Senate, the "Reply to Hayne" of 1830:

> When my eyes shall be turned to behold for the last time the sun in heaven, may I not see him shining on the broken and dishonored fragments of a once glorious Union; on States dissevered, discordant, belligerent; on a land rent with civil feuds, or drenched, it may be, in fraternal blood! Let their last feeble and lingering glance rather behold the gorgeous ensign of the republic, now known and honored throughout the earth, still full high advanced, its arms and trophies streaming in their original lustre, not a stripe erased or polluted, nor a single star obscured, bearing for its motto, no such miserable interrogatory as "What is all this worth?" nor those other words of delusion and folly, "Liberty first and Union afterwards"; but everywhere, spread all over it in characters of living light, blazing on all its ample folds, as they float over the sea and the land, and in every wind under the whole heavens, that other sentiment, dear to every true American heart,—Liberty *and* Union, now and for ever, one and inseparable!

Customarily many who commended the great oratory of the day cited this passage or similar ones. Our appreciation for such flights is tepid. The reason is that there has been a change in taste during the last century.

In the years before the Civil War, there were already some portents of the change in taste which eventually was to take place. In 1857, Edward G. Parker, in his book *The Golden Age of American Oratory*, indicated that the age which he had in mind was then, after exactly a hundred years, about to end. He saw two reasons for its conclusion. First, what he called "the age of chivalry" was closing and, said he, "A brazen age, antisentimental, succeeds; an age when sordid, calculating interest rather than conscious merit dares to run after reason." Secondly, "the growing taste of our people for reading" was bringing into prominence a new kind of persuasive composition—"accurate rhetorical composition, rather than the dashing vigor and vivacious sparkle of spontaneous oratory."

Whether for the reasons he suggested or not, Parker's prophecy about the changes in American taste was, in general, to come true. Even as he wrote, some had begun to lose their liking for what Parker characterized as "the oratory of America . . . bursting from the lips of Prophets" and to prefer, as he feared they might, "the less contagious influences of logic, and figures and facts." The style of this transitional period is well represented by the Clay Compromise addresses of Calhoun and Webster (1850).

By 1850, Webster had developed what students of his work call his "mature style"—a style which, compared with his earliest efforts, had greatly gained in simplicity. Edwin P. Whipple, in "Daniel Webster as a Master of English Style" (1879), wrote: "The mature style of Webster is perfect of its kind, being in words the express image of his mind and character,—plain, terse, clear, forcible; and rising to the level of lucid statement and argument into passages of superlative eloquence only when his whole nature is stirred by some grand sentiment. . . ." Modern readers, of course, will shy away from the passages of "superlative eloquence" which Whipple obviously admired. But they will be pleased to find that Webster does not indulge in such eloquence too often and that the bulk of his oratory is concerned with expressing thoughts clearly. They will be pleased to find that most of the speech of March 7, 1850, is devoted to Webster's version of history, to arguments justifying his attitude, set forth massively to be sure, but for the most part simply and moderately—at least for the times—and that the address is excellently organized. Only when they reach the most famous passage in the speech —that on "peaceable secession"—will they be made painfully aware of Webster's eminence in the florid school of oratory. John C. Calhoun, who was generally ranked below Webster at the time, may be preferred by readers today. The reason was suggested by a comment made upon his style by a critic of oratory in 1849. "Mr. Calhoun," E. L. Magoon wrote in *Living Orators in America*, "flaunts in no gaudy rhetorical robes of scarlet and gold, but comes into the forum clothed in the simplest garb, with firm hands grasping the reins of fancy, and intent only on giving a reason for the faith that is in him." Readers today will admire the relatively simple dress and the tight grip upon the reins, will find Calhoun's logic and his clarity admirable.

Lincoln

Although modern readers can endure the reading of Webster and Calhoun, they will probably find more moving the one speaker of the Golden Age of Oratory who, by general consent, has become a classic author — Abraham Lincoln. At least four of Lincoln's speeches between 1861 and 1865 — *Farewell to Springfield, First Inaugural Address, Gettysburg Address*, and *Second Inaugural Address* — whether one agrees or disagrees with their interpretation of history, were great utterances.

A student of Lincoln's collected speeches will find that a surprising amount of his work is far below these masterpieces in excellence. His first speech, delivered in 1832 when, as a gangling, ill-dressed youth of twenty-three, he was running for the state legislature, went this way:

I presume you-all know who I am. I am humble Abe Lincoln. I have been solicited by many friends to become a candidate for the legislature. My politics are short and sweet like the old woman's dance. I am in favor of a national bank. I am in favor of the internal improvements system, and a high protective tariff. These are my sentiments and political principles. If elected I shall be thankful. If not it will be all the same.

The speech, to be sure, is somewhat better than that of Candidate Earth, but clearly its eloquence is in a similar style. And many of Lincoln's later speeches, among them the historic debates with Douglas, now appear to have little more than a certain homespun straightforwardness, well adapted to public debate, to recommend them. At times, by contrast, especially during his early career, Lincoln indulged in spread-eagle melodramatic oratory as tawdry as any produced at the time. There was, for instance, a campaign speech of 1840, in which he said:

I know that the great volcano at Washington, aroused and directed by the spirit that reigns there, is belching forth the lava of political corruption in a current broad and deep, which is sweeping with frightful velocity over the whole length and breadth of the land, bidding fair to leave unscathed no green spot or living thing; while on its bosom are riding, like demons on the wave of hell, the imps of the evil spirit, and fiendishly taunting all who dare to resist its destroying course with the hopelessness of their efforts; and knowing this, I cannot deny that all may be swept away. Broken by it, I, too, may be; bow to it, I never will. The probability that we may fall in the struggle ought not to deter us from the support of a cause we believe to be just. It shall not deter me. If ever I feel the soul within me elevate and expand to those dimensions not wholly unworthy of its Almighty Architect, it is when I contemplate the cause of my country, deserted by all the world beside, and I standing up boldly alone, hurling defiance at her victorious oppressors.

Clearly the figurative language here used was meant to appeal to the current taste. But although many contemporaries did not sufficiently appreciate him, Lincoln did manage, at least in his later years, to achieve greatness as a composer of speeches.

Just why Lincoln managed to steer away, as he did, from both the crude utterances of a small-town politician and the fustian elegance of the popular orator is something of a problem. The very fact that he, unlike many of the leaders of the day, was self-schooled probably was important. While others among his contemporaries had studied the classical rules and examples of oratory in college, Lincoln had learned his art chiefly in frontier political debates and in clashes in law courts. Because he relied upon the teachings of experience, he shared the democratic belief in common sense and its direct expression, and that fact, too, was significant. Literary influences upon Lincoln, nevertheless, were important, and fortunately some of the most notable were those of authors who achieved forceful expression by means of simplicity and restraint—Robert Burns, William Shakespeare, and the translators of the Bible into the King James version. Finally, Lincoln's own character and feeling, as they developed during the trying years of his Presidency, were strongly reflected in his thought and the form of its expression. As Edgar Dewitt Jones remarks, somewhat flossily, in his study of orators, *Lords of Speech*, "The graces of an orator's presence, the charm of his voice and manner, are ephemeral; while the grandeur of his thoughts, the magnanimity of his soul and the soundness of his reasoning live after him. It is the substance of his speeches, together with the chaste beauty of a style which matches the sheer beauty of his spirit, that lifts Abraham Lincoln into the small and elect company of the world's supreme masters of public speech." Lincoln, despite the intemperance of the times in which he lived, was a temperate man, and he was an extremely sincere man. He was also something of a poet. His utterances, therefore, could outlast both the crude mouthings of the folksy politicians and the highly ornate orations of less temperate, less sincere, and less poetic speakers.

Two Styles in the Drama

In drama as in oratory there were, between 1829 and 1865, two styles—the romantic literary style and the realistic vernacular style. These were utilized to portray characters to whom they were appropriate in dramas of two sorts — poetic plays usually of foreign scenes and of past times and comedies of native American types. In some plays, *Uncle Tom's Cabin* for instance, the two styles and the two types of character were brought together.

A famous actor, Edwin Forrest (1806-1872), was active in stimulating authors to produce some of the most notable romantic plays of the period. After making his debut at fourteen in the Chestnut Street Theater of Philadelphia, his home city, Forrest served an apprenticeship in frontier theaters. Upon returning to the East, he was a sensational success. He was a great figure of a man with a voice of extraordinary melody and volume, whose style of delivery reflected that of such impassioned orators as Clay and Webster. His favorite roles were those of intense characters who, every few scenes, gave thunderous utterance to passionate feelings.

Forrest offered prizes and other inducements to native playwrights in order to secure dramas suitable for his robust acting. In 1829, for example, he awarded a prize to John Augustus Stone (1800-1834) for a drama entitled *Metamora, or the Last of the Wampanoags*. The part of an Indian chief in this drama gave Forrest such fine chances to rant and swagger about the stage that he continued to play it, at intervals, to the end of his long career. Equally successful was one of several plays written for the actor by Robert Montgomery Bird (1806-1854), a Philadelphia doctor who had turned to writing. *The Gladiator* (1831) was based upon Plutarch; in unfolding the story of the insurrection of the gladiators, it provided Forrest, in the role of Spartacus, their leader, with several excellent scenes and many sonorous blank-verse lines. The close of Act II, one of several climaxes in the play, invariably brought the house to its feet wildly cheering. When Spartacus found that his opponent in the arena was his own brother, he stood, stripped to the waist, his deep chest heaving, and issued the call to rebellion in these words:

> Death to the Roman fiends, that make their mirth
> Out of the groans of bleeding misery!
> Ho, slaves, arise! it is your hour to kill!
> Kill and spare not — for wrath and liberty!
> Freedom for bondsmen — freedom and revenge!

The Gladiator was given hundreds of successful performances. This play and *Metamora* were typical of many written for other actors as well as for Forrest. Dramatic scenes and poetic lines combined to tell romantic stories of distant lands or of the America of the past. Robert T. Conrad's *Jack Cade, the Captain of the Commons* (1835), N. P. Willis' *Bianca Visconti* (1837) and *Tortesa the Usurer* (1839), Epes Sargent's *Velasco* (1837), and George H. Miles' *Mohammed* (1850) were some with foreign settings. Charlotte Barnes Conner, *The Indian Princess* (1830), Cornelius Mathews, *Witchcraft, or the Martyrs of Salem* (1846), George H. Miles,

Hernando de Soto (1852), Oliver Bell Bunce, *Love in '76* (1857)—these offer a sampling of many dealing poetically with American history. The best among all plays of both sorts, by general consent, was *Francesca da Rimini* (1855) by George Henry Boker (1823-1890), a play which has been successfully revived several times. Like other dramas of the era, this transports its audience to a distant time and place; it tells a romantic story —the medieval tale of Paolo and Francesca—in five acts, numerous scenes, and blank verse, a form modeled after Elizabethan dramas. Boker's ability for characterization and his real talent as a poet made this play outstanding, but inevitably it suffers when compared with the great British dramas.

Crude by comparison but nevertheless more instinct with the life and spirit of our country were a vast number of plays of a quite different sort which were being produced during the period—plays which appealed to audiences because, instead of poetically portraying the past, they realistically set before the public recognizable native types. Some, continuing the tradition of *The Contrast* (1787), made capital of the stage Yankee; some represented frontiersmen; some portrayed still other types. Yankees such as Lot Sap Sago in *Yankee Land* (1834) by Cornelius A. Logan, Solon Shingle in *The People's Lawyer* (1839) by Joseph Stevens Jones, and Calvin Cartwheel in *The Brazen Drum* (1841) by Silas S. Steel, played by character actors, delighted thousands of playgoers. Frontier characters who were similarly prominent were rather infrequent, but one such figure who made a hit was boastful Nimrod Wildfire, a backwoodsman patently modeled after Davy Crockett, in J. K. Paulding's *The Lion of the West* (1831).

Beginning in the 1840's the city as well as the farm and the frontier was the source of numerous character representations on the stage. The political connivers of New York were comically drawn in *The Politicians*, by Cornelius Mathews, in 1840; those of the capital city in *Fashions and Follies of Washington Life*, by Henry Clay Preuss, in 1857. A gallery of New York types was offered by an outstanding play comparable with *The Contrast*, Anna Cora Mowatt's *Fashion*, in 1845—the social climber, the coquette, the poet, and the important merchant. Probably the most popular (and often the crudest) dramas of city types were those in which a swashbuckling figure of the New York Bowery, the volunteer fireman, and his fellow Manhattanites appeared. Mose, as this comic figure was called, was a leading attraction in B. A. Baker's *A Glance at New York* (1848), W. B. Chapman's *Mose in California* (1849), and more than a dozen others. As Richard M. Dorson remarks in "Mose the Far-Famed and World-Renowned" (*American Literature*, November 1943), Mose was a "unique compound of East Side swell, gutter bum, and volunteer fire laddie," and his queer ways, queer talk, and heroic deeds caught the fancy not only of New Yorkers familiar with his living prototype but also of theatergoers in every part of the country.

George L. Aiken's dramatization of *Uncle Tom's Cabin* (1852) was very popular (and therefore important in the slavery controversy) because it combined so many details of plot and character found in both kinds of plays. Like Aiken, of course, other authors in this period saw no reason for separating the romantic characters and their flowery speeches from the earthy native types. As a result, just as racy "low" characters mingled with stiff heroes and heroines in the fiction of the time, numerous localized comedy figures often appeared on the same stage as did romantic heroes and heroines. Prominent in S. E. Glover's *The Cradle of Liberty; or Boston in 1775,* produced in 1832, is Yankee Seth Sage, whose nature and style of talk is suggested by his remark, "I calculate we shall give the reg'lars a considerable damned smart drubbing." Again, in J. G. Burnett's *Blanche of Brandywine* (1858), we encounter both heroic characters (including Generals Washington and Greene) and two native types, Seth Hope, a Yankee, and Krout, a Pennsylvania Dutchman. Several of the plays about Indians showed aborigines who indulged in highly poetic orations mingling with frontier character types whose talk was spiced with racy backwoods phrases. But *Uncle Tom's Cabin* goes about as far as a play could in alternating hilarious scenes with thrilling or pathetic ones and in drawing together ideal characters and a variety of realistic ones.

In Aiken's long-lived play, we have the type hero and heroine; we have also the saintly little Eva and the pious Uncle Tom. We have a bloodcurdling villain, Simon Legree, and a minor villain or two for good measure. There is, too, a varied collection of low comedy types—the frontiersman, the Yankee bumpkin (Gumption Cute), the Yankee spinster (Ophelia), and the Negro comic straight from the minstrel shows of the day (Topsy). Scenes are arranged so that audiences may indulge alternately in the two favorite pastimes of theatergoers in this country—laughing and weeping—time after time. The speeches in the play range between the realistic echoes of everyday speech and the grandiloquent orations of romanticized characters. Consider the extremes in style in two speeches of Act I. The first is a shout of the comic frontiersman, Phineas:

> Halloa, thar! bring us a jug of whiskey instantaneously, or expect to be teetotally chawed up! Squat yourself, stranger, and go in for enjoyment.

The second is a prayer and soliloquy uttered by Eliza as she prepares to make her hazardous journey across the ice-filled river:

> Powers of mercy, protect me! How shall I escape these human bloodhounds? Ah! the window—the river of ice! That dark stream lies between me and liberty! Surely the ice will bear my trifling weight. It is my only chance of escape—better sink beneath the cold waters, with my child locked in my arms, than have him torn

from me and sold into bondage. He sleeps upon my breast — Heaven, I put my trust in thee!

No better summary of the taste of the day could be found than *Uncle Tom's Cabin*, and no play of the past can teach us more about the sure-fire devices of melodrama which have to be modernized only slightly to enthrall moving-picture audiences in our own time.

Poetry

Two passages of verse by James Russell Lowell, one published in 1845, the other in 1846, show how one author active in this period could use both the high style and the low style of poetry in persuasive compositions. Lines in "The Present Crisis" (1845) read:

> Slavery, the earth-born Cyclops, fellest of the giant
>   brood,
> Son of brutish Force and Darkness, who have
>   drenched the earth with blood,
> Famished in his self-made desert, blinded by our
>   purer day,
> Gropes in yet unblasted regions for his miserable
>   prey; —
> Shall we guide his gory fingers where our helpless
>   children play?

The first of the *Biglow Papers*, the next year, had this stanza:

> Aint it cute to see a Yankee
>   Take sech everlastin' pains,
> All to git the Devil's thankee
>   Helpin' on 'em weld their chains?
> Wy, it's jest ez clear ez figgers,
>   Clear ez one an' one make two,
> Chaps that make black slaves o' niggers
>   Want to make wite slaves o' you.

Few other authors could switch at will, as their contemporary Lowell could, from one extreme of style to the other, and in general the writers of the period tended toward one or the other of the two styles of popular appeal. Some of the popular songs also show how both styles might be adapted to a single tune, "John Brown's Body" and "The Battle Hymn of the Republic" (1862), for instance, as well as the two versions of "Dixie" (1859, 1861).

Grayson and Henry Timrod, though they warmly disagreed about the definition of poetry, both followed the literary rather than the illiterate tradition in their verse. Grayson modeled his versification after what he called the "School of Dryden and Pope," writing his most representative poetry in heroic couplets. "I have faith," he wrote in his unpublished "Autobiography," "in the ancient classical models, the masters directly or indirectly of all the great poets of modern times." Timrod, by contrast, frankly acknowledged indebtedness to such authors as Milton, Wordsworth, and Tennyson. In some poems—"Charleston" (1862) and "Ode" (1866), for example—he used the simple ballad stanza or a slight adaptation; in more, perhaps—notably "Ethnogenesis" and "The Cotton Boll"—he employed the irregular ode form which had been employed by Wordsworth and Tennyson with marked success. But Grayson, disciple of Neoclassical poets, and Timrod, disciple of nineteenth-century poets and the seventeenth-century poet Milton, were alike in using diction of a highly literary nature.

John Greenleaf Whittier tried at times to write "literary" verse, and his use of dialect in poetry was infrequent. Nevertheless, at his most effective he was a writer of songs which were relatively simple—almost in the manner of folk songs—both in metrical form and in the kind of words used. The Quaker poet's country rearing, his brief schooling, and his particular admiration for the seemingly artless songs of Robert Burns all led him to write unpretentious poems. Never, it appears, did he give much consideration to matters of technique. His aim, as he stated it, was

> To paint, forgetful of the tricks of art,
> With pencil dipped alone in colors of the heart.

As a rule, therefore, no sign appeared of his striving for novelty of effect. All his life, his favorite measures were ballad measure, octo-syllabics, and iambic pentameter—quite conventional forms of verse; and he used a vocabulary and figures of speech which were far from complex. His were "journalistic" poems which, because of their almost rustic directness and simplicity, appealed greatly to many untutored readers.

Whittier's songs resemble most other poems of the period, both literary and unliterary, proslavery and antislavery, in their depiction of the friends and the foes of the poet. Sure that his Quaker Inner Light had shown him what attitudes to take, Whittier conceived of the abolitionists as engaged in a "moral warfare," girded "in God's own might" and "in conflict with unholy powers," and he constantly pictured the struggle in such terms. Vouchsafed similar visions, as they believed, other poets on both sides were similarly intemperate. The author of a famous version of "Dixie" urged Southerners to battle "Till the spoilers are defeated,/Till the Lord's work is completed." Julia Ward Howe saw the Northern army clothed in righteousness and proclaimed that "God was marching on." Timrod saw the enemy as "the Goth," and confidently expected the Lord to release the Confederacy from "the great burthen of our country's wrong." For both North and South, the issue was as clear-cut as that. Such were the signs of bitter partisanship in many melodramatic poems.

Walt Whitman, War-Born Poet

Although, like other poets, he was a controversialist, Walt Whitman made no contribution worth noting to the argument about slavery. His poems about the Civil War are concerned with the experiences and the sufferings shared by men and women of both sides. However, Whitman found himself as a poet in the years when the nation was deeply engaged in the controversy about slavery, and he himself saw his own wartime experiences as the "final reasons-for-being" of his mature songs. Hence, despite the fact that he lived and wrote for many years after Appomattox, Whitman was in a very real sense a war-born poet. His poetry, though it seemed strange to readers when it first appeared, was, we now can see, molded by the literature being produced at the time he began to write. Emerson's poetry, for example, obviously left its mark. Perhaps even more important, the oratory and the styles of the 1840's and 1850's left their imprint upon the form of Whitman's poetry.

Whitman was like the orators of the day in that he wanted to preach to men the ways of righteous thinking and living. In notebooks which he filled when he was working toward the writing of *Leaves of Grass*, he voiced his determination to "elevate, enlarge, purify, deepen and make happy the attributes of the body and soul of man." Furthermore, as he considered how he would deliver this message to his countrymen, evidently he was not sure, for some time, whether his medium was to be oratory or poetry. His considering oratory was hardly surprising, since the accepted medium for social or religious preachments was the oration or the sermon, and he was fascinated all his life by public speaking and public speakers. Possibly Whitman's inability to succeed as an orator was an important factor leading to his final decision to become a poet. In his early New York days, so he said, he "haunted the courts to witness notable trials, and . . . heard all the famous actors and actresses." Over the years, he listened to Webster, Garrison, Beecher, Clay, Everett, and Phillips, as well as less famous orators. His "Poem of Joys" contains an interesting description of the great speaker swaying his audience:

> O the orator's joys!
> To inflate the chest — to roll the thunder of the voice
>   out from the ribs and throat,
> To make the people rage, weep, hate, desire, with
>   yourself,
> To lead America — to quell America with a great tongue.

He enjoyed the declamatory interpretations of Shakespeare by Booth and Forrest which were then fashionable, and he himself loved to intone sonorous lines from the dramas while riding Broadway omnibuses, tramping with friends, and strolling by the seashore. He knew and greatly admired, too, literature which approximated the oratorical effect he wanted — the lecture-essays of Emerson, the songs of Ossian, translations of Greek and Latin dramas and epics, the exhortatory parts of the Bible and their adaptations and paraphrases in sermons.

In the notes that Whitman wrote for his early works, there were passages which might have done for either lectures or poems. One scrap of paper bears the caption "Poem — Religious," and then, underneath this title is written "or lecture on Religion"; and one note, though it was headed "lecture," eventually was utilized as part of a poem. As a reciter of his own poetry, he attempted (though unfortunately with questionable success) to use the resonant tones, the modulations, the gesticulations of an old-school public speaker. As late as 1888, in his final Preface, he spoke of his art as a "new and national declamatory expression." There can be little question that the methods of oratory were important in shaping Whitman's style. In a note on "style" for his projected lectures he wrote: "besides direct addressing *to You* another leading trait of Lectures may well be — strong assertion — ('I say') it is so?) — launched out with fire, or emphasis, or enthusiasm, or anger." This oratorical device occurs frequently in the poems, as in the line, "And I say to any man or woman, Let your soul stand cool and composed before a million universes." Other oratorical devices which are used time after time include apostrophes, rhetorical questions, aphorisms, exclamations, alliterative phrases, and parenthetical asides. Often the phrasal order is that of oratory — lines which loosely balance on both sides of a pause, or series of parallel structures all of which contribute to a periodic sentence. (See, for example, the opening stanza of "Out of the Cradle Endlessly Rocking.") Devices such as these, in Whitman's poems, pretty regularly perform functions of rhymes and stanzas in more conventional poems: they hold lines together and set off units of thought.

The scheme of *Leaves of Grass* as a whole and the schemes of individual poems, moreover, have noteworthy resemblances to oratory. Whitman evidently hoped that the impact of the book would be comparable to that of the dynamic presence of a great orator — that it would, as he said, "possess, more than any other known book, the magnetism of living flesh and blood, sitting near the reader, & looking & talking." Like the collected works of a great orator, it would convey, in addition to the personality of the speaker, his gospel, developed and modulated in a number of individual compositions on varied topics. There is evidence, in the whole book, that Whitman attempted to unfold his beliefs in this fashion. In quite a few of the poems, too, there are organizations typically used by orators as well as by some poets — ideas developed by analogy, by passages of narrative, by comparison and contrast, and quite a number which are developed in the style of Emerson's lectures and poems.

But although eventually Whitman's poems, in their form, thus resembled oratory, even as he conceived of them they differed from oratory. In one of his self-criticisms the poet found fault with his method of composing and delivering lecture-. "The trouble," he said, "is often the endeavor (from the habit of forming the rhythmic style of *Leaves of Grass*) involuntarily to preserve a sort of rhythm in the Lecture sentences, —It seems to me this rhythm, for them, is not only not necessary, but is often dangerous to their character-requirements—which, for speaking purposes, need to be abrupt. . . ." Whitman conceived of his free verse poems as "chants" more rhythmical than spoken discourses and corresponding, in some ways, to the arias or recitatives of operas. Toward his free verse, after starting as a quite conventional poet, he worked his way slowly. According to Emory Holloway, in his Introduction to *The Uncollected Prose and Poetry of Walt Whitman*, "he began versifying with the simplest of forms . . . then made use of more difficult stanza forms . . . ; next he wrote a little blank verse . . . ; then he made private experiments with some of the very material he was to work over, through several years, for the 1855 edition of *Leaves of Grass.* . . ." When this first edition appeared, concludes Holloway, his verse was disciplined, "poise and sweeping rhythm were added, and a standard of line length was adopted which would fit the bold but delicate burden of his song." What he evolved was a form blending prose and poetry, which carried still further liberating tendencies in poetry which had been initiated by a number of his predecessors including, notably, Emerson and Thoreau. His lines, characteristically, corresponded to the grammatical-phrasings or at least the thought-phrasings of speech. His rhythms were, as he put it, "in a loose and free metre of his own, of an irregular length of lines, apparently lawless at first perusal, although on closer examination a certain regularity appears, like the recurrence of lesser and larger waves on the sea-shore, rolling in without intermission, and fitfully rising and falling." And he found, as later poets were to find, that patterns of repeated vowel and consonant sounds could do much to unify parts and wholes.

Whitman not only broke away from some of the conventions of versification; he also broke away from some of the conventions of style. He was distressed by "stock poetical touches" and by ornamentation as such in poetry. "*No ornaments,*" he sternly enjoined himself, "especially no ornamental adjectives, unless they have come molten hot, and imperiously prove themselves. No ornamental similes at all—not one: *perfect transparent clearness.* . . ." His dislike for what he called "drawing room poetry" led him, in general, to use relatively simple words and to avoid an excess of figurative language. His feelings about common speech led him to interject it into a style not then thought hospitable to it. Most orators who employed the more literary style, as we have seen, tended to disdain the use of words in the vernacular. Whitman, however, from the early days of his career, appreciated the force of humble speech, and praised such speech as growing out of human life. In his youth, he was an avid searcher after colloquial and slang phrases with life to them, and his early prose is dotted with expressions such as "loaded down to the guards," "they do say," "some pumpkins," and "a great place and *no* mistake." "Slang," he wrote, "profoundly consider'd, is the lawless germinal element, below all words and sentences, and behind all poetry, and proves a certain perennial rankness and protestantism in speech . . . an attempt of common humanity to escape from bald literalism, and express itself illimitably, which in highest walks produces poets and poems." He reveled in nicknames for men of different states (Kentucky Corn Crackers, Michigan Wolverines, Connecticut Wooden Nutmegs, etc.); in original place-names (Hog-eye, Lick-skillet, Rake-pocket, and Steal-easy, Texas, for instance); in the racy and imaginative phrases of bus drivers, laborers, railroad men, and boatmen. The result was that with the rolling periods and some of the more elegant diction characteristic of oratory, Whitman intermingled localisms, bits of slang, common talk. In Section 6 of "Song of Myself" (1855), for instance, along with sonorous and dignified lines comparable to those of oratory, occur lines like these:

> Or I guess it [the grass] is the handkerchief of the Lord,
> A scented gift and remembrancer designedly dropt. . . .
>
>   *   *   *
>
> Kanuck, Tuckahoe, Congressman, Cuff. . . .
>
>   *   *   *
>
> And now it seems to me the beautiful uncut hair of
>   graves.
>
>   *   *   *
>
> The smallest sprout shows there is really no death. . . .

To mingle such homely phrasings, as Whitman typically did, with the highfalutin style of heightened oratory represented a daring experiment.

These details about the form of Whitman's poetry suggest that in several ways he was a culmination of some important literary tendencies of his period. They may, perhaps, also suggest to modern readers ways of approach to him. They imply that he should be read differently from most poets — as a man with a message, as a chanting orator, as an experimenter with a form which blends poetry with prose and mingles the words of everyday talk with those of more formal literature. He should be read not only as a wartime poet of the past but also as a pioneer breaking a trail toward modern poetic achievements.

W.B.

This chronological table carries back to the year 1838 in order to give a more complete background of the events leading up to the Civil War

1838	■ John P. Kennedy's *Rob of the Bowl*
	Atherton resolutions in Congress, a second "gag" on discussions of slavery
1840	■ William G. Simms' *Border Beagles*
	1200 cotton factories in the United States, two thirds being in New England · United States census: population 17,000,000, including 400,000 free Negroes and 2,500,000 slaves · William Henry Harrison elected ninth President
1841	■ Thomas B. Thorpe's "Big Bear of Arkansas"
	Death of Harrison; succeeded by John Tyler as tenth President
1842	■ Henry W. Longfellow's *Poems on Slavery*
1843	■ William T. Thompson's *Major Jones's Courtship*
1844	Repeal of "gag" rule against slavery discussions in Congress · James K. Polk elected eleventh President
1845	Florida and Texas, the twenty-seventh and twenty-eighth states, annexed to the Union with slavery, making fifteen slave states to thirteen free states
1846	■ John G. Whittier's *Voices of Freedom* · Thorpe's *Mysteries of the Backwoods*
	Treaty with Great Britain determined the Oregon boundary line · War with Mexico, "by act of Mexico" · Wilmot Proviso, prohibiting slavery in any territory to be acquired from Mexico, passed the House but was defeated in the Senate · Iowa, the twenty-ninth state, admitted as a free state
1848	Mexican cession of what is now California, Nevada, Utah, and Arizona · Gold discovered in California, resulting in the famous "rush" · Wisconsin, the thirtieth state, admitted as a free state, restoring the balance of free and slave states · Zachary Taylor elected twelfth President
1850	■ Nathaniel Hawthorne's *The Scarlet Letter* · John C. Calhoun's *Speech*

on the Slavery Question · Daniel Webster's *Seventh of March Speech*

Death of President Taylor; succeeded by Millard Fillmore as thirteenth President · Compromise of 1850: admission of California, the thirty-first state, as free state · A drastic Fugitive Slave Law · First act of Congress making land grants to aid in construction of railroads—in this case, the Illinois Central · United States census: population 23,000,000

1851 ■ Hawthorne's *The House of the Seven Gables* · Herman Melville's *Moby Dick*

Slavery prohibited in the District of Columbia

1852 ■ Mrs. Stowe's *Uncle Tom's Cabin*, greatest literary stimulus to the antislavery movement

Franklin Pierce elected fourteenth President

1853 ■ Joseph G. Baldwin's *Flush Times of Alabama and Mississippi*

1854 ■ Henry D. Thoreau's *Walden*

Kansas-Nebraska Act establishing "squatter sovereignty" in those territories; bloody conflicts between free-state and slave-state settlers; emergence of John Brown · Republican Party organized as protest against the Kansas-Nebraska Act · Anthony Burns, fugitive slave, captured in Boston and returned to his owner despite the efforts of a Boston mob to rescue him from the police · Preston Brooks of South Carolina assaulted Senator Charles Sumner of Massachusetts in the Senate chamber

1855 ■ Simms' *Forayers* · Whittier's "Barefoot Boy" · Whitman's *Leaves of Grass*

1856 ■ Simms' *Eutaw* · Whitman's *Leaves of Grass* (second edition, containing Emerson's letter)

James Buchanan elected fifteenth President

1857 ■ Founding of the *Atlantic Monthly* in Boston, with Lowell as editor · Founding of *Russell's Magazine* (1857-1861) in Charleston, with Paul Hamilton Hayne as editor

Chief Justice Taney's Dred Scott decision: a Negro was not a citizen and therefore had no right to bring suit in a federal court · Financial panic

1858 The Lincoln-Douglas debates in Illinois on the questions arising from the slavery issue · Minnesota admitted as thirty-second state

1859 | Oregon admitted as thirty-third state · Silver discovered in the Comstock lode, Nevada · First oil well, Oil Creek, Pennsylvania · John Brown's raid on Harper's Ferry

1860 | ■ Thoreau's "Plea for John Brown" · Whitman's *Leaves of Grass* (third edition) · William D. Howells' campaign biography of Lincoln

United States census: population 31,500,000 including 450,000 free Negroes and 4,000,000 slaves · South Carolina seceded from the Union · Abraham Lincoln elected sixteenth President

1861 | ■ Henry Timrod's "Ethnogenesis," and "The Cotton Boll"

Kansas, thirty-fourth state, admitted as a free state · Mississippi, Florida, Alabama, Georgia, Louisiana, and Texas seceded from the Union · Confederate States of America organized at Montgomery with Jefferson Davis president · The Civil War began when the Confederates fired on Fort Sumter, 12 April · Virginia, Arkansas, Tennessee, and North Carolina joined the Confederacy · Great Britain and France recognized the belligerency of the Confederate States · The First Battle of Bull Run

1862 | *Merrimac-Monitor* engagement in Hampton Roads, first battle of ironclads · The Battles of Shiloh, Seven Days, Second Bull Run, Antietam, Murfreesboro · Slavery abolished in the territories · The Lancashire cotton famine in England · Pacific Railway Act to promote by land grants the construction of a railroad between Missouri points and California

1863 | ■ Whittier's "Barbara Frietchie" · Lincoln's "Emancipation Proclamation" and *Gettysburg Address*

West Virginia admitted as thirty-fifth state; formed by secession from Virginia · Death of Stonewall Jackson, great Confederate general, at Battle of Chancellorsville · Battle of Gettysburg (1-3 July) and surrender of Vicksburg (4 July), the turning point of the war

1864 | ■ William C. Bryant's *Thirty Poems*

Battles of the Wilderness, Spottsylvania Courthouse, Cold Harbor · Grant versus Lee in Virginia · Farragut at Mobile Bay · Sherman's March to the Sea · Nevada admitted as thirty-sixth state · Lincoln reëlected President

1865 | ■ Lincoln's *Second Inaugural* · Whitman's *Drum-Taps* · Mark Twain's "Celebrated Jumping Frog of Calaveras County"

Surrender of Lee to Grant at Appomattox, 9 April · Assassination of Lincoln, 14 April; succeeded by Andrew Johnson as seventeenth President · Thirteenth Amendment, abolishing slavery, ratified by 27 states

5 ————————————————————————

THE RISE OF MODERN AMERICA
1865 – 1914

"As a strong bird on pinions free,
Joyous, the amplest spaces heavenward cleaving. . . ."

WHITMAN

"Are we the eagle nation Milton saw . . . ?"

MOODY

INTELLECTUAL CURRENTS

Reunion

The Civil War, which terminated when Lee surrendered to Grant
at Appomattox in April 1865, left the nation sadly disrupted. The restoration of unity — at best a long and difficult process — was made longer and
more difficult by the Era of Reconstruction, which imposed the rule of
ill-qualified Negroes and of carpetbaggers and scalawags upon the
Southern states and maintained this rule by the presence of federal troops.
When President Hayes withdrew the troops in 1877, reconstruction
governments collapsed and the "tragic era" ended.

Much ill feeling was engendered on both sides by sectional controversy, civil war, and tyrannical misrule. On the other hand, many
forces were working inexorably for the restoration of national unity.

The states were bound together by a common language, common traditions, and a close interdependence of economic interests. The establishment of schools and colleges in the South by Northern philanthropy contributed much to the growing unity of feeling; the abandonment by the national government after 1883 of the attempt to control race relations in the South contributed still more. Not the least of the unifying influences was our postwar literature. Some writers preached the gospel of union, while others contributed less directly to the same end by exemplifying in the local color story the admirable qualities to be found in the rank and file of people in various regions.

Among those who celebrated unity and reunion, three writers stand out above the others: Lowell in New England, Whitman in the Middle Atlantic States, and Lanier in the South. On July 3, 1875, Lowell read in Cambridge his poem "Under the Old Elm," which celebrated the hundredth anniversary of Washington's taking command of the Colonial army. After paying eloquent tribute to the greatness of Washington, the poet held out the hand of reconciliation and friendship to Virginia.

> Virginia gave us this imperial man . . .
> She gave us this unblemished gentleman:
> What shall we give her back but love and praise
> As in the dear old unestrangèd days
> Before the inevitable wrong began?
> Mother of states and undiminished men,
> Thou gavest us a country, giving him,
> And we owe alway what we owed thee then . . .
> A great man's memory is the only thing
> With influence to outlast the present whim
> And bind us as when here he knit our golden ring.

A great man's memory. Lowell was right. The common memory of Washington helped to restore national unity after the schismatic years. Mount Vernon soon became a national shrine. So important to a nation's well-being is the principle enunciated by Lowell that in the years to follow, other great Americans, such as Jefferson, Lincoln, and Lee, irrespective of sectional differences, were to become national heroes.

Whitman's plea for reunion took the characteristic form of an inspiring prophecy of the future greatness of the United States. This greatness would be the achievement of states which are "varied" and "different" and at the same time united in "one identity." In the famous poem ("As a Strong Bird on Pinions Free," which was later changed to "Thou Mother with Thy Equal Brood") read at Dartmouth College in 1872, Walt Whitman expressed unbounded confidence in the future progress of America — a progress which would be not only political and material, but scientific, aesthetic, and moral as well:

Thee in an education grown of thee, in teachers, studies,
   students, born of thee,
Thee in thy democratic fêtes en-masse, thy high original
   festivals, operas, lecturers, preachers . . .
Thee in thy pinnacles, intellect, thought, thy topmost
   rational joys, thy love and godlike aspiration,
In thy resplendent coming literati, thy full-lung'd orators,
   thy sacerdotal bards, kosmic savans,
These! these in thee, (certain to come,) to-day I prophesy.

It was a vision calculated to make men forget the quarrels of the past
and unite in the achievement of a splendid civilization.

Although Sidney Lanier fought through the Civil War and spent
several months as a federal prisoner, there was no bitterness in his soul.
He saw clearly that the South could not attain well-being in isolation and
estrangement from the North. In the centennial year of 1876, he attempted
in two poems to draw the sections together in loving harmony: "The Psalm
of the West" and "The Centennial Meditation of Columbia," the second
of which was sung at the Philadelphia Exposition by a great chorus with
orchestral accompaniment. Both poems employ the historical approach:
a backward glance over the events which have brought us to this good
hour should awaken a new sense of pride and responsibility. In "The
Psalm of the West" Lanier surveyed the early voyages to the New World
(the eight sonnets on Columbus are especially notable), the settling of
New England, the progress of the Revolutionary War from Lexington to
Yorktown, and the Civil War between "Heart-strong South" and "Head-
strong North." The "Psalm" concluded with a prophecy of America's
future glory as ardent as Whitman's. The "Centennial Meditation" suggested more briefly the same historical evolution and concluded likewise
with a prophecy which was also a prayer for America's future:

Long as thine Art shall love true love,
   Long as thy Science truth shall know,
Long as thine Eagle harms no Dove,
   Long as thy Law by law shall grow,
Long as thy God is God above,
   Thy brother every man below,
So long, dear Land of all my love,
   Thy name shall shine, thy fame shall glow.

If James Russell Lowell, Walt Whitman, and Sidney Lanier aided
the process of reunion by emphasizing the solidarity of a new and glorious
America, the fictionists of the local color school contributed to the same
end with perhaps even greater effectiveness by drawing attention to the
innate virtues of Americans everywhere and by adding to their under-

standing of one another. During the two or three decades following the Civil War, our most popular form of literature was the regional short story. Bret Harte and Hamlin Garland in the West, George Washington Cable, Joel Chandler Harris, and Mary Noailles Murfree in the South, Sarah Orne Jewett and Mary E. Wilkins Freeman in New England—all portrayed with tender sympathy the lives of the inhabitants of their respective regions. One effect of this body of literature was to reassure Southern readers that there was much natural goodness in the North, and Northern readers that there was much natural goodness in the South. Only the most stubborn of hard feelings could persist under such an emollient.

Consider, for example, the reputedly flinty New England character as seen in the soft light of Miss Jewett's tales. Describing a family reunion on the Maine coast, Miss Jewett wrote in *The Country of the Pointed Firs:* "Each heart is warm and every face shines with the ancient light. Such a day as this has transfiguring powers, and easily makes friends of those who have been cold-hearted, and gives to those who are dumb their chance to speak, and lends some beauty to the plainest face." Miss Jewett assured her readers that beneath the plain, taciturn, and cold exterior of the New England character could be discovered, on propitious occasions, beauty, ampleness of speech, and warmth of heart. These were the points on which non-New Englanders were likely to entertain serious doubts. It is reasonable to suppose that Miss Jewett's stories substantially increased the amount of good feeling in America toward New England.

Or take the character of the Southern highlander—reputedly wild and lawless—as seen through the sympathetic eyes of Miss Murfree. She saw that friendliness, charity, the domestic virtues can be found in abundance in the hill and mountain country of the South. It is a natural goodness, produced not by schools and the higher civilization, but by Nature herself, and therefore the more worthy of recognition and admiration. "The grace of culture is, in its way, a fine thing," Miss Murfree said in one of the stories in *In the Tennessee Mountains*, "but the best that art can do—the polish of a gentleman—is hardly equal to the best that Nature can do in her higher moods."

Or look (to mention only one more example) at the Southern planter —by report a brutal and tyrannical man—as he is reflected in the genial pages of *Uncle Remus*. More effectively than any other single writer, Joel Chandler Harris reassured the world of the essential kindliness which had existed between master and slave on the ante-bellum plantation and implied that not even emancipation and reconstruction could destroy the friendly relations of the two races. Harris' stories had an effect similar to that produced in one of his tales by Mr. Benjermun Ram's fiddling:

W'en ole man Benjermun Ram sorter let up wid he fiddlin', he don't see no Brer Wolf, en he don't year no ole Miss Wolf. Den he look in de back room; no Wolf dar. Den he look in de back po'ch; no Wolf dar. Den he look in de closet en de cubbard; no Wolf ain't dar yit.

The infectious laughter of Uncle Remus and the pervasive good humor and kindliness expressed by Harris did much toward putting to flight (as Benjermun Ram put to flight Brer Wolf and Miss Wolf) the ill will which persisted in partisans both North and South in the postwar years.

It is not too much to say.that the writers of the period contributed greatly to the reëstablishment of national unity. The local color stories, in particular, were for many readers a fresh and exciting discovery of America, and the writers of this school might have taken for their motto the words spoken by Senator Lamar of Mississippi in his eulogy of Charles Sumner: "My countrymen, know one another and you will love one another."

The remarkable extent to which reunion had been achieved by the end of the century was dramatically demonstrated in the war with Spain, in which Northerners and Southerners fought side by side and ex-Confederate generals held positions of command. World War I and World War II were to afford even more impressive evidence of the growing solidarity of the American nation.

Social and Economic Problems

Industry and agriculture expand. American social and economic life changed radically and rapidly during the years between 1865 and 1914. The railroad was a typical achievement of the age and powerful in its influence on economic and social life. In 1865 there were only thirty-five thousand miles of track in the United States; by 1900 this mileage increased to nearly two hundred thousand. The Westinghouse air brake and other inventions improved the efficiency of railroad transportation. Enormous land grants by the government financed the building of the transcontinental lines: the Union Pacific, the Northern Pacific, and the Santa Fe, all of which had reached the Pacific Coast by 1884. If the cost in land grants was high, the railroads made substantial returns by peopling and developing the vast region west of the Mississippi. The roads, however, often abused their great power, and the Interstate Commerce Act of 1887 marked the beginning of federal regulation.

The railroad was only one factor in the economic revolution which followed the Civil War. A great transportation system presupposed commodities to transport, and these were supplied by an expanding industry and an expanding agriculture.

Industrial expansion was stimulated by a variety of factors: the exploitation of our resources in iron, coal, and oil; the development of improved machinery; the procurement of cheap labor through immigration; and the government's policy of protecting infant industries by high tariffs and allowing a free hand to business. There were many marvels of scientific invention: Andrew Carnegie was using the improved Bessemer process in the manufacture of steel by 1875; Alexander Graham Bell demonstrated the telephone at the Philadelphia Centennial Exposition in 1876; Thomas A. Edison and others made possible the dynamo, which was exhibited at the World's Columbian Exposition in Chicago in 1893 and which, as Henry Adams declared, "gave to history a new phase." Expanding industry required an abundance of labor, and this was supplied by a growing stream of immigrants, who, at the turn of the century, came in larger proportions from the southern and eastern than (as they had done previously) from the northern and western European countries. They were motivated in part by hardships at home, but even more by inducements proffered by agents of American factories and transportation lines. Immigration continued without drastic reduction until 1921.

Under these favorable conditions, our rapidly expanding industry soon got out of hand, and toward the end of the century it became increasingly apparent that some form of government regulation was necessary. Trusts and monopolies exceeded reasonable bounds. The railroads of the entire country were controlled by only a half-dozen small groups of men. A disproportionate part of the wealth of the nation became concentrated in the pockets of a relatively few people. Big business had formed a corrupt alliance with politics. Abuses were rampant. Attempts at regulation and reform — at first ineffective — began with the Sherman Anti-Trust Act of 1890, and in response to growing social criticism became more effective after the turn of the century: among other things, the powers of the Interstate Commerce Commission were increased, and in 1906 a Pure Food and Drug Act heralded a new era in the responsibilities of business to society.

Agriculture also underwent a revolution during the post-Civil War years. Vast new lands in the West were opened to farming. New machines — reapers, binders, threshers — and new scientific devices — fertilizers, insecticides, improved strains — greatly increased the yield of the land. The methods of big business invaded the farm: the cash crop supplanted subsistence farming. But fewer people were needed to do the work, thanks to the improved machinery; the financial returns were precarious; and migration from the farms to the cities grew steadily.

Growth of cities. Perhaps the most conspicuous change of all during these years was the rapid growth of cities, fed by immigrants from abroad and by farm and village folk from the American countryside. In 1860 one sixth of our population was urban; in 1900, one third. Between 1880 and 1900 the population of Chicago grew from a half million to a million and a half, and the number of American cities with a population of one hundred thousand or more increased from nineteen to thirty-six. City life gained, while country life suffered, in prestige. It was supposed by thousands of young Americans that a better life, somehow, could be lived in the city than in the country, and the bigger the city, the better the life. Many novels of the time — especially those of Theodore Dreiser — show the error of this supposition. The sudden growth of great urban centers created new social and economic problems, and municipal government broke down under the strain. The evils of the slums appeared for the first time in American life.

Labor organizes. The new industry exploited labor, and it was inevitable that labor should organize to combat the exploitation. A beginning was made by the Knights of Labor, founded in 1869; but the movement did not gain appreciable strength until 1886, when the American Federation of Labor was organized under the leadership of Samuel Gompers. The A. F. of L. continued to gain steadily until 1920, when it reached a peak of more than four million members. As organized labor grew in strength, industrial conflicts increased in number and intensity. The first of these was the railroad strike of 1877. Others worthy of note are the Pullman strike of 1894 and the strike in the Pennsylvania coal fields in 1902. Strikes have often been an effective weapon, and much has been accomplished to improve the lot of labor by social legislation. Since the Massachusetts "Ten Hour Act for Women and Children in Factories" in 1874, much progress has been made in the working conditions, hours, and wages of labor. Early reform legislation was often declared unconstitutional on the disingenuous principle that "a person has the right to sell his labor upon such terms as he deems proper." But after 1900, more liberal judges, like Louis D. Brandeis, were instrumental in reversing many of the decisions which had blocked social reform.

The Literature of Social Criticism

St. Paul said that "the love of money is the root of all evil," and the history of America after the Civil War exhibits the truth or near-truth of that statement. Perhaps never before was a nation so engrossed in the business of making money. Perhaps never before was materialism so rampant, or so much pride taken in material achievements.

The writers of the period pointed out forcefully the evils of this crass materialism. In *Democratic Vistas* (1871) Walt Whitman warned his readers that material wealth alone would not make a nation great:

I hail with joy the oceanic, variegated, intense practical energy, the demand for facts, even the business materialism of the current age, our States. But woe to the age or land in which these things, movements, stopping at themselves, do not tend to ideas. As fuel to flame, and flame to the heavens, so must wealth, science, materialism—even this democracy of which we make so much—unerringly feed the highest mind, the soul.

Lanier in "The Symphony" (1875) pleaded eloquently for a Christian and chivalric code in place of the unfeeling relations between employer and employed:

'Thou Trade! thou king of the modern days!
   Change thy ways,
   Change thy ways;
Let the sweaty laborers file
   A little while,
   A little while,
Where Art and Nature sing and smile.
Trade! is thy heart all dead, all dead?
And hast thou nothing but a head?
I'm all for heart,' the flute-voice said.

In "these cold, merchantable days," the poet declared, even the love of the sexes is tainted by mercenary motives:

Now, comes a suitor with sharp prying eye—
Says *Here, you Lady, if you'll sell, I'll buy:*
Come, heart for heart—a trade? What! weeping? why?
Shame on such wooers' dapper mercery!

While Whitman and Lanier were voicing their spiritual protests, Mark Twain was ridiculing, typically without mercy, the get-rich-quick schemes of his money-mad countrymen. In *The Gilded Age* (1873)—a book whose name has been given to the Grant era (1869-1877) and by extension to the twenty or thirty years following the Civil War—the author presented at once hilariously and devastatingly Colonel Sellers' designs for moneymaking. At one and the same time, Sellers was scheming to corner the corn and hog crops, buy up the wildcat banks, and market an "Optic Liniment" (his own concoction) throughout the world. He and his associates attempted to sell a large tract of worthless land ("the Tennessee land") to the government. Despite skillful lobbying in Washington, they failed, though by a narrow margin, and the book ends with the moral that sober industry and contentment with a modest income honestly earned are infinitely preferable to frantic schemes to get rich quick. It was a good moral, but one which the author himself never learned, and one which millions of Americans had not learned as late as 1929.

The Gilded Age also exposed political corruption in the national capital, where votes were bought and sold. Henry Adams, in his novel

Democracy (1880), turned a censorious eye on similar political phenomena. He portrays a distinguished United States senator, the leader of his party, who accepted a bribe of $100,000. His reasons were good "political" ones, but they did not satisfy Adams' heroine, whose break with the senator parallels Adams' own withdrawal from the corrupt politics of the Gilded Age. But Adams remained a fascinated observer and refused to surrender his belief in democracy despite its current evil manifestations. "I grant it is an experiment," he said through one of the characters in the novel, "but it is the only direction society can take that is worth its taking. . . . Every other possible step is backward."

Our writers were not long content with a general censure of materialism and political corruption. Growing ills awakened the social conscience and called forth specific indictments which became increasingly prominent in the literature of the late nineteenth and early twentieth centuries. Prepared by his own unhappy experience on an Iowa farm and indoctrinated in the economic theories of Henry George, Hamlin Garland in *Main-Travelled Roads* exposed, with strong emotional appeal, the hardships and injustices suffered by the farmers in the Iowa-Wisconsin country. An angry and anger-arousing book, *Main-Travelled Roads* suggests the gathering strength of the Populist Movement and helps explain the spectacular rise of William Jennings Bryan in 1896. An important phase in the history of the railroad's exploitation of the farmer is presented in Frank Norris' *The Octopus* (1901), which powerfully portrays the struggle between the Southern Pacific Railroad (the "octopus") and the wheat farmers of California. The triumphant force is neither the railroad nor the farmers, but the wheat, which Norris represents in both *The Octopus* and *The Pit* (1903) as more powerful than any man or combination of men.

Criticisms of industrialism. With the opening of the new century, the exposure of injustices and abuses in our national life became the most popular of literary subjects. In politics, the 1900's were the era of Theodore Roosevelt's progressivism and "trust-busting"; in literature, the era of the "muckrakers." Literature was dedicated to the exposé, and scores of books revealed all sorts of malpractices to an indignant public. Perhaps the greatest of the muckraking books was Upton Sinclair's *The Jungle* (1906), which dealt graphically with the life of a Lithuanian immigrant employed in the Chicago stockyards. This sturdy young man is gradually broken, and his family completely ruined, by the inhuman cruelties of the stockyards. The book's exposure of unsanitary practices in the processing of meat undoubtedly hastened the enactment of the Pure Food and Drug Act.

The leader among the muckrakers was Lincoln Steffens, whose *The Shame of the Cities* (1904) brought to focus the problems created by the sudden emergence of great urban communities and contributed to the movement for municipal reform. Steffens' book drew attention to the corruption in city government and attempted to fix the blame on certain prominent citizens. The growing problems of the Big City had been noticed before Steffens and were to be further exposed after his notable book. As early as 1890 William Dean Howells had exhibited, though somewhat conservatively, the grime and squalor of New York City in *A Hazard of New Fortunes*. Less conservatively, Stephen Crane's novel *Maggie: A Girl of the Streets* (1893) exposed the ugly life of New York's Bowery. In *Sister Carrie* (1900) and *Jennie Gerhardt* (1911) Theodore Dreiser told affectingly of the hard lot of the underpaid working girl in the big cities of the Middle West. Henry Blake Fuller in *The Cliff-Dwellers* (1893) and Robert Herrick in *The Common Lot* (1904) underscored the degrading effect on Chicago's social life of greed and cutthroat competition. Possibly the apogee of the literary attack on the Big City as a monster of corruption and vice was reached in David Graham Phillips' *Susan Lenox* (1917), whose heroine encounters (and miraculously survives) nearly all the evils of our modern Babylons.

The most prominent and commanding figure in the new industrial scene was the captain of industry. The years following the Civil War saw the amassing of unprecedented private fortunes. Financiers like Jay Cooke, the first great American banker; John D. Rockefeller, the Oil King; Andrew Carnegie, monopolist of iron and steel; and Jay Gould, Commodore Vanderbilt, and Collis P. Huntington, railroad magnates, became the real rulers of America. The reputations of these great entrepreneurs are now tarnished; their money was often acquired unethically; they have been called, with a good deal of justice, the "robber barons."

The type early attracted the attention of our novelists, but the literary treatment was for a good many years comparatively gentle. In Howells' *The Rise of Silas Lapham* (1885), Lapham, a wealthy Boston paint manufacturer, is crude but honest. At the great crisis of his career, he loses his business rather than accept a price for properties which is greater than he knows them to be worth. Howells would have defended his portrait of Lapham by saying that the great majority of American financiers were honest, that robber barons were the exception, not the rule. In *A Hazard of New Fortunes*, Dryfoos, the millionaire, is less amiable in his domestic and social relations than Lapham, and less honorable in business, though we are told that he never "wrecked a railroad" or belonged to a "swindling company or grinding monopoly."

Because he lived abroad, Henry James had the opportunity of knowing only those prosperous and emancipated Americans who took a vacation in Europe. His Christopher Newman (*The American*, 1877) and Adam Verver (*The Golden Bowl*, 1904) are men of integrity and charm. Although James does not enter at all into their business careers — a subject on which he is always vague — we see Newman and Verver behaving decently and even magnanimously. Newman is devoted to culture in a limited way; Verver has built in "American City" a museum of art which he has filled with priceless treasures. Both are men of honor as well as of cultural aspirations.

The balance has never been struck between the portraits drawn by Howells and James and the authentic careers of the "robber barons." Were all successful businessmen in the Gilded Age boors and scoundrels? Some social historians have implied as much. But the modern reader— unless he is a cynic—is still free to believe that the Gilded Age produced Laphams and Newmans as well as Cookes and Goulds.

The emphasis of the muckrakers on the exposé resulted in much less flattering portrayals of the American businessman after the turn of the century. The most elaborate study of the type was made by Dreiser in two voluminously documented novels, *The Financier* (1912) and *The Titan* (1914), in both of which the business career of Frank Cowperwood more closely approximates the unsavory records of the barons. The literary pendulum was to swing back to a more favorable picture of the American millionaire in *Dodsworth* (1929), where Sinclair Lewis' hero (recalling James' Newman in many ways) is an admirable person despite his wealth.

The reformers. While emphasizing the blight of materialism upon the soul, and the injustices and abuses of the new industrial order, the literature of social criticism was not entirely destructive; there were constructive elements as well. Specific utopias were proposed. The greatest and most influential of these was Edward Bellamy's *Looking Backward* (1888): "Not since *Uncle Tom's Cabin*," declares V. L. Parrington, "had an American novel reached so many readers." Believing that economic inequality was the cause of all social ills, Bellamy described a Socialist utopia in which the wealth was distributed with exact equality among its members. A benevolent state controlled public and private economy in the minutest detail; it assigned members to tasks according to their aptitudes; it provided incentives through special recognition of public service. A planned and cooperative society produced sufficient wealth to permit the early retirement of its members and the free enjoyment of cultural pursuits. *Looking Backward* has made many converts to Socialism. Other writers of the period also proposed the Socialist solution: among them, Howells in *A Traveler from Altruria* (1894) and Upton Sinclair in *The Jungle*—after the incredible woes of the stockyards, Sinclair's hero embraces Socialism and becomes an active worker for the cause.

The great body of the literature dealing with social problems, however, proposes not a radical alteration of the American system of free enterprise, but reforms and ameliorations. If men would be honest and fair, if they would be satisfied with a modest income, if they would spend their money unselfishly, if they would be Christians imbued with the spirit of the Sermon on the Mount—then all would be well: this is the burden of many writers who have concerned themselves with the subject.

Charles M. Sheldon's *In His Steps* (1896), which had an amazing sale of more than fifteen million copies, recommended that everyone when confronted by a problem should ask himself, "What would Jesus do?" Less popular and better writers also emphasized the importance of the Christian attitude. Robert Herrick advised in *The Common Lot* (1904) a quiet withdrawal from the market place into a Wordsworthian simplicity. William Vaughn Moody, who was the first of our poets to examine the new social problems with critical insight, urged in "Gloucester Moors" (1900) the necessity of a social conscience among the more fortunate members of society. The results of the Machine Age, he pointed out in "The Brute" (1900), had been disappointing: contrary to expectations, the Machine (the "brute") had not brought prosperity and leisure to all, but only to "the strong and cunning few." The solution lay, Moody thought, not in the rejection of the Machine (as some nineteenth-century Romantics had believed), but in a better control of the Machine and a fairer distribution of the wealth which it produces:

> For the Brute must bring the good time on . . .
> He must loose the curse of Adam from the worn neck
> of the race.
> He must give each man his portion, each his pride and
> worthy place.

Substantial progress was to be made in the new century toward the realization of these aims.

The Frontier Versus Europe: A Question of Values

The freedom of the frontier. "Westward the course of empire takes its way," wrote Bishop Berkeley in his "Verses on the Prospect of Planting Arts and Learning in America" published in 1752. The Westward movement in America was a fulfillment of the prophecy beyond anything which the good bishop could have foreseen. Before the end of the eighteenth century, pioneers had crossed the Alleghenies; by the middle of the nineteenth century, they had settled the Mississippi Valley as far as Texas and the upper reaches of the Missouri and had invaded California and Oregon; by the end of the century, only the Rocky Mountains and the arid tracts of Arizona and Nevada remained unsettled; and by the beginning of World War I, there was no more frontier. The "epic of America" before 1914 was in no small part the epic of the ever advancing frontier. The treatment of the frontier in literature has been of two kinds: romantic, and realistic and critical. In the nineteenth century the romantic treatment predominated; the realistic and critical treatment did not prevail until after World War I.

Whitman sounded the dominant nineteenth-century note in

"Pioneers! O Pioneers!" (1865). Whitman's pioneers were heroes — "tan-faced children," "youthful and sinewy," armed with "pistols and sharp-edged axes."

> We primeval forests felling,
> We the rivers stemming, vexing we and piercing deep
>   the mines within,
> We the surface broad surveying, we the virgin soil
>   upheaving,
> Pioneers! O Pioneers!

(A century later it was to appear that the pioneers had done too thorough a job in upheaving the soil and felling the forests.) They were "impatient" and "full of action" — a "resistless, restless race." Such was Whitman's glorification of the Westward movement. Other poets of the nineteenth century — Emerson and Lowell in New England, Lanier in the South, and Joaquin Miller in the West — echoed Whitman's praise and admiration.

The distinguished historian Frederick Jackson Turner was almost as romantic as the poets in his treatment of the subject in "The Significance of the Frontier in American History" written in 1893. "Stand at Cumberland Gap," he wrote, "and watch the procession of civilization, marching single file — the buffalo following the trail to the salt springs, the Indian, the fur trader and hunter, the cattle raiser, the pioneer farmer — and the frontier has passed by. Stand at South Pass in the Rockies a century later and see the same procession with wider intervals between." Turner defined the frontier as "the line of most rapid and effective Americanization." The American character was largely formed by the frontier; frontier traits became the traits most distinctive of America:

> To the frontier the American intellect owes its striking characteris-
> tics. That coarseness and strength combined with acuteness and
> inquisitiveness; that practical, inventive turn of mind, quick to
> find expedients; that masterful grasp of material things, lacking
> in the artistic but powerful to effect great ends; that restless,
> nervous energy, that dominant individualism, working for good
> and for evil, and withal that buoyancy and exuberance which comes
> with freedom — these are the traits of the frontier, or traits called
> out elsewhere because of the existence of the frontier.

Turner's sentences are almost a prose paraphrase of Whitman.

When we come to the literature written by frontiersmen, we find much that is sordid and unattractive in the life described, but the total effect is still romantic. Frontier life was vital, expansive, exuberant; it was in the full tide of growth; here was no Indian summer, no sere and yellow leaf.

The life portrayed in the books by Mark Twain's precursors —

Davy Crockett's *Autobiography* (1834), A. B. Longstreet's *Georgia Scenes* (1835), W. T. Thompson's *Major Jones's Courtship* (1843), Johnson J. Hooper's *Some Adventures of Captain Simon Suggs* (1846), J. G. Baldwin's *The Flush Times of Alabama and Mississippi* (1853), G. W. Harris' *Sut Lovingood Yarns* (1867) — contains much that is vulgar, brutal, and unprincipled. The bloody athletic contests described by Longstreet, the low chicanery of Simon Suggs, and the rough practical jokes of Sut Lovingood may repel the delicate reader. But there is no denying the vitality, the sturdy strength and individualism, and above all, the high spirits and love of fun in these pioneer tales. Life on the frontier must have been good to produce so much solid enjoyment; perhaps no other early settlements in the world's history have been enlivened by such hilarity. The literary apex of the hilarity was *Sut Lovingood;* nowhere else, even in our own literature, will one find quite so much of that quality, or the qualities it connotes — good health and an inexhaustible enjoyment of physical living. Sut Lovingood and his fellows were a remarkably healthy and uninhibited race.

Lincoln liked to read the Southwestern Yarnspinners, for he was one of them; and from their writings runs a straight line of genealogical descent to the great works of Mark Twain: *Roughing It* (1872), in which he told with gusto the tall tales of his sojourn in the Far West, and *Life on the Mississippi* (1883), *The Adventures of Tom Sawyer* (1876), and *The Adventures of Huckleberry Finn* (1884), in which he immortalized the Mississippi River from Hannibal to New Orleans. Mark Twain did not omit the seamy side of the Mississippi River region in the 1850's — the squalor, the vulgarity, the lawlessness; but this aspect is not too depressing because there was so much that was splendid and exhilarating. The splendor was symbolized for Mark Twain in the steamboat, and "the boat *was* rather a handsome sight!" The exhilaration was owing to the freedom symbolized by Huck and Jim on the raft:

> I never felt easy till the raft was two miles below there and out in the middle of the Mississippi. Then we hung up our signal lantern, and judged that we was free and safe once more. I hadn't had a bite to eat since yesterday, so Jim he got out some corn-dodgers and buttermilk, and pork and cabbage and greens — there ain't nothing in the world so good when it's cooked right — and whilst I eat my supper we talked and had a good time. I was powerful glad to get away from the feuds, and so was Jim to get away from the swamp. We said there warn't no home like a raft, after all. Other places do seem so cramped up and smothery, but a raft don't. You feel mighty free and easy and comfortable on a raft.

It is important to note, however, that the freedom symbolized by Huck and his raft is social as well as individual. Despite his revolt against Miss Watson's "civilization," Huck's behavior is not irresponsible. The freedom of *Huckleberry Finn* turns out to be, paradoxically, a qualified freedom, a freedom complicated by responsibilities and social ties. As Lionel Trilling has acutely observed, "Huck is always 'in a sweat' over the predicament of someone else." It was with good reason that William Dean Howells called Mark Twain "the Lincoln of our literature."

The European tradition. The Westward movement was a powerful driving force which settled the American continent. But there has been another, a counter-force, less powerful but insistent, which has operated throughout our history. As Ferner Nuhn pointed out in *The Wind Blew from the East*, there has been in American life and literature from the beginning "the everpresent pullback toward modes of culture that lie in our past . . . the desire to retrace the racial steps. . . the nostalgic tradition." The Atlantic seaboard has felt drawn constantly to Europe; the Middle West and the Far West, to the Atlantic seaboard. In colonial times, Increase Mather and William Byrd — each in his own way — enjoyed London. In the nineteenth century, Irving and Longfellow and Lowell assimilated the culture of Europe, and Hawthorne felt acutely the ancestral ties to "our old home." Among our major writers, only Thoreau and Whitman — those staunch Americans — never traveled abroad. In the latter half of the century, the Eastward pull began to be felt in the newly settled West: Howells and Garland were drawn from their Western habitats to Boston by the lodestone of the East; Mark Twain settled in Hartford.

The counter-pull has produced two kinds of literary subjects: comparisons of the Eastern and the Western parts of the United States, and comparisons of Europe and America. Although the first subject may be found here and there in our literature (*A Hazard of New Fortunes* transplants several Midwesterners to the East and suggests some comparisons of the two sections; Moody's *The Great Divide* studies the contrasting moralities of New England and the West), it does not attain the importance of the second: Europe versus America is one of the more significant themes in American literature.

Mark Twain treated Europe with unorthodox scorn in *The Innocents Abroad* (1869). He had a frontiersman's hatred of tyranny, and Europe to him meant the twofold tyranny of church and state, of priests and kings. The best thing that had ever happened in Europe, he thought, was the French Revolution, and he regretted that it had not done its work more thoroughly. He could not enjoy the great art of Florence when he recalled the sycophantic attitude of the artists toward the Medicis. Not only in *Innocents Abroad* but in other works as well (*A Connecticut Yankee in King Arthur's Court, Life on the Mississippi, Huckleberry Finn*) he lashed out against feudalism and its survivals wherever he found them, whether in Europe or in Walter Scott's novels or in the ante-bellum South. It was primarily Mark Twain's love of freedom and his sense of the dignity of the common man which blinded him to the glories of Europe.

Two great contemporaries of Mark Twain were not so blinded: Henry James spent most of his life in England because he felt that "it takes an old civilization to set a novelist in motion"; Henry Adams, the historian, was drawn to medieval France as an example of "unity," against which he set the "multiplicity" of the modern world.

Though James admired the "items of high civilization" which he professed to find in Europe and failed to find in America, he wrote in large part about Americans — Americans in Europe. In novel after novel (*The American, The Portrait of a Lady, The Ambassadors, The Golden Bowl*) he shows us Americans, admirable though unsophisticated, in the process of exposure to European influences. These influences make for social and aesthetic enrichment; they are, at the same time, often questionable morally. James' innocent Americans — Christopher Newman, Isabel Archer, Lambert Strether, Maggie Verver, in, respectively, the four novels just named — are shocked by the evil which they discover in Europe. But they do not succumb to the evil; indeed, they are triumphant over it. Lesser Americans in James' stories may be corrupted by Europe or may remain impervious to its culture, but his American heroes and heroines, though not always happy or successful, emerge from their European experiences culturally enriched and strong of soul. Perhaps James meant to suggest that the ideal civilization would combine the freshness and moral strength of America with the rich culture of the Old World.

Henry Adams was not interested in the richness of contemporary Europe so much as in the richness of its medieval past. In his attempt to establish historical lines of force — his "dynamic theory of history" — by which he might explain the modern world and perhaps predict its future course, Adams centered his interest in twelfth-century France and in the Cathedral of Chartres as the epitome of that time and place. In Chartres he found the perfect symbol of unity. In that distant age, the Virgin, in whose worship Chartres was built, exerted a dominating influence over all men. She was the greatest force of the age — energizing, controlling, comforting, beatifying.

If the Virgin was the symbol of medieval unity, the dynamo, Adams thought, was the symbol of modern multiplicity. The Virgin was a unifying spiritual force; the dynamo was obviously a force, but neither spiritual nor unifying. As religion decayed, enormous, incalculable forces unleashed by science — steam power, electricity, radioactivity — threatened to destroy mankind. It was a serious question, Adams thought in the *Education*, whether there was enough intelligence and moral character in the world to control these new forces and use them for man's welfare. The release of atomic energy makes the question an even more serious one today. *The Education of Henry Adams* (1907) is perhaps the best statement in our literature of the background of our present problems.

In *Mont-Saint-Michel and Chartres* (1904) Adams, the disillusioned intellectual, almost surrendered to the spell of Chartres and the Virgin:

One sees her personal presence on every side. Anyone can feel it who will only consent to feel like a child. Sitting here any Sunday afternoon, while the voices of the children are chanting in the choir — your mind held in the grasp of the strong lines and shadows of the architecture; your eyes flooded with the autumn tones of the glass; your ears drowned with the purity of the voices; one sense reacting upon another until sensation reaches the limit of its range — you, or any other lost soul, could, if you cared to look and listen, feel a sense beyond the human ready to reveal a sense divine that would make that world once more intelligible, and would bring the Virgin to life again, in all the depths of feeling which she shows here — in lines, vaults, chapels, colours, legends, chants — more eloquent than the prayerbook, more beautiful than the autumn sunlight.

Europe to Adams was a bright symbol of something eminently valuable — possibly essential to man's prosperity and happiness — which the modern world has lost.

Europe retained a good deal of prestige throughout the nineteenth century and after, despite *Innocents Abroad* and the frontier school; but European prestige lost ground steadily as the twentieth century advanced, despite a growing disposition of Americans to be critical of frontier values.

Science and Religion

The march of science in the nineteenth century profoundly affected religious thought. Geology established the antiquity of the earth, thus discrediting the chronology of Genesis. Evolution, as set forth in Darwin's *The Origin of Species* in 1859, saw man as the result of a slow development from simpler forms of animal life, thus challenging the Christian belief in his special creation. Astronomical science seemed to point to an infinite universe, in the face of which man appeared insignificant. Before the end of the period 1865-1914, sociological, biological, and psychological investigations still further reduced man's importance and autonomy. William Graham Sumner argued that human behavior was largely determined by "folkways," the mores of one's environment. Biology emphasized the determining influence of physical inheritance, of glandular secretions; psychology, the determining influence of automatic responses to stimuli. So effective was the combined onslaught of the sciences that by the end of the period, man appeared to be — from the scientific point of view — little more than an ingenious mechanism. Modern science seemed to leave no room for the soul, or God, or the transcendental perception of truth — for those religious beliefs, in short, which had motivated most Americans for nearly three centuries and which had found eloquent expression in the writings of Edwards, Emerson, and Whitman. The inspired view of the psalmist—"What is man that thou art mindful of him? . . . For thou hast made him a little lower than the angels, and hast crowned him with glory and honor"—became little short of absurd to the scientific mind. All phenomena, we were to suppose, were naturalistic phenomena, and were explicable on purely naturalistic, as opposed to spiritual or transcendental, grounds.

Early resistance to science. The scientific movement did not capture our literature immediately, and, as one might expect, the poets offered a sturdier resistance than other writers. Although Whitman accepted the evolutionary idea, it was the Emersonian (which was in turn the Lamarckian) concept, rather than the concept of Darwin, which emphasized the struggle for survival. For Whitman, as for Emerson, the evolutionary idea exalted man by enlarging his future possibilities:

> My feet strike an apex of the apices of the stairs,
> On every step bunches of ages, and larger bunches be-
> > tween the steps,
> All below duly travel'd, and still I mount and mount.

As the scientific movement advanced in the post-Civil War years, Whitman became not less but more Transcendental. His Transcendentalism reached its highest points in the late poems, "Passage to India" (1871):

> O my brave soul!
> O farther farther sail!

and the "Prayer of Columbus" (1876):

> Shadowy vast shapes smile through the air and sky,
> And on the distant waves sail countless ships,
> And anthems in new tongues I hear saluting me.

Lanier was a spiritually minded person who had no intention of surrendering his Christian faith to the new science. But partly as a natural reaction against his strict Calvinistic upbringing in Macon, partly through the influence of his professor of science, James Woodrow, at Oglethorpe, and partly because of the liberal atmosphere at Johns Hopkins, he welcomed science with an open mind. His copy of Darwin, we are told, was copiously annotated. He made a special study of the physics of sound in connection with his investigation of prosody in *The Science of English Verse*. Science, then, was an unmixed good. An intelligent man, he thought, must be, above all else, "catholic" (see "The Marshes of Glynn," 1878): he must eschew the narrowness of creed and cultivate breadth. The ideal soul is characterized by its "loves," its points of receptivity, and excludes neither science nor any other good thing ("My Springs"):

> And home-loves and high glory-loves,
> And science-loves and story-loves.

He was aware (in "The Mocking Bird") that science might have its limitations:

> Sweet Science, this large riddle read me plain:
> How may the death of that dull insect be
> The life of yon trim Shakspere in the tree?

He admitted (in "Acknowledgement") that possibly his age was dazzled by the new science: "blinking at o'er bright science." These, however, were small reservations in Lanier's mind; no writer of the period was more hospitable to science. Lanier's eager search for truth was thoroughly admirable. But one cannot avoid a suspicion of indiscrimination and naïveté. Lanier did not recognize the contradictions involved; like more able thinkers than himself in the 1870's, he advocated the reconciliation of religion and science. Unlike some other reconcilers, he was apparently unaware that such a reconciliation would entail a diminution of Christian doctrine.

The breadth which Lanier extolled and exemplified seemed vicious to the quiet and then all but unknown New England poetess, Emily Dickinson. In liberalism, she thought, lurked an insidious and fatal danger to religion. Religion was being watered down to the point of insipidity. Her satire of the liberal clergyman — and she must have had in mind the popular advocates of reconciliation between the old religion and the new science — is a telling indictment: "He preached upon 'breadth' till it argued him narrow. . . ." Miss Dickinson was scarcely touched by the scientific movement. Her religion was the older Puritanism modified somewhat by Emersonian Transcendentalism. For her, the things of religion still lay beyond the realm of scientific demonstration; they were still the objects of faith:

> I never spoke with God,
> Nor visited in heaven;
> Yet certain am I of the spot
> As if the chart were given.

If religious faith transcends the world of science, so does the individual life, on occasion, transcend the mechanisms with which science strives to hem it in:

We never know how high we are
    Till we are called to rise;
And then, if we are true to plan
    Our statures touch the skies.

The "plan" Miss Dickinson refers to is not the scientist's but God's.

The spread of mechanistic philosophy. Lanier died in 1881; Emily Dickinson, in 1886; Whitman, in 1892; and with them died in American literature a religious faith untroubled by science. By the end of the century, our poets and prose writers were feeling the full impact of the scientific movement.

Stephen Crane inferred from the biological struggle for survival and the astronomical immensity of the universe that man is unimportant:

A man said to the universe
"Sir, I exist!"
"However," replied the universe,
"The fact has not created in me
A sense of obligation."

"A high cold star on a winter's night" (see "The Open Boat") is the symbol of the indifference of Nature and Nature's God. It seemed ironical to Crane, who found intense irony everywhere in human experience, that the discoverer of the universe should be dwarfed by his discovery, that the chief spiritual result of man's scientific achievements should be the conviction of his own insignificance.

Mark Twain, late in life, became a convert to the mechanistic philosophy. Partly through the influence of the new agnosticism as expounded by Robert G. Ingersoll and others, and partly, perhaps, in the attempt to stifle the deep-seated feeling that his literary performance had not been in keeping with his creative powers, he declared and attempted to prove that "man is a machine." In *What Is Man?* (1906) he summarized his argument as follows:

To me, Man is a machine, made up of many mechanisms, the moral and mental ones acting automatically in accordance with the impulses of an interior Master who is built out of born-temperament and an accumulation of multitudinous outside influences and trainings; a machine whose one function is to secure the spiritual contentment of the Master, be his desires good or be they evil; a machine whose will is absolute and must be obeyed; and always *is* obeyed.

If to Henry Adams man himself was something more than a machine, man at least seemed to be impelled along lines of force. "Modern politics," he said in the *Education*, "is a struggle not of men but of forces. The men become every year more and more creatures of force, massed about central power-houses." He began to "see lines of force all about him, where he had always seen lines of will," and thus "before knowing it," he confessed, "the mind stepped into the mechanical theory of the universe." The future which Adams envisioned for the race was not too hopeful. There was a fair possibility of man's being engulfed in the new forces: "In the earlier stages of progress, the forces to be assimilated were simple and easy to absorb, but, as the mind of man enlarged its range, it enlarged the field of complexity, and must continue to do so, even into chaos, until the reservoirs of sensuous or supersensuous energies are exhausted, or cease to affect him, or until he succumbs to their excess."

Like Adams, Theodore Dreiser believed that men were creatures of force. With the turn of the century, the mechanistic philosophy began to appear in the naturalistic novel, which soon became its chief literary vehicle. Many naturalistic novelists felt a profound sympathy with the unfortunate members of modern society, who appeared to be the helpless and blameless victims of forces beyond their control. The mechanistic philosophy afforded a means of complete exoneration: if a person was dominated by chemical forces from within and social forces from without, he was not morally responsible for his acts or culpable for his misdeeds. In accordance with this view Dreiser wrote his great naturalistic novels: *Sister Carrie, Jennie Gerhardt, The Financier, The Titan,* and *An American Tragedy*. "All of us," declared Lester Kane in *Jennie Gerhardt*, "are more or less pawns. We're moved about like chessmen by circumstances over which we have no control." The world seemed utterly without purpose to Dreiser:

> In distant ages a queer thing had come to pass. There had started on its way in the form of evolution a minute cellular organism which had apparently reproduced itself by division, had early learned to combine itself with others, to organize itself into bodies, strange forms of fish, animals and birds, and had finally learned to organize itself into man. Man, on his part, composed as he was of self-organizing cells, was pushing himself forward into comfort and different aspects of existence by means of union and organization with other men. Why? Heaven only knew.

The obvious tendency through Crane, Mark Twain, Adams, and Dreiser was a growing pessimism.

Mechanistic materialism, so prominent in the literature of the 1900's, was not unchallenged after its apparent triumph. Josiah Royce expounded at Harvard an idealism reminiscent of Emerson's. William James, another Harvard professor, brother of the novelist and America's first great authority in the new science of psychology, emphasized in

The Varieties of Religious Experience (1902) the energizing power of religious faith. This power could hardly be accounted for, he thought, in terms of a mechanistic universe. The creative individual need not succumb to Adams' lines of force or Dreiser's weight of circumstance. James set up the pragmatic test of truth: "The ultimate test for us of what a truth means is the conduct it dictates or inspires." And, finally, Herrick among the novelists and Moody among the poets in the first decade of the century presented the religious view of life. But despite these dissenting voices, it appeared likely that the determinism of mechanistic science would continue to gain in popular and literary acceptance.

The New Imperialism

Throughout the nineteenth century, expansionist doctrines had been urged sporadically. Certain prominent Americans had advocated in the name of "manifest destiny" the desirability of annexing the entire North American continent. Out of this agitation had come the war with Mexico and the acquisition of large territories in the Southwest in 1845-1853 and the purchase of Alaska in 1867. But this expansion could hardly be called flagrantly imperialistic since, Alaska excepted, the new territory seemed necessary to round out our natural boundaries.

The Cuban Revolution of 1895 afforded a plausible excuse for American intervention, and the quick victory over Spain in 1898 stimulated imperialistic sentiments. The spectacular and exciting events of the war—Dewey's victory in Manila Bay, the crushing defeat of Cervera's squadron as it attempted to escape from Santiago, the charge of Roosevelt's Rough Riders up San Juan Hill—evoked a dubious mixture of patriotism and jingoism. After the defeat of Spain, the Filipinos resisted our rule and General Miles' army put down the insurrection. Many thoughtful Americans were alarmed at the new imperialistic policy upon which our nation seemed to be embarking. The crisis called forth protests from persons as various as William Jennings Bryan, Jane Addams, Charles W. Eliot, Finley Peter Dunne, and William Vaughn Moody.

Through the inimitable "Observations of Mr. Dooley" (1898), Dunn satirized the whole American imperialistic policy:

> "An there ye ar-re, Hinnissy. I hope this here lucid story will quite the waggin tongues iv scandal an' that people will let th' Ph'lippeens stew in their own happiness."
>
> "But sure they might do something f'r thim," said Mr. Hennessy.
>
> "They will," said Mr. Dooley. "They'll give thim a measure iv freedom."
>
> "But whin?"
>
> "Whin they'll stand still long enough to be measured. . . ."

Moody lashed out against the conquest of the Philippines in one of the most impassioned poems of our literature, "An Ode in Time of Hesitation" (1900):

> Are we the eagle nation Milton saw
> Mewing its mighty youth,
> Soon to possess the mountain winds of truth,
> And be a swift familiar of the sun . . .
> Or have we but the talons and the maw,
> And for the abject likeness of our heart
> Shall some less lordly bird be set apart? —
> Some gross-billed wader where the swamps are fat?
> Some gorger in the sun? Some prowler with the bat!

But neither the humor of Dunne nor the Miltonic fervor of Moody could stem the tide — we took the Philippines. The immediate outcome notwithstanding, the protests need not be regarded as futile: they may very well have had the effect of making our rulers more careful, for our record in administering the Islands proved to be creditable.

Secretary of State Hay made partial amends to the anti-imperialists by his Chinese policy, and Moody's tone changed from condemnation in the "Ode" to pride in "The Quarry." Having declared the policy of the "Open Door," Hay backed it up by thwarting the obvious intention of the European powers to use the Boxer Rebellion as a favorable opportunity for the dismemberment of China. The American eagle — no longer a "gross-billed wader" — now appeared in a heroic role. When China — backward, helpless, unaware (the description of China in the poem is extraordinarily fine) — was about to be pounced upon by the "brutes of prey," the "grand circler," uttering a cry of warning, drove them away:

> . . . stiller-tongued, with eyes somewhat askance,
> They settled to the slot and disappeared.

A distinguished historian has recently declared that "'The Quarry' is worth all of the literature of imperialism together."

The United States emerged from the war with Spain a world power. National pride centered to an unprecedented degree (except possibly during the War of 1812) in the Navy. Alfred T. Mahan's *Influence of Sea Power upon History*, whose doctrine was espoused by Theodore Roosevelt, helped to make us navy-minded; the victories over Spain raised naval patriotism to a high pitch; Theodore Roosevelt dramatized the role of the "big stick" by sending the fleet around the world in 1907. But the great majority of Americans were not imperialists at heart, and by 1910 pacifism seemed to be gathering strength: Bryan, thrice Democratic candidate for the Presidency, advocated disarmament; David Starr Jordan, president of Stanford, argued that war was the reversal of evolution — the survival of the unfit; William James attempted to discover "a moral equivalent of war." Not deeply affected by the flare-up of 1898-1900, the national temperament preferred peace with isolation.

R.S.

LITERARY TRENDS

"The eight years in America from 1860 to 1868," wrote Charles Dudley Warner and his collaborator, Mark Twain, in *The Gilded Age* (1873), "uprooted institutions that were centuries old, changed the politics of a people, transformed the social life of half the country, and wrought so profoundly upon the entire national character that the influence cannot be measured short of two or three generations." Although many writers continued to follow older patterns, these changes in American life brought changes in at least some forms of the literature. Some changes adapted forms to the tastes of the growing middle-class reading public. Others helped in the expression of the nostalgia, the puzzlement, or the distress of people living in a transitional period.

Authors continued to write old-fashioned essays, but this form began to date as it was crowded from magazines by journalistic articles. By the end of this period, muckraking reports by Lincoln Steffens and many others had become much more typical. A great deal of poetry—some of it weak and imitative, some redeemed by individual qualities of its creators—was poured into prewar molds. But the period saw the rise to prominence of much popular poetry, some created by the people for the people, some written by more literate poets who consciously tried to please the growing group of readers who enjoyed poetry in dialect. Preeminently, though, this was an age of fiction, and fiction changed more than any other type of literature. There were some developments in the drama, too, which paralleled developments in fiction and which foreshadowed some achievements of the modern period.

Older Patterns of Poetry

Much poetry—"literary" poetry as contrasted with folk songs and folk poetry—showed remarkably few effects of the changing intellectual climate. Poetry in general somehow lost its vitality for many intelligent readers; it awaited a rebirth, portents of which began to appear in the final years of the period. This was partly because many poets—Bryant, Longfellow, Holmes, Lowell, Emerson, and Whittier—whose careers had begun in an earlier period continued to satisfy and to determine tastes after the war. It was partly because these established artisans and their British contemporaries were imitated in innocuous, genteel poems by hosts of inferior poets — Richard Henry Stoddard (1825-1903), Bayard Taylor (1825-1878), Edmund Clarence Stedman (1833-1908), Thomas Bailey Aldrich (1836-1907), and Richard Watson Gilder (1844-1909), to name but a few. Even on a higher level, Sill, Hayne, and Moody — all of whom had important things to say and said them with real eloquence — were well satisfied with established verse forms. Crane was a minor, though arresting, exception in his use of free verse. With the exception of Whitman, who was generally ignored, even the leading poets of the period — Sidney Lanier and Emily Dickinson — usually shaped their poetry to conform with accepted schemes. Each, however, sang with a noteworthy difference.

Sidney Lanier: musician and poet. Sidney Lanier, in his conception of poetry, was much closer to prewar New England poets than he was to Walt Whitman. "Whitman," he charged, "is poetry's butcher. Huge raw collops slashed from the rump of poetry, and never mind gristle — is what Whitman feeds our souls with." In his lectures on *The English Novel* Lanier devoted a good deal of time, a bit irrelevantly, to attacks upon Whitman's heresies. And when Lanier himself wrote free verse, as he frequently did, he did not think of publishing it. Instead, he conceived of himself as writing not poems but outlines for poems which awaited more conventional artistic clothing before they were fit to appear in public. Whitman, he held, had been at his best when writing "O Captain, My Captain" because in it he had "abandoned his theory of formlessness and written in form." Like the Brahmins, Lanier saw the poet achieving greatness when he used his supreme artistry to fuse beauty and truth. "Art, to be free," he wrote, "is not to be independent of form but to be master of many forms."

Lanier's departures from conventional versification came, therefore, less because he disagreed with the older poets than because he had individual tastes and talents. Because, even better than Emerson, he knew and loved the Elizabethans, he tended to use many images and conceits which were Elizabethan in their daring. Because he was a musician and a lover of the forms of music, in several poems, notably "The Symphony," he employed organizations analogous to those of musical compositions. And also because he was a musician, he tended, as he showed in his *Science of English Verse*, to think of poetic rhythms as essentially the same as musical rhythms. The result of this belief was that, though he kept within the limits which he had defined, he was a master of more complex modulations of meter, of more artful handlings of vowels and consonants for melody, than any of his predecessors, save Poe.

Emily Dickinson: meaning in miniatures. Emily Dickinson, despite the fact that only a few of her poems were published before 1890, actually was almost contemporaneous, as a writer, with her idol, Ralph Waldo Emerson (1803-1882): she began to write poetry, it appears, in the mid-fifties and continued until her death. She was probably as innocent of theories about technique as any poet could possibly be, as her test for poetry shows — "If I read a book and it makes my body so cold no fire can ever warm me, I know that is poetry. If I feel physically as if the top of my head were taken off, I know that is poetry." In all probability, when such an impressionistic critic conceived of what she was doing, she did not self-consciously consider herself a rebel against established forms. Like Lanier, therefore, when she diverged from conventional procedures, she did so less because she had new theories than because, even for a poet, she was an unusual personality.

One belief of Emerson which his admirer in Amherst did share and enunciate was that a task for the poet was, as Emerson put it, to "embrace the common, . . . explore and sit at the feet of the familiar, the low." "Give me," said Emerson, "insight into to-day, and you may have the antique and future worlds." Miss Dickinson saw the poet as one who distills attars "from the familiar species that perished by the door." So in stanzas ordinarily like those of Emerson and, incidentally, like those of church hymns, she tried to tell (again as Emerson phrased it) the "meaning" of "the meal in the firkin; the milk in the pan; . . . the glance of the eye . . . every trifle bristling with the polarity that ranges it instantly on an eternal law. . . ."

The common, for her, included a household group of men, women, and children; New England nature in the small range of nearby fields; and the rooms of a house as they were known to a housekeeper. She saw these with eyes focused to minute details — with intimate knowledge comparable to a nun's knowledge of each stone and lichen in her narrow cell. And when she announced what the details in her world of miniatures meant, the revelations were very personal ones — the discoveries of a mind which was both serious and playful, both mystical and whimsical. Novel imagery was the result, much of it predicted by nothing else in literature so well as by the poem "Huswifery" by seventeenth-century Edward Taylor, which had told of faith by employing conceits derived from household tasks.

"I'll Tell You How the Sun Rose" is in some ways typical of Miss Dickinson's poetry. Like many of the poems by this introspective recluse, it begins with "I," and goes on to record highly individual insights into a common experience. In the second line she playfully interprets the sunrise in terms of feminine fineries — "A Ribbon at a time" — a conceit paralleled, in the next stanza, by the image of ladylike hills "untying their Bonnets." A comparison of the light with darting squirrels, two details of the commonplace scene — steeples "swimming" in "Amethyst" and bobolinks bursting into song — then the soft soliloquy of the watcher ("That must have been the Sun"!) give the effect of the dawn. The end of the day is impressionistically represented, in the next two stanzas, by figures which involve children climbing a stile and a "Dominie" putting up pasture bars and leading away his flock. All the details come from ordinary observations, and their very commonplaceness gives the interpretation a unique appeal.

Though this poem is less intense in thought and feeling than many by Miss Dickinson, its imagery is fairly representative. As Henry W. Wells remarks in *The American Way of Poetry*, "Children playing in the garret or asleep in their beds at dawn, New England customs at Thanksgiving, apples snug in the cellar through the winter, the loud ticking of the clock at night, signs on chimneys and doors, needle and thread, the little girl shut in the closet and told to be still—such images take on the most piquant and unexpected emotional meanings. . . . Her microscope requires only one clover and one bee to make a prairie; one flake of snow debating whether it will cross a rut suffices her to create at once a mood and a winter's day." The fusion of such homespun imagery with the thoughts and whimsies of a poet made Emily Dickinson's work a new thing.

Folk Songs and Folk Poetry

One of the glories of the period 1865-1914 was the discovery, by many, of one aspect in particular of our rich native folklore—the folk songs. The scholars active before and after 1914 did not, to be sure, create the songs. The ballads had been made by humble, uneducated folk, and the scholars merely collected them and made them known. Even before the war there had been some interest in such lore, indicated by sporadic studies. Notably, young Francis James Child (1825-1896), newly appointed to the Harvard faculty, had been inspired by his study in Germany in the 1840's to carry on research in British balladry. His lifelong work, climaxed by his five-volume collection, *English and Scottish Popular Ballads* (1882-1898), made such work "respectable" and aroused the interest of many scholars in the subject. Postwar interest in sectional life and in national history stimulated new enthusiasm. By the end of the period, therefore, knowledge about folk songs had increased tremendously.

During the war and the years after it, the songs which had been chanted by soldiers were collected in such volumes as *Songs of Soldiers* (1864), *Poetry of the Civil War* (1866), and *Southern Poems of the War* (1867). At least some of the verses drawn together in such volumes were of folk origin. Concurrently, several writers began to introduce the public to Negro spirituals in magazine articles such as "Negro Spirituals" (*Atlantic Monthly*, 1867) and in books such as *Slave Songs of the United States* (1867), *Jubilee Songs* (1872), and *Cabin and Plantation Songs* (1875). The last two volumes contained versions of folk songs as sung by the students of two newly founded institutions, Fisk and Hampton.

In the following decades, more songs of the people came slowly to light. In 1880, for example, when Joel Chandler Harris issued his first collection of Uncle Remus stories, themselves valuable as folklore, he included a number of plantation songs as he had heard them sung in Georgia. In 1883 a fine study, *Games and Songs of American Children*, was published by W. W. Newell. The American Folk-Lore Society began in 1888 the regular publication of its *Journal*, which from time to time published, along with other lore, folk songs as they were sung by the Negroes, the folk of New England, or the Southern mountaineers. Other learned journals printed occasional articles. Stedman and Hutchinson included several sections of folk songs in their anthology, *A Library of American Literature* (1889-1890). In 1894, Alfred M. Williams included in his *Studies in Folk-Song and Popular Poetry* not only the ballads of other nations but also Civil War songs and American sea-chanteys. In 1908 a new vein was opened when N. Howard Thorp, Southwestern cowhand and himself a maker of ballads, published a little pamphlet, *Songs of the Cowboys*, a collection in which he stated, whenever possible, exactly where, when, and from whom he had picked up each. Two years later John Lomax, who had learned at Harvard to prize the ballads he had heard as a boy and a youth in Texas, published a better-known collection, *Cowboy Songs and Other Frontier Ballads*.

During the year between these two collections, a folk song very different from cowboy ballads swept the country, carried from coast to coast by vaudeville singers and gramophone records. This was the famous "Casey Jones," a railroad song which had been composed some years before by some anonymous lyricist to celebrate "a brave engineer," and which was published, in a somewhat refined version, by T. L. Siebert and E. Newton. During 1909, too, a writer in the *Journal of American Folk-Lore*, Louise Rand Bascom, published the opening lines of another railroad song, as heard in North Carolina:

> Johnie Henry was a hard-workin' man,
> He died with his hammer in his hand.

These, she said, were all the words of the song she had heard. A few years later (1913) in "Songs and Rhymes from the South," an article in the same publication, E. C. Perrow printed fragments or complete versions of songs about this same John Henry which he had collected in east Tennessee, Indiana, Mississippi, and Kentucky. All these, as well as others to be recorded later, were apparently based upon the exploits of a giant Negro who had driven steel for the Chesapeake and Ohio Big Bend Tunnel in West Virginia in the early 1870's.

This record of a few milestones tells only the beginnings of the American study of folk songs which, in the modern period, was to engage the attention of both careful scholars and lovers of poetry and music.

Two rather different reasons for the awakened interest in such lore may be suggested. The study of folklore, thanks largely to the efforts of Child and his students, had become both respectable and scientific. For another thing, in those days when life was beginning to show its present pace and complexity, there was an attraction in the arts and cultures of the primitive, unlearned folk who sang such songs. Their traditional creations, at least, were not marred by the harassing problems of a transitional period.

The makers of the songs, naturally, plied their art for reasons which had nothing to do with either the science of ballad collecting or the distress of city folk during a time of change. Their songs came directly from their own experiences, their way of living, their feelings. To express what they had to say, they fitted poetic words of the only kind they knew to music of the only sort with which they were familiar. Thus the Negroes amalgamated the old-time hymns which whites had taught them with African rhythms which had been passed along to them by their enslaved forebears; and the isolated whites of the mountains or the prairies fashioned their compositions after the example of current songs or of ballads which had been brought to America from England or Scotland by early settlers.

These folk songs probably had few appeals to a sizable group which thought that poetry had to be elegant, genteel, and ornamental. Appreciation of balladry was usually confined to a pair of audiences differing greatly from one another. One audience, like the makers of the songs, was, in some ways, naïve — shy on book knowledge, although probably learned in the emotions and behavior of real men and women. Such an audience appreciated the songs much as had their original audiences. The other audience was highly sophisticated — one which could perceive the historical value of balladry as a cultural expression, and one which could appreciate simplicity of style, suggestiveness of detail, and music which, though it differed from the music currently fashionable, had a beauty of its own.

Some poets who were not folk poets took hints about writing from ballad makers and wrote what might be called not folk songs but "folk poetry." Some of these — Whittier, for instance — used ballad verse or metrical forms resembling it, and employed language with balladlike simplicity. Others, in various parts of the country, wrote dialect verse.

In the South a number of poets continued the tradition which had been started before the war by Stephen Collins Foster, and wrote poetry echoing Negro melodies and employing Negro dialect. Irwin Russell (1853-1879) of Mississippi, in his *Christmas Night in the Quarters* (1878), produced a masterpiece of this genre, a sympathetic mingling of the Negroes' religion and humor in authentic dialect. Hayne and Lanier, as well as other less famous Southerners, also wrote poetry using Negro dialect. During the period, too, Paul Laurence Dunbar (1872-1906) in *Lyrics of Lowly Life* (1896) showed himself to be, as Howells held, the first writer of pure African descent "to feel the Negro life aesthetically and to express it lyrically."

The most popular dialect poetry, however, was written in the Far West and the Middle West. Outstanding were John Hay (1838-1905), author of *Pike County Ballads*; Bret Harte, whose most famous poem in this style was the popular "Plain Language from Truthful James" (1870); and James Whitcomb Riley (1849-1916), whose first book was *The Old Swimmin' Hole and 'Leven More Poems* (1883). At their best, such poems caught some of the flavor of rural life and some of the tang of American speech; they had wholesome humor and sentiment. At their worst, they were maudlin in their sentimental nostalgia for the "olden times." At both their best and their worst, however, they were interesting reflections of the tastes and the expressions of the feelings of the period. The extraordinary success of such writings showed that a large class of readers had come into being who were happy to buy the writings of even "humbler poets" than those Longfellow had praised — poets whose "simple and heartfelt lays" were, indeed, extraordinarily simple.

Humor

The period 1865-1914 is noteworthy as one during which humor perceptibly contributed to the development of fiction and merged with that type of literature. Thus our most admired humorist to date, Mark Twain, whose works were written in this period, was praised not only for making people laugh but also for writing great fiction. His mingling, in some of his work, of the techniques of comedy with the techniques of the short story and the novel was typical: many authors found the procedures of some of the humorists useful in creating postwar fiction. Some humor, by contrast, moved further and further from fiction, in the end becoming almost divorced from it.

In the years before the Civil War, magazines and newspapers — "exchanges" — came from all over the country to the office of the little Hannibal, Missouri, newspaper run by Mark's brother, Orion Clemens. Young Samuel Clemens, in the days when he was learning the printer's trade, read humorous writings in these publications and set some of them up in type. Some of the humor was that of New England — sketches and stories of Yankee characters like Jack Downing. More often it was the fine brand of humor then being produced in the part of the country with which he was familiar, the old Southwest — Tennessee, Georgia, Alabama, Louisiana, Mississippi, Arkansas, and Missouri.

One important thing about much of this Southwestern humor was its relationship to a favorite frontier pastime, yarnspinning. Traveling across country, moving down river, resting at night by campfires, household firesides, or by glowing stoves, the people of the section (like rural folk elsewhere in the country) found that good stories helped pass the time pleasantly. Able storytellers were greatly admired, and political figures like Davy Crockett and Abe Lincoln, who were masters of the art, could win votes by spinning yarns for their constituents. So the art of oral narration flourished on the frontier.

The stories ranged all the way from wild fantasy to fairly straightforward accounts of everyday happenings. Some yarns were playful lies comparable to their modern survivors, "fish stories" or Walt Disney animated cartoons. Their tellers, like Ovid Bolus, described in Joseph G. Baldwin's *The Flush Times of Alabama and Mississippi* (1853), "lied with a relish . . . lied with a coming appetite, growing with what it fed on . . . lied from the delight of invention and the charm of fictitious narrative." They lied about the astonishing fertility of the soil, about encounters with huge beasts, as did Jim Doggett in Thomas B. Thorpe's "The Big Bear of Arkansas" (1841). Almost as often, in some parts of the country, they imaginatively exaggerated the poverty of the soil, telling of land so poor that birds flying across it had to carry rations, so poor that if a buyer couldn't read he was likely to learn to his sorrow that the seller had got rid of two sections instead of the one contracted for.

Such lies about land, climate, and beasts were inventive and fantastic, and so were those about certain mythical heroes — gigantic comic demigods capable, so the stories asserted, of superhuman deeds. Among these were Mike Fink, keelboat king on Western rivers; Davy Crockett, hunter, congressman, and warrior; John Henry, the Negro steeldriver; Pecos Bill, the rootin-tootin Texas cowboy; Paul Bunyan, mighty logger of the whole north country from Maine to Washington. Some of the tall tales which gifted truth-stretchers recounted about a few of these worthies began to get into print as early as the 1820's. Mike Fink, for instance, was introduced in a short story in the *Western Souvenir* in 1828, and between that date and 1914 stories about him were told in a hundred varied publications — books, magazines, almanacs, and newspapers. Davy Crockett, who became prominent about the same time, was yarned about in even more publications. As the period ended, Paul Bunyan stories began to appear, and after 1914 all three heroes were to be celebrated by a number of authors.

The printed yarns about these men and others of their ilk were definitely influenced by the forms of the oral tales. Many details were products of the soaring frontier imagination; some of them were indeed fantastic (see the tall stories in the *Crockett Almanacs*). But the incongruity which made the tales comic was the incongruity between the actual and the impossible. Thus though whole sequences of events were completely impossible, happening was made to arise from happening in an elaborately logical fashion. An earthy dialect style rather than the majestic language of inspired poetry matter-of-factly recounted astonishing feats. Details painstakingly rendered — highly authentic details — gave added verisimilitude. Sometimes, even touches which were quite vulgar heightened contrasts between the earthy and the unearthly. A few lines after Jim Doggett had poetically evoked a giant bear of Arkansas which "loomed like a black mist," Jim was shamefacedly telling about losing his pants. And frequently, though the tale was impossible by any sane standards, the character of the teller, and his motives for inventing his lie, were most plausibly rendered. The playfulness of tall tales was underlined, in short, by the constant reminders of actuality.

Even more of actuality entered into stories of another sort told by Western firesides and eventually translated into print—comic tales about more commonplace frontier characters and happenings. Several reasons for authenticity in such narratives may be cited. There was a desire on the part of some sophisticated storytellers and writers to show that they, like eighteenth-century British humorists, could detachedly perceive and appreciate "originals" and "eccentrics." Again, there was a wish, on the part of many, to write history—as A. B. Longstreet put it, in his pioneer book, *Georgia Scenes*, ". . . to supply a chasm in history which has always been overlooked—the manners, customs, amusements, wit, dialect, as they appear in all grades of society to an eye and ear witness. . . ." Finally, of course, there was a desire to entertain one's fellows. Lawyers, for instance, riding the circuits, said Samuel A. Hammett, in 1853, "living as they do in the thinly inhabited portion of our land, and among a class of persons generally their inferiors in point of education . . . are apt to seek for amusement in listening to the droll stories and odd things always to be heard at the country store or bar-room."

Whatever their motivation, authors who wrote such tales managed among them to record in extraordinary detail many aspects of frontier life. Franklin J. Meine, in his excellent anthology, *Tall Tales of the Southwest*, lists a group of subjects that is strikingly inclusive—local customs, games, courtships, weddings, law circuits, political life, hunting, travel, medicine, gambling, religion, fights, and oddities in character. As Bernard De Voto claims, in *Mark Twain's America*, "No aspect of the life in the simpler America is missing from this literature." The details about backgrounds, costumes, mores, and dialect are plentiful and vivid. Regardless of their crudities and exaggerations, such authors as David Crockett, Thomas Bangs Thorpe, William Tappan Thompson, and George Washington Harris represent the first American achievement of what later was called "realism."

Although some humorists, for instance Finley Peter Dunne, continued the older style, humor in general after the Civil War followed two channels. That which was generally classified as "humor" lost much of its prewar localized quality—tended in fact to become divorced from fiction. The new professional humorists such as Josh Billings and Artemus Ward managed to appeal to much larger audiences than ante-bellum humorists had by replacing much of the humor of regional scene and individualized characters with humor which depended almost exclusively upon expression; and background, character, and plot became unimportant. Characters became generalized so that it was practically impossible for readers to tell where they lived (except somewhere on the North American continent) and whether they were good or bad, wise or foolish. The source of laughter, rather, was the style—ludicrously assembled sentences, words badly spelled, malapropisms, puns, and the like. This, then, was the first type of humor that developed after the war. The second type merged with a kind of fiction which flourished between about 1868 and 1900—local color.

Local Color

In the decade following the end of the Civil War, Whittier and Harriet Beecher Stowe of New England, Bret Harte of the Far West, Edward Eggleston and Mark Twain of the Middle West, and George Washington Cable of the Deep South all won enthusiastic praise for their depictions of life and character in their particular corners of the country. This was the beginning of a great movement in fiction in the United States. In 1894, critic Edward E. Hale, Jr., could write, in *The Dial*, "Everybody writes 'local' stories nowadays; it is as natural as whooping cough." There was a slight exaggeration in this statement, but beyond question a vast number of authors were so engaged. Mary Noailles Murfree of Tennessee, Joel Chandler Harris of Georgia, Sarah Orne Jewett of Maine, Mary E. Wilkins Freeman of Massachusetts, and O. Henry of Texas and New York City are only a few of scores who wrote such fiction.

Directly or indirectly, much of this writing was influenced by the prewar humor of New England or the old Southwest. Mrs. Stowe's best work took the form of fireside yarns, many of them humorous, spun by a quaint Yankee character, Sam Lawson. It seems probable that Edward Eggleston learned much of his art from such dialect humorists as Jack Downing, Hosea Biglow, and various Southwestern practitioners. Miss Murfree admittedly was indebted to Sut Lovingood. Joel Chandler Harris, too, and O. Henry knew American humor well, and actually wrote a good deal of it themselves before they began to write fiction. And it is noteworthy that Bret Harte, who was so successful that many fictionists paid him the tribute of imitation, definitely believed that the humorous story of "bar-rooms, gatherings in the 'country store,' and . . . public meetings" was "the parent of the American 'short story.'"

Naturally, it was not so simple as that. Many influences which had shaped our fiction in the past continued to shape it. The genial essays of Irving, sentimental novels, the writings of Scott, Cooper, Dickens, and others left their imprint. Yet the prewar humorous story was influential in ways which Harte suggested when he described it: "It was concise and condensed, yet suggestive . . . delightfully extravagant—or a miracle of understatement. It voiced not only the dialect, but the habits of thought of a people or locality. . . . It went directly to the point." Many details in this formula applied to representative local color stories.

So far as the local colorists, in their narratives, lived up to this description, they tended to be recorders of actuality. Several thought of themselves as merely reflectors of life. Typical was Mrs. Stowe's claim that in her New England fiction she tried to "make her mind as still and passive as a looking-glass, or a mountain lake," in order that she might reflect "New England life and character." "My studies for this object," she said, "have been . . . taken from real characters, real scenes, and real incidents." But perhaps because of the example set by romantic fictionists, perhaps, also, because of the nostalgia which most writers felt for the past, local colorists tended to write not of the scene of the day but of a day that was ended. So Mrs. Stowe wrote of the New England of her childhood, Eggleston of the Indiana of frontier days, Harte of the California of the Gold Rush, and others of happy ante-bellum plantations. The mists of time blurred the mirrors somewhat, and the local colorists as a rule avoided the sordid and the tragic in favor of geniality, sentiment, and pathos.

Mark Twain: Humorist and Local Colorist

Reared on the frontier and instructed in writing by prewar Yankee and Southwestern humorists, Mark Twain came into national prominence in the years when postwar professional humorists and local colorists were flourishing. In his varied writings the student of humor may see evidence of the influences of all these schools. But since Samuel L. Clemens happened to be a genius, he frequently managed to surpass his teachers.

Most of Twain's ephemeral works and passages are the creations of a "Funny Man" who was working rather too hard to get laughs. At their worst such creations were typified by the "Thomas Jefferson Snodgrass Letters," which he wrote in the late fifties, newspaper screeds soon forgotten and not reprinted until they were dug up by scholars as specimens of his youthful efforts. The style was like that of Artemus Ward and his cohorts of the postwar period—a style notable for cacography and for outlandish expressions. Later, Clemens, like other humorists of the school, refined this style somewhat—dropping bad spelling, for instance—in various sketches and in parts of his travel books. Often, in using the later style, he was quite funny. At its best, nevertheless, this type of humor never marked his highest reaches. And now and then—as in some later chapters of *Huckleberry Finn*—burlesque and buffoonery struck discordant notes.

The artistry of the frontier oral story, by contrast, was one of Twain's most important assets. Having lived in the frontier town of Hannibal, traveled around the whole country, and worked on river boats and in mining camps, he had, by 1865, heard as well as read a great number of humorous stories told by master storytellers. He knew, as he said in "How to Tell a Story," that ". . . the humorous story is strictly a work of art, high and delicate art — and only an artist can tell it." He knew important aspects of the technique: "The humorous story is told gravely; the teller does his best to conceal the fact that there is anything funny about it. . . ." Again, "To string incongruities and absurdities together in a wandering and sometimes purposeless way, and seem innocently unaware that they are absurdities, is the basis of the American art. . . ." Finally, he knew how the introductory framework of an enclosed narrative, as well as the language and thoughts of the yarnspinner, might be made to reveal the narrator as an appealing or amusing character. When, therefore, Clemens heard the "Jumping Frog" story unfolded by a mining-camp fireside in 1865, he was able to write it out in a masterly form. And when later, in "Baker's Blue-Jay Yarn" (1880) and elsewhere, he created tall tales in the style of Thompson's "A Coon Hunt in a Fency Country" (1847) and Thorpe's "The Big Bear of Arkansas," his were even better than those ante-bellum masterpieces.

Twain's travel books and to some extent his novels were combinations of similar brief narratives with longer chronological accounts. As De Voto remarks, in *Mark Twain's America*:

> He took the humorous anecdote, combined it with autobiographical reminiscence, and so achieved the narrative form best adapted to his mind. . . . *The Innocents Abroad* is structurally an autobiographical narrative. Descriptive passages . . . interrupt the narrative from time to time but its steady progress is accomplished by means of stories. Some of them are brief, unelaborated anecdotes, in no way different from the type out of which they proceed, but others already show Mark's perception that this form can be utilized for more intricate effects. . . . The same framework produces *Roughing It*, *A Tramp Abroad*, *Life on the Mississippi*, and *Following the Equator*.

Similarly in novels such as *The Gilded Age* and *Huckleberry Finn*, Twain constructed mosaics made up of anecdotal units.

Just as anyone familiar with humor sees these resemblances, so anyone familiar with local color writing notices resemblances to writings of that type. The material for all of Twain's best narratives was his boyhood home, Hannibal, or the great river which rolled before it. More accurately, the stuff of his best works was not the actuality but his memory of the scenes and of the life he had known in childhood and youth. Memory often had blurred away the most sordid and unlovely details, leaving an idyll to be set forth in nostalgic fiction. The localized details and the longing for times past were completely typical of local color fiction.

Two skills in particular give Twain's best fiction, long or short, much of its distinction: ability to characterize and ability to use words in a masterly fashion. Other humorists in America before Twain had managed, at best, to create only a few memorable characters. Twain dotted his pages with them with a prodigality comparable to that of Chaucer or Dickens. And he had such descriptive skill, such a knack for portraying actions, such an accurate ear for speech that he could make both characters who appeared for a few lines and characters whose stories occupied many pages come alive for readers. As a stylist, also, he was outstanding. He took great pains with style; it is remarkable that a large share of his remarks about literature touch knowingly upon this aspect of writing. Some of his reasons for praising a sentence which he quotes are illuminating: "For compactness, simplicity, and vigor of expression, I will 'back' that sentence against any in literature." He praises a letter from his daughter Susan for "clearness of statement, directness, felicity of expression, photographic ability in setting forth an incident — style — good style — no barnacles on it in the way of unnecessary, retarding words." He came close to living up to the ideal implied by these comments. He wrote very much as he talked, transferring to the printed page the natural rhythms of unpretentious speech, both when he set down his own thoughts and when he quoted the words of characters. His words were simple; almost always they were distinctly American; and he used them economically. Perhaps even more important, without any appearance of being "literary," he was able to find words which gave full scope to his exuberant, poetic imagination. It makes some sense, therefore, to claim, as some critics do, that Mark Twain was the first great stylist who wrote purely in the American language.

Varied Types of Realism

Comic tall tales, by juxtaposing the workaday world with the world of fantasy, made fun of imaginative excesses, and even the most extravagant American humor was in some ways anti-romantic. Since funny character sketches drew many details directly from actuality, some of the humor led the way toward fiction which was concerned with ordinary characters and scenes. Local color writing, which had a similar concern, also departed to some extent from the romantic fiction of the ante-bellum period. Scholars, therefore, see in both humorous writing and local color writing a trend toward "realism" which culminated, toward the end of the century, in numerous realistic and naturalistic fictional works.

The term "realism," like its counterpart "romanticism," is a vague term which has been variously defined. The group pursuing it in this period differed in theory and practice. They generally agreed, probably, that realistic fiction truly presented "actuality" — "real life" — and that it was concerned with the near, rather than the distant, in time and place. Most realists, therefore, believed that the probability of happenings in novels might properly be tested, not by rules set up by the inventor of an imaginative world but by what was likely in the actions of living men and women. Alice might properly dwindle to a minute size in Wonderland, but not in a realistic novel, since there the laws of physics and of biology as well as the stern limitations of heredity and environment were constantly operative. So far there was agreement; but disagreement naturally arose when authors tried to define "actuality." Where was the "real" to be found—in the world itself, in the inductively discovered scientific truths about the nature of the world, in the impression which the world made upon the observer's mind, or in a combination of these? The methods of authors depended upon their answer to this question and upon their ability to portray what they considered to be reality.

Clemens clearly indicated how he thought art should portray actuality when, in a newspaper letter of 1867, he thus criticized a painting by Bierstadt: "Now, to sum up the picture's merits, those snow-peaks are correct—they look natural; the valley is correct and natural; the pine trees clinging to the bluff on the right, and the grove on the left, and the boulders, are all like nature. . . . But when I got around to the atmosphere, I was obliged to say 'This man has imported this atmosphere . . . from some foreign country, because nothing like it was ever seen in California.'" Steadfastly Twain believed that the artist in colors or in words did his work best when he was "true to nature," accurately and honestly recording what he saw. "There is nothing," he wrote in a personal letter of 1868, "that makes me prouder than to be regarded by intelligent people as 'authentic.'" So far as he could, therefore, he made his fiction an exact transcript of life. Only because his memory changed things, because his notions of propriety changed things, and because he was something of a poet did he (to use his own terms) "import" the "atmosphere" in his best narratives.

William Dean Howells, Twain's close friend, had at the start of his career a similar conception of the task of the fictionist. Fiction, Howells also thought, should be lifelike. Moreover, it should concern itself only with the most ordinary facets of life. A passage in *Their Wedding Journey* (1872) concerning the people in a railway car suggests the attitude: "It was in all respects an ordinary carful of human beings, and it was perhaps the more worthy to be studied on that account. As in literature the true artist will shun the use even of real events if they are of an improbable character, so the sincere observer of man will not desire to look upon his heroic or occasional phases, but will seek him in his habitual moods of vacancy and tiresomeness. To me, at any rate, he is at such times very precious. . . ." Since he followed this formula, the literalness of Howells' transcripts in his early writings was significant. But he recognized certain limitations—limitations which kept his literalness from being complete. It is important to recall that he first glimpsed the possibilities of realism while reading the comedies of Carlo Goldoni and that he was extremely fond, all his life, of the witty novels of Jane Austen. Like these two writers, he tended to concern himself, at the start of his career, more with the comedies of human experience than with the tragedies. In addition, because he believed that the typical American life was relatively pure, and because he held that it was wrong for an American novelist "to deal with certain facts of life which are not usually talked of before young people, and especially young ladies," he rather prudishly limited his treatment of sex.

Harold Frederic and Joseph Kirkland, both admirers of William Dean Howells, had much the same attitude Howells had about the fiction writer: his task was to serve up "a slice of life." Kirkland's *Zury: The Meanest Man in Spring County* (1887), he told an acquaintance, was authentic: "I know farm life. All the characters in *Zury* have their prototypes in my down-state acquaintances. The book is as true as I could make it. Many of its incidents are literally exact." But both Frederic and Kirkland were less convinced of the need for limitations upon subject matter than Howells was. Frederic, as he demonstrated clearly in *Seth's Brother's Wife* (1887) and *The Lawton Girl* (1890), was not averse to treating sex in a fashion which might distress young ladies; *The Damnation of Theron Ware* (1896) dealt in an equally frank way with religion. And Kirkland admitted his indebtedness to an English novelist who was in those days considered quite daring. "This novel," he wrote of *Zury*, "is a palpable imitation of Thomas Hardy's *Far from the Madding Crowd*; an attempt to reproduce on American soil the unflinching realism given by that remarkable work of English low life down in actual contact with the soil itself." The word "unflinching" as well as Kirkland's uninhibited treatment of moral problems in *Zury* showed that he had an attitude toward frankness in the novel closer to that of Hardy than to that of Howells.

When Hamlin Garland met Howells in Cambridge, Massachusetts, in 1885, Garland had, so Howells said later, "convictions flatteringly like mine." As Garland made clear in his *Crumbling Idols* (1894), he believed in what a French critic had dubbed "veritism." The true artist, he held, "must consciously stand alone before life" and must sincerely set down "the drama of the average type of character." In two ways, however, he departed from the early Howells. In the first place, Garland was moderately frank in his consideration of sex. ("I am old-fashioned," wrote Howells of this tendency in 1912, "and I have moments when I could wish that the author had not been of such unsparing conscience.") In the second place, Garland, under the tutelage of a group of assorted nineteenth-century thinkers, acquired the belief that "to fiction is given the task of subtilely embodying the splendid creed" of improvement — social, moral, and philosophical. "It is safe to say," he prophesied in *Crumbling Idols*, "that the fiction of the future will grow more democratic in outlook and more individualistic in method. . . . The higher art would seem to be the art that perceives and states the relations of things, giving atmosphere and relative values as they appear to the sight." Hence, *Main-Travelled Roads* not only pictured some of the harsher aspects of Middle-western farm life; it also crusaded against conditions and suggested remedies.

By the time this first collection of Garland's stories appeared, Howells, too, had come to believe that fiction should have an element — one of great importance — which had been lacking in his early fiction. His first encounter — at fifty — with Tolstoy's writings had, as Howells indicated in *My Literary Passions*, brought about a change in his thinking. "He," wrote Howells, "has been to me that final consciousness which he speaks of so easily in his essay on Life. I came in it to the knowledge of myself in ways that I had not dreamt before, and began at last to discern my relations to the race, without which we are nothing. The supreme art in literature had its highest effect in making me set art forever below humanity. . . ." What this meant was that Howells, in *Annie Kilburn* (1889), *A Hazard of New Fortunes* (1890), *The World of Chance* (1893), and his other mature novels, became a novelist of social purpose — selecting characters not only because they were typical but also because their characteristics and their stories preached sermons about society and economics.

Naturalism

Just as the line between some local color fiction and some realism is hard to draw, it is difficult to distinguish clearly and surely between realism and some "naturalism," another "ism" about which there was, in this period, a great deal of discussion. In general, the American naturalists — Crane, Norris, Dreiser, and others — took at least some of their cues from a group of authors, led by Émile Zola (1840-1902), who were important in France after 1880. The characteristics of the French group have been admirably summarized by Professors Nitze and Dargan in their *History of French Literature*:

> Naturalism . . . is an excessive form of Realism and is usually considered as possessing the following characteristics. First, it allows a still larger variety of subjects, emphasizing the lower and coarser forms of life; it presents this material in a form which is often revolting; it rejects ideality, it minimizes heart-interest and plot interest in favor of "facts" and notations; it magnifies the study of the industries and seeks to apply to fiction the processes of the natural sciences; from these, taken in their application to heredity and environment, it draws its conception of life — deterministic, fatalistic, essentially pessimistic. The laws of brute Nature are viewed as grimly controlling the destinies of helpless and hopeless men.

An interesting fact about this accurate description of a literary method is that it deals more with the philosophical views of novelists than with their fictional technique. The reason may well be that, for the naturalistic writers, "actuality" is located not merely in life itself but also in the philosophical interpretation of life. For Zola, art was nature, yes, but nature as it was interpreted by the artist. In a fashion comparable to that of the scientist, theoretically, the naturalist exposed his sensibility to life and then "scientifically" worked with characters and actions known through his experience. But the vast difference between the artist and the scientist whom he thought he was imitating was that the artist, unable really to prove his hypotheses in the laboratory, took them for granted and merely illustrated them from his experience.

American naturalists resembled their French prototypes in treating subjects barred even from realistic writings, in treating lower forms of life — thus differing from realists in their details. Also each American naturalist, on the basis of his own reading and his own thinking, created characters and plots illustrative of his own peculiar "scientific" convictions. Thus Dreiser, believing that men's actions were "chemical compulsions," pictured situations and happenings which made clear that characters had no control over their actions. Believing, further, that "the race was to the swift and the battle to the strong," he devised plots which showed weak characters conquered by ruthless and mighty opponents. Norris, excitedly perceiving both unconquerable forces of Nature and the relentless man-made power of the soulless railroad, devised in *The Octopus* a plot which showed Force at work:

> Men were mere nothings, mere animalculae, mere ephemerides that fluttered and fell and were forgotten between dawn and dusk. . . . Men were nought, death was nought, life was nought. Force only existed — Force that brought men into the world — Force that crowded them out to make way for the succeeding generation — Force that made the wheat grow — Force that garnered it from the soil to give place to the succeeding crop.

And Stephen Crane showed the hero of *The Red Badge of Courage* discovering naturalistic truths on the blood-drenched field of battle, or showed the correspondent in "The Open Boat" becoming aware of the complete indifference of Nature to puny men.

Theodore Dreiser, unlike the French naturalists, had a good deal of contempt for niceties of style. Not so Norris and Crane. Norris used a great deal of symbolism, some of it quite explicit, and some a bit obvious. (The slaughter of the sheep in *The Octopus* is an example.) Crane, rather more subtle as a poet, was sometimes less labored in his handling of symbolism, but much of it came into his work — usually in the form of images seen through the eyes and interpreted by the minds of his characters. Such images both pictured and interpreted details. The correspondent in "The Open Boat," for instance, thus saw a wind-tower on the tantalizing beach: "This tower was a giant, standing with its back to the plight of the ants. It represented in a degree, to the correspondent, the serenity of nature amid the struggle of the individual — nature in the wind, and nature in the vision of men. She did not seem cruel to him then, nor beneficent, nor treacherous, nor wise. But she was indifferent, flatly indifferent." Touches similar to this were to give significance, later, to backgrounds and actions in the writings of such diverse authors as Willa Cather, Ernest Hemingway, and John Steinbeck.

Henry James

To Stephen Crane, one of the most intuitive fictional artists of the period, thoughts and feelings of characters, then, were important. To Henry James, probably the most conscious artist, they were even more important. As his work "The Art of Fiction" (1884) shows, James was a careful thinker about the nature of reality, the nature of art, and the relationship between the two. His belief was that "reality," as a story presented it, was twice translated, once through the author's experiencing of it, again through the artistic representation of it. Both the initial impression and the execution were important.

For him a novel "in its broadest definition" was "a personal, a direct impression of life: that, to begin with, constitutes its value, which is greater or less according to the intensity of the impression." For a person with the kind of sensitivity needed in writing great fiction, he went on, "Experience is never limited, and it is never complete; it is an immense sensibility, a kind of huge spider-web of the finest silken threads suspended in the chamber of consciousness, and catching every air-borne particle in its tissue." Since "impressions were experience," James did not hesitate to advise the novice, "Try to be one of the people on whom nothing is lost!"

But having gained such a sensitive and complete impression of life, the artist, James contended, also had the problem of giving his fiction "that air of reality (solidity of specification)" which he felt was "the supreme virtue of the novel — the merit on which all its other merits . . . helplessly and submissively depend." James was aware throughout his career that to achieve this end through artistry was a highly complicated and delicate business. A brilliant series of Prefaces which he wrote, in his maturity, for the volumes of his collected works showed in detail how, during his artistic lifetime, he struggled with problems of form to give his writings exactly the intended "effects."

Such a conception of fiction clearly sets James off from those practitioners who believed that the best fiction was the exact reproduction of life as well as from those who believed that it was an embodiment of naturalistic generalizations about life. Since he saw reality — even generalizations about reality — as a series of impressions, and since he saw fiction as the artistic rendition of such impressions, his sort of realism was essentially a complicated psychological process. In his writings, more than others, therefore, one sees the impact of the newer psychology upon which his brother, William James, was a leading authority. One sees, too, progress in the development of a technique which had been notably advanced even before James by George Eliot in England and Gustave Flaubert in France — the technique of making new psychological insights a vital part of fiction.

How James' notions led him to shape the form of a narrative is shown in some of the details in his 1907 Preface to *Roderick Hudson* (1876), wherein he told how that book had been written. After a "story idea" had come to him, the chief difficulty, he suggested, was to decide exactly how to limit "developments" so as to interrelate them. "Up to what point," he asked himself, "is such and such a development *indispensable* to interest? . . . When, for the complete expression of one's subject, does a particular relation stop — giving way to some other not concerned in that expression?" The complexity of experience made this problem difficult: "Really, universally, relations stop nowhere, and the exquisite problem of the artist is eternally but to draw, by a geometry of his own, the circle within which they shall happily *appear* to do so." Selection and arrangement therefore were absolutely necessary. He needed to hit upon exactly the right details of background; he needed (though later he felt he had failed, in this particular book) to devise an adequate time scheme; he needed — and this was very important — to find a "centre, the point of command of all the rest." In this story, such a center was the impression of the whole action received by someone other than Hudson:

> From this centre the subject has been treated, from this centre the interest has spread, and so, whatever else it may do or may not do, the thing has acknowledged a principle of composition and continues at least to hang together. . . . The centre of interest throughout . . . is Rowland Mallet's consciousness — which I had of course to make sufficiently acute to enable it, like a set and lighted scene, to hold the play.

James believed that what Mallet saw, felt, or guessed could, if properly rendered, be made to give the story unity, movement, and meaning. Though James gave details about a number of additional procedures, this summary traces a main line of his typical thought about his artistry.

An author with such concerns was bound to write narratives which differed greatly from those by most contemporaries. James was horrified by the formlessness of many fictional works. He believed that ". . . a novel is a living thing, all one and continuous, like any other organism, and in proportion as it lives it will be found, I think, that in each of the parts is something of the other parts." And he learned that often his most useful step in achieving selectivity and arrangement necessary for such an organic entity was the location of the story in a consciousness "connected intimately with the general human exposure, and thereby bedimmed, befooled and bewildered, anxious, restless, fallible," in short "not *too* acute," but endowed "with such intelligence that the appearances reflected in it, and constituting together there the situation and the 'story,' should become by that fact intelligible." Thus the sensitive author had, in the story, a sensitive counterpart whose limitations and perceptions both bounded and filled in the pattern. Working in such a fashion, James became a leader in calling attention to the importance of the "fictional point of view" — to the values to be derived from letting a narrative unfold as it was experienced by some character. Psychology thus became of central importance, particularly in such masterpieces as *The Wings of the Dove* (1902), *The Ambassadors* (1903), and *The Golden Bowl* (1904), and its hitherto unexploited potentialities for writers were suggested to a great number of authors who followed James.

The Drama

In general, the period between the Civil War and 1914 was one of depression in the history of American drama. Hundreds of plays, to be sure, were produced, and many were admired; but few have proved to be worthy of memory. As Barrett Clark says of the plays of the period in *An Hour of American Drama:* "It is not the quaintness of the language and the labored style of these plays that has caused them to be forgotten, it is the fundamental fact that they are the products of superficial writers, of men who could believe that 'plays are not written but rewritten,' an epigram appropriately attributed to [such popular playwrights of the period as] Boucicault, Bronson Howard, Augustin Daly, Augustus Thomas, and a dozen other able playmakers. The kind of plays these men wrote were indeed rewritten: they had to be. But here 'rewritten' means picked apart, built up, 'lifted,' like a dowager's face, put on a diet, painted, and rouged." During this comparatively arid period, productive chiefly of melodramas and slick plays cunningly designed to lure cash customers, there were three tendencies of some significance, each comparable to some contemporary development in fiction: toward realism, toward the more intelligent consideration of serious problems, and toward symbolism.

Hamlin Garland, lecturing on "Local Color in Fiction and Drama," was able, so he said later, to consider quite a few playwrights who, like his favorite fiction writers, were moving toward realism via stage representations of the life and character of certain regions. Examples — typical, though in some ways superior — were Bronson Howard (1842-1908), who in *Shenandoah* (1888) vividly pictured the valley of the title as it had been during the war; James A. Herne (1839-1901), who made a noteworthy effort to draw true-to-life characters against a homely background in *Margaret Fleming* (1890) and *Shore Acres* (1892); and Augustus Thomas (1857-1934), who dramatized the life of varied sections in plays such as *Alabama* (1891), *In Mizzouri* (1893), *The Capitol* (1895), and *Arizona* (1899).

These same authors serve as well as others to show how the drama, like the novel of purpose, began to consider various problems. Here, Americans were particularly influenced by the Norwegian Henrik Ibsen (1828-1906), who became world-famous during this period as an author of problem plays. Herne's *Shore Acres* was much discussed not only because it was realistic but also because it contained references to advanced scientific and social ideas, and *Margaret Fleming* dealt with family relationships in a fashion then considered quite daring. Bronson Howard's *The Henrietta* (1887) satirized the fever and the greed of financial and social life. And Thomas treated pseudo-scientific topics such as hypnotism, psychological domination, and mental healing in plays including *The Witching Hour* (1907) and *As a Man Thinks* (1911).

Toward the end of the period, many critics of the day found in Clyde Fitch (1865-1909) a man who could fuse sincerity and artistry with good theater. Fitch's creed, as he expressed it in "The Play and the Public," sounded like one of the definitions of realism then current in writings about fiction:

> In the modern play, I feel myself very strongly the particular value — a value I can't help feeling inestimable — of reflecting absolutely and truthfully the life and environment about us. Be truthful, and then nothing can be too big, nothing should be too small, so long as it is here, and there. Every class, every kind, every emotion, every motive, every occupation, every business, every idleness. . . . Apart from the question of literalism, apart from the question of art, reflect the real thing with true observation and with sincere feeling for what it is and what it represents, and that is art and literature.

Fitch tried to follow this formula in a varied group of plays, dramas which not only tried to be "true to life" but which also commented upon various problems. *The Climbers* (1901) and *The City* (1909) were serious portrayals of various aspects — political, financial, and social — of New York life. *The Girl with the Green Eyes* (1902) and *The Truth* (1907) were interesting psychological studies, the first of a character abnormally jealous, the second of a congenital liar. The feeling of a reader today is likely to be that these plays have fine stuff in them — as fine as anything to be found in the theater of the era — but that they suffer because Fitch, like other dramatists, had to shape his work to make it appeal to theatergoers who were a little too fond of broad effects.

Two authors were ranked with Fitch, or even above him: Langdon

Mitchell and William Vaughn Moody. In *The New York Idea* (1906), Mitchell, active contemporaneously with Fitch, showed rather more of a tendency to deal with problems than a tendency toward realism. Nevertheless, since this drama, like Royall Tyler's *The Contrast* and a host of other plays, was a social comedy, it was essentially realistic in a good many of its details. And its deft construction and witty dialog made it more memorable than many dramas of its day which were heavily serious.

William Vaughn Moody, a poet and a professor, started his career as a "practical dramatist" after having written poetic dramas which were profound in their ideas and impressive as poetry, but which had no chance of professional presentation. When he tried his hand at writing plays which might be produced, his very aloofness from the commercial theater helped him avoid some of its bad tendencies. As Walter Prichard Eaton remarks in *The Drama in English:* "The superficial traits of modern drama meant little to him, one way or the other. It was its deeper spirit he was after." Having such an attitude, and having, moreover, a real flair for dramatizing the psychologies of characters and for representing ideas by action, he wrote for the stage *The Great Divide* (1906), a surprisingly successful play. This drama had in it, to be sure, elements of sensationalism and melodrama; but these were means to an end rather than ends themselves. Actually *The Great Divide* was a symbolic representation of the conflict between the Puritanical tradition of New England on the one hand and, on the other, the frontier's impulsive gusto for life. It showed the approach of a poet. "Poetry," Moody believed, "is the salvation of the stage. . . . It is the poetry in a play that makes it great." A play written in such a spirit, although in retrospect it might seem a bit crude, pointed to a better period in the American theater. As Mr. Eaton asserts, "With a play like this the modern drama in America was coming of age." It was not to come fully of age, however, until after 1914. The greatest achievements of the era between the Civil War and World War I were decidedly not in drama or (except in a few instances) in poetry, but in fiction.

W.B.

Chronological Table of LITERATURE AND HISTORY

1866 ■ Whittier's *Snow-Bound* · Charles H. Smith's *Bill Arp, So Called* · John W. DeForest's *Miss Ravenel's Conversion*

Civil Rights Bill passed, designed to assure equal treatment of Southern Negroes · Ku Klux Klan organized

1867 ■ Henry Timrod's "Ode" · George W. Harris' *Sut Lovingood Yarns* ·

Lowell's *The Biglow Papers, Second Series* · Bret Harte's *Condensed Novels*

Alaska purchased from Russia · Nebraska admitted as the thirty-seventh state · Reconstruction Act passed, providing conditions of the return of the Confederate States to the Union

1868 ■ *The Overland Monthly* (1868-1933) established in California · Harte's "The Luck of Roaring Camp"

Fourteenth Amendment, guaranteeing fair trial for all persons, ratified · President Johnson impeached, acquitted · Ulysses S. Grant elected eighteenth President

1869 ■ Harte's "Tennessee's Partner," "The Outcasts of Poker Flat" · Mark Twain's *The Innocents Abroad*

Fifteenth Amendment, ensuring Negro suffrage, ratified · Union Pacific Railway completed first transcontinental line, 10 May · "Black Friday" in New York, caused by gold corner, 24 September · Opening of the Suez Canal, 15 November

1870 ■ Lowell's *Among My Books* · Bronson Howard's *Saratoga* · Harte's "Plain Language from Truthful James" · Joaquin Miller's *Songs of the Sierras* · Emerson's *Society and Solitude*

United States census: population 38,558,371

1871 ■ Edward Eggleston's *The Hoosier Schoolmaster* · Walt Whitman's *Democratic Vistas* · Harriet Beecher Stowe's *Oldtown Fireside Stories*

1872 ■ Mark Twain's *Roughing It* · Holmes' *The Poet at the Breakfast-Table* · William D. Howells' *Their Wedding Journey*

Grant reëlected

1873 ■ Mark Twain and Charles Dudley Warner's *The Gilded Age* · Howells' *A Chance Acquaintance*

Financial panic began, 19 September

1875 ■ Sidney Lanier's "Corn," "The Symphony" · Howells' *A Foregone Conclusion* · Mary Baker Eddy's *Science and Health*

1876 ■ Twain's *The Adventures of Tom Sawyer* · Henry James' *Roderick Hudson*

Rutherford B. Hayes elected nineteenth President · Colorado admitted as the thirty-eighth state

1877 ■ James' *The American* · Lanier's *Poems* · Sarah Orne Jewett's *Deephaven*

1878 ■ James' *Daisy Miller* · Lanier's "The Marshes of Glynn," "The Revenge of Hamish"

1879 ■ James' *Hawthorne* · George W. Cable's *Old Creole Days* · James A. Herne's *Hearts of Oak* · Frank R. Stockton's *Rudder Grange* · Howells' *The Lady of the Aroostook* · Henry George's *Progress and Poverty*

1880 ■ Twain's *A Tramp Abroad* · Henry Adams' *Democracy* · Lew Wallace's *Ben Hur* · Lanier's *The Science of English Verse* · Joel Chandler Harris' *Uncle Remus: His Songs and Sayings* · Steele MacKaye's *Hazel Kirke*

United States census: population 50,155,783 · James A. Garfield elected twentieth President

1881 ■ James' *The Portrait of a Lady*

Garfield shot, 2 July; died, 19 September; succeeded by Chester A. Arthur as twenty-first President · Tuskegee Institute founded · Federation of Organized Trades and Labor Unions, forerunner of the American Federation of Labor, founded

1882 ■ Stockton's "The Lady or the Tiger?" · Twain's *The Prince and the Pauper* · Howells' *A Modern Instance*

1883 ■ Edgar Watson Howe's *The Story of a Country Town* · Harris' *Nights with Uncle Remus* · Twain's *Life on the Mississippi*

1884 ■ Twain's *Huckleberry Finn* · Lanier's *Poems* · Mary Noailles Murfree's *In the Tennessee Mountains* · Lowell's "Democracy" · Helen Hunt Jackson's *Ramona*

Grover Cleveland elected twenty-second President

1885 ■ Murfree's *The Prophet of the Great Smoky Mountains* · Howells' *The Rise of Silas Lapham*

1886 ■ James' *The Princess Casamassima*

Haymarket Riot in Chicago turned public opinion against labor organizations · American Federation of Labor organized under the leadership of Samuel Gompers

1887 ■ Harold Frederic's *Seth's Brother's Wife* · Joseph Kirkland's *Zury* · Mary E. Wilkins Freeman's *A Humble Romance* · Thomas Nelson Page's *In Ole Virginia*

1888 ■ Edward Bellamy's *Looking Backward* · Howard's *Shenandoah* · Whitman's *November Boughs* and *Complete Poems and Prose* (1888-1889)

Benjamin Harrison elected twenty-third President

1889 ■ Twain's *A Connecticut Yankee*

North Dakota and South Dakota admitted as thirty-ninth and fortieth states, Montana as forty-first, Washington as forty-second

1890 ■ Emily Dickinson's *Poems* · James' *The Tragic Muse* · Howells' *A Hazard of New Fortunes*

United States census: population 62,979,766 · Sherman Anti-Trust Act · Idaho admitted as forty-third state, Wyoming as forty-fourth

1891 ■ Hamlin Garland's *Main-Travelled Roads* · Howells' *Criticism and Fiction* · Freeman's *A New England Nun and Other Stories* · Ambrose Bierce's *Tales of Soldiers and Civilians*

1892 ■ Herne's *Shore Acres*

Grover Cleveland reëlected

1893 ■ Frederick J. Turner's "The Significance of the Frontier in American History" · Stephen Crane's *Maggie: A Girl of the Streets*

1894 ■ Twain's *Pudd'nhead Wilson* · James Lane Allen's *A Kentucky Cardinal* · Howells' *A Traveler from Altruria*

Pullman strike; widespread sympathetic strikes called by American Railway Union; Federal troops called out and Sherman Anti-Trust Act invoked in settlement of Pullman dispute

1895 ■ Crane's *The Black Riders, and Other Lines* and *The Red Badge of Courage* · Garland's *Rose of Dutcher's Coolly*

1896 ■ Jewett's *The Country of the Pointed Firs* · Edwin A. Robinson's *The Torrent and the Night Before* · Twain's *Joan of Arc* · Frederic's *The Damnation of Theron Ware*

William McKinley elected twenty-fifth President · Utah admitted as forty-fifth state

1897 ■ Henry James' *What Maisie Knew* and *The Spoils of Poynton* · Robinson's *The Children of the Night* · William James' *The Will to Believe* · Twain's *Following the Equator*

1898 ■ Crane's "The Open Boat" · Finley Peter Dunne's *Mr. Dooley in Peace and in War* · Henry James' *The Turn of the Screw*

Destruction of the battleship *Maine* precipitated Spanish-American War, which resulted in United States' acquisition of Puerto Rico, Guam, and the Philippines

1899 ■ Frank Norris' *McTeague* · James' *The Awkward Age* · Crane's *War Is Kind* and *The Monster and Other Stories* · Dunne's *Mr. Dooley in the Hearts of His Countrymen* · Edwin Markham's "The Man with the Hoe" · Thorstein Veblen's *The Theory of the Leisure Class*

1900 ■ Theodore Dreiser's *Sister Carrie* · Crane's *Whilomville Stories* · Howells' *Literary Friends and Acquaintance* · Ellen Glasgow's *The Voice of the People* · William V. Moody's "An Ode in Time of Hesitation"

United States census: population 76,303,387 · President McKinley reëlected

1901 ■ Norris' *The Octopus* · Moody's *Poems* · Clyde Fitch's *The Climbers* · Booker T. Washington's *Up from Slavery*

McKinley shot, 6 September; died, 14 September; succeeded by Theodore Roosevelt as twenty-sixth President

1902 ■ Robinson's *Captain Craig* · Owen Wister's *The Virginian* · James' *The Wings of the Dove* · Fitch's *Girl with the Green Eyes* · Glasgow's *The Battleground* · Edith Wharton's *The Valley of Decision*

1903 ■ Norris' *The Pit* · James' *The Ambassadors* · Jack London's *The Call of the Wild*

1904 ■ Lincoln Steffens' *The Shame of the Cities* · Ida Tarbell's *History of the Standard Oil Company* · Paul Elmer More's *Shelburne Essays* (1904-1935) · Adams' *Mont-Saint-Michel and Chartres* · O. Henry's *Cabbages and Kings* · James' *The Golden Bowl*

Theodore Roosevelt elected President

1905 ■ Howells' *The Kentons* · Wharton's *The House of Mirth* · David Belasco's *The Girl of the Golden West*

1906 ■ Augustus Thomas' *The Witching Hour* · Upton Sinclair's *The Jungle* · Langdon E. Mitchell's *The New York Idea* · Moody's *The Great Divide* · O. Henry's *The Four Million*

1907 ■ Adams' *The Education of Henry Adams*

Oklahoma admitted as forty-sixth state

1908 William Howard Taft elected twenty-seventh President

1909 ■ William Allen White's *A Certain Rich Man* · Gertrude Stein's *Three Lives* · Moody's *The Faith Healer* · Percy MacKaye's *The Scarecrow*

1910 ■ Robinson's *The Town Down the River* · John A. Lomax' *Cowboy Songs* · Irving Babbitt's *The New Laokoön*

United States census: population 93,402,151

1911 ■ Dreiser's *Jennie Gerhardt* · Wharton's *Ethan Frome*

1912 ■ Dreiser's *The Financier* · Amy Lowell's *A Dome of Many-Coloured Glass* · Robinson Jeffers' *Flagons and Apples* · *Poetry: A Magazine of Verse* founded

Woodrow Wilson elected twenty-eighth President · New Mexico admitted as forty-seventh state, Arizona as forty-eighth

1913 ■ Robert Frost's *A Boy's Will* · Vachel Lindsay's *General William Booth Enters into Heaven and Other Poems* · Willa Cather's *O Pioneers!*

Sixteenth (income tax) and Seventeenth (direct senatorial election) Amendments ratified

6

U. S. A.
1914 to the present

"U.S.A. is the slice of a continent. . . . U.S.A. is the world's greatest rivervalley fringed with mountains and hills. . . . But mostly U.S.A. is the speech of the people."

DOS PASSOS

INTELLECTUAL CURRENTS

The Modern Pessimism

Thinking of the Civil War, Hawthorne spoke of the tragedy in the lives of the women whose husbands and sweethearts were killed in battle: "The girls that would have loved them," he said, "and made happy firesides for them, will pine and wither, and tread along many sour and discontented years, and at last go out of life without knowing what life is. Every shot that takes effect kills one and worse than kills the other." This aspect of war's aftermath found expression in many literary works during and after World War I. Two illustrations will suffice: Amy Lowell's "Patterns" (1915) and Eugene O'Neill's *Strange Interlude* (1928). The poem is a powerful expression of sexual frustration:

> For the man who should loose me is dead,
> Fighting with the Duke of Flanders,
> In a pattern called a war.
> Christ! What are patterns for?

In the "strangled explosion" of the last line, "half-oath, half-prayer" (as Foster Damon, Miss Lowell's biographer, aptly describes it), is compressed much of war's misery. Instead of the rigid self-control described in Miss Lowell's poem, O'Neill, in a similar situation, shows breakdown. After the death of her fiancé in the war, Nina Leeds went to pieces, giving herself promiscuously to the men in an army hospital. One of the characters in the play attributed her behavior to "a desire to be kind" and "a morbid longing for martyrdom." In both instances the psychological effects of war on women are poignantly portrayed.

Other literary works deal with actual participants in World War I. John Dos Passos' *Three Soldiers* (1921) is concerned chiefly with the irksomeness of army life to a man of aesthetic temperament. John Andrews, graduate of Harvard, wanted to write great music. When he was arrested for desertion at the end of the story, the wind scattered about the room the leaves of the musical score on which he had been working. War is hateful to the artist, Dos Passos said, and destructive of his art. In the minds of many men — whether artists or persons of average sensitivity — the war left memories of experiences which they tried in vain to forget. The case of the war veteran, Stetson, in T. S. Eliot's *The Waste Land* (1922) is a classic instance. Stetson's tragic experience is likened to a corpse "planted" in a garden, which will either be dug up by "the Dog" of memory or "sprout" and "bloom" in the subconscious mind.

The tragic effects of World War I are best epitomized, perhaps, in Ernest Hemingway's *The Sun Also Rises* (1926) and *A Farewell to Arms* (1929). In *The Sun Also Rises* we are shown the "lost generation" of expatriates who, with shattered nerves and illusions, sought amusement and forgetfulness at bullfights in Spain and in the cafés of Paris. The chief character, Jake Barnes, had been made sexually impotent by a physical injury received in the war. His condition is symbolic of the spiritual impotence of the "lost generation." In *A Farewell to Arms* the war again deprived its victims of high aims and ideals. After the "Retreat from Caporetto" (which has been justly called the finest account in all literature of the collapse of an army) Frederic Henry, the American ambulance driver, could see nothing worth living for except physical satisfactions. In the wreckage of the world about him, thought became a torment and a futile occupation. Hence his famous conclusion: "I was not made to think. I was made to eat. My God, yes. Eat and drink and sleep with Catherine."

A new criticism of America. We had entered World War I, as Woodrow Wilson optimistically expressed it, "to make the world safe for democracy," and the failure of that high mission produced a cynical reaction in many minds. Possibly the United States was hardly qualified to play such an exalted role. It was natural that many writers should turn a critical — sometimes a jaundiced — eye upon the American scene and that they should see much more to condemn than to admire. "Debunking" became a favorite literary approach; after Pearl Harbor it was called "selling America short."

Biographers of the 1920's attempted to show that our national idols had feet of clay. Historians insisted that materialistic rather than idealistic motives had determined the entire course of our history since Jamestown and Plymouth Rock. The most popular magazine of the period among the literate was H. L. Mencken's *American Mercury*, which exposed in a monthly department called "Americana" a wealth of current stupidities —at once laughable and deplorable—culled from the newspapers of the forty-eight states.

The most effective and the most popular criticism of the American scene of the twenties was written by Sinclair Lewis. His *Main Street* (1920) satirized the small town of the Middle West, where Lewis found "dullness made God." *Babbitt* (1922) ridiculed the American businessman so successfully that the words "Babbitt" and "Babbittry" were added to the dictionary. The hard-hitting satire got under the skins of many Rotarians and boosters. Among the items in Lewis' indictment were questionable business ethics, an undeveloped literary taste, commercial criteria of success, and ultraconservatism in social and political thinking. *Babbitt* epitomized the unlovely aspects of the Harding era. *Arrowsmith* (1925) showed an America inimical to scholarship and pure research. Heroically devoted to medical experimentation, Dr. Martin Arrowsmith found many stupid obstacles in his path. *Dodsworth* (1929) satirized the American woman. Fran Dodsworth was unmercifully exposed as a pampered, selfish, superficial, pretentious snob; she is the most damning portrait in Lewis' entire gallery. Reading between the lines today, one can see that Lewis really enjoyed many of the people whom he ridiculed and relished much in the life which he professed to view with contempt, and that he would not exchange his Gopher Prairie or his Zenith for Utopia. But readers in the 1920's saw only the devastating satire; they hailed him as the greatest of all debunkers, being unaware that he transcended the narrow boundaries of the debunking age. His greatness may very well lie in the subtle quality which escaped his current readers.

Though Lewis was the chief of the satirists in the 1920's, many other writers presented indictments of America. Theodore Dreiser's *An American Tragedy* (1925) showed a society vitiated by perverted notions of the good life. Though the reader might wonder if Clyde Griffiths would have amounted to much under ideal conditions, the mores of his materialistic and class-conscious world were bad enough to corrupt a stronger character. Carl Sandburg clearly described the increasing evils of capitalism: "people living in shanties," "$6 a week department store girls," "steel trust wops, dead without having lived, gray and shrunken at forty years of age." Allied with Big Business, the Church, Sandburg charged, travestied the teachings of Jesus. Following Sandburg's lead, other writers directed attention to conditions among the workers, and the word "proletariat" came for the first time into general American use. O'Neill's *The Hairy Ape* (1922) presented the worker's increasing dissociation from his work, his growing feeling of not "belonging." Carlyle had pointed out nearly a hundred years earlier the inadequacy, from the human standpoint, of the "cash-payment nexus": a feeling of loyalty, of belonging, is necessary to a man's satisfaction in his work. It is still perhaps the central problem of modern industrialism. While O'Neill expressed the problem in stirring modern terms, he offered nothing constructive: the conclusion of *The Hairy Ape* is futile and defeatist. In another remarkable play of the twenties (*The Adding Machine*, 1923), Elmer Rice argued that the modern machine had a degrading effect upon the worker, that machine-tending is the lowest of all serfdoms in human history, and that man deteriorates as the machine improves. It seemed bitterly ironical to the author that "the finest triumph of the evolutionary process" should be a machine-tender, "operating a super-hyper-adding machine with the great toe of his right foot." A distinguished anthropologist expressed a similar view of the problem when he said: "There is real danger that the engineers will make apes of all of us. By the invention of tools, engineers brought man up from the level of an ape, but the human curve starts downward when tools can be used without cerebral exertion, when the individual is allowed not only to stop sweating but also to stop thinking."

Despite these and other searching criticisms, the general public of the 1920's was relatively complacent. For the three consecutive administrations of Harding, Coolidge, and Hoover, political conservatism was predominant. Successful investors enjoyed a rapidly mounting "prosperity." Yale undergraduates (see Lewis' *Dodsworth*) aspired to become Wall Street brokers and owners of yachts. Poor boys with ability and nerve, like Fitzgerald's Gatsby (*The Great Gatsby*, 1925), amassed wealth quickly and spent it gaudily in the attempt to realize the dreams of their youth; Fitzgerald's novel, indeed, is a brilliant representation of the tinsel and corruption of this whole fabulous era. A few economists foresaw the crash of 1929, but their warnings were overridden by the mania for money. Irving Fisher and President Hoover assured us to the bitter end that the economic structure of the country was "fundamentally sound." After the crash came the Great Depression.

During the years of the Great Depression, criticism of America in literature became more serious, more bitter, and more brutal. Whether the accounts presented were of contemporary life or of life in an earlier period, many writers joined in a strident, damning chorus. With lurid, Gothic power, William Faulkner's novels told of violence and moral perversion in "Jefferson," Mississippi. These works were to acquire for readers rich symbolic meanings: in the words of his best early interpreter, George Marion O'Donnell, Faulkner "projected in fiction the conflict between his inherent traditional values and the modern world." Nearer the naturalistic level was James T. Farrell's *Studs Lonigan* (1932-1935), which showed the collapse of middle-class morality in south-side Chicago. The traditional character-building institutions—the home, the school, and the church—were powerless to prevent the moral ruin of Studs. Again starkly, but with human warmth, John Steinbeck's *The Grapes of Wrath* (1939)—perhaps the best single expression in our literature of the difficulties peculiar to the Depression—told of the Joads of Oklahoma, who were tractored off the land, of their westward migration in a jalopy, and of their sufferings in California, where the family of seven workers, including women and children, were able to earn the sum total of $3.50 a day. The book gives an impression of a powerful mass movement: the Okies are less arresting as individuals than as representatives of the mass. The proletarian novel "arrived" in *The Grapes of Wrath*.

The dominance of science and quasi-science. Not only the wreckage of war and the mounting criticism of American economic and social life, but science too contributed to the dominant mood of pessimism between the wars. Perhaps it would be more correct to say "popular science," for the reference is not to science as such, but to its embodiment in literature, where it is easily susceptible of misconstruction and falsification. In any case, the scientist is hardly to blame. It is regrettable that some of his discoveries had unfortunate results.

The new physics gave the impression to the lay mind that the universe is somehow doomed. Historians and interpreters of science had much to say in the twenties and thirties about the second law of thermodynamics or the law of entropy, which seemed to mean that energy is deteriorating or becoming less available, that the universe is cooling off and running down, and that the earth will someday be unfit for human habitation. The ultimate destination of man on this planet appeared to be the "heat-death." This view of things colored the thinking of many moderns, writers and readers alike; it found its most forceful literary expression in the pessimistic poetry of Robinson Jeffers who wrote in "To the Stone Cutters":

> . . . man will be blotted out, the blithe earth die,
>   the brave sun
> Die blind, his heart blackening.

It was better so, the poet reasoned, for he saw in man's deepest nature a subconscious desire to return to the prenatal darkness and silence of the womb. In "Night" he declared,

> The sun-lovers have a blond favorite,
> A father of lights and noises, wars, weeping, and
>   laughter,
> Hot labor, lust and delight and the other blemishes.

Quietness
Flows from her deeper fountain; and he [the sun] will
    die; and she [the night] is immortal.

Inspired by the new physics, Jeffers regarded life as a "blemish," and extinction as the greatest good.

Freudian psychology, too, left its mark everywhere in the literature between the wars. Possibly the first fictional work in America to exemplify the conscious and deliberate use of Freudian principles was Sherwood Anderson's *Winesburg, Ohio* (1919), where almost everyone is abnormal and the abnormalities are explained in terms of sexual repression. O'Neill's *Strange Interlude* (1928) and *Mourning Becomes Electra* (1931) appear to have been constructed from Freudian blueprints. The new psychological principles were employed also in biography and literary history. Psychoanalyzing Poe (*Edgar Allan Poe*, 1926), Joseph Wood Krutch believed that Poe's sexual impotence accounted for much that is distinctive in his poems and tales. Applying Freud to American literary history (*Expression in America*, 1932), Ludwig Lewisohn was able to reveal an amazing number and variety of psychological maladies among men of letters: Hawthorne's sense of guilt, for example, was "precipitated by the incest wish of infancy." By the middle thirties many sophisticated moderns, through a kind of "scientific" mania for sex-analysis and sex-experimentation, had succeeded in making themselves almost as morbid on the subject as the prudish, hypocritical Victorians, whom they regarded with unmitigated horror (note Lewisohn's remarks on Howells in *Expression in America*).

Closely associated in the popular mind with Freudian psychology was the biology of glandular secretions, which, to many, seemed a new source of tyranny. Oversexed persons, like Lady Brett in Hemingway's *The Sun Also Rises*, could blame the endocrine or some other glands for their immoral behavior. Stupid, brutal persons, like Lennie in Steinbeck's *Of Mice and Men* (1937), could point to hypothyroidism as the sign of their fate. Little by little, the modern sciences, which had begun as a great liberating force, seemed to be imprisoning man as tightly as he had ever been imprisoned by the pseudosciences of the Middle Ages.

The new sciences of economics and sociology also tended to overplay their legitimate roles. Charles A. Beard (*An Economic Interpretation of the Constitution*, 1913) and his successors exaggerated the importance of economic factors in American history. V. L. Parrington (*Main Currents in American Thought*, 1927-1930) and his disciples likewise exaggerated the importance of economic elements in American literature. It is not surprising that in much of the fiction of the period economic pressure appeared decisive or that before the end of the period man's life appeared to consist, contrary to Holy Writ, of the commodities which he possessed. Meanwhile, social pressures vied strenuously with the economic ones for the honor of being the chief determinant in human destiny.

William Graham Sumner had declared that folkways were decisive, and his successors elaborated and illustrated the proposition. Clyde Griffiths in Dreiser's *An American Tragedy* and Studs Lonigan in Farrell's trilogy demonstrated brilliantly enough the apparent impossibility of escape from the environment.

The helplessness of the individual. Many signs, in short, seemed to point to the growing helplessness of the individual. There no longer appeared to be any such thing as an autonomous and morally responsible person. In actual life, of course, there were many such persons, but the species well-nigh disappeared from books written in the spirit of the age. This spirit found its best philosophical statement in Joseph Wood Krutch's *The Modern Temper* (1929). Modern civilization, to Krutch, was decadent, for thought itself is a mark of decadence. The future belongs, as always, to the barbarians, "absorbed in the processes of life for their own sake, eating without asking if it is worthwhile to eat, begetting children without asking why they should beget them, and conquering without asking for what purpose they conquer."

The poets brilliantly expressed the mood of failure and despair. Robinson's "man against the sky" was by no means sure that he was not pursuing a

> blind atomic pilgrimage
> Whereon by crass chance billeted we go. . . .

Eliot gave the classic picture of futility in "The Love Song of J. Alfred Prufrock":

> "I have measured out my life with coffee spoons. . . ."

The Hamlet of A. MacLeish (1928) echoed, with modern mutations and overtones, the despair of Shakespeare's Hamlet:

> Thou wouldst not think
> How ill all's here about my heart!

These three poems may be taken as sufficiently characteristic of the period. The Hamlet mood was congenial to all of them, but they exemplified Hamlet's confusion and indecision rather than his capacity for heroic action. Submerged in endless debate, the man against the sky or Prufrock or MacLeish's Hamlet could never have killed the king.

While Krutch and the intellectual poets were displaying the helplessness of the thinking man, entangled in the toils of thought, the novelists were discovering another kind of helplessness in the masses of men — a helplessness obviously not explicable by intellectualism, but by biological and social determinism. Several novels already mentioned — *An American Tragedy, Studs Lonigan, The Grapes of Wrath* — abundantly illustrate the tyranny of social and economic pressure and the impotence of the individual in the face of overwhelming circumstance. But the most complete illustration in American fiction of the modern determinism is Dos Passos' trilogy *U.S.A.* (published in one volume in 1937), which is at once — in the apt description of Alfred Kazin — "the dominant social novel of the thirties" and "the coldest and most mechanical of tragic novels." It is indeed our largest and most comprehensive fictional gallery of human automatons. The reader finds it difficult, if not impossible, to take an interest in its people as persons: it has been justly said that Dos Passos did not create character. The twenty-odd people in *U.S.A.* exhibit the mechanical behavior, the unawareness, the moral irresponsibility, of robots, as they are pushed about over the continents by irrational force. A contradiction in the novel, of which the author may not have been aware, affords the only ground for hope: unlike the fictional characters, the subjects of the "biographies," which were taken from contemporary history, are by no means helpless. The discrepancy suggests how far the pattern of the social novel in the middle thirties had deviated from life.

Counter Attitudes

American literature between the wars was thus predominantly pessimistic. It would be a mistake, however, to suppose that all American literature in this period was negative and despairing. The old positive forces were not dead; they were rooted too deeply in man's nature to die. It goes without saying that certain names appearing among those supporting the prevalent pessimism will reappear among those expressing more positive views, for few writers were entirely negative or completely pessimistic.

First among the positive forces was what Browning called "our manhood's prime vigor": "How good is man's life, the mere living!" exclaimed that now unfashionable Victorian poet. However outmoded his message, one would not expect to find an entire generation of American writers silent on this theme. In fact, it appears frequently in the literature of the period between the wars. The most notable examples of *élan vital* are found in the writings of those incorrigible romanticists, Ernest Hemingway and Thomas Wolfe. Whatever the state of the world at large might be, these writers were still able to enjoy living. No author has ever shown a greater spirit of youth than Wolfe. In this respect he stands at the opposite pole from Jeffers. No author has ever celebrated friendship and love with greater ardor and tenderness than Hemingway. At the end of *For Whom the Bell Tolls* (1940), Robert Jordan "told himself," "You had a lot of luck to have had such a good life."

Other instinctive forces which would not stay down, no matter how mechanical or scientific the age, were the love of the earth, the love of humanity, the love of country—they appeared separately and combined in a variety of patterns. The good earth was never better than in the poems of the late Robert Frost, and was never exhibited with greater tang or economic urgency than in the essays of the Southern Agrarians (*I'll Take My Stand*, 1930), who brilliantly argued for the way of life of Thomas Jefferson and John Taylor of Virginia. Love of humanity still manifested itself, ranging from individuals to the mass, from personal kindness to faith in the common man. Sandburg was devoted to "the people" with an ardor as warm as Whitman's and more militant. People were "beautiful" to William Saroyan. Steinbeck's characters had a friendly warmth: human kindness could hardly go further than in the concluding scene of *The Grapes of Wrath*. Love of country still flourished, ranging between a lively sense of the past and its historic glories and a passionate, instinctive attachment to the place of one's birth. Stephen Vincent Benét was inspired by the history of the Civil War to write our most praised historical verse narrative in *John Brown's Body* (1928). Wolfe's devotion to America was more instinctive. To him, it was the "fabulous country—the place where miracles not only happen, but where they happen all the time" (*Of Time and the River*, 1935). Like Whitman, he tried to take in all of America equally, though neither quite succeeded; for just as Whitman's affection was intensely localized in Manhattan and the Brooklyn Ferry, so Wolfe's was rooted deepest in "old Catawba, there in the hills of home," the hills of North Carolina.

The positive forces thus far considered were largely instinctive, but there were also positive intellectual and moral forces at work in the literature of the twenties and thirties. In the midst of a world which appeared given over to naturalism and lawlessness, the "neohumanists" —Paul Elmer More, Irving Babbitt, and Norman Foerster—argued for the necessity of discipline, of standards of excellence, and of traditional values. Control must come from within, they reasoned; the "inner check" is the only saving virtue, and the most available sources of that virtue are the classic disciplines (*Humanism and America*, 1930, by Foerster and others). Less "humanistic" but more human and genuinely fortifying was the note sounded with charm and firmness by two of the finest novelists of the period—Ellen Glasgow and Willa Cather. While most of the male novelists were advertising failure, Miss Glasgow and Miss Cather preferred to show the possibility of success. In *Barren Ground* (1925), Miss Glasgow reversed two stock pictures of failure: failure on the farm and failure through disappointment in love. It had been generally supposed that success of any sort on a farm was no longer possible, but Dorinda Oakley actually reclaimed the barren ground, thereby fulfilling Lanier's prophecy in "Corn" fifty years earlier. It had been generally supposed, too—especially in the South—that a girl could scarcely survive disappointment in love, but Dorinda survived. "Dorinda exists," Miss Glasgow declared, "wherever the spirit of fortitude has triumphed over the sense of futility." Miss Cather also showed the triumph of fortitude. *My Ántonia* (1918) portrayed a pioneer immigrant woman, passionately devoted to her family and to her life on the Nebraska prairie, triumphant over difficulties which would have defeated a less robust soul. It is a beautiful and heart-warming picture. *Death Comes for the Archbishop* (1927) is likewise a story of heroism—the heroism of two Catholic missionaries in the Spanish Southwest. They made a great team: Latour curbing Vaillant's rashness, Vaillant stimulating and inspiring Latour. The building of the cathedral in Santa Fé was a splendid culmination of their efforts to succeed in a strange environment. Even in the pessimistic gloom of the years between the wars, Miss Cather and Miss Glasgow—brave women—were able to say: Success is the reward of the strong-hearted. This is the meaning of America, and of life.

One other force on the positive side must be mentioned, religious faith. In the literature of no other period in our history had the note of religious faith been so nearly absent. Its rare occurrence seemed anachronistic to many readers, though later generations may judge otherwise of—to mention two commanding examples—*Death Comes for the Archbishop* and *Ash-Wednesday* (1930). "Where there is great love," Father Latour said, "there are always miracles. The miracles of the Church seem to me to rest not so much upon faces or voices or healing power coming suddenly near to us from afar off, but upon our perceptions being made finer, so that for a moment our eyes can see and our ears can hear what there is about us always." If Miss Cather's case for religion was chiefly emotional and aesthetic, T. S. Eliot's was chiefly intellectual. After the futility of "The Love Song of J. Alfred Prufrock" (1917) and the despair of *The Waste Land*—the most powerful single statement of the aridity of the world between the wars and the most influential poem of the century—Eliot moved firmly on to the religious position of *Ash-Wednesday* (1930). The poem does not record an easy victory. There is no disposition to nurse the illusion that the modern man can recover the spontaneous, unquestioning faith of an earlier age: the poet does not "hope to know again the infirm glory of the positive hour." The road to belief is a tortuous one, and is symbolized in the poem by a staircase which one climbs with difficulty, and down which one can see the "twisted shapes" left below. Final attainment is possible only through realizing the necessity of surrendering the individual will to the divine will. *Ash-Wednesday* concludes with Dante's words, "Our peace in His will," which are themselves a rephrasing of the words of Jesus, "Not my will but thine be done."

The usual contemporary comment on the religious attitudes of Miss Cather and Eliot was that they were impossible because they were essentially medieval attitudes inapplicable to modern times. The objection loses its weight if the values of religion are timeless.

The Political Struggle

The years between 1914 and the present seem to fall into a series of periods each of which profoundly affected the lives of all Americans: World War I, reluctantly entered by the United States in 1917; the period of peacemaking, which ended with general disillusionment about the value of the war; the boom-time era, which, after several portents had been unnoted, ended with the stock-market crash of 1929; the period of depression, followed by slow recovery; then the period during which the world drifted toward another war; and finally World War II and its aftermath.

Each of these eras was marked by political disputes, some of them unusually bitter. Looking back, we may see that the domestic conflict centered upon the role of the state versus the role of the individual, while the conflict concerning our foreign relations set isolationism against participation in world affairs.

The domestic policies of the Democrats under President Woodrow Wilson were thus summarized by the party in 1916: "We found our country hampered by special privilege, a vicious tariff, obsolete banking laws and an inelastic currency. . . . Under our administration, under a leadership that has never faltered, these abuses have been corrected and our people freed therefrom." Such was the work of Wilson's "New Freedom," as seen by his followers. The Republican presidents who came into office after the war, by contrast, tended to give business a freer hand and to increase tariffs. Harding, Coolidge, and Hoover tended to emphasize free enterprise and minimize governmental control. Hoover wrote in 1922: "Salvation will not come to us out of the wreckage of individualism. What we need today is steady devotion to a better, brighter, broader individualism — an individualism that carries increasing responsibility and service to our fellows." Those who took an opposing point of view, championed by Franklin D. Roosevelt, came into power after Hoover's policies failed to end the depression which had begun in 1929. Their position was that the federal government had to assume a greater responsibility in curbing a ruthless economic individualism and in assisting its victims. The "New Deal," as a result, comprised many measures which limited the scope of free enterprise. On into the 1940's and 1950's the battle of free enterprise versus a modified form of collectivism continued.

The attitude of the general public moved more in harmony in the discussion of international affairs. At the end of World War I, the public was in favor of the League of Nations and the participation of the United States in world affairs. After the disillusionment of the peace, however, the country tended toward pacifism and isolationism. As Fascism and Nazism developed in the 1930's, and as the inevitability of war became increasingly apparent, a growing and soon dominant group became convinced that the United States could no longer separate itself, either in war or in peace, from the rest of the world.

The Impact of World War II

The outbreak of war in Europe in 1939, our Lend-Lease to Britain
and to Russia, and our own entrance into the war following Japan's surprise attack on Pearl Harbor in December 1941 had the effect of stepping
up American production. In what turned out to be a war for survival, the
criticism of capitalism and its "boom and bust" cycles, so common in the
depression years, all but disappeared. American technological know-how
was turned to the logistic problems of global war. Out of American factories rolled the airplanes, the tanks, the guns and ammunition necessary
to wage war in remote corners of the world; from American farms, which
were becoming more and more mechanized, came much of the food to
keep the allied armies battle-ready. Eventually the power of the Nazis,
who had occupied the greater part of Western Europe, was broken, and
the Japanese were pushed back from the islands of the western and southern Pacific, the Philippines, and Malaya. The fighting ended in Europe on
May 8, 1945, and in the Pacific, except for scattered pockets of resistance,
on August 14, 1945.

Like most wars, World War II settled some issues but raised others
in their place. The Nazi concept of a Europe ruled by a superior race, with
its horrifying anti-Semitism and its bland assumption that the end justified
any means, was effectually destroyed, as was the Japanese dream of a
vast Asian and Pacific empire. It soon became evident, however, that the
United States was going to have to worry for a long time over four questions, which may be stated as follows:

(1) What is to be done with "The Bomb," as we have come to call
the vast complex of possibilities, most of them frightening, which have
been opened up by the discovery of the power within the atom?

(2) What is the best way of preserving constitutional or representative democracy, in a world which has proven easy prey for dictators and
which is in large part dominated by Marxist and collectivist convictions?

(3) What is to be the machinery for preserving peace among nations, in a world wherein time and space, thanks to incredibly swift
transportation and communication, mean less than they ever have before?

(4) What, if the United States is to maintain its leadership and influence among those who believe in an open and free society, is to be done
about its internal imperfections, those failures to square its practices with
its theories which its critics have been pointing out for generations?

These have been the major problems of the past fifteen years: the
use of atomic energy, the cold war, the role and adequacy of the United
Nations, and the persistence of racial strife. One needs only to read a
newspaper to see that they are all still with us, and that they are all still
unsolved. Since these problems are probably responsible for most of the
tensions observable in contemporary literature, their origins are worth
recalling.

"The Bomb"

The first atomic bomb was exploded at Alamogordo, New Mexico, on July 14, 1945. Scientists of many nations other than the United States participated in the development of theoretical physics, which lay behind nuclear fission, and there is every reason to believe that other nations would have built the Bomb (as Russia did later), no matter what happened in America. Americans, however, bear the responsibility for its first use in warfare. At Hiroshima on August 8, 1945, 79,000 persons died, and over 73,000 were killed at Nagasaki on the day following. Thousands more were horribly injured by the accompanying effects of radiation. President Truman, who made the decision, has said that the American use of the Bomb saved as many lives as it destroyed, for it brought an abrupt end to a war which might otherwise have dragged on for years. No historical event, however, has made the world at large more critical of the United States than this demonstration of what would almost certainly happen to civilian populations in the event of a third World War.

Nor is the Bomb the only instrument which terrifies men and women today. New sources of power and ingenious electronic devices have made possible the construction of guided missiles, some with a range of thousands of miles and capable of delivering atomic warheads anywhere on the earth. Others can be fired from beneath the surface of the ocean. The armed forces now have an arsenal and a missile delivery system that are able to reduce to rubble any great city on any continent within a short time.

The official American position has been that this arsenal is the chief deterrent against attack from Russia or any other possible enemy, and for ten years the superiority of American arms inspired widespread confidence. On October 4, 1957, however, the Russians launched into orbit the first earth satellite, Sputnik I. A painful reëxamination of the American situation immediately followed. Is our educational system adequate? Do we train enough engineers, enough mathematicians? Because satellites and space stations are obviously readily adaptable to military purposes, a series of subsequent Russian "firsts" in space exploration has added to American insecurity.

Progress has been made in the use of the atom for peaceful aims and of space vehicles for weather prediction and communication. The development of technology in the last fifteen years, however, has unquestionably added to world-wide anxiety about the future. Can the instruments of death be destroyed or banned? Can the vast new sources of power be used to improve the human condition rather than to set the stage for a world-wide holocaust? These are questions which all Americans, and all thoughtful and informed men everywhere, continue to ask. Their effect upon the American psyche is well summed up by the central character in Steinbeck's *The Winter of Our Discontent* (1961):

When a condition or a problem becomes too great, humans have the protection of not thinking about it. But it goes inward and minces up with a lot of other things already there and what comes out is discontent and uneasiness, guilt and a compulsion to get something—anything—before it is all gone. Maybe the assembly-line psychoanalysts aren't dealing with complexes at all but with those warheads that may one day be mushroom clouds.

Fear of the Bomb and distrust of a society which could allow its production are seen everywhere in contemporary literature, most conspicuously perhaps in the work of the "beats," whose rejection of all values but those of sensation displays anti-intellectualism in a strength new to the American experience.

The Cold War

The rivalry between democracy and closed societies, such as that of Communism, is as old as political theory. In 1945, however, it took new shape. During the first week of February, Stalin, Churchill, and Roosevelt met at Yalta, in the Crimea. As a result of their conference, Russia entered the final phase of the war against Japan, with the promise of the strategic Kurile Islands and the restoration of the southern half of Sakhalin, lost to her at the end of the Russo-Japanese War of 1904-1905. The Yalta meeting immensely strengthened Stalin's hand in postwar settlements. The crucial decision, however, was made at Potsdam between July 17 and August 8. Stalin, Churchill, and Truman (Roosevelt had died on April 12) agreed to divide the occupation of Germany among Russia, Great Britain, France, and the United States. Russia was understandably anxious to protect herself by extending her sphere of influence to the west, and the democracies were determined to demilitarize a nation which twice in twenty-five years had destroyed the peace of the world. Before long, however, the one-time allies were battling over ideological issues.

The Russian plan unfolded as the extension of the Communist system by political methods, including infiltration and subversion. Communists took over the governments of Hungary, Rumania, and Poland in 1947, that of Czechoslovakia in 1948, and in 1949 were in control of the East German Democratic Republic and the People's Republic of China.

To this rapid spread of Communist influence the United States opposed an enormous foreign aid program, the pros and cons of which continue to be incessantly debated. Foreign aid began with the Truman Doctrine of 1947, under which military aid was sent to Greece and Turkey. In the same year the massive economic assistance of the Marshall Plan, which in a period of four years amounted to approximately twelve billion dollars, was offered to the free nations of Western Europe. In addition, the

United States entered into elaborate military alliances in several parts of the world, most importantly under NATO (North Atlantic Treaty Organization, 1949) and SEATO (Southeast Asia Treaty Organization, 1954).

In some areas, notably western Europe, economic aid was spectacularly successful, and since the formation of EEC (European Economic Community, 1956, better known as the Common Market), the strength of the free world has grown steadily. In other places, such as Egypt, the Russians have adopted the American technique of economic aid to keep up the contest for the good will of neutral nations. Military assistance, which has meant the establishment of American bases in many parts of the world, has been aimed at helping free nations maintain their independence. Its critics have felt that it has sometimes assisted undemocratic governments to remain in power, but it has unquestionably been a major factor in confining armed conflict to "little" wars.

The most obvious effect of the cold war upon American writers, who often with quasi-diplomatic assignments have traveled widely in the last fifteen years, are the novels, poems, and plays which they have written displaying both the ease of travel in the jet age and the tensions which exist in a world divided into two mutually suspicious political and economic systems.

The Instruments of Peace

From the early days of the Republic, scattered Americans have displayed an interest in the elimination of war through international cooperation. In 1799, for example, Dr. Benjamin Rush devised *A Plan of a Peace-Office for the United States*, one of whose purposes was to "subdue that passion for war, which education, added to human depravity, have made universal." In the nineteenth century, Elihu Burritt, a self-educated blacksmith, devoted his life to pacifist activities, proposing in *Olive Leaves* (1848) both a world congress and a world court for settling international disputes. The only alternative to these organizations that he saw was a world-wide strike of workingmen against any war—an idea he may have derived from the *Communist Manifesto*. Burritt organized a long series of world peace conferences; his example led Czar Nicholas II of Russia to call the Hague International Peace Conference. From that meeting came the International Court of Justice at The Hague, eventually housed in a building for which Andrew Carnegie donated $1,500,000. It provided a place for the arbitration of disputes among those nations which subscribed to the Hague Convention of 1899.

With these precedents, the League of Nations was conceived in 1920 as a part of the Treaty of Versailles. It incorporated the world court at The Hague as a part of its structure and, despite Woodrow Wilson's failure to convince the Senate that the United States should join, was a significant instrument of peace for nearly twenty years.

World War II appreciably lessened the "isolationist" sentiment among Americans, so that one of the chief war aims of the United States became the establishment of more effective international communication and control. The scheme for the United Nations was devised at the Dumbarton Oaks Conference in 1944, and the charter was adopted at San Francisco in June of 1945, with fifty nations participating. The organization began its work in the following October and in 1952 occupied its permanent headquarters on the East River in New York City. It has since been a major forum for the discussion of international problems. Its power has been enhanced by distinguished executive officers, notably Trygve Lie and Dag Hammarskjöld, and by the possession of its own military forces. The Cuban blockade of 1962 showed that the United States was not willing to relinquish its right to unilateral action in matters of great concern to its safety, but by and large the effort to preserve the peace by collective decision has been maintained.

Many Americans are still critical of the form, the expense, and the possible effects of the United Nations, but a majority appears to believe that its work has been on the whole beneficial and that American participation is a necessary part of peaceful existence in the atomic age. Under United Nations auspices, the United States is at least taking its part in the effort to minimize international friction. The problems of a population explosion, in part the result of advances in medical science, and of the dislocation attendant upon technological change are world problems in which Americans are deeply involved.

A new sense of international responsibility is reflected in much contemporary literature and will continue to be. One of its results has been to arouse an intense interest in the United States and its literature throughout the free world. Programs of exchange of teachers and students, such as that devised by Senator Fulbright, have taken hundreds of Americans abroad to lecture and have interested thousands of young people, from West Germany to Japan and India, in American literature. The image of America is being conveyed by the nation's literary art more than it ever has been before.

Internal Problems

The new internationalism, with its concern for the good opinion of the peoples of the less fortunate countries, has led Americans to an agonizing appraisal of their own internal problems. The greatest of these continues to be that of finding the best means of eliminating the second-class citizen in a nation which prides itself on its democracy. Primarily, this means doing something about the Negroes, who now number over ten per cent of the total population.

The generation following the Civil War thought it had settled the Negro question by the abolition of slavery and the adoption of the Fifteenth Amendment to the Constitution (1870), which asserted that "The right of citizens of the United States to vote shall not be denied or abridged by the United States or any State on account of race, color, or previous condition of servitude." The underlying conviction was that the right of suffrage would enable the Negroes to secure the fairness of treatment and equality of opportunity to which all citizens in a democracy are theoretically entitled.

The American Negroes made remarkable economic progress in the last decades of the nineteenth century. The Fifteenth Amendment, however, was circumvented in some states by literacy tests and poll taxes, and in cities where the Negroes voted they were often the victims of "machine" politics and unscrupulous political bosses. In time it became clear that suffrage was not the only civil right which the Negroes needed. As the social responsibility of government broadened, "Jim Crowism" or the segregation of the races in humiliating ways did not disappear. As Wallace Stegner has said in *One Nation*, Jim Crowism made the function of the Negro

> to do the dirtiest job, get the least pay, live in the poorest shacks, receive an inferior education, have the least protection from the law, and serve as a whipping boy when white men need one.

In the aftermath of World War II strong feelings about this situation stirred both whites and Negroes. The white Americans were sensitive to the accusation that, while they roundly condemned the apartheid policy of the Union of South Africa, they permitted similar discriminatory practices in their own land. The American Negroes, on the other hand, began to feel more keenly the discrepancy between the official pronouncements of democratic society and the hard facts of discrimination — and they began to do more about it. They may, indeed, have gained a new sense of destiny by the upsurge of Negro nationalism in Africa, where since World War II a large number of the former colonies of France, Great Britain, and Belgium have become, or are about to become, Negro republics. African nationalism has doubtless fostered extremist elements such as the Black Muslims, who prophesy Negro separatism or even Negro supremacy as just recompense for the many years of degradation.

The identification of the vast majority of American Negroes with the Christian church and with the aims and ambitions of democracy is probably an adequate safeguard against actual insurrection, but the unrest of the last fifteen years is the most remarkable feature of American social conflict. This unrest became apparent in the thirties when the pressure for municipal, state, and federal "fair employment" legislation began to be felt. Laws passed since then are meant to make sure that citizens are not discriminated against because of their race or religion. They forbid advertising that jobs are open to whites or Gentiles only, or that rental housing is not available to just anyone who is capable of paying for it, or that an employer requires an applicant for a position to provide a photograph of himself. The intent is to see that a man be judged on his merits, not on the color of his skin or on his faith. After World War II the National Association for the Advancement of Colored People, an organization founded in 1909, began to take a more militant position, particularly on the matter of educational segregation. Its legal battle for equal and unsegregated educational opportunities culminated in a unanimous decision of the Supreme Court in 1954, which declared racial segregation in American public schools unconstitutional. This decision was reaffirmed by the court in 1955 and 1958 and was the cause of such widely publicized incidents as those at Little Rock, Arkansas, in 1958, and at Oxford, Mississippi, in 1962. The persistence of Jim Crowism in bus terminals, lunch counters, and rest rooms has been the prime concern of another organization, CORE (Congress of Racial Equality), a biracial group committed to improving the condition of Negroes by the technique of passive resistance. Its methods were followed with dramatic results in the "sit-in" demonstrations of 1960 and in the "freedom riders" expeditions of 1961. Clearly the doctrine of "gradualism," or acceptance of the principle that the improvement of racial relations must be a step-by-step process, is no longer acceptable to large portions of the American Negro population.

There is no consensus on how this social problem is to be solved. The literature of the last decade, however, shows the almost universal concern about it, a concern which has been the more immediate among the readers of new and talented Negro writers. Ralph Ellison's *Invisible Man* (1952) and James Baldwin's *Another Country* (1962) are among the most discussed books of recent years.

R.S.
T.II.

LITERARY TRENDS

Twentieth-century American literature, like twentieth-century American life, divides into three periods, with the two World Wars marking the transitions. Between 1910 and 1917, modern American drama and poetry came of age, in an idyllic moment wherein innocence and maturity blended. The second decade of the century was a time of rebellion and experiment which produced writers with extraordinary literary talent. Many of the writers of that awakening have left marks upon subsequent literature in the United States. World War I marked a hiatus, but it was followed by a similar awakening in fiction which, particularly after the stock market crash of 1929, became strongly social in flavor. With the appearance of

Fitzgerald, Hemingway, and Faulkner, the American novel commanded a new respect around the world. Drama and poetry developed steadily between the wars, and there arose what amounted to a revolution in criticism. Since 1945, finally, while there has been no sharp break with the earlier periods, American writers have in a sense turned inward, toward an appraisal of what an honest man can do in a world all but fractured by the overwhelming complexities of contemporary life.

The "Little" Movement

If names meant anything, the literary movement which began shortly after 1910 was at first a "little" movement. In cities and towns all over the nation, and after World War I in Paris and London, "little groups" devoted themselves to the modest project of revolutionizing literature. They produced plays in "little theaters" and published poems and stories in "little magazines." The oft-repeated word "little" proclaimed hostility to "big" theatrical producers and "big" national magazines and publishing houses which catered to masses of people.

The word "little" also implied rebellion against the alleged conservatism and shallowness of writers for large audiences. Such writers, the rebels contended, prolonged the thoughtless optimism, the prudishness, and the simple and unlifelike depictions of "The Victorians." Like literary rebels who had started movements in previous ages, the new young writers looked to other times and other lands for models which met their peculiar needs. Dramatists turned for instruction to the experimental playwrights of Europe. Poets turned to radical American poets of the past (such as Emily Dickinson, Walt Whitman, and Stephen Crane) and to the poets of France and Great Britain. Novelists looked back to American realists and naturalists or looked abroad for contemporary models. Adapting the methods of a host of un-Victorian authors, American writers between World Wars I and II produced highly experimental works which they believed represented life more truly than older writings had.

And, though the movement, at the start, was "little," in the end it tended to dominate our national literature. Group theaters developed leading playwrights; and several poets and fiction writers who had started as contributors to *Poetry, The Little Review, transition, Story,* or other little magazines eventually won national or even international recognition.

The experiences of 1910-1940 show how crucially necessary to the health of American literature are the relatively uncommercial outlets for the work of new writers. The situation against which the writers of that decade were rebelling has intensified with the development of new mass media — the movies, radio, and television. All of these are too big, cost too much for the luxury of experimenting with the innovations of inexperienced writers, and tend to aim their offerings at the lower levels of popular taste. Even today, therefore, playwrights of the new generation are writing their plays for the college and regional theaters or the off-Broadway houses, and the foremost poets of tomorrow are publishing their first work in periodicals seldom if ever seen on the newsstands. Without the "little" movement there would have been almost no twentieth-century American literature worth studying.

Experiments in Drama

Although the theater was popular in America from colonial times (there were probably more theaters in the country in the nineteenth century than there are now), and although many Americans wrote plays which were produced, American drama of a quality to command respect abroad is the product of the twentieth century. It began in rebellion.

By 1910 the movies had all but killed the legitimate theater everywhere except in the largest cities. "Road shows" were a thing of the past, and New York theatrical producers were too concerned with box-office receipts to give art much of a chance. In Europe, however, the drama was flourishing, with a lively experimental theater centering around the Théâtre-Libre of Paris (founded in 1887), the Abbey Theater of Dublin (1894), the Moscow Art Theater (1897), and the Kleines Theater of Berlin (1902). Americans traveling abroad observed this vigor and came home to ask why the United States could not have something like it.

Finding others who agreed with them, they helped to establish numerous community playhouses or workshops — little theaters — all over the country, from Boston, where the Toy Theater operated, to Palo Alto, California, where the Stanford University Theater was active. A number of colleges, simultaneously, offered work in playwriting and production under such teachers as George Pierce Baker of Harvard, Thomas Wood Stevens of Carnegie Institute of Technology, A. M. Drummond of Cornell, E. C. Mabie of Iowa, and Frederick Henry Koch of North Carolina. In the little theaters, some of them most active in the summer months near popular resort areas, and in the college workshops, amateur authors, actors, and producers carried on experiments more radical than any which commercial theatrical folk were likely to attempt. Both the little theater movement and the college theater have gained momentum almost year by year, some of them branching out into productions especially for children or with touring companies to play in school auditoriums. The summer theaters flourished and in a few cases elaborate regional theaters were established, with generous support from local drama-lovers or even from foundations. In these essentially noncommercial theaters amateurs and apprentices often had a chance to act with professionals or under professional direction.

In time, the results of the grass-roots drama experiments were very considerable. Three little theater groups which later became leading commercial producers were responsible for this drama's earliest importance. The Washington Square Players, founded in Greenwich Village in 1915, became the Theatre Guild in 1919; the Provincetown Players, also founded in 1915, left their fishing-shack playhouse on Cape Cod to go to New York City and to become active in production there; and the Group Theatre, founded by some insurgent Theatre Guild members, became professionally active in 1931. These organizations, successful both commercially and artistically, were responsible for initial productions of plays by such outstanding authors as Paul Green, Eugene O'Neill, and Clifford Odets.

Imagination and realism. Authors writing for the new theater not only tried to avoid the clichés of plot, characterization, dialog, acting, and staging which had stultified the older drama, but they experimented imaginatively in numerous ways. Even when they were highly successful with one type of play, a number of authors gladly tried their hands at completely different types.

For instance, two men trained by Professor Baker of Harvard, alternated between writing highly successful social comedies and the writing of fantasies: Philip Barry won success with his sparkling *You and I* (1923), then wrote a poetic play about street cleaners—*White Wings* (1927); and S. N. Behrman, after making a hit with *The Second Man* (1927), offered a comic version of a classic legend in *Amphitryon 38* (1937). Later, both wrote additional social comedies. Marc Connelly, who began his career as a collaborator with George S. Kaufman in writing satirical comedies such as *To the Ladies* (1922), turned, with Kaufman, to the writing of the expressionistic play *Beggar on Horseback* (1924) and later wrote, solo, the prize-winning folk Biblical play, *The Green Pastures* (1930), based upon Roark Bradford's Negro Sunday-school stories. Elmer Rice, trained by the Morningside Players, a little theater group, succeeded equally well in writing his expressionistic *Adding Machine* (1923) and his realistic *Street Scene* (1929). Maxwell Anderson, a graduate of Stanford, collaborated with Laurence Stallings in the realistic play *What Price Glory?* (1924) and later wrote verse dramas such as *Elizabeth the Queen* (1930) and *Winterset* (1935); the prose satire, *Both Your Houses*; and a musical comedy satire, *Knickerbocker Holiday* (1938). Paul Green, trained in the playwrighting courses of the University of North Carolina, became widely known for his realistic Negro play, *In Abraham's Bosom* (1927), but followed it with *Roll, Sweet Chariot* (1934), "a symphonic play of the Negro people," and then with *Johnny Johnson* (1937), a musical comedy fantasy.

Clearly, the writers and the public of the period before World War II saw values in both realistic modes of writing and the more imaginative. Such hospitality led to one development, evident in some dramas, which was more or less peculiar to the period—the mingling of the realistic with the romantic or the fanciful. The "folk plays" of Paul Green are one example, since they show life close to the soil but employ songs and poetic dialog. Another instance, now somewhat better known, is the work of Thornton Wilder, sharply focused on the problems of everyday American life but staged with little or no scenery and with deliberate intentions of greater audience involvement than the traditional drama permitted, in the hope of transcending time and space. *The Happy Journey to Trenton and Camden* (1931) and *Our Town* (1938), both one-act plays, and the longer but highly unconventional *The Skin of Our Teeth* (1942) continue to be enormously popular with little theater and college groups.

Expressionism. The mingling of the realistic and the fantastic or symbolic is generally ascribed to the influence of August Strindberg (1849-1912), an enormously productive Swedish dramatist whose work ranges from such studies of abnormal psychology as *The Father* (1887) to masterpieces of symbolism such as *The Dream Play* (1902). What expressionism means can best be seen, however, by analysis of some American examples.

Connelly and Kaufman's *Beggar on Horseback*, for instance, starts with a scene in the apartment of the hero, Neil, a penniless composer. The settings are realistic. The characters are introduced as true-to-life figures — the workingwoman with whom the hero is in love, the rich Gladys Cady, whom he is tempted to marry, and Gladys' money-grubbing family. Then the hero takes a sedative and has a dream forecasting the life he is to have if he marries the rich girl. The dream, thereafter, is presented objectively on the stage, with the distortion, the stylization, the symbolism of some dreams, set forth in dialog which often has the repetitious quality, the rhythmic cadences, and the vocabulary of poetry. The costumes and settings are not realistic but are like those in dreams. A few lines of the stage directions at the time the dream starts suggest the technique:

> . . . it begins to grow light again — but it is no longer Neil's room. It is a railway station, with the arch of Track 37 prominently visible, and other arches flanking it at the side. A muddled train schedule is printed on the station walls, with strange towns that never existed. Neil's piano, however, has remained where it was, and so has his easy chair. Then, down the aisles of the lighted theater, there comes suddenly a double wedding procession. One section is headed by Mr. Cady and Gladys — Mr. Cady in golf knickers and sox, knitted vest, and frock coat, with a silk hat prominently on his arm. Gladys is the gorgeously attired bride, bearing proudly a bouquet that consists entirely of banknotes. Behind them stream four ushers — spats, frock coats, and high hats, to say nothing of huge bridal veils, draped over their heads.

When the dream has concluded, the scene again becomes the composer's apartment, and the action returns to the realm of the everyday world.

Experiments of this kind abound in the work of Eugene O'Neill, the outstanding dramatist of the interwar period. He studied playwriting in Professor Baker's class at Harvard, and he had his first plays produced by the Provincetown Players, his later ones by the Theatre Guild. Starting with realistic writing in such plays as *Beyond the Horizon* (1920) and *Anna Christie* (1922), he shifted to expressionistic writing in *The Emperor Jones* (1921), wherein the uneasy conscience of a fleeing Negro dictator is dramatized by such symbolic devices as "little formless fears." In *The Hairy Ape* (1922) some of the scenery and much of the dialog and action are realistic. In some scenes, however, masked characters, marionette-like processions, monologs, and choric effects lift the action into the realm of fantasy. The primitive Yank, despite his tough vocabulary, has an articulateness which is more in character for O'Neill than for the battered stoker. The rhythms of much of the dialog are much more poetic than those of ordinary speech.

In other plays O'Neill experimented with devices now familiar but relatively new in American drama at the time he wrote. *Desire under the Elms* (1925) uses a set showing four rooms of a farmhouse, two downstairs and two up, together with an exterior dominated by the symbolic trees which give the play its name. The action weaves in and out, sometimes in one room, sometimes in another, sometimes in two at once, and sometimes in connection with what is going on outside. *The Great God Brown* (1926) employs a Greek device, the portrayal of its characters in masks, to which O'Neill resorted in a few other plays. *Strange Interlude* (1928) seeks to extend the bounds of drama by portraying, in addition to the speech of its characters, their inner thoughts, by means of lengthy soliloquies spoken as the other onstage characters "freeze" into the background — a device which many theater-goers found more ridiculous than rewarding. O'Neill continued to be fond of symbolism, which he nowhere handled more effectively than in *Mourning Becomes Electra* (1931), a trilogy of plays retelling in an American setting the story of Orestes and his sister's vengeance on their faithless mother, Clytemnestra. Yet he could on occasion return to realism, as in *Ah, Wilderness!* (1933), or try his hand at mystical poetry, as in *Lazarus Laughed* (1927). His great ingenuity, supported by the steady advances in theater technology, particularly in lighting, together with his philosophical turn of mind, make him the dominant figure thus far in twentieth-century American drama. His shadow lingered long after his death in 1953, for among his manuscripts were *Long Day's Journey into Night* (1956), which won for him posthumously his fourth Pulitzer Prize, and *A Touch of the Poet* (1957), which has had considerable success as an off-Broadway production.

The drama as social criticism. The new drama was marked not only by its experimentation but also by its greater concern with social problems. Many of the plays already mentioned testify to this fact.

O'Neill's *The Hairy Ape* deals forcefully with the need for a man to believe that his work is meaningful—a need which in an industrial society is seldom easily satisfied. *What Price Glory?* was only one of many plays showing the American disillusionment with a war which was supposed to make the world safe for democracy. The manifestations of American materialism, as exemplified by the *nouveaux riches* and the code of big business, were the object of satire in *Beggar on Horseback* and in numerous other plays, among them O'Neill's *Marco Millions* (1927).

The heyday of the social drama, however, was the thirties. From the hardships which followed the breakdown of the vaunted American economic system came innumerable plays which glorified the common man at the expense of his leaders or which were thinly veiled socialistic tracts. Some of them came out of the WPA Theatre (officially the Federal Theatre Project of the Works Progress Administration), a New Deal agency which lasted from 1935 to 1939. At its height the WPA Theatre was operating in forty states and employing 10,000 persons. Other social dramas were the contribution of the little theater groups, notably the Group Theatre, which introduced the work of Clifford Odets. *Waiting for Lefty* (1935), a depiction of a strike of taxicab drivers requiring such devices as action in the auditorium as well as on the stage, the unfolding of the story in episodic blackouts, and the employment of rhetorical language, remains the best known of the so-called proletarian plays. Strong social overtones are also audible in Odets' *Awake and Sing* (1935) and *Golden Boy* (1937), other Group Theatre productions.

Lillian Hellman's strike play, *Days to Come* (1936), failed, but *The Little Foxes* (1939) is among the most memorable Broadway plays of social protest. Taking her title from the Song of Solomon (2:15: "Take us the foxes, the little foxes, that spoil the vines: for our vines have tender grapes"), Miss Hellman created a Southern family, the Hubbards, whose love of money and the power it brings has smothered all humane values. She returned to the Hubbards, somewhat less successfully, in *Another Part of the Forest* (1946). Miss Hellman's prophetic *Watch on the Rhine* (1941), in which she indicated that Americans soon would have to deal with Fascism, was likewise socially oriented.

Psychology and integrity. Many of the dramatists who won respect in the twenties and thirties were still active after the end of World War II in 1945. O'Neill, as we have seen, continued to be important; but most of the others had little new to say. Their chief successors seem to be William Inge, Edward Albee, Tennessee Williams, and Arthur Miller.

Inge is an interesting product of the college theater movement. A graduate of the University of Kansas, he was associated in play production at Stephens College with Maude Adams, the famous actress, and just after the war he taught a playwriting course at Washington University in St. Louis. His first play, *Farther Off from Heaven*, was produced at Margo

Jones' little theater in Dallas in 1947. His second effort, *Come Back, Little Sheba* (1949), had a highly successful Broadway production by the Theatre Guild and was followed by *Picnic* (1952), *Bus Stop* (1955), and *The Dark at the Top of the Stairs* (1957). More recent plays have quickly failed. Inge's specialty is the study of the personal adjustment of frustrated "little" people, and he has tended to write to a popular but not very profound formula. Doc, the alcoholic in *Come Back, Little Sheba*, is perhaps his best character thus far. There is a good deal of sex and symbolism in Inge's work which makes good theater, but most critics have complained about a lack of depth.

Albee reflects a significant change in the theatrical situation in New York as well as the psychic state of the post-Bomb world. His treatment of personal problems is on a somewhat more sophisticated level than Inge's. Like the boyhood of Holden Caulfield, in J. D. Salinger's novel *The Catcher in the Rye*, Albee's boyhood left him at odds with his family and with most of the schools he attended, including Trinity College, which he attended for only a year and a half. He began to write poetry as a schoolboy and, although he had ample private means, continued to write after settling down, in a fashion, in Greenwich Village in 1949. He was then twenty. In 1958 he showed his first short play, *The Zoo Story*, to a friend, who sent it to an acquaintance in Germany, where it was produced and published the following year. It and three other brief plays were produced in off-Broadway theaters in New York in 1960 and 1961.

"Off-Broadway" needs brief definition, for it differs today from what it was when the Washington Square Players and the Group Theatre were making their marks. Although the little theaters of New York are still experimental and more open to exciting new talents from abroad and at home than the large long-run houses, their plays are nevertheless commercial in spirit. They produce plays on smaller budgets, but when the productions are successful, they are likely to move into the higher rental theaters. In fact, it is difficult to draw a clear line between the "off-Broadway" and the "big" Broadway theater of 1963. Albee crossed it in 1962 with *Who's Afraid of Virginia Woolf?*

The feeling of personal isolation in Albee's plays is probably characteristic of our age; but he heightens his effects by exaggeration and violence — at times something not unlike surrealism — which his audiences have found remarkably exciting. Of his work he has himself recently said:

> What happens in my plays is, I think, an accurate mirror of reality. There's always a certain amount of selection and hyperbole in art, but not so much that what I say is less than true. What people object to in my plays is a certain objectivity. I suffer for my subjects of course, but I do not slop over into sentimentality. Everything must be measured against something else, I feel, to be understood. One enlarges the canvas to see what the separate

elements are. I have a faculty for objectivity even in my own life. Half the time I find my own rages and anxieties quite funny. Maybe . . . I don't exist at all.

The search for identity in a complex and confusing age, which Albee's statement suggests as his main concern, is best presented, probably, in his *The American Dream* (1961).

An unhappy childhood and a good deal of knocking about at odd jobs in the lower Mississippi valley underlie the remarkable creative work of Tennessee Williams. He also had some work in the academic world of theater, first under Professor Mabie at Iowa and later with Theresa Helburn and John Gassner at the New School for Social Research. Since the success of *The Glass Menagerie* (1945), which many critics still consider his best effort, scarcely a season has lacked a new Williams play, and two of them, *A Streetcar Named Desire* (1947) and *Cat on a Hot Tin Roof* (1955), have been Pulitzer Prize winners. All of Williams' seventeen plays are marked by his concern for warped personalities, many of them regarded by his audiences as physically or psychically abnormal, so that he has accustomed the public to relatively unpleasant experiences in the theater. Like Theodore Dreiser's, however, Williams' preoccupation with the sordid and the sickly is combined with considerable tenderness for the victims of life, and his gallery of queer people, looked at as a whole, is a commentary on the fragility of happiness in a hostile world. Along with undertones of social criticism, a strong strain of violence has added to Williams' shock value in the theater. Not yet fifty, Williams still has great opportunities in theater, and the probability is that he will be a force in American drama for some time to come.

Arthur Miller, a New Yorker by birth, studied playwriting under Professor Kenneth E. Rowe at the University of Michigan, where two years in succession he won Hopwood Awards. He got out of college in 1938, just in time to join in the last months of the WPA Theatre. He worked during the war in the Brooklyn Navy Yard, continuing his writing. His first play was *The Man Who Had All the Luck* (1944), but his first success was *All My Sons* (1947), a study of the results of failure in family and social responsibility. Remarkable for its tightness of structure and its honest facing of the problem of how a man should act in the complicated modern world, this play established Miller as the dramatist with the most to say in the post-Bomb era. He quickly followed it with *Death of a Salesman* (1949), generally considered the strongest single play of the last fifteen years. Although a family play with a depression background, it is a remarkably subtle utilization of the facility with which the modern stage can create the illusion of blending past and present, and it ends with a moving statement of the theme that "There, but for the grace of God, go I." Man's search for identity and honesty and integrity in family and social relations is the theme, also, of *The Crucible* (1953), in which Miller went back to the Salem witchcraft episode of the seventeenth century to say what badly needed to be said about the Communist-hunting hysteria of 1954, which ended with the censure of Joseph R. McCarthy of Wisconsin by the United States Senate for his abuse of witnesses in the course of his widely publicized investigation of subversive activities. Finally, in *A View from the Bridge* (1955), enlarging what was originally a one-act play, Miller developed his favorite theme, "I want my name," in a more universal context, even though the setting was the Brooklyn waterfront. Although Miller's total product has not been great, *Death of a Salesman*, *The Crucible*, and *A View from the Bridge* are read and performed all over the world. Of all our contemporaries, he comes closest to rivaling Eugene O'Neill.

The Poetic Renaissance

Although various dates have been mentioned as marking the beginning of the poetic renaissance, the date most widely accepted is 1912, the year of the founding of *Poetry, A Magazine of Verse* by Harriet Monroe (1860-1936) and a group of subscribers. The motive of this publication, as the first issue stated it, was "to give to poetry her own place, her own voice." "The popular magazines," explained the editors, "can afford her but scant courtesy — a Cinderella corner in the ashes — because they seek a large public which is not hers, a public which buys them not for their verse but for their stories, pictures, journalism, rarely for their literature even in prose. . . . We believe that there is a public for poetry, that it will grow, and that as it becomes more numerous and more appreciative the work produced in this art will grow in power, in beauty, in significance."

The magazine, from its founding down to the present, has admirably fulfilled its function, and in time its prophecy was justified. *Poetry* introduced many new poets to the public. The books of some poets, notably Masters' *Spoon River Anthology* (1915), which was extraordinarily popular for poetry, attracted additional readers. Poets who lectured — Frost, Sandburg, and Lindsay, in particular — won a wider audience. Then there were various little magazines which, following the lead of *Poetry*, devoted much space to poems and to critical discussion: *Contemporary Verse* (1916-1929), *The Double Dealer* (1921-1926), *The Fugitive* (1922-1925), *Palms* (1923-1940), and others. Books on the new poetry by persuasive critics (Amy Lowell, Louis Untermeyer, John Crowe Ransom, Cleanth Brooks, and Allen Tate, to name but a few) helped cultivate understanding and appreciation. The result was the creation of a sizable cultured public which bought books of contemporary poetry and read it with enthusiasm.

Critics of modern poetry, many of whom urged the detailed analysis of poems (illustrated by Tate's "Narcissus as Narcissus," 1938), found that a common attitude among the new poets was one of rebellion against

Victorian poetry. Sometimes, as in the works of E. A. Robinson, this rebellion was visible chiefly in *what* the poet said—the voicing of un-Victorian philosophical attitudes. More often, however, the poets rebelled not only against conventional beliefs but also against conventional poetic techniques—a rebellion indicated by *how* the poet expressed himself.

In poetry, as in the drama, there were innumerable experiments. As Frost observed humorously, "Poetry . . . was tried without punctuation. It was tried without capital letters. It was tried without any image but those to the eye. . . . It was tried without content under the name of poesie pure. It was tried without phrase, epigram, coherence, logic, and consistency. It was tried without ability. . . . It was tried without feeling or sentiment. . . ." The sources of these experimental techniques were also numerous—the English metaphysical poets of the seventeenth century, the symbolists of France, the "radical" American poets of the nineteenth century, and others. A complete consideration of the period, therefore, would deal with innovations and influences by the score. Our more limited consideration will deal with three of the chief rebellions against older techniques: (1) against the older ideas about the "seriousness" proper to poetry, (2) against conventional versification, and (3) against conventional "poetic" diction.

"Serious humor." During the last decades of the nineteenth century and the early years of the twentieth century, poets in general lagged behind radical realistic and naturalistic fiction writers in adapting their methods to changing views of life in the United States. The more advanced novelists, dissatisfied with what they had thought were romantic simplifications, had turned to realism and naturalism partly because they believed that these modes made possible more inclusive—and truer—representations of life. But most poets had continued to write romantic poetry. Love or hate or sorrow had continued to be an "all out" business with them, completely disconnected from workaday concerns such as digging ditches, say, or sipping coffee, or selecting neckties. The attitude of the best poetry, in literal accordance with the urgings of Matthew Arnold and other leading critics, was one of "high seriousness." Poets had values about which they cherished no doubts, and though their poems sometimes showed vacillations, they moved forward steadily to firm conclusions.

There had been some exceptions: Walt Whitman had fused "fleshly" and "spiritual" viewpoints; Emily Dickinson had been simultaneously playful and serious while writing of love, nature, religion, or even death; William Vaughn Moody had assumed the comic role of "a little man in trousers, slightly jagged," to discuss the serious problem of evolution; Stephen Crane had told with irony of man's sense of self-importance in the face of the indifferent universe. These poets, it now developed, foreshadowed the conception of "seriousness" combined with humor which was to shape interwar poetry. Cleanth Brooks, in *Modern Poetry and the Tradition*, interestingly contrasts the new conception with the older one:

> The two conceptions are almost diametrically opposed. Arnold's sincerity expresses itself as a vigilance which keeps out of the poem all those extraneous and distracting elements which might seem to contradict what the poet wishes to communicate to his audience. It is the sincerity of the conscientious expositor who makes his point, even at the expense of suppressions and exclusions. . . . The second conception of poetry, on the other hand, reveals itself as an unwillingness to ignore the complexity of experience. The poet attempts to fuse the conflicting elements in a harmonious whole.

Modern poets, in other words, feeling that life is more complicated than most romantic poets have admitted, reveal its conflicting aspects, its colliding values. Inevitably, therefore, their poems — excepting those of Jeffers and others who view life as completely tragic — deal with incongruities; and humor, wit, or irony of varied shades become important even in very serious poems. The poet is not necessarily vacillating indecisively; in making up his mind, he is trying to take into account manifold aspects of life.

Incongruity in many of Lindsay's best poems, for instance, is akin to that in American folklore. In such poems, one may hear echoes of the fireside talk of frontier yarnspinners. Lindsay is a mythmaker, and though his myths stop short of the most inventive tall tales, they achieve comparable fusings of the real and the imagined. His Andrew Jackson "was eight feet tall. . . . His sword was so long he dragged it on the ground." His General Booth enters a Heaven which is part supernatural, part Illinois country town. His Simon Legree is the legendary creation of a Negro poet, and his Congo blacks are a white man's fabulous interpretation of savagery. Even his Lincoln, stalking through Springfield at night, assumes the guise of a folk creation.

Sandburg, likewise, embodies playful myths and imaginative tall tales in serious poems. His "Chicago" (1916) is a giant personification comparable to the frontier braggarts; he re-creates a half-mythical Lincoln by giving folk pictures of him; he praises the people by telling of their folklore. In addition to frontier or rural humor, however, he makes use of the wry humor of the dispossessed as it is voiced in hobo ballads which he has reproduced in his *American Songbag:* it mingles hate, bitter contempt, and tenderness in "To a Contemporary Bunkshooter" and "A.E.F." (1920).

The humor of two New England poets, Robinson and Frost, as Constance Rourke has remarked in *American Humor*, also prolongs an older tradition:

For companions in the legendary village of Tilbury Town Robinson has chosen types recurrent throughout early American comedy, ne'er-do-wells, liars, the quirky, the large-hearted and lost, spendthrifts of time and money and love. Robinson is master of that unobtrusive irony that has belonged to the Yankee; like the older Yankee he turns constantly to a dry metaphor — "an old vanity that is half as rich in salvage as old ashes.". . . . A reticent humor runs through much of Robinson's poetry, so quietly as to pass unnoticed by many readers, yet producing a constant lightning and relief and change, with a balance of forces against the impending tragedy. . . . Frost [too] has kept the native humor, often deepened to a bitter irony, but delicately infused; most of his humor, like that of the early Yankee tradition, is so deeply inwoven with his further speech as to be almost inseparable from it.

These poets of New England, then, show relationships to the Yankee humor of the *Farmer's Almanacs* and of Seba Smith.

In summary, four modern poets, Lindsay, Sandburg, Robinson, and Frost, re-create in serious poetry the extravagant humor of the old West or the dry humor of Down East. Another group — claiming T. S. Eliot, Wallace Stevens, Hart Crane, Karl Shapiro, and many others as part of its membership — embodies more subtle (albeit ironic) incongruities in its poetry. Cleanth Brooks sees "wit" as the instrument used by these poets in fusing disparates; and his definition of wit shows how it may be used for serious purposes:

Wit is not only an acute perception of analogies; it is a lively awareness of the fact that the obvious attitude toward a given situation is not the only possible attitude. Because wit, for us, is still associated with levity, it may be well to state it in its most serious terms. The witty poet's glancing at other attitudes is not merely "play" — an attempt to puzzle or show off his acuteness of perception; it is possible to describe it as merely his refusal to blind himself to a multiplicity which exists.

The perception of such multiplicity has frequently caused poets in this group to discard or greatly modify older ways of organizing poems in favor of "witty" organizations which emphasize ironic incongruities. Contrasting aspects or values are placed side by side, and their disparate qualities are emphasized by the omission of most transitions. What Eliot calls "'links in the chain,' of explanatory and connecting matter" are left out. Though such arrangements may, for a time, puzzle readers used to Victorian poetry, they are inevitable considering the poets' assumptions about reality. As Eliot has pointed out, "Such selection of sequences of images and ideas has nothing chaotic about it. There is a logic of imagination as well as a logic of concepts." Eliot and others of his group, in their poems seek to arrange details in accordance with what he calls "the logic of the imagination."

A poem held together by what Eliot calls "the logic of concepts" might begin with a poetic statement of the idea that modern man is less romantic than man was in the past. "Look upon modern man," it might continue, and thereupon it might describe modern man in unromantic terms. The description might be followed by a transition—"It was not so with man in other days"—and the transition might introduce a description of a romantic character of the past. Possibly the poet might thereafter summarize the whole idea of the poem, and then lament the departure of romance. In such a structure no "links in the chain" would be missing and the meaning would be explicitly formulated. Contrast Eliot's "logic of imagination" in a terse passage in *The Waste Land* (1922). Note that there are no transitions, generalizations, or statements of attitudes— simply juxtaposed images, with those of the opening two lines providing a meaningful ironic contrast with those of the last four:

> At the violet hour, the evening hour that strives
> Homeward, and brings the sailor home from sea,
> The typist home at teatime, clears her breakfast, lights
> Her stove, and lays out food in tins.
> Out of the window perilously spread
> Her drying combinations touched by the sun's last rays. . . .

The opening two lines here connote the romance of purple twilight for adventurous sailors turning homeward; the remaining lines show the drab office worker clearing up dirty breakfast dishes, dining on canned food, and then washing and hanging out her underwear.

Comparable ironic contrasts or ironic parallelisms—or, more often, parallelisms and contrasts combined—are implied in the order of the images in many modern poems. In "The Love Song of J. Alfred Prufrock" (1917), "The Hippopotamus" (1920), or "Gerontion" (1920) the images are much more complex, but the juxtaposition is the essential thing. Thus "the logic of the imagination" which shapes these poems expresses irony, and in its "serious humor" Eliot's poetry shows its kinship to that of even such a broadly humorous poet as Vachel Lindsay. Similar juxtapositions involving irony are used by Wallace Stevens, often for a purpose somewhat similar to that of the early Eliot—to underline the tawdriness of modern life. And younger poets such as Hart Crane, Karl Shapiro, and Gwendolyn Brooks, all doubtless acquainted with their predecessors among modern poets, have employed the device in ways of their own.

New rhythms. During the early years of the poetic renaissance, one great battle was for the recognition of free verse. Keith Preston, a Chicago newspaper columnist, implied what was a widespread belief when he wrote, in a witty quatrain:

> Of all the literary scenes,
> The saddest that I see
> Are graves of little magazines
> That died to make verse free.

Casual readers, for a long time, thought that "the new poetry" and "free verse" were synonymous. Many leaders in the movement did for a time write much free verse — Amy Lowell, Edgar Lee Masters, John Gould Fletcher, Hilda Doolittle, and others. Among the writers of such verse, obviously in the tradition of Walt Whitman, are Carl Sandburg and Wallace Stevens.

By degrees, poets won this battle. They were aided by the growth of Whitman's reputation which took place during this period, by the popular success of the *Spoon River Anthology*, by critics, poets, and teachers who championed vers libre. By 1940, radio plays written in free verse appealed to wide audiences, and many an amateur poet who mailed his early efforts to the home-town newspaper wrote, without any sense of being daring, in free verse.

Free verse won its spurs, but after a period during which it was used by more and more poets, there came a period during which it was used by fewer and fewer, and by 1941 many leading poets considered it rather old-fashioned. Having won all the freedom they wanted, many poets eventually decided that they could do with less freedom than vers libre allowed. Nevertheless, free verse had important effects, for it offered clues about possible variations in verse forms. Robinson, for instance, in some ways highly conventional in his prosody, diverged from regularity rather more than he probably would have done in an earlier period — and was less criticized for his divergences. And other poets, when they departed from established prosodic methods, did so without a twinge and without disastrous consequences.

Even so "classical" a poet as Robert Frost was not untouched by the new tendency toward freedom. His theory of prosody, as Lawrance Thompson explains in *Fire and Ice*, attempted to reconcile "three separate planes of sound" which affect rhythms:

> The first of these is the basic and theoretically rigid meter, which Frost is willing to reduce "virtually" to "strict iambic" and "loose iambic." These basic accents, fitted to the variable structure of the line and of the stanza, offer an underlying foundation of words and phrases. The second plane of sound is derived from the words and phrases as they might be pronounced without regard to meaning, without regard to context. The third plane of sound is

derived from the tones of voice which give particularly intended shades of meaning to the words when they are spoken as units in their contexts of phrases and sentences.

For example, in the opening lines of "Mending Wall" (1914) the "basic pattern" is iambic pentameter. However, normal accentuation, regardless of contexts, in such words as "something," "ground-swell," and "makes gaps" causes deviations from the regular iambic pattern. A proper reading of the poem, also, will suggest the character of the speaker and the quizzical, teasing tone of his remarks: such a character, probably, would maliciously emphasize and caress with his tongue the word "spills"—a word which embodies the whole playful destruction of walls by nature which so distresses the orderly neighbor. And later, in line 15, the word "between," important as it is in the concept being developed, may properly be given a stress—may properly be set off by significant pause—suggestive of its contextual importance. The sense Frost revealed, here and in other poems, of these three different planes of sound doubtless does much to account for a quality which many critics have seen in his poems: for poetry, they are often extraordinarily close in their rhythms to the everyday talk of New England farmers.

Vachel Lindsay, as his remarks here and there about metrics indicate, learned a great deal about versification from three poets: John Dryden (1631-1700), Edgar Allan Poe (1809-1849), and Algernon Charles Swinburne (1837-1909). Each of these achieved noteworthy effects by varying established rhythms and by exploiting, to the full, possibilities of tone-color—vowel and consonant arrangements. Dryden's "A Song for St. Cecilia's Day" brilliantly utilizes variations possible in an irregular ode to contrast the sounds of musical instruments, and it is not difficult to imagine Lindsay writing a gloss for Dryden comparable to that on "The Congo" offering instructions like those below for the reading of the lines:

The trumpet's loud clangor	Shrilly and with
Excites us to arms	increasing speed.
With shrill notes of anger	
And mortal alarms.	
The double, double, double beat	To be chanted in
Of the thundering drum	deep bass, all the
Cries hark! the foes come;	heavy accents
Charge, charge, 'tis too late to retreat!	very heavy.
The soft complaining flute	To be read slowly and
In dying notes discovers	softly in the manner of
The woes of hopeless lovers,	insinuating music, all the o
Whose dirge is whispered by the warbling lute.	sounds very golden.

So glossed, Dryden's lines show clearly the source of some of Lindsay's practices.

But Lindsay's rhythms also had more immediate sources. During his boyhood in Springfield, Lindsay came to know well the rhythms of church oratory, both white and Negro, and also those of open-air political oratory. While at Hiram College, he was well trained in the florid public speaking fashionable during his young manhood. The rhythms of the Gregorian Chant were also, he acknowledged, influential. "From Boston to Los Angeles," he wrote, "we American versifiers, democratic poets, face the problem of our potential audiences of one million or one hundred million that we have never conquered, but which the Chatauqua orator like Bryan . . . may reach any day. From this standpoint, Bryan is the one living American poet till we make a few songs sturdy enough to endure the confusion of the Chatauqua tent. . . ." To capture such audiences, Lindsay wrote such poems as "General William Booth Enters into Heaven" and "The Congo"—experiments in what he called "The Higher Vaudeville"—designed to attract popular attention. Recited as this poet recited such poems,* these and other songs proved attractive to unsophisticated high-school students and even to tired businessmen.

Although T. S. Eliot, Wallace Stevens, Hart Crane, Allen Tate, and others of their "school" probably are not overfond of Lindsay, they adapt rhythms to materials in a comparable fashion. Eliot, who wrote a few poems close to free verse in form during his early career, eventually came to use rhyme and fairly conventional meters. Like Lindsay, however, he found contrasts in rhythms useful to enforce contrasting moods, attitudes, or materials. That Tate conceives of rhythm similarly is indicated by his discussion of his own prosody in "Narcissus as Narcissus."

Jeffers started his career as a conventional versifier, but his later poetry—that most admired by his critics—follows a metrical scheme which, as he said, is a "compromise" avoiding both "arbitrary form and capricious lack or disruption of form." Jeffers says of his meter:

> I want it rhythmic and not rhymed—moulded more closely to the subject than in older English poetry—but as formed as alcaics if that were possible too. The event is of course a compromise. . . . My feeling is for the number of beats to the line. There is a quantitative element too in which the unstressed syllables have part.

Taking this statement as a clue, Herbert Klein made a study reported in *The Prosody of Robinson Jeffers* (1930). His finding was that, considered carefully, the rhythms of this poet are much less chaotic than, at first glance, they appear to be. The reason is that Jeffers was aware not only of the patterns of English verse but also of the quantitative patterns common to classical poetry. Says Klein:

*Some of his readings are available on records issued by Columbia University. Caedmon has issued many recordings of poets reading their own works, including Frost, Sandburg, and Eliot.

Briefly, my conclusion is that Jeffers uses stress to define and limit the line; quantity to regulate it. That is to say, the sheer possible syllabic length of the line is set (within exceptionally broad limits) by the number of stresses which the beat pattern of the poem permits. But the tempo of the lines, the contrast of breathless haste in one line (or joyful skipping) with sonorous deliberation (or hard wrenching plodding) in another is due to quantity.

Because of a knowledge of ancient poetry rather uncommon for modern American poets (with the exception of Frost), Jeffers achieved metrical effects which are new, individual, and arresting.

The effect, in the end, of all the experimentation with rhythms was to give modern poets a very wide range indeed in their handling of rhythms. Patterns of emphasis could be adjusted in many ways to the thoughts and emotions expressed in poems, and readers accustomed to the new poetry readily accepted any metrical patterns, no matter how bizarre, which justified themselves by their achievements. And the flexible rhythms became highly appropriate to the expression of the contrasts and the incongruities so important in many modern poems.

The language of modern poetry. After 1914 there was about as much variety in the kinds of language used as there was in the kinds of rhythms. Robinson, in general, used the same sort of diction as had been used in the Victorian period, though shorn of clichés and many of its ornaments, and so did some other poets. However, at the start of the period, some poets — like Dryden, Wordsworth, and Whitman before them — consciously rebelled against what they believed to be "unnatural" or ineffective ways of saying things, characteristic of older poetry. The rebellion was justified, so writers said, by several convictions: that a new language was needed to cope in a real way with the modern world, that expressions not worn threadbare had particular impact, that concrete rather than abstract words were best for stating truth, and that poets did well to draw upon the common speech which still was a great source of poetry.

The ways of rebelling, however, differed. They differed, quite often, in accordance with the poets' ideas about the ways "common speech" should be translated into poetry. For in this period when the talk of various classes differed greatly, naturally it was possible to disagree about the class of men whose talk should be imitated. Should it be the class of the factory worker, say, of the farmer, or of the learned scholar? And naturally, even after deciding upon the kind of speech to be used in poetry, poets differed about the selection, the intensification necessary if ordinary talk was to be transmuted.

Robert Frost conceived of himself as a user of the talk of New Hampshire farmers. He approvingly quoted R. W. Emerson's lines about Down East talk in "Monadnock," lines which point out that country folk, with their paltry vocabularies of a hundred words or so, are "the masters who can teach" the poet our "ancient speech," and he admired the dialogs in Shakespeare, made up as they are of "lean sharp sentences, with the give and take, the thread of thought and action quick, nor lost in a maze of metaphor and adjective." Frost usually lived up to his implied ideal. He used an extraordinarily large proportion of monosyllables (forty in a row, for instance, at one point in "The Death of the Hired Man," 1914), and very few long words; he often employs provincialisms. His lines, whether they serve as dialog or as first-person voicings of the poet's thought, often have a sparse epigrammatic quality like that of folk speech. (Note, for instance, ll. 1, 27, 32-33 in "Mending Wall," 1914.) Since Frost deliberately used such simple, undecorated diction, very close to ordinary speech, he perforce suggested poetic meanings in subtle and delicate ways; and the unwary reader is likely to miss complexities firmly embodied in his laconic poems.

Lindsay and Sandburg employ words in a fashion in some ways comparable to Frost: some of their poems are couched in the Middlewestern counterpart of New England farm language. Each of these poets, however, following the example of Whitman (whom both admire), mingles poetic words with more vernacular expressions. And each experiments with somewhat different elements in our national speech. The language which Lindsay calls "really American" is the pure and simple English of the Elizabethan period, still spoken in unspoiled rural districts: he cites as an example of it Mark Twain's *Roughing It* (1872). But he conceives of this language as potentially "eloquent" since its speakers "are all orators and preserve in eloquent periods the United States language." Such are the elements in our speech which Lindsay tries to utilize in his poetry—"the Grand Style," but employed with earthiness and native humor. Sandburg draws upon the talk of common men for the epigrams and sayings in some of his poems. He draws, in addition, upon the language of the factory or of the city sidewalk for such expressions as "where do you get that stuff"; "the . . . bunch backing you"; "a good four flusher"; and "he starts people puking" (all in "To a Contemporary Bunkshooter")—language highly appropriate to express the proletarian sentiments of the speaker.

Jeffers, over the years, varied his diction. His earlier poems are, on the whole, pretty conventional: they embody expressions typical of older poetry and contain frequent inversions. Later poems are couched in a larger vocabulary which draws upon science—physics, biochemistry, geology, botany—for many words. But mingled with these are colloquial phrases and contractions. And the style also is richly figurative.

Jeffers, at times, wrote moderately obscure lines—one may cite these in "Roan Stallion" (1925):

> The atom bounds-breaking,
> Nucleus to sun, electrons to planets, with recognition

Not praying, self-equaling, the whole to the whole,
the microcosm
Not entering nor accepting entrance, more equally,
more utterly, more incredibly conjugate
With the other extreme and greatness; passionately
perceptive of identity. . . .

But he is not alone in being obscure. Even such an old-fashioned poet as Robinson is obscure now and then, and so are such ordinarily forthright poets as Lindsay and Sandburg. Modern poetry, as a matter of fact, has been much criticized for the obscurity of its language.

Such obscurity is not, as some claim, the result of a deliberate attempt to blur meaning: actually it attempts to express meaning which is hard to decipher chiefly because it is complicated. Many difficult passages are at least as justifiable as those explained by Tate in his convincing apologia for their use in a specific poem. Tate—like Stevens, Crane, Shapiro, and Brooks—works in a fashion similar to that of Eliot, and though Eliot writes poetry not immediately clear even to sophisticated readers, he amply justifies his diction, and that of other modern poets, in notably intelligent critical writings.

Difficult though some of his poetry is, Eliot indicates in his writings that he shares the belief that poets do well to write verse after the manner of the actual talk of men. He praises Donne, the seventeenth-century British metaphysical poet, for "managing to maintain a tone of direct and informal address"; he commends Dryden for having a talent which is "exactly the same" as Donne's; he holds that "no serious critic" will disapprove of Wordsworth's avowed attempt "to imitate, and as far as possible, to adopt, the very language of men." In general, carrying out his own theories, Eliot does achieve a conversational tone in his poems.

But Eliot sees clearly that at times certain demands of poetry may make conversational language unsatisfactory. "There is," he says, "no conversational or other form which can be applied indiscriminately": some ideas and feelings may be best expressed in other styles. Moreover, he feels that the poet cannot "talk like *any* class of society," since he has to talk "like himself—rather better, we hope, than any actual class; though when any class of society happens to have the best word, phrase, or expletive for anything, then the poet is entitled to it."

And indeed the poet who achieves all that Eliot sees him doing must be an artist in manipulating language. The language important to the poet, Eliot feels, "is that which is struggling to digest and express new objects, new groups of objects, new feelings, new aspects. . . ." Such living language, this poet holds, combines traditional with novel meanings: "whatever words a writer employs, he benefits by knowing as much as possible of the history of those words, of the uses to which they have already been applied. . . . The essential of tradition is this: in getting as much as possible the whole weight of the history of the language behind his word." Hence a sense of the traditional is valuable. The essential of novelty, by contrast, is the expression of that which is characteristic not only of the age but also of the individual poet. The modern poet, aware of the complexity of his period and of his reactions to it, must "become more and more comprehensive, more allusive, more indirect, in order to force, to dislocate if necessary, language into his meaning." In addition to thus expressing what is traditional and what is unique, the language of today's poetry, Eliot thinks, fuses two other elements—feeling and thought. Poets of today will be condemned if, like Tennyson and Browning, "they do not feel their thought as immediately as the odour of the rose." Instead each should reveal in his words "a direct sensuous apprehension of thought, or re-creation of thought into feeling, which is exactly what we find in Donne," greatly admired by Eliot as well as other modern authors.

The title and one of the lines of a poem by Eliot offer examples of these fusings in diction. The words "love song" in the title, "The Love Song of J. Alfred Prufrock," have *traditional* signification: in past periods, they stood for an expression of affection which was direct and passionate. This *individual* love song, by contrast, represents our peculiar era by not expressing affection and by being indirect and unimpassioned. Similarly, the word "song," which in the past stood for simple singing, in this poem stands for complex thinking. Again, in "J. Alfred Prufrock" (one of those names "parted on the side," today typical of some pretentious people), "Alfred" has been *traditionally* associated with the man of action, Alfred the Great; but in this *individual* poem, it applies to a "hero" who is exactly the opposite of a man of action. Fusion of *thought* and *feeling* is illustrated by line 51, in which Prufrock thinks "I have measured out my life with coffee spoons." Prufrock's thought is that he has wasted his life in meaningless social rituals; but this is expressed in sensory terms—terms of feeling—in the image of annoyed frustration: the delicate handling of ineffectual little spoons from which coffee cannot be savored but must be sipped.

Some modern poets, then, for all their approval of the use of conversational language, often depart from the simplicities of social talk in order to express complex meanings. Therefore the language aids the "serious humor" and the varied rhythms in appropriately voicing the ideas and feelings poets have about the modern world.

Poetry since World War II. A considerable number of the leading figures of the poetic renaissance were still alive in 1963—Ezra Pound, T. S. Eliot, Carl Sandburg, John Crowe Ransom, and also Allen Tate. In the twenties and thirties they perfected their technique and idiom. Although Sandburg and others continued the effort to take poetry to the people, the verse of the interwar period was on the whole relatively abstruse. The influence of the dominant school of Eliot, the delight of the New Critics in the more intricate and difficult examples of poetic art, and the welcome which colleges began to give to poets in residence or to poets willing to become full-time teachers may all have had something to do with the greater subtlety of American poetry. Among the many fine poets whose work the public found hard to understand were William Carlos Williams, Wallace Stevens, Marianne Moore, E. E. Cummings, Archibald MacLeish, Delmore Schwartz, and Robert Penn Warren.

Between these writers and the younger ones who have achieved solid reputations since 1945, the line is very thin. Karl Shapiro, Robert Lowell, Randall Jarrell, Peter Viereck, Theodore Roethke (d. 1963), Richard Eberhart, Richard Wilbur, and W. D. Snodgrass are all basically intellectualist poets, and a great many of them, at some time have been college teachers. What is new in their work is the sense of living on the brink of disaster. Their visions are for the most part bleak, if not black; their awareness of the forces arrayed against common humanity is keen. Shapiro, Lowell, Jarrell, and Viereck all reflect in their early work their war experiences and express more or less contempt for the bungling which has brought man to his present state. The others are less explicitly critical, occasionally finding consolations of one sort or another in their observation of modern life, but their visions are for the most part pessimistic. Snodgrass and Wilbur, almost alone among them, appear to find some charm and beauty in their personal world. Yet the academic poets still have a good deal to tell us about the dislocations and frustrations of our time. They are intelligent, thoughtful men, making the best of what everyone admits is a desperately bad situation.

The movement sometimes called the "New Bohemianism" but more often referred to as the "beat" or "beatnik" complex, first developed in the early fifties in San Francisco, with some encouragement from Kenneth Rexroth, San Francisco correspondent for *The Nation* and an old-time radical. Housed in such places as the City Lights Bookstore and in the small jazz night clubs, it spread to Greenwich Village and to other places. For the thoroughgoing beat there is not much point in writing anything, since he holds that he might better be employed in scrutinizing his own emotions. Yet the beats, like other rebel groups, have felt the need to communicate their protest, at least to their fellow spirits. They have written more fiction than poetry, but two of them have become well known for their verse. Lawrence Ferlinghetti is the author of *A Coney Island of the Mind* (1958), a curious piece meant to be recited, full of parody and jazz lingo. It is a more interesting poem than Allen Ginsberg's *Howl* (1956), of which the first line is "I saw the best minds of my generation destroyed by madness, starving hysterical naked." With such a vision, understandable as it is, few of us can be wholly satisfied. The beats have been somewhat less conspicuous since 1960, but they are still with us, and some of them may grow enamored enough with poetry to pursue it more persistently.

The New Criticism

Possibly the outstanding new trend in literature during the 1940's and 1950's was the prominence given to the so-called "New Criticism." For the first time in our literary history, there seemed to be more practicing critics than poets, or novelists, or dramatists. Literary quarterlies like *The Kenyon Review, The Sewanee Review, The Partisan Review, The Hopkins Review,* and *The Hudson Review*—and many others of a similar kind—were so largely devoted to criticism that some midcentury observers said that our age had become more critical than creative.

The New Criticism was, in its inception, primarily a protest against the historical approach emphasized by professors and graduate schools. The new critics rightly insisted that a literary work—whether poem, play, story, or novel—is a work of art, that it has a uniqueness, an independent life of its own, that it is its own excuse for being. They deplored the historical emphasis, which substituted for the close analysis of a literary work a biographical and historical commentary on the author's life and his age, the circumstances of composition, textual variants, and other matters which the new critics maintained were irrelevant to the aesthetic question. Allen Tate threw down the gauntlet in his "Miss Emily and the Bibliographers" (1940). For a good many years there were lively skirmishes between "historians" and "critics."

The most valuable product of the movement was a considerable body of important critical writing, writing which subjected literature—particularly individual works of literature—to a new kind of scrutiny. Critics had not often before examined literary texts so closely and so perceptively. T. S. Eliot and I. A. Richards were early leaders. They were soon followed by such expert practitioners as Yvor Winters, R. P. Blackmur, Allen Tate, John Crowe Ransom, Kenneth Burke, Cleanth Brooks, Robert Penn Warren, Philip Rahv, and Lionel Trilling, to name only a few. These critics differ a good deal among themselves: Brooks, for example, has been concerned largely with the tensions and paradoxes of the individual poem; Burke, with semantic suggestiveness; Trilling, with symbolic overtones; and so on. But they all agree in placing the individual work at the center and in focusing our attention upon that. Meanwhile, *Understanding Poetry* (1938) by Brooks and Warren, and many subsequent volumes modeled after it, brought about important changes in the reading and teaching of literature in America.

The new critical movement for a time seemed in danger of carrying its principles too far when it tended to divorce the literary work from its milieu. A more recent trend seems to recognize the fact that history as well as analysis has its place in literary study, and many signs now point to a rapprochement between the warring schools. But the contribution of the New Criticism remains a solid one. Thanks to the efforts of its practitioners, the literary work itself has regained its rightful primacy.

The New Fiction

During the period 1912 to 1920, then, "the new drama," "the new poetry," and "the new criticism" reached notable heights. "The new fiction," by contrast — at least that which people bought and talked about a great deal — lagged behind. Consistent authors of best sellers included Gene Stratton Porter, Harold Bell Wright, Zane Grey, and Eleanor H. Porter. The most popular novels left out the less savory aspects of American life, and their optimistic plots showed virtuous characters triumphant, after a struggle, over vicious villains. Obviously this fiction, although written in the twentieth century, prolonged the tradition of nineteenth-century sentimentalism.

Early in the 1920's, though, the beginnings of a change became apparent. On the best-seller list appeared F. Scott Fitzgerald's *This Side of Paradise*, Edith Wharton's *The Age of Innocence*, and Sinclair Lewis' *Main Street*, books in sharp contrast with previous best sellers. The last of these shortly became sensationally successful. In an article in *Bookman*, September 1921, a British novelist, Archibald Marshall, considered "half a dozen novels said to represent a new development in American fiction, all of which are now being widely read." There was, indeed, "a new development." During the years that followed pre-1920 novelists tended slowly to recede in importance while very different writers such as Sinclair Lewis, Ernest Hemingway, William Faulkner, John Dos Passos, John Steinbeck, and Thomas Wolfe replaced them not only in critical esteem but also — at least at times — in general popularity.

Probably the huge audience which fictionists had was in large measure responsible for the late burgeoning of "the new fiction." More numerous than for either poetry or drama, fiction readers for a long time were still content with old-fashioned narratives. They preferred "pure" and "sweet" stories to the more rugged works of the Stephen Cranes and the Theodore Dreisers. But after many readers had been disillusioned by the outcome of World War I or had been converted by preachers of disillusionment such as Henry Adams and H. L. Mencken, a part of the older audience seceded and began to demand fictional works of a different sort. These were joined by a large share of the younger readers. Increasing numbers approved of the tendency which Archibald Marshall saw in best sellers "to portray the meanness of life in a particular [American] community." Attacks made by older neglected novelists, voiced anew, were considered with respect. Interest in Howe, Kirkland, and Crane was reawakened and redoubled. Dreiser's reputation prospered, and in 1925, when Dreiser published *An American Tragedy*, he found to his pleased surprise that the new audience was large enough to make that book for a time a best seller. By the 1930's, many books as stern as Dreiser's managed to win wide and appreciative audiences — not such as escapist novels like *Anthony Adverse* and *Gone with the Wind*, but very respectable audiences nevertheless.

Readers, then, who turned to fiction writers of the newer sort did so less because of their manner than because of their matter. But the authors of the new fiction, like the interwar poets, rebelled against older techniques, and they naturally needed new techniques appropriate to their preachments. Looking back to their most sympathetic predecessors, the realists and naturalists of the period 1880-1920, they found useful hints. And considering their new views of life, they hit upon methods of unfolding narratives which served their purposes.

Regardless of the sources of their procedures, fiction writers tended to drop the old argument concerning the relative merits of romanticism, realism, naturalism, expressionism, and other "isms," and to agree with Percy Lubbock, an admired critic of fiction, when he wrote: "The best form is that which makes the most of its subject—there is no other definition of the meaning of form in fiction." Authors and critics admired equally the novels of Dreiser and Farrell, cast in the form of naturalism; those of James Branch Cabell, written after the pattern of romances; and those of Robert Nathan, in the form of fantasy. What mattered most was that the fiction, as the phrase constantly had it, should "tell the real truth about life as it was." Detail, plot, and characterization were manipulated chiefly to achieve the end Mencken had in mind when he spoke of the "fundamental purpose" as being "to make the novel true."

Detail in modern fiction. Two ways of handling detail, perhaps, are outstanding in modern fiction—the "documentary" way and the "poetic" way. The documentary method, discoverable in Fitzgerald's *This Side of Paradise* and in the writings of Sinclair Lewis, John Dos Passos, and many other modern novelists, is notable for its mass of detail. Probably Dreiser, as much as any previous author, is its parent, and its ideal is something like scientific accuracy and completeness. An example of this method in an extreme form is the chapter in *Main Street* wherein Lewis tells of Carol Kennicott's stroll down the street after which the novel is named. A grocery is thus described:

> Howland & Gould's Grocery. In the display window, black, over-ripe bananas and lettuce on which a cat was sleeping. Shelves lined with red crêpe paper which was now faded and torn and concentrically spotted. Flat against the wall of the second story the signs of lodges—the Knights of Pythias, the Maccabees, the Wood-men, the Masons.

In similar detail, for several pages, Lewis tells about building after building along the street—a total of twenty-five of them. The method is almost photographic in the multiplicity of descriptive touches used. The intention behind it, apparently, is to give such overwhelming documentation that the reader feels that the picture must be accurate.

Similarly, when Lewis records conversations, he sets down something close to a complete transcript: the repetitions of phrase and the peculiarities of expression seem to be mimicked to perfection. Consider this snatch of conversation between Babbitt and Littlefield, after Babbitt has brought up the subject of politics:

> "In my opinion, what the country needs, first and foremost, is a good, sound, business-like conduct of its affairs. What we need is — a business administration!" said Littlefield.
>
> "I'm glad to hear you say that! [said Babbitt] I certainly am glad to hear you say that! I didn't know how you'd feel about it with all your associations with colleges and so on, and I'm glad you feel that way. What the country needs — just at this present juncture — is neither a college president nor a lot of monkeying with foreign affairs, but a good — sound — economical — business — administration, that will give us a chance to have something like a decent turnover."

The details in this speech and others monotonously repeating phrases and "thoughts" seem almost stenographic in their accuracy and their completeness.

Of course, there is selection even in such passages as these, and other authors who use this method are likely to be somewhat more selective than Lewis. The basis of the selection is the author's view of the scene or speech he is presenting. Lewis, for instance, gives an impression of the tawdriness, the dullness of Main Street in the first passage, and an impression of the unintellectual, standardized attitudes of Americans in the second. The abundant details are so chosen as to document amply each interpretation.

The "poetic" handling of detail, by contrast, is very highly selective, and although the details are likely to be literally accurate, they are also likely to be symbolically, i.e., poetically, significant — reminiscent not so much of Dreiser as of Stephen Crane and Frank Norris.

Willa Cather discusses the problem of detail in "The Novel Démeublé" (the unfurnished novel). She quotes approvingly Mérimée's dictum to the effect that the art of choosing from innumerable details is more important than attentive observation or exact rendition, and scoffs at the "popular superstition that 'realism' asserts itself in the cataloguing of a great number of material objects . . . and in minutely and unsparingly describing physical sensations." Balzac, she holds, failed as an artist in so far as he "tried out the value of literalness . . . to the uttermost." Tolstoy, by contrast, succeeded because he made the physical details "so much a part of the emotions of the people that they are perfectly synthesized." Hawthorne, too, used details sparsely but made all he used unobtrusively valuable to the mood of the story. Miss Cather concludes:

> Whatever is felt upon the page without being specifically named there—that, one might say, is created. It is the inexplicable presence of the thing not named, of the overtone divined by the ear but not heard by it, the verbal mood, the emotional aura of the fact or the thing or the deed, that gives high quality to the novel or the drama, as well as to poetry itself.

The implication, of course, is that the details in a novel by Miss Cather should have an "emotional aura," an implicit value, comparable to that of the images in poetry.

Ernest Hemingway, although unlike Miss Cather in many respects, had similar theories about the handling of details. In all save one of his books (*To Have and Have Not*, 1937, wherein he briefly tries, with dubious success, to write like Dos Passos), Hemingway reduced descriptive detail to the minimum. His problem—the problem of all writers—as he saw it, consists of "knowing what you truly felt, rather than what you were supposed to feel," and then setting down "the real thing, the sequence of motion and fact which made the emotion." Details, in other words, primarily are valuable to suggest the experiencing of feelings, and Hemingway believed that if these are stated "purely enough," they will be "valid . . . always." "All good books are alike," he has said, "in that they are truer than if they had really happened and after you are finished reading one you will feel that all that happened to you and afterwards it all belongs to you: the good and the bad, the ecstasy, the remorse and the sorrow, the people and the places and how the weather was. If you can get so you can give that to people, then you are a writer." The details, selected with the lyric skill necessary for such an achievement, ideally get what this author called "a fourth and a fifth dimension"—perhaps the prototype of Miss Cather's "whatever is felt upon the page without being specifically named." The fact or the detail becomes a symbol, and Hemingway, like his master, the Mark Twain of *Huckleberry Finn*, achieved poetry in what appears to be matter-of-fact prose.

This may be seen in the opening paragraph of "In Another Country" (1927):

> In the fall the war was always there, but we did not go to it any more. It was cold in the fall in Milan and the dark came very early. Then the electric lights came on, and it was pleasant along the streets looking in the windows. There was much game hanging outside the shops, and the snow powdered in the fur of the foxes

and wind blew their tails. The deer hung stiff and heavy and empty, and small birds blew in the wind and the wind turned their feathers. It was a cold fall and the wind came down from the mountains.

The paragraph is factual, but it contrasts with Lewis' description of *Main Street* because of the nature of its details. Hemingway's details are sparse, and they are more than literal: they are symbolic as well as accurate. Poetically they stand for the "other countries" which the lonely characters portrayed in the story sense but do not enter—the country of battle from which their wounds have removed them, that of peace which they glimpse through lighted windows from darkened streets, the country of nature symbolized by the game, and the country, finally, of death—connoted by the cold, the dark, and by the wind which blows from the mountains.

Poetic details comparable to those in the passage by Hemingway just quoted are to be found, as one would expect, in the writings of Willa Cather. They are to be found in Steinbeck and Wolfe (although both of these writers often employ the literal method characteristic of Lewis) and in the packed long stories of Katherine Anne Porter. In fact, if a trend in the handling of detail is to be discovered in the modern period, it is a trend toward selectivity and poetic suggestion rather than exhaustive documentation. F. Scott Fitzgerald interestingly represents this trend: one may see it very clearly by contrasting his handling of detail in *This Side of Paradise* (1920) and *The Great Gatsby* (1925). Between the two novels, he revised his method in the direction to be followed by many major writers of the period.

Plot patterns. When, in December 1930, Sinclair Lewis accepted the Nobel Prize, he made an address, "The American Fear of Literature," in which he catalogued conservative criticisms of contemporaneous writers. Eugene O'Neill, for instance, who had transformed American drama "from a false world of neat and complete trickery to a world of splendor and fear and greatness," was criticized because "he has seen life as not to be neatly arranged in the study of a scholar but as a terrifying, magnificent, and often quite horrible thing akin to the tornado, the earthquake, the devastating fire." The description applies not only to this dramatist but also to a number of fiction writers. They, too, refused to arrange happenings in neat and complete patterns comparable to those in older fiction. It was this fact, probably, that Archibald Marshall had in mind when he accused the new fictionists of failing to tell a story. "There is no progress," he complained.

Like Marshall, readers fond of Victorian plots believe that many modern novels, especially those of the twenties, bewilderingly depart from established narrative forms. Often, novelists like Dreiser, whom many of them admire, are satisfied to write simply the biographies of characters — sometimes from birth to death, sometimes from day to day over a shorter but not particularly exciting period. Such biographies often tell of characters who do not change: like picaresque figures they merely do various things and meet a series of people. Marshall used as an example Carol Kennicott in *Main Street*, who, he said "remains at the end much as she was at the beginning." "And her successive revolts," he added, "have little dramatic quality in them." Similarly, in *Babbitt, Arrowsmith, Elmer Gantry, Dodsworth*, and other novels, as Carl Van Doren notices, Lewis "employs an easy arrangement nearer chronicle than drama." James T. Farrell and Thomas Wolfe, in their novels, also use such arrangements as are supplied by apparently unmanipulated biography, although they continue their biographies through several volumes. In *All the King's Men* by Robert Penn Warren, the narrative thread is the biography of the demagogue chief character, Willie Stark.

John Dos Passos uses a similar technique in *Three Soldiers*, but he tends to complicate his story element by unfolding, simultaneously, several biographical chronicles — moving briskly and without transitions from one to the other. *"Manhattan Transfer,"* as Professor J. W. Beach remarks in *American Fiction, 1920-1940*, "is a picture of chaos, moral and social; and the narrative technique corresponds to the theme. Each chapter is a loose bundle of incidents from the lives of many different persons or groups, anywhere from four or sixteen in number, completely unrelated save in time and their common involvement in the chaos of Manhattan." *U.S.A.* does much the same thing with a broader picture screen, the entire nation, as a background. The biographies of twelve people, scattered from the East to the West coast, are presented in fragmentary parts. These people encounter many characters who move into and out of their lives. In addition, at intervals, "Newsreels," "The Camera Eye," and biographies of leading public figures are interspersed. The newsreels present impressionistic pictures of the nation of the day. The "Camera Eye" passages offer stream-of-consciousness interpretations. The brief biographies show, with selected details, the lives of leaders in ways which emphasize the trends of the times. These thumbnail biographical accounts are comparable, as a result, to the biographies of major characters, although their parts are drawn together — are not separated by stretches of narrative.

But there are many modern narratives, nevertheless, which do show developments, developments which occur when the characters learn something — discover something. Faulkner's narratives often show a discovery of the terrible in human existence. "A Rose for Emily" (1930), although it is comparatively uncomplicated, shows the method in miniature, for it tells how the villagers learn, detail by detail, of the horror of Miss Emily Grierson's life. Sometimes it is not the characters so much as the readers who make the discovery. *The Sound and the Fury* (1929), for example, one of Faulkner's best works, follows a jumbled plan, even as to time, which is justifiable largely because it makes such an unfolding possible. The order and relationships of happenings are further obscured because the story is told as it is seen not by one character but by three characters, in turn, and then the author. But the result of the whole procedure is a parading of various fragments which finally cease to be disconnected and become, instead, interrelated parts of a terrible picture. The discovery, therefore, takes place in the mind of the reader rather than in that of anyone in the story. Faulkner uses similar schemes — in eventual effect, at any rate — in other narratives.

The plot of discovery may be useful, of course, for affirmative as well as negative fictional works. Willa Cather often shows characters seeking and finding satisfactory self-fulfillment — the artist in *Song of the Lark*, the pioneer in *My Ántonia*, the soldier in *One of Ours*, the intellectual in *The Professor's House*, religious men in *Death Comes for the Archbishop*. When, in the latter part of the 1930's, fiction writers (like writers in other fields) began to forsake critical attacks in favor of positive preachments, this pattern tended to be prevalent.

Hemingway marks this transition. His "The Killers" (1927) shows the youthful Nick apprehending some of the terror of the world — apprehending ruthlessness and violence, not through books and motion pictures but through first-hand experiences. Hemingway's earlier novels (*The Sun Also Rises*, 1926 and *A Farewell to Arms*, 1929) and various short stories show characters making discoveries, usually of such a primitive sort that they indicate not the rehabilitation of human values so much as their disintegration. The chief characters in *To Have and Have Not* and *For Whom the Bell Tolls* (1940) find a social faith. The simple fisherman in *The Old Man and the Sea* (1952) finds fulfillment even in defeat. Increasingly, as the United States moved toward World War II, and affirmations became more important for some novelists than attacks, fictional narratives tended to show similar discoveries — in Lewis' *Work of Art* (1934) and *It Can't Happen Here* (1935), in Steinbeck's *The Grapes of Wrath* (1939), and in Wolfe's *You Can't Go Home Again* (1940). In the later part of the period, nevertheless, as in the earlier, the plots of discovery served admirably for the development of the authors' ideas.

Characterization and psychology. From the beginning, authors of fiction have had certain limited ways of characterizing — showing the characteristics of the people about whose lives they wrote: they could comment upon them, describe their physical backgrounds and their outward appearance, tell of their actions or of their thoughts, set forth their conversations or the conversations of others about them. During the interwar period, fictionists did not manage to hit upon any new devices, but in various ways they manipulated and modified the older ones. One older device tended to disappear altogether: the comment of the author upon the characters. Fearful of appearing to moralize, and dubious, as a matter of fact, about their ability to state positive values, the authors in these years tended to drop out of their stories and to become relatively dramatic — objective — in their characterization. Description, too, was used less frequently as a characterizing device, although some authors (as has been suggested) continued to rely upon detailed description of background and physical appearance. For the most part, however, modern fiction writers depended for characterization upon the presentation of the words, deeds, and thoughts of their characters.

The handling of these characters was shaped largely by the science of psychology, which, as has been stated, was of great importance in modern fiction. Seemingly, like Henry James before them, modern authors found central to their writing problem the selection of a fictional point of view — the kind of insight or insights they as authors were to have into the minds of their characters. And, of course, the statement of the insights was determined by the authors' concepts of psychology. Sherwood Anderson, for instance, was strongly influenced by the Freudian concept of human behavior, and stories in *Winesburg, Ohio,* his most famous collection, almost all dealt with complexes or phobias.

Hemingway, in some of his writings, seems to follow one lead suggested by behavioristic psychologists* when they scoffed at the scientific value of a study of "consciousness" and urged, instead, the observation of human activity — behavior. Often, Hemingway objectively sets down remarks and actions of the characters, or, as he puts it, "what really happens in action" — but he leaves to be inferred what the characters feel or think. "The Killers" is a perfect example, set forth as it is without a single glimpse into its characters' thoughts: it has the dramatic objectivity of a play. "In Another Country," though a first-person narrative, holds to a minimum the unfolding of the narrator's thoughts. When such a technique is used, whether Hemingway's characters are sophisticates or prize-fighters, the subtle nuances of their thoughts and feelings — exactly the things with which Henry James was chiefly concerned — are not and cannot be presented. Hemingway's belief, apparently, is that such subtleties are relatively unimportant — that the primitive and universal emotions related to physical pleasure or pain are those most significant both in life and in art. Hence Hemingway, at times, has been classified as a "primitivist."

Steinbeck, too, is often a primitivist in his psychology. His tendency, as Edmund Wilson notices in *The Boys in the Back Room* (1941), is "to present life in animal terms," to deal "either with the lower animals or with human beings so rudimentary that they are almost on the animal level." In consequence, as Wilson says, "The chief subject of Mr.

*The chief scholarly consideration is J. B. Watson's *Behavior: An Introduction to Comparative Psychology*, New York, 1914; the chief popular study is a best-selling book by G. A. Dorsey, *Why We Behave Like Human Beings*, New York, 1925. In the 1920's, behaviorism was quite influential in psychological study.

Steinbeck's fiction has been . . . not those aspects of humanity in which it is most thoughtful, imaginative, constructive, nor even those aspects of animals that seem most attractive to humans, but rather the processes of life itself. . . . And it is only, as a rule, on this primitive level that Mr. Steinbeck deals with moral questions: the virtues like the crimes for Mr. Steinbeck are still a part of . . . planless and almost aimless, of . . . almost unconscious, processes of life." Even the psychology of labor movements, as this author sees it, is animal-like. Striking fruit-pickers become "groupmen," and a character thus describes them: "It was like all of them disappeared, and it was just one big animal, going down the road. Just all one animal. . . ."

The somewhat similar psychological technique employed by Dos Passos also might well have stemmed from the "animal psychology" of the behaviorists—a psychology which tends to reduce action to two elements, stimuli and responses. His vast collection of human beings, though varied, seem (as Professor Beach suggests) to be capable of only a few responses to basic stimuli. "The presence of a given organism within the field of vision provokes the response of 'love'; discomfort drives one to a more comfortable attitude; a feeling of emptiness provokes boredom and sets one on the track of entertainment and novelty; a business opportunity releases effort and ambition." Dos Passos' human beings are comparable to laboratory mice which react one way when a bell rings, another way when a light flashes.

This type of psychology tends to make characterization simpler in modern fiction than it was in the older fiction. In some instances, by contrast, modern psychological concepts tend to make characterization rather more complex. Freud and his various followers have made authors aware of the complexity of some human motives and of the strangely illogical processes of the subconscious. Therefore, when some writers peer into the minds of characters, they see thoughts following devious pathways. These complicated mental processes the writers may reproduce by the "stream-of-consciousness" technique, the strange digressions, the random associations, which take place in the mind. In *The Sound and the Fury*, Faulkner, using the "floating point of view" described earlier, records different happenings as they are held or considered in the thoughts —both conscious and unconscious—of a series of characters. (The device, incidentally, is very helpful to the gradual unfolding of horror which his narrative achieves.) Katherine Anne Porter, in a number of outstanding stories—for example, "Flowering Judas" (1930)—has focused upon the happenings by showing the thoughts a leading character has about them. Hemingway, in some of the most important passages of *A Farewell to Arms*, *To Have and Have Not*, and *For Whom the Bell Tolls*, momentarily departs from his characteristic dramatic method. Peering into the excited minds of his characters, he uses the stream-of-consciousness technique to tell what thoughts and fragments of thoughts are running through their minds. And Wolfe, when he tells what a leading character is thinking, may resort to poetic prose suggestive of both thought and emotion.

Such are some of the varied methods of characterization which have been suggested to modern fictionists by psychology. Psychological insights characteristic of the modern period have had, as we have seen, profound effects upon the form of drama (notably expressionistic drama), upon the form of poetry, and upon the forms of novels and stories.

Fiction Since World War II

Hemingway died in 1961, Faulkner in 1962. Nobel Prize winners both, they were the outstanding figures among the many competent novelists who appeared in the interwar era. Their high reputations overshadowed all the others, although their actual production after 1945 was not great. In *Across the River and Into the Trees* (1950) Hemingway described the reflections of a fighting man on war and on many other matters. For the setting he chose Italy and the landscape of *A Farewell to Arms. The Old Man and the Sea* (1952), a parable of man's relation to nature and "luck," a favorite word of his, explored the emotions of a stout-hearted fisherman in deadly danger, as he had in his accounts of bull fighting and big game hunting. Faulkner added materially to his Yoknapa-tawpha County series with *Intruder in the Dust* (1948), *Knight's Gambit* (1949), *The Town* (1957), and *The Reivers* (1962). He also returned to the characters of *Sanctuary* in *Requiem for a Nun* (1951) and added a new dimension to his work with *A Fable* (1954), his fullest treatment of religion. Judging by the extent of critical interest in his work, Faulkner was easily the most significant novelist of the era.

Other novelists of the twenties and thirties are still active. Dos Passos, although turning more and more to interpretations of American history, continued his studies of political and economic strife in a number of books, of which *Midcentury* (1961) is the most interesting because of its use of "Documentary" inserts, which recall the "Newsreels" and "Camera Eye" of *U.S.A.* Steinbeck has been consistently popular, al-though most critics found his work after *The Grapes of Wrath* inferior and uneven. Some surprise was expressed when he was awarded the Nobel Prize in 1962. The public, however, followed him faithfully through *East of Eden* (1952), *Sweet Thursday* (1954), *The Winter of Our Discontent* (1961), and a number of lesser pieces, widely circulated in paperback. Steinbeck's autobiographical account of a highway ramble, *Travels with Charley in Search of America* (1962), was also a best seller.

The novels of World War II. As one would expect, novels of World War II were numerous and highly popular, most of them being made into movies. Some of them were by new writers, others by experienced storytellers.

The first to attract wide attention was *A Bell for Adano* (1944) by John Hersey, who as correspondent for *Time* covered both the Pacific and the European theaters of the war. Its portrait of a well-intentioned officer dealing with the civilians of a small Italian town may have strengthened in his readers the new sense of international destiny which Americans have acquired. Hersey's account of the effects of the Bomb, *Hiroshima* (1946), is a classic of factual reporting. His later novels have not won much critical admiration.

In 1948 came the first two large-scale war novels. One, *The Young Lions*, was the work of Irwin Shaw, who had previously written a number of plays and short stories. His use of a multiple point of view enabled him to study the mentality of some Nazi participants as well as that of several American soldiers; it is perhaps the most original of World War II novels. Later, Shaw published *The Troubled Air* (1950), a study of the fear of Communist influence in the radio world, and *Two Weeks in Another Town* (1960), which portrays Americans in postwar Europe. The second 1948 sensation among war novels was Norman Mailer's *The Naked and the Dead*, a description of a minor but typical military operation on a Pacific island. It employs some of the unconventional devices pioneered by Dos Passos and, like *The Young Lions*, has a multiple point of view. Its concern centers on the hierarchical structure of the army. *The Naked and the Dead* was Mailer's first book, and the only one which can be called a story in the conventional sense. Of a philosophical turn of mind, Mailer has since devoted himself to reflecting on the wrongs of the world. In *Barbary Shore* (1951), *The Deer Park* (1955), *The White Negro* (1958), and *Advertisements for Myself* (1959), he is largely on the side of the beats, with whom, indeed, he has been closely associated.

Herman Wouk's *The Caine Mutiny* and James Jones' *From Here to Eternity* were both published in 1951. Wouk was no novice. He had graduated from Columbia in 1934 and had done some radio writing before the war. In *Aurora Dawn* (1947) and *The City Boy* (1948), moreover, he had shown promise of comic talent in his handling of the advertising business and summer camp life, respectively. *The Caine Mutiny*, however, was a lengthy study of men on a small naval vessel in the Pacific, in which the theme of discipline versus individual responsibility was studied meticulously. Wouk's tendency toward prolixity was not curbed in *Marjorie Morningstar* (1955), one of the longest seduction tales in literature.

Jones was largely self-taught, and *From Here to Eternity* was evidently the result of a determination to tell the truth about army life, even to its language. Of all the war stories, it probably catches best the monotony and unbearable boredom of barracks life, with its carelessness about individual dignity. It has been followed by *Some Came Running* (1957), *The Pistol* (1959), and *The Thin Red Line* (1962). Jones has continued to be interested in the psychology of the military cadre, and his blunt honesty is generally acknowledged as rare in contemporary writing.

The final World War II novel worth special mention is Joseph Heller's *Catch-22* (1955), an air force story which alternates widely between sheer horror and grim, fantastic comedy. The short chances of survival of combat airmen led to condoning their off-duty recklessness, a fact of which Heller makes good use in a narrative which has surrealistic touches resembling those in Albee's plays.

The World War II novels form an interesting contrast to the World War I stories by Hemingway, Dos Passos, E. E. Cummings *(The Enormous Room)*, and others. The irksomeness of army life ("Hurry up, hurry up — and wait" as its tempo has been called) is portrayed in much the same terms at both periods, and there are stupid officers in both, but the second group lacks the tinge of self-pity which World War I writers tended to have. War was still horrible, but it was less so than the ovens at the Jewish concentration camps in Germany.

The fiction of the South. A conspicuous feature of the interwar period, and of that since 1945, is the Southern Renaissance. It has had important consequences in poetry and criticism, through the work of John Crowe Ransom, Donald Davidson, Allen Tate, Cleanth Brooks, Robert Penn Warren, and Randall Jarrell. Its contribution to fiction, however, has probably been equally significant, especially in the short story.

Faulkner, of course, leads the list, but also important, in the order of their birth, are Katherine Anne Porter, Caroline Gordon, Robert Penn Warren, Eudora Welty, Carson McCullers, Truman Capote, William Styron, and Flannery O'Connor. The number of women should not surprise anyone; the Southern woman is a vigorous subspecies in the American branch of *homo sapiens*.

Misses Porter, Gordon, Welty, and O'Connor are primarily short story writers, and exceptionally fine ones, although they have all written at least one novel. The novels of Mrs. McCullers *(The Heart is a Lonely Hunter*, 1940; *Reflections in a Golden Eye*, 1941; *The Member of the Wedding*, 1946; and *Clock without Hands*, 1961) are among the most widely admired works of fiction of our time, with much the same sense of the tragic beauty of life that one finds in the work of Sherwood Anderson.

Capote's work *(Other Voices, Other Rooms*, 1948; *Tree of Night*, 1949; *The Grass Harp*, 1951; and *Breakfast at Tiffany's*, 1958) does not go beyond the *novella* in length and, as several critics have observed, is hard to distinguish from that of other Southern short story writers. Warren and Styron, however, have worked on a larger scale. Both are highly literate and self-conscious novelists, and it is likely that readers will continue to return to Warren's major works *(All the King's Men*, 1946; *World Enough and Time*, 1950; *Brother to Dragons*, 1953; *Band of Angels*, 1955; and *The Cave*, 1959) as well as to Styron's *(Lie Down in Darkness*, 1951; *The Long March*, 1952; and *Set This House on Fire*, 1960).

 The footloose "beats." No protest novel of the last fifteen years has rivaled in word-of-mouth reputation Jack Kerouac's *On the Road* (1957). No book better expresses the determination of the beats to establish themselves outside the frame of conventional behavior. The utter irresponsibility of the characters would be repellent were it not for their ability to enjoy the humor of the moment. Although far from carefully structured, *On the Road* is a very funny book.

 The search for identity. The fifties, finally, have been distinguished by a number of serious efforts to answer the question of how a man should live in the fragmented and fractured society of our times. What is the individual, after all, and how does he stand in relation to his family, his friends, and the innumerable complexes to which he at one time or another is related, briefly or at length? A major theme of recent fiction has been this search for identity.

 Of many authors who might be chosen to represent this theme, four are outstanding, for somewhat different reasons. In the order of their birth dates they are Bernard Malamud (1914), Saul Bellow (1915), J. D. Salinger (1919), and John Updike (1932).

 Malamud grew up in Brooklyn. In short stories (collected as *The Magic Barrel*, 1958 and *Idiots First*, 1963) and in an impressive novel (*The Assistant*, 1957), he has depicted the Jews and Italians of New York City's slums. Bruised in spirit by their hopeless struggle with circumstances and unscrupulous neighbors, they attain human dignity in Malamud's presentation, which is marked by severe clarity and unsentimental compassion. *The Assistant* is the story of Frank Alpine, a young Italian who moves into the home and failing grocery store of Morris Bober, a Jew. Although Alpine cannot keep his hands off Bober's daughter or out of Bober's till, he undergoes a degree of moral illumination and at the end of the book is converted to Judaism. Malamud's other novels are *The Natural* (1952) and *A New Life* (1961). The former describes the downfall of a baseball player; the latter follows a Jewish teacher from New York through an eventful year in the English department of a small university on the west coast. These books contain episodes which are more sensational, and also more predictable, than anything in *The Assistant*. Their strength lies in the characterization. Both Ray Hobbs and S. Levin are men of conscience, a fact which gets them into trouble in a world where corruption and accident are prevalent. Malamud's fiction as a whole seems to say that the individual's best chance of accommodation to the world is to abide by his dreams and his faith, his religion in the broad sense of the word.

 Although Bellow was born in Canada, he has spent much of his life in Chicago. To his credit are four substantial novels: *Dangling Man* (1944), *The Victim* (1947), *The Adventures of Augie March* (1953), and *Henderson the Rain King* (1959). All use a first-person narrative point of view, and all fit into the theme of the search for identity. The "dangling man" tells his story in a journal which extends from December 12, 1942, through April 9, 1943. He is awaiting a call for induction. Separated by his condition from his former world, and not yet caught up in that of the army, he can look at himself, his friends and relatives, and the whole matter of human life with thoughtful detachment. One of his central questions — and Bellow is full of questions — is "How should a good man live; what ought he to do?" *The Victim* pursues the same theme in a New York setting, and on a somewhat smaller scale. Asa Leventhal, the protagonist, is the busy editor of a trade magazine, puzzled about his relations to his family and to his associates. In *The Adventures of Augie March*, Bellow's most ambitious work thus far, and undoubtedly one of the finest novels about Chicago, many persons and factors are posed in their relation to the hero, and his reactions and judgments are analyzed. Finally, in *Henderson the Rain King*, Bellow sends his hero to Africa where he becomes involved in a fantastic series of events designed to get him thoroughly acquainted with himself. In combination with Bellow's exploration of the theme of identity is a good measure of the comic spirit; he sees a great deal of what George Meredith called the "overblown, affected, pretentious, bombastic, hypocritical, pedantic, fantastically delicate" in human life.

For Meredith's adjectives, Holden Caulfield, the teen-age hero of Salinger's *The Catcher in the Rye* (1951), has a single synonym — *phony*. To avoid the phony has been the goal of the rebels in numerous school and college generations since Holden Caulfield emerged as the twentieth-century rival of Huck Finn. Not the first youth to discover a difference between appearance and reality, Holden is allowed by his creator to tell his story in his own terms, which are so ritualistically vulgar that students continue to think them the height of honesty and school boards to cringe at the very thought of the book in one of their classrooms. The closest approach to a second novel by Salinger is an unfinished chronicle of the Glasses, a New York family of Irish-Jewish descent. The parents were once vaudeville actors; each of their seven children is a genius or close to it; the family *esprit de corps* is high but edgy. Seven stories or character studies relating to the Glasses have been published, four of them in *Franny and Zooey* (1961) and *Raise High the Roof Beam, Carpenters; and Seymour: An Introduction* (1962). The only other collection is *Nine Stories* (1953). Although Salinger at one time wrote for mass market magazines such as *Cosmopolitan* and *The Saturday Evening Post*, for the last fifteen years he has written chiefly for *The New Yorker*. His audience there is highly sophisticated and ordinarily shock-proof; for it he has perfected a kind of psychological thriller. Many of his characters are a little off balance, and some of them are way off. They are, however, highly intelligent, sensitive, and perceptive, and tend to seek to understand their rather complicated selves. The Glasses, for example, are students of Zen Buddhism, and the writing brother is bewitched by his idol, Seymour, who committed suicide.

Salinger is evidently fascinated by braininess and family affinities. He is, one should add, almost the only contemporary who has specialized successfully in short fiction rather than the novel.

Updike has thus far published two volumes of poems (*The Carpentered Hen*, 1958, and *Telephone Poles*, 1963), two collections of short stories (*The Same Door*, 1959, and *Pigeon Feathers*, 1962), and three novels (*The Poorhouse Fair*, 1959; *Rabbit, Run*, 1960; and *The Centaur*, 1963). His approach to the problem of personal identity most often is by means of the description of elderly people and their relationship to others, although in *Rabbit, Run* the hero is a young man. Updike is rather more of an experimentalist than those of his elders so far discussed, and he likes to have a neat time line. *The Poorhouse Fair*, in which the action covers a single day, winds up with a series of flashes more poetic than most narratives. *The Centaur*, finally, is a curiously contrived overlay of a contemporary story upon a mythological base explained by an index at the end. The impression of creative power is seldom lacking in Updike's work, and his literary production in the last five years is probably as great as that of any contemporary. With him, as with the other three seekers for identity, the hope is that the best is yet to come.

W. B.
T. H.

Chronological Table of
LITERATURE AND HISTORY

1914 ■ Theodore Dreiser's *The Titan* · Robert Frost's *North of Boston* · Vachel Lindsay's *The Congo and Other Poems* · Amy Lowell's *Sword Blades and Poppy Seed* · Eugene O'Neill's *Thirst and Other One Act Plays*

World War I began in Europe, 1 August

1915 ■ Willa Cather's *The Song of the Lark* · Dreiser's *The "Genius"* · Edgar Lee Masters' *Spoon River Anthology*

The Provincetown Players, Washington Square Players, The Playhouse established · *Lusitania* sunk, 7 May, with loss of American lives

1916 ■ Sherwood Anderson's *Windy McPherson's Son* · Frost's *Mountain Interval* · Robinson Jeffers' *Californians* · Lindsay's *A Handy Guide for Beggars* · O'Neill's *Bound East for Cardiff* · Edwin Arlington Robinson's *The Man Against the Sky* · Carl Sandburg's *Chicago Poems* · Mark Twain's *The Mysterious Stranger*

Woodrow Wilson reëlected President

1917 ■ Anderson's *Marching Men* · T. S. Eliot's *Prufrock and Other Observations* · Hamlin Garland's *A Son of the Middle Border* · Lindsay's *The Chinese Nightingale and Other Poems* · Robinson's *Merlin*

Germany began unrestricted submarine warfare, 1 February · United States severed diplomatic relations with Germany, 2 February; declared war, 6 April · Czar Nicholas of Russia abdicated, 15 March · First troops of American Expeditionary Force landed in France, 26 June · Bolshevists under Lenin assumed power in Russia, 7 November

1918 ■ Stephen Vincent Benét's *Young Adventure* · Cather's *My Ántonia* · Sandburg's *Cornhuskers* · *The Education of Henry Adams* first made available to the general public, became a best seller

Wilson outlined Fourteen Points for peace, 8 January · Russia, with treaty of Brest-Litovsk, made separate peace with Central Powers, 3 March · Revolution in Germany, 7 November; Kaiser Wilhelm abdicated, a German Republic proclaimed, 9 November · Armistice signed, 11 November

1919 ■ Anderson's *Winesburg, Ohio* · Irving Babbitt's *Rousseau and Romanticism* · H. L. Mencken's *Prejudices* (first series) and *The American Language* · O'Neill's *The Moon of the Caribbees, and Six Other Plays*

The Theatre Guild established · Communist International (Comintern) organized in Russia · Benito Mussolini organized Italian Fascist movement, 23 March · Treaty of Versailles signed, 28 June; rejected by United States Senate, 19 November

1920 ■ Anderson's *Poor White* · Benét's *Heavens and Earth* · Clarence Day's *This Simian World* · John Dos Passos' *One Man's Initiation—1917* · Eliot's *The Sacred Wood* · F. Scott Fitzgerald's *This Side of Paradise* · Sinclair Lewis' *Main Street* · O'Neill's *Beyond the Horizon* · Robinson's *Lancelot* · Sandburg's *Smoke and Steel*

League of Nations established at Geneva, Switzerland, 10 January · Warren Gamaliel Harding elected twenty-ninth President · Transcontinental airmail service and commercial radio broadcasting initiated · United States census: population 105,710,620

1921 ■ Anderson's *The Triumph of the Egg* · Dos Passos' *Three Soldiers* · O'Neill's *The Emperor Jones*

Washington Conference opened, 11 November; concluded 6 February 1922, after which President Harding submitted to the Senate seven treaties designed to ease tensions with Japan in the Pacific

1922 ■ Benét's *Young People's Pride* · Eliot's *The Waste Land* · Fitzgerald's

The Beautiful and Damned · Lewis' *Babbitt* · O'Neill's *Anna Christie* and *The Hairy Ape*

Mussolini and the Fascists took over the government of Italy, 28 October · Russian government organized as the Union of Socialist Soviet Republics, December

1923 ■ Anderson's *Many Marriages* and *Horses and Men* · Cather's *A Lost Lady* · Frost's *New Hampshire* · Robinson's *Roman Bartholow* · Wallace Stevens' *Harmonium*

President Harding died, 2 August; Calvin Coolidge became thirtieth President · Munich "Beer-Hall Putsch" by German National Socialists failed, 9 November; Adolf Hitler captured and imprisoned, 12 November

1924 ■ Kenneth Burke's *The White Oxen* · Eliot's *Homage to John Dryden* · Ernest Hemingway's *In Our Time: Stories* · Jeffers' *Tamar and Other Poems* · Herman Melville's *Billy Budd, Foretopman* first published

Lenin died, 21 January; after some years Joseph Stalin emerged as virtual dictator of Soviet Russia · Coolidge elected to full term as President

1925 ■ Anderson's *Dark Laughter* · Cather's *The Professor's House* · Dos Passos' *Manhattan Transfer* · Dreiser's *An American Tragedy* · Fitzgerald's *The Great Gatsby* · Jeffers' *Roan Stallion* · Lewis' *Arrowsmith*

1926 ■ Cather's *My Mortal Enemy* · Hart Crane's *White Buildings* · William Faulkner's *Soldiers' Pay* · Hemingway's *The Sun Also Rises* and *The Torrents of Spring* · O'Neill's *The Great God Brown* · Sandburg's *Abraham Lincoln: The Prairie Years*

Germany admitted to League of Nations

1927 ■ Cather's *Death Comes for the Archbishop* · Faulkner's *Mosquitoes* · Hemingway's *Men without Women* · Jeffers' *The Women at Point Sur* · Lewis' *Elmer Gantry* · O'Neill's *Marco Millions* and *Lazarus Laughed* · Robinson's *Tristram* · Sandburg's *The American Songbag*

Chiang Kai-shek, leader of the Kuomintang government, established capitol at Nanking and became virtual ruler of China until 1949

1928 ■ Benét's *John Brown's Body* · Eliot's *For Lancelot Andrewes* · Frost's *West-Running Brook* · Jeffers' *Cawdor and Other Poems* · O'Neill's *Strange Interlude* · Sandburg's *Good Morning, America* · Allen Tate's *Mr. Pope and Other Poems*

First Russian Five-Year Plan for industrialization organized by Stalin · Herbert Hoover elected thirty-first President

1929   ■ Faulkner's *Sartoris* and *The Sound and the Fury* · Hemingway's *A Farewell to Arms* · Jeffers' *Dear Judas and Other Poems* · Lewis' *Dodsworth* · Robinson's *Cavender's House* · James Thurber and E. B. White's *Is Sex Necessary?* · Thomas Wolfe's *Look Homeward, Angel: A Story of the Buried Life*

Postwar prosperity ended with stock market crash, 29 October, the beginning of the Great Depression

1930   ■ Crane's *The Bridge* · Dos Passos' *The 42nd Parallel* · Eliot's *Ash-Wednesday* · Faulkner's *As I Lay Dying* · Twelve Authors (the Southern Agrarians), *I'll Take My Stand: The South and the Agrarian Tradition*

Sinclair Lewis became the first American to win the Nobel Prize in Literature · United States census: population 122,775,046

1931   ■ Anderson's *Perhaps Women* · Burke's *Counter-Statement* · Cather's *Shadows on the Rock* · Faulkner's *Sanctuary* · O'Neill's *Mourning Becomes Electra* · Lincoln Steffens' *Autobiography* · Thurber's *The Owl in the Attic* · Edmund Wilson's *Axel's Castle*

King Alfonso XIII forced to leave Spain, 14 April, and a republic proclaimed · Japanese troops invaded Manchuria, 18 September; a puppet state, Manchukuo, was created 18 February 1932

1932   ■ Anderson's *Beyond Desire* · Day's *God and My Father* · Dos Passos' *1919* · Faulkner's *Light in August* · Hemingway's *Death in the Afternoon* · Jeffers' *Thurso's Landing and Other Poems* · Tate's *Robert E. Lee*

Secretary of State Henry L. Stimson protested Japanese occupation of Manchuria · Congress authorized, 2 February, establishment of Reconstruction Finance Corporation (RFC) to aid railroads and financial institutions affected by the depression · Franklin Delano Roosevelt elected thirty-second President

1933   ■ Hemingway's *Winner Take Nothing* · Jeffers' *Give Your Heart to the Hawks and Other Poems* · Lewis' *Ann Vickers* · O'Neill's *Ah, Wilderness!* · Robinson's *Talifer*

Hitler became Chancellor of Germany, January, was granted dictatorial power in March and began persecution of Jews and proscription of anti-Nazi parties · Roosevelt inaugurated numerous measures to relieve severe economic distress: National Industrial Recovery Act (NRA), Agricultural Adjustment Act (AAA), Civilian Conservation Corps (CCC), Tennessee Valley Authority (TVA) · Japan signified intent to withdraw from the League of Nations

1934   ■ Lewis' *Work of Art* · O'Neill's *Days Without End*

Securities Exchange Act (establishing SEC), Home Owners' Loan Act

(HOLC) enacted for recovery from depression · After death of President von Hindenburg, Hitler combined presidency and chancellorship of Germany and assumed title of "Der Fuehrer," 16 August

1935 ■ Burke's *Permanence and Change—Anatomy of Purpose* · Cather's *Lucy Gayheart* · Day's *Life with Father* · Eliot's *Murder in the Cathedral* · Jeffers' *Solstice and Other Poems* · Lewis' *It Can't Happen Here* · Robinson's *King Jasper* · John Steinbeck's *Tortilla Flat* · Stevens' *Ideas of Order* · Wolfe's *Of Time and the River*

Works Projects Administration (WPA), National Youth Administration (NYA) set up to provide "work relief" · NRA declared unconstitutional · Social Security Act passed · Committee for Industrial Organization (CIO) founded · Italian forces invaded Ethiopia, 3 October, having been massed on Somaliland border since December 1934; economic sanctions against Italy applied by fifty-three nations after Ethiopian appeal to League · German rearmament begun

1936 ■ Faulkner's *Absalom, Absalom!* · Frost's *A Further Range* · Sandburg's *The People, Yes* · Steinbeck's *In Dubious Battle* · Stevens' *Owl's Clover* · Robert Penn Warren's *Thirty-six Poems*

AAA declared unconstitutional · King George V of England died, 20 January; his eldest son, Edward VIII, succeeded, but abdicated, 11 December, and was in turn succeeded by George VI · German troops began to occupy the Rhineland, 7 March, defying treaty agreement · Revolt against Spanish Republican Government began in Morocco, 17 July; Gen. Francisco Franco invested with title of Chief of the Spanish Nationalist Government, 1 October · Roosevelt reëlected President

1937 ■ Benét's *The Devil and Daniel Webster* · Dos Passos' *The Big Money* · Hemingway's *To Have and Have Not* · Jeffers' *Such Counsels You Gave to Me and Other Poems* · Steinbeck's *Of Mice and Men* · Stevens' *The Man with the Blue Guitar and Other Poems* · Thurber's *Let Your Mind Alone*

Japan invaded China, 7 July, occupying both Peiping and Shanghai before the end of the year · Roosevelt called for "quarantine" of aggressors in Chicago address, 5 October

1938 ■ Benét's *Johnny Pye and the Fool-Killer* · Faulkner's *The Unvanquished* · Hemingway's *The Fifth Column and the First Forty-nine Stories* · Lewis' *The Prodigal Parents* · Steinbeck's *The Long Valley* · Wilson's *The Triple Thinkers*

Hitler invaded Austria, 11 March; German-Austrian union (Anschluss) proclaimed two days later · Prime Minister Neville Chamberlain of Britain signed a "Peace Declaration" with Hitler at Munich, 30 September, yielding to Nazi demands that Czechoslovakia cede the Sudetenland to

Germany; Czechoslovakia subsequently partitioned among Germany, Hungary, and Poland

1939 ■ Dos Passos' *Adventures of a Young Man* · Eliot's *The Idea of a Christian Society* · Faulkner's *The Wild Palms* · Katherine Anne Porter's *Pale Horse, Pale Rider* · Sandburg's *Abraham Lincoln: The War Years* · Steinbeck's *The Grapes of Wrath* · Warren's *Night Rider* · Wolfe's *The Web and the Rock*

Franco completed conquest of Spain, 29 March · Italian troops invaded Albania, 7 April · Germany and Italy announced military and political alliance, 7 May · Germany and Soviet Russia signed ten-year nonaggression pact, 24 August · Germany attacked Poland, 1 September · Britain and France declared war on Germany, 3 September · Roosevelt proclaimed a national emergency, 8 September · Poland occupied by Germany and Russia, September · Russia invaded Finland, 30 November; Finland made peace and ceded territory, March 1940

1940 ■ Cather's *Sapphira and the Slave Girl* · Faulkner's *The Hamlet* · Hemingway's *For Whom the Bell Tolls* · Lewis' *Bethel Merriday* · Carson McCullers' *The Heart is a Lonely Hunter* · Mencken's *Happy Days, 1880-1892* · Thurber's *The Male Animal* (with Elliott Nugent) · Wolfe's *You Can't Go Home Again*

German armies swept across Europe, conquering Holland, 13 May; Belgium, 28 May; France, 22 June · Winston Churchill replaced Chamberlain as Prime Minister of Britain · Italy and Germany invaded Greece · First peacetime conscription inaugurated in the United States, 29 October · Roosevelt elected President for third term · United States pledged aid to Britain "short of war" · United States census: population 131,669,275

1941 ■ Burke's *The Philosophy of Literary Form* · Dos Passos' *The Ground We Stand On* · Fitzgerald's *The Last Tycoon* · McCullers' *Reflections in a Golden Eye* · Mencken's *Newspaper Days, 1899-1906* · Steinbeck's *Sea of Cortez* (with E. F. Ricketts) · Wilson's *The Boys in the Back Room* and *The Wound and the Bow*

Roosevelt proclaimed the Four Freedoms, 6 January · Congress passed the Lend-Lease Act, March · Russia and Japan signed a five-year neutrality treaty, 13 April · German troops invaded Russia, 22 June · Atlantic Charter announced, 14 August · Pearl Harbor attacked by Japan, 7 December; Japanese troops simultaneously occupied Guam and Wake Island and landed in the Philippines · United States declared war on Japan, 8 December · Germany and Italy declared war on the United States, 11 December · United States declared war on Germany and Italy, 13 December

1942 ■ Frost's *A Witness Tree* · Marion Hargrove's *See Here, Private Hargrove*

· Randall Jarrell's *Blood for a Stranger* · Karl Shapiro's *Person, Place, and Thing* · Steinbeck's *The Moon Is Down* and *Bombs Away* · Stevens' *Parts of a World* · Thurber's *My World — and Welcome to It* · Eudora Welty's *The Robber Bridegroom*

Declaration of the United Nations issued, 1 January · Japanese occupied Singapore, 15 February · Threat of invasion of Australia lessened by naval air engagement, Battle of the Coral Sea, 4-8 May · Last American troops in the Philippines surrendered Corregidor Island, 6 May · Japanese invasion fleet turned back at Midway Island, 4-7 June · American and Australian troops began offensive, establishing bases in New Guinea and on Guadalcanal in the Solomon Islands · Allied troops occupied French North Africa, 7-8 November · German armies pushed to the Caucasus and threatened both Leningrad and Moscow, being held there and at Stalingrad

1943 ■ Dos Passos' *Number One* · Eliot's *Four Quartets* · Lewis' *Gideon Planish* · Mencken's *Heathen Days, 1890-1936* · Frederick Prokosch's *The Conspirators* · Ernie Pyle's *Here Is Your War* · Thurber's *Men, Women, and Dogs* · Wendell Willkie's *One World*

Roosevelt and Churchill conferred at Casablanca, Morocco, 14-24 January, choosing Dwight D. Eisenhower as supreme commander for attack on Italy · Russia announced, 3 February, destruction of German army of 300,000, encircled at Stalingrad since November · Allies occupied Tunis and Bizerte, last Axis positions in North Africa, 8-12 May; conquered Sicily, 10 July-17 August · Mussolini resigned, 23 July · Pietro Badoglio, Mussolini's successor, signed armistice, 3 September; Allies landed on Italian mainland · Roosevelt, Churchill, and Chiang Kai-shek conferred at Cairo, Egypt, 21-26 November, agreeing that postwar Korea should be independent · Roosevelt, Churchill, and Stalin conferred at Teheran, Iran, 22 November-2 December, guaranteeing independence of postwar Iran

1944 ■ Dos Passos' *State of the Nation* · John Hersey's *A Bell for Adano* · Robert Lowell's *Land of Unlikeness* · Katherine Anne Porter's *The Leaning Tower* · Shapiro's *V-Letter and Other Poems* · Jean Stafford's *Boston Adventure*

American troops invaded Marshall Islands, 2 February · Rome liberated, 5 June · Allied invasion of Western Europe began, 6 June (D-Day), with landings in Normandy, Eisenhower, supreme commander · American troops returned to Guam, 20 July · Paris liberated, 29 August · Germany invaded from the west, 12 September · American troops returned to the Philippines, landing on Leyte, 19 October · Roosevelt elected for fourth term as President

1945 ■ Benét's *Western Star* · Gwendolyn Brooks' *A Street in Bronzeville* · Burke's *A Grammar of Motives* · Frost's *A Masque of Reason* · Jarrell's

Little Friend, Little Friend · Mencken's *The American Language, Supplement One* · Shapiro's *Essay on Rime* · Steinbeck's *Cannery Row*

Russian troops invaded Germany from the east, 19 January · Yugoslavia became a federated republic, after the soviet model, with Marshall Tito as head of state · Roosevelt, Churchill, and Stalin conferred at Yalta, in the Crimea, discussing postwar policies, 4-11 February · Manila liberated, 3 February · American troops landed on Iwo Jima, 18 February · American troops crossed the Rhine, 8 March · American troops invaded Okinawa, 325 miles from Japan, 1 April · Roosevelt died, 12 April; Harry S. Truman became thirty-third President · Russians occupied Vienna and entered Berlin, April · Death of Hitler announced, 1 May; Admiral Doenitz proclaimed himself successor · Germany surrendered unconditionally, 7 May (V-E Day) · Labor Party won British general election, 26 July; Clement R. Atlee became Prime Minister · Truman, Churchill, and Stalin, with their foreign ministers, conferred at Potsdam, 17 July-2 August, providing for occupation of Germany, reparations, and procedure for peace treaties · Charter of the United Nations issued by the San Francisco conference, 26 June; ratification completed by the United States, 8 August, and by Russia, 24 October · Atomic bomb dropped on Hiroshima, Japan, 6 August · Russia declared war on Japan, 8 August · Unconditional surrender of Japan announced by President Truman, 14 August (V-J Day)

1946 ■ Dos Passos' *Tour of Duty* · Dreiser's *The Bulwark* · Hersey's *Hiroshima* · Jeffers' *Medea* · Lowell's *Lord Weary's Castle* · McCullers' *The Member of the Wedding* · O'Neill's *The Iceman Cometh* · Warren's *All the King's Men* and *Blackberry Winter*

First Assembly of the United Nations met at London, 10 January · League of Nations dissolved itself, 18 April, turning over its assets to the United Nations · Philippines became independent, 4 July · First convictions of high-ranking Nazis for war crimes announced by International Military Tribunal, at Nuremberg, 30 September

1947 ■ Dreiser's *The Stoic* · Frost's *A Steeple Bush* and *A Masque of Mercy* · A. B. Guthrie's *The Big Sky* · Lewis' *Kingsblood Royal* · James Michener's *Tales of the South Pacific* · Shapiro's *Trial of a Poet and Other Poems* · Steinbeck's *The Pearl* and *The Wayward Bus* · Stevens' *Transport to Summer* · Warren's *The Circus in the Attic and Other Stories*

Foreign ministers of Britain, France, the United States, and Russia ended a six-week conference in Moscow, 24 April, without reaching agreement on peace terms for Germany and Austria · "Truman Doctrine" inaugurated by Congressional appropriations for economic and military aid to Greece and Turkey, where Communist coups were feared · "Marshall Plan" of aid to free nations announced by Secretary of State George C. Marshall, 5 June · Rumanian People's Republic (Communist) proclaimed

1948 ■ Cather's *The Old Beauty and Others* · Faulkner's *Intruder in the Dust* · Jeffers' *The Double Axe and Other Poems* · *Literary History of the*

United States, ed. R. E. Spiller and others · Norman Mailer's *The Naked and the Dead* · William Van O'Connor's *Sense and Sensibility in Modern Poetry*

Communists seized Czechoslovakia, 25 February · Britain, France, and Benelux countries signed a fifty-year mutual defense treaty, 17 March · Western Berlin blockaded by Soviets, 1 April; supplies delivered by air-lift · Organization of Economic Cooperation Administration (ECA) to supervise aid to free nations, 2 April · Korea partitioned into northern People's Democratic Republic (Communist), 1 May, and southern Republic of Korea, 10 May · Yugoslavia expelled from the Cominform and denounced by Soviet Russia, June · Truman elected to full term as President.

1949 ■ Nelson Algren's *The Man with the Golden Arm* · Gwendolyn Brooks' *Annie Allen* · Faulkner's *Knight's Gambit* · René Wellek and Austin Warren's *Theory of Literature* · Welty's *The Golden Apples*

Chiang Kai-shek resigned as President of China, 21 January · North Atlantic Defense Treaty (NATO) signed 4 April by U.S., Canada, Britain, France, Belgium, Netherlands, Luxemburg, Norway, Denmark, Iceland, Italy, and Portugal · Federal Republic of West Germany proclaimed, 23 May · German Democratic Republic (Communist) proclaimed in East Germany, 7 October · People's Republic of China (Communist) set up in Peiping, 21 September · Chinese Nationalist government fled to Formosa, 7 December

1950 ■ Burke's *A Rhetoric of Motives* · Hersey's *The Wall* · Steinbeck's *Burning Bright* · Stevens' *The Auroras of Autumn* · Viereck's *Strike Through the Mask!*

Britain recognized Peiping Communist regime, 6 January · Security Council rejected Reds' resolution to oust Nationalist China from U. N., 10 January; Russian member boycotted the U. N. for six months · Mao Tse-tung and Stalin signed a mutual defense treaty, 15 February · North Korean troops invaded South Korea, 25 June; Security Council called upon all U. N. members to aid in enforcing its order for withdrawal of North Koreans to the 38th parallel; MacArthur ordered by Truman to assist South Koreans and guard Formosan waters · U.S. census: population 150,697,261

1951 ■ Truman Capote's *The Grass Harp* · Faulkner's *Requiem for a Nun* · James Jones' *From Here to Eternity* · Lewis' *World So Wide* · J. D. Salinger's *The Catcher in the Rye* · Richard Wilbur's *Ceremony and Other Poems* · Herman Wouk's *The Caine Mutiny*

U.N. General Assembly named Communist China the aggressor in Korea, 1 February · Chinese Communists "liberated" Tibet, 27 May · Japanese Peace Treaty signed by U.S. and forty-eight other nations, 8 September · Greece and Turkey admitted to NATO, September · Conservative

Party won general election in Britain, 25 October, Churchill returning as Prime Minister

1952 ■ Ralph Ellison's *Invisible Man* · Hemingway's *The Old Man and the Sea* · William Inge's *Picnic* · MacLeish's *Collected Poems, 1917-1952* · O'Connor's *An Age of Criticism* · O'Neill's *A Moon for the Misbegotten* · Steinbeck's *East of Eden*

King George VI of Britain died, 6 February; Elizabeth II proclaimed Queen · NATO Council approved a European army, with use of German troops, February · Communist Party in Russia reorganized, 5-15 October · Dwight D. Eisenhower elected thirty-fourth President of the U.S.

1953 ■ Aiken's *Collected Poems* · Saul Bellow's *The Adventures of Augie March* · Roethke's *The Waking: Poems 1933-1953* · Sandburg's *Always the Young Strangers* · Shapiro's *Poems, 1940-1953*

First hydrogen bomb exploded, 2 February · Stalin died, 5 March; succeeded by Georgi M. Malenkov · Hammarskjöld replaced Lie as U.N. secretary-general, 7 April · Hillary scaled Mt. Everest, 29 May · Workers declared general strike in East Berlin, 17 June · Korean armistice signed, 27 July

1954 ■ Louise Bogan's *Collected Poems, 1922-1953* · Cummings' *Poems: 1923-1954* · Faulkner's *A Fable* · Stevens' *Collected Poems* · Welty's *The Ponder Heart*

First nuclear submarine, *Nautilus*, launched, 21 January · Nasser became Egyptian Premier, 25 February · Army-McCarthy hearings, April-June · U.S. Supreme Court outlawed school segregation, 17 May · Southeast Asia Treaty Organization (SEATO) formed, 8 September

1955 ■ Auden's *The Shield of Achilles* · Elizabeth Bishop's *Poems: North and South* · Jarrell's *Selected Poems* · John O'Hara's *Ten North Frederick* · Warren's *Band of Angels* · Sloan Wilson's *The Man in the Gray Flannel Suit* · Wouk's *Marjorie Morningstar*

Malenkov replaced by Bulganin and Khrushchev, 8 February · Eden succeeded Churchill as British Prime Minister, 6 April · Afro-Asian Conference at Bandung, 18-24 April · Geneva Big Four Conference, 18-23 July

1956 ■ John Berryman's *Homage to Mistress Bradstreet* · John F. Kennedy's *Profiles in Courage* · Marianne Moore's *Like a Bulwark* · Wright Morris' *The Field of Vision* · O'Neill's *Long Day's Journey into Night*

Stalin denounced by Khrushchev, 24 February · Eisenhower Doctrine proclaimed, 9 April · Nationalization of Suez Canal announced by Nasser, 26 July · Hungarian revolution, October-November · Eisenhower re-elected · Cease-fire declared in Egypt after Suez crisis, 7 November

1957 ■James Agee's *A Death in the Family* · John Cheever's *The Wapshot Chronicle* · James Gould Cozzens' *By Love Possessed* · Faulkner's *The Town* · Kenneth Rexroth's *In Defense of Earth*

Creation of European Common Market and Euratom, 25 March · International Geophysical Year opened, 1 July · Molotov, Malenkov, Kaganovich ousted from Presidium, 3 July · Soviet Sputnik sent into orbit — space age begins, 4 October · U. S. ICBM Atlas fired, 17 December

1958 ■Capote's *Breakfast at Tiffany's* · Stanley Kunitz's *Selected Poems, 1928-1958* · MacLeish's *J. B* · Bernard Malamud's *The Magic Barrel* · Mark Van Doren's *Autobiography*

U.S. satellite Explorer I sent into orbit, 31 January · United Arab Republic formed, 1 February · Khrushchev became Soviet Premier, 27 March · Brussels International Exhibition, April-October · U.S. Marines arrived in Lebanon, 15 July · Pasternak refused Nobel Prize, 29 October · First All-African People's Conference, 8-13 December · De Gaulle elected French President, 21 December

1959 ■Jacques Barzun's *The House of Intellect* · Bellow's *Henderson the Rain King* · Faulkner's *The Mansion* · Leslie A. Fiedler's *Love and Death in the American Novel* · Lorraine Hansberry's *A Raisin in the Sun* · Delmore Schwartz's *Summer Knowledge* · Warren's *The Cave*

Castro and rebels took over Cuban government, 1 January · Alaska and Hawaii became 49th and 50th states of the Union, 3 January and 18 March · Big Four met in Geneva to discuss reunification of Germany, May-August · Sukarno assumed dictatorial powers in Indonesia, 5 July · Large-scale French offensive against Algerian rebels · Khrushchev visited U. S., 15-27 December · European Free Trade Association set up, 20 November

1960 ■Flannery O'Connor's *The Violent Bear It Away* · Sandburg's *Harvest Poems, 1910-1960* · Shapiro's *In Defense of Ignorance* · Irwin Shaw's *Two Weeks in Another Town* · William Styron's *Set This House on Fire* · Updike's *Rabbit, Run*

Riots in South Korea led to resignation of President Syngman Rhee, 27 April · U-2 incident, 1 May · Big Four Paris summit collapses, 16 May · Regime of Menderes overthrown in Turkey, 27 May · John F. Kennedy elected thirty-fifth President of the U.S. · U.S. Census: population 179,323,175

1961 ■John Cheever's *Some People, Places, and Things That Will Not Appear in My Next Novel* · Dos Passos' *Midcentury* · Ginsberg's *Kaddish* · McCullers' *Clock Without Hands* · Phyllis McGinley's *Times Three* · Malamud's *A New Life* · Salinger's *Franny and Zooey* · John Steinbeck's *The Winter of Our Discontent*

U.N. forces enter the Congo · Mounting tension with the Cuban invasion, April · Berlin Crisis, closing of the border and the building of the Berlin Wall, August · First American astronaut in suborbital flight, 5 May · Twenty-third Amendment ratified, permitting citizens in Washington, D. C. to vote in presidential elections

1962 ■ Albee's *Who's Afraid of Virginia Woolf?* · Baldwin's *Another Country* · Alan Dugan's *Poems* · Faulkner's *The Reivers* · Frost's *In the Clearing* · James Jones' *The Thin Red Line* · Mailer's *Death for the Ladies* · Katherine Anne Porter's *Ship of Fools* · Salinger's *Raise High the Roof Beam, Carpenters; and Seymour: an Introduction* · Updike's *Pigeon Feathers*

Telestar, communications satellite, sends live TV picture from the U.S. to Europe · First American manned orbital flight, 20 February · Supreme Court decision that the reading of an official prayer in schools is unconstitutional · Cuban Crisis and U.S. quarantine of shipments of military supplies to Cuba, 22 October

BIOGRAPHIES AND BIBLIOGRAPHIES

HENRY ADAMS 1838-1918

Henry Adams, born in Boston of very wealthy parents, inherited from his illustrious family not only a brilliant mind but also the cherished tradition of culture and useful service. It was not surprising that, after he had been trained in a Boston private school, then in Harvard, and finally—for some years—in centers of European culture, he showed real talents for several different kinds of endeavor. During the Civil War period he efficiently acted as secretary to his father, who served for a time as United States congressman and later as minister to England. Between 1868 and 1870 he was a journalistic commentator, of much promise, upon domestic and foreign affairs. Between 1870 and 1876 he was the competent editor of a long-established and distinguished magazine, the *North American Review*. Simultaneously he was a highly successful teacher of medieval history at Harvard, where, among other important innovations, he introduced the graduate seminar.

Adams is noteworthy as a social theorist and as a historian whose philosophy of history was based on a deterministic outlook. His *Education of Henry Adams* is significant not primarily as an autobiography but as a record of his search for a satisfactory world view. Though it describes the scepticism of a man living in a chaotic age, the book is not without order; subtlety and sureness make it an outstanding masterpiece among American works of its genre.

Novels:
Democracy (1880)
Esther (1884)
Nonfiction:
Life of Albert Gallatin (1879)
John Randolph (1882)
History of the United States During the Administrations of Jefferson and Madison (1889-1891)
Mont-Saint-Michel and Chartres (1904, revised in 1913)
Autobiography:
The Education of Henry Adams (1907; publicly printed, 1918)

GEORGE L. AIKEN 1830-1876

Few details are known about George L. Aiken's life. He was born in Boston, but how much education he had is not known. Eventually, however, he was attracted to the stage, and in 1848 he made his debut in Providence, Rhode Island. By 1851 he had begun to write for the stage: his *Orion*, based upon a novel, was produced that year. In 1852 G. C. Howard, manager of the Museum in Troy, New York, decided that a play based upon Mrs. Harriet Beecher Stowe's famous novel, *Uncle*

Tom's Cabin (1852), would provide excellent roles for his daughter and his wife, and he commissioned Aiken to write such a dramatization. The play was a notable success. From Troy it moved to Albany and then to New York where it ran for 325 consecutive performances. It became one of the great stand-bys for itinerant companies and has continued to be popular down to the present. After this success, Aiken continued to write plays, but most of them were undistinguished, evanescent dramas.

Orion (1851)
Uncle Tom's Cabin (1852)

EDWARD ALBEE   1928–

Edward Albee was born in Washington, D.C. Abandoned by his parents, he was adopted when two weeks old by Reed and Frances Albee, the millionaire owners of a chain of theaters. He spent some time at Trinity College but at twenty-one left school and went to live in New York City, where he drifted from one odd job to another while he tried to find himself as a writer. He wrote much poetry and worked on a novel and, when he was almost thirty, turned to playwriting. With *The Zoo Story*, his first play, and the four that immediately followed it, Albee achieved recognition and was held by some to be a new Tennessee Williams.

Many feel that Albee's plays are characteristic of the theater of the absurd. Yet much of their excellence lies in the author's ability to render dialog precisely and to create believable and interesting characters.

The Zoo Story (1958)
The Sandbox (1959)
Fam and Yam (1960)
The Death of Bessie Smith (1960)
The American Dream (1961)
Who's Afraid of Virginia Woolf? (1962)

SHERWOOD ANDERSON   1876–1941

Sherwood Anderson was born in Camden, Ohio, and much of his boyhood was spent in Clyde, another small Ohio town. The poverty of his family was perhaps the chief reason why he quit school at the age of fourteen and got a job. Thereafter, for a good many years, he worked at a great variety of jobs (all requiring manual labor), first in Clyde and then in Chicago. In 1898 he joined the National Guard, and his company was sent to Cuba for patrol duty after the defeat of the Spanish forces. Upon his return from Cuba in 1899, he enrolled (somewhat belatedly—he was twenty-three) in Wittenberg Academy, a preparatory school in Springfield, Ohio, and was graduated the following year. Soon thereafter, he became a writer of advertising copy. He was so successful in this line that he organized, in 1907, in Elyria, Ohio, the Anderson Manufacturing Company, which specialized in roof paint. In 1912 Anderson—though married and the father of three children, and eminently successful in the manufacture and sale of roof paint—left his factory and did not return. Anderson went at once to Chicago, where he soon became a member (though he perforce continued for a good many years to write advertising copy for a living) of the circle of writers who were making the "Chicago Renaissance."

Though the Midwest was his rightful milieu, and Chicago his proper cosmopolitan center, Anderson moved restlessly to this place and that, always seeking a fulfillment which he could never achieve: to New York, which he mistakenly regarded as a better place for him than Chicago, and where he sought the guidance of Waldo Frank and Van Wyck Brooks; to Paris, where he met Ernest Hemingway and Gertrude Stein; to New Orleans, where his association with William Faulkner probably contributed little to his literary career. After 1927 he lived (with his fourth wife) on a farm near Marion, Virginia, and, having bought the two newspapers in the town, gave much of his time to journalism. Even here, in a handsome house of native stone built into the Virginia hillside, he was unhappy, presumably because of the failure of his creative powers and the decline of his literary reputation. During his later years he espoused with noble (if sometimes ingenuous and misguided) fervor the cause of the Southern textile workers.

In *Winesburg, Ohio* and in the two collections (*The Triumph of the Egg* and *Horses and Men*) which followed it, Anderson created stories which, because of their intensity and unconventionality, are his special contributions to American literature.

Short Stories:
Winesburg, Ohio (1919)
The Triumph of the Egg (1921)
Horses and Men (1923)
Novels:
Poor White (1920)
Many Marriages (1923)
Dark Laughter (1925)
Autobiography:
A Story Teller's Story (1924)
Tar: A Midwest Childhood (1926)
Nonfiction:
Perhaps Women (1931)
Puzzled America (1935)

IRVING BABBITT 1865–1933

Irving Babbitt was born in Dayton, Ohio, and educated at Harvard and abroad. He taught a year at Williams College (1892-1893) and then returned to Harvard to teach there in the romance languages department the rest of his life. A few years after his death, the general impression was that "The New Humanists" movement which he had led had pretty well ended. But in the late 1930's and the 1940's, when social changes and World War II stimulated affirmative thinking, an increasing number of American writers were echoing Babbitt's plea for firmly held and interrelated critical and ethical standards.

Literature and the American College (1908)
The New Laokoön (1910)
The Masters of Modern French Criticism (1912)
Rousseau and Romanticism (1919)
Democracy and Leadership (1924)
On Being Creative (1932)

JOEL BARLOW 1754–1812

Joel Barlow was a teacher and editor before he was admitted to the bar in 1786. In 1788 he went to Europe to sell Ohio real estate but while in Paris was caught by the French Revolution. Somewhat surprisingly for a native of Federalist Connecticut who had collaborated in *The Anarchiad* (1786), an attack on populist tendencies in the government, Barlow emerged in 1792 as an ardent Radical. He lived through the Reign of Terror without inconvenience and from 1795 to 1797 served as American Consul in Algiers. He spent most of the remainder of his life writing, working especially on his not too impressive epic, *The Columbiad*. Later generations have regretted that the time spent on *The Columbiad* did not go instead into something like his *Advice* and *Hasty-Pudding*—less pretentious but more immediate works.

Pamphlets:
A Letter to the National Convention of France (1792)
Advice to the Privileged Orders (1792)
Poetry:
The Anarchiad (with Timothy Dwight and John Trumbull, 1786-1787)
The Hasty-Pudding (1796)
The Columbiad [*The Vision of Columbus*, 1787] (1807)

EDWARD BELLAMY 1850-1898

Edward Bellamy was born in Chicopee Falls, Massachusetts. At eighteen he spent the better part of a year in Europe, where, as he wrote later, "my eyes were first fully opened to the extent and consequences of man's inhumanity to man." After two years of study he was admitted to the bar, but he gave up law almost at once in favor of journalism. In 1875 Bellamy began to contribute short stories to the national magazines and by 1880 had published nine times in *Scribner's Monthly*, *Lippincott's*, and *Appleton's*. Then, late in 1886, the year of the Haymarket affair, he began to compose *Looking Backward*, which convinced thousands of Americans that the society it described was just what they wanted. Bellamy soon became the leading force in the Nationalist movement which followed. In January 1891 he founded his own weekly, *The New Nation*, and it is probable that his followers lent their influence to the formation of the People's Party, founded in May 1891. There is scarcely an aspect of present-day social planning with which Bellamy did not deal in some detail in his novels. Like Henry George, he had a "call" to reaffirm the philosophy of the rights of man and a "vision" of a society in which there would no longer be economic injustice.

Six to One: A Nantucket Idyl (1878)
Dr. Heidenhoff's Progress (1880)
Miss Ludington's Sister: A Romance of Immortality (1884)
Looking Backward: 2000-1887 (1888)
Equality (1897)
The Duke of Stockbridge: A Romance of Shays' Rebellion (mostly written
  before 1880; completed and published, 1900)

SAUL BELLOW 1915-

Saul Bellow, one of the most admired of the contemporary novelists, was born in the province of Quebec in Canada and reared in Chicago; he considers himself a Chicagoan. He studied at the University of Chicago—which later supplied some of the background of his picaresque novel, *The Adventures of Augie March*—and at Northwestern University, where he received his B.A. in 1937. His first work, published in the 1940's, was well received, and in the fifties, following the publication of *The Adventures of Augie March*, *Seize the Day*, and *Henderson the Rain King*, he became a leading avant-garde writer. Although he has lectured and taught at the University of Minnesota and is currently teaching at the University of Chicago, Mr. Bellow discourages formal criticism of his work, holding that his writings should be regarded as "entertainment." Nevertheless, his books adroitly develop themes and criticize life in the modern world.

Short Stories:
Seize the Day (1956)
Novels:
Dangling Man (1944)
The Victim (1947)
The Adventures of Augie March (1953)
Henderson the Rain King (1959)

STEPHEN VINCENT BENÉT 1898–1943

Stephen Vincent Benét was born in Bethlehem, Pennsylvania, the descendant of three generations of professional soldiers. A frail youngster, Benét early became an avid reader and a writer of stories and poems, some of which were published while he was still a schoolboy. He left Yale in his junior year to enlist for World War I. Rejected because of defective eyesight, he became a code clerk in the State Department, serving for a time in the same office as James Thurber. After the war he returned to college for his B.A. and M.A.

As an undergraduate, Benét had published his first book of poems, *Five Men and Pompey*, in 1915. His first novel, *The Beginning of Wisdom* (1921), he wrote the summer after leaving Yale; his second, *Young People's Pride* (1922), after a period in Paris. After 1923 he resumed the writing of poetry and became a successful writer of magazine stories. A Guggenheim fellowship enabled him to go to France and to concentrate upon *John Brown's Body* (1928), an epic which not only became a best seller but also won a Pulitzer Prize.

When, in the 1930's and 1940's, Benét felt that the attitudes and the safety of the United States were endangered, he devoted much of his energy to the writing of poems, stories, and radio dramas dealing with social and political ameliorations and with American participation in World War II. He died in March 1943, leaving uncompleted an epic account of the settlement of the Eastern seaboard, *Western Star*, published in incomplete form in 1943.

Humor found its way into most of Benét's varied and extensive writings. It figures importantly even in his youthful poems and in his epic, *John Brown's Body*. Probably more admired and possibly more durable than any of his other popular writings was a series of stories in which he made use of materials and methods of writing typical of old-time tall tales.

Poetry:
Five Men and Pompey (1915)
Young Adventure; a Book of Poems (1918)
Heavens and Earth (1920)
John Brown's Body (1928)
Burning City (1936)
Western Star (1943)
Novels:
The Beginning of Wisdom (1921)

Young People's Pride (1922)
Spanish Bayonet (1926)
James Shore's Daughters (1934)
Short Stories:
Thirteen O'Clock (1936)
Twenty-Five Short Stories (1943)

JOSH BILLINGS: see Henry Wheeler Shaw

HUGH HENRY BRACKENRIDGE 1748–1816

Hugh Henry Brackenridge was born in Scotland and came to a frontier region in Pennsylvania when he was five. At the age of twenty he entered the College of New Jersey (now Princeton), a classmate of James Madison and Philip Freneau, and there he dabbled in satirical verse and fiction. A schoolteacher, then an army chaplain, he tried magazine publishing and finally turned to law with the ambition of becoming a legislator and political leader. However, he could never go all the way with either Federalists or Republicans, with national or local interests; and more than once he found himself defeated at the polls, vilified in the local newspapers, and suspected by party leaders. His recourse, fortunately, was to satire, both in verse and in prose. His most notable work, the comic novel *Modern Chivalry*, well demonstrates his craftsmanship as a writer and the quality of his belief in democracy.

Poetry:
The Rising Glory of America (with Philip Freneau, 1772)
A Poem on Divine Revelation (1774)
Drama:
The Battle of Bunkers-Hill (1776)
The Death of General Montgomery (1777)
Novel:
Modern Chivalry (1792-1815)

WILLIAM BRADFORD 1590–1657

William Bradford sailed on the *Mayflower* in 1620. Following the landing at Plymouth in December of that year, Bradford, as his *History of Plymouth Plantation* (1620-1647) records, took a leading part in the affairs of the colony. He was chosen governor in the annual elections no less than thirty times, serving continuously from 1622 to 1656, except for five years when he was relieved at his own urgent request. Whether his art was conscious or not, Bradford's prose is worthy of a distinguished place in the English tradition of his century.

Mourt's Relation (with Edward Winslow, 1622)
History of Plymouth Plantation, 1620-1647 (published, 1856)

ANNE BRADSTREET 1612–1672

Anne Bradstreet and her husband, Simon, a graduate of Cambridge, came to Massachusetts with John Winthrop and other prominent first settlers of the Massachusetts Bay Colony. Her husband became a noted leader in the affairs of the Massachusetts Bay Colony. Anne Bradstreet had eight children; hers was the busy, heroic life of a wife and mother in a pioneer community. She found time, nevertheless, for the writing of verse, a considerable quantity of which was published in London in 1650 with the title, *The Tenth Muse Lately Sprung up in America*. Mrs. Bradstreet's most original poems, and some may think her best, are her private domestic pieces, unpublished until after her death, in which she reveals her religious difficulties and her wifely and maternal devotion.

The Tenth Muse Lately Sprung up in America (1650)
The Works of Anne Bradstreet, ed. J. H. Ellis (1867; reprinted, 1932)

GWENDOLYN BROOKS 1917–

Miss Brooks (since 1939 Mrs. Henry Lowington Blakely) was born in Kansas but taken only a month later to Chicago. There she grew up, went to college, worked, married, lived through World War II. She never lost an early pleasure in poetry, and in 1944 some of her writing was printed in *Poetry, A Magazine of Verse*. A year later *A Street in Bronzeville* was published, bringing her a number of fellowships and grants-in-aid which were amply rewarded by *Annie Allen*, the story of a Negro girl's life from childhood to maturity. In 1949 it won the Pulitzer Prize for Poetry.

Technically Miss Brooks' poetry is impressive for range and variety of form. She delicately combines direct and vivid sense impressions with the somewhat elliptical style characteristic of T. S. Eliot and his admirers.

Poetry:
A Street in Bronzeville (1945)
Annie Allen (1949)
The Bean Eaters (1960)
Novel:
Maud Martha (1953)

CHARLES FARRAR BROWNE (Artemus Ward) 1834–1867

Born in Waterford, Maine, Charles Farrar Browne started out as a printer's devil and in time moved from his printer's case to the editorial desks of various newspapers. He was an editor of the Cleveland, Ohio, *Plain Dealer* in 1858 when some playful letters he composed started him on his way to fame. Artemus Ward, the purported author of the letters, introduced himself as the illiterate, humorless owner of an itinerant waxworks and menagerie. After these pieces had won a large following for him, Browne went to New York to work on the comic magazine *Vanity Fair*, and in 1861 he embarked on a highly remunerative career as a comic lecturer. Browne was typical of a majority of the humorists of his day — professional funnymen, literary comedians who exploited the humor of diction rather than the humor of character. Their writings are interesting as social documents and as works foreshadowing much of the "free association humor" of such authors as Benchley, Thurber, and Perelman.

Artemus Ward: His Book (1862)
Artemus Ward: His Travels (1865)
Artemus Ward in London (1867)

WILLIAM CULLEN BRYANT 1794–1878

William Cullen Bryant was born at Cummington, in western Massachusetts. Brought up in a Calvinistic and Federalist environment, he took himself and the world very seriously as soon as he knew anything about them. His first verses appeared in a newspaper when he was ten, and he saw his first book in print five years later, when his father arranged for the publication of *The Embargo*, an attack on Jefferson's methods of avoiding entanglement in the Napoleonic conflict. He had only one year of college, at Williams, and then, because there was no livelihood in poetry, he turned to the study of law. Admitted to the bar in 1814, he practiced in several Massachusetts towns with moderate success, occasionally using his leisure for composing poems. After 1817, when his father sent some of his poems to a Boston friend and "Thanatopsis" came out in the *North American Review*, he became known as poet and reviewer for that periodical and others. In 1821 he married Fanny Fairchild, the "fairest of the rural maids"; theirs was an unusually happy marriage.

In 1825 Bryant had the courage to give up the law for the uncertainties of a literary life and deserted Massachusetts for New York City. Within a few months he formed a connection with the *Evening Post*, a daily newspaper which had been founded by Alexander Hamilton; in 1829 he became the editor-in-chief and held the position until his death in 1878. As a part owner of the paper, he grew wealthy and was able to afford much European travel for himself and his family, as well as to establish a comfortable home at Roslyn on Long Island.

Bryant's poetry, although apparently simple, does, in fact, defy categorization. Although his concern for form and clarity, harmony and serenity is typically "classical," his poetic theories and his themes — the past, death, freedom, nature — have much in them that is ordinarily called "romantic."

The Embargo (1808)
The White Footed Deer and Other Poems (1844)
Poems (1821, 1832, 1836, 1847, 1854, 1871, 1876)

KENNETH BURKE   1897–

Kenneth Burke was born in Pittsburgh, Pennsylvania. He studied at Ohio State and Columbia universities but in his twenties plunged into the New York world of letters as reviewer, translator, and roving critic. His first book, *The White Oxen* (1924), was fiction, but he made his real reputation as a music critic, first on the avant-garde magazine of the twenties, *The Dial*, in 1927-1929, and then in 1934-1936, on *The Nation*. He gradually emerged, however, as a notable theorist on aesthetics in general and on literary criticism in particular. He has lectured at the New School for Social Research, at the University of Chicago, and at Bennington College. In 1957-1958 he was a Fellow of The Center for Advanced Study in the Behavioral Sciences. One of the best of the New Critics, Burke is a man of great breadth. He knows music, psychology, and political philosophy as well as other special fields.

Essays:
Counter-Statement (1931)
Permanence and Change — Anatomy of Purpose (1935)
Philosophy of Literary Form — Studies in Symbolic Action (1941)
A Grammar of Motives (1945)
A Rhetoric of Motives (1950)
Novel:
The White Oxen (1924)
Poetry:
Book of Moments (1956)

WILLIAM BYRD 1647–1744

Although William Byrd's birthplace was a tidewater plantation, he was educated in England and on the Continent. He was trained not only in business and law but also in the social graces and in classical and Neoclassical literature. Shortly after his return from England to America in 1692, Byrd assumed his place as a member of the ruling circle in Virginia. He served several times as a representative in the House of Burgesses; on various occasions he represented the colony in England; he was also appointed member of the Supreme Council and held that dignified position for the remainder of his life. His journal writings, in which his witty perceptions are recorded in well-turned phrases, reveal not only his admiration of Neoclassical literature but also the complexity of a Virginian who was not only an aristocrat but also a businessman and a man of the world.

The History of the Dividing Line (1728)
The Secret History of the Line (1728)
A Progress to the Mines (1732)
A Journey to the Land of Eden (1733)

GEORGE WASHINGTON CABLE 1844–1925

George Washington Cable's father came from an old slaveholding family in Virginia; his mother was a native of New England and a strict Puritan. Cable himself was born in New Orleans, where he spent much of his life. For more than ten years after the Civil War, in which he had served and had been wounded, he was clerk and bookkeeper for a cotton firm. During these years, however, he read much, delved into the old French and Spanish records of New Orleans, and began to write. His first story appeared in *Scribner's Monthly* in 1873 and was followed by other stories of New Orleans in the early nineteenth century, a colorful mélange of races. Despite the success of his early local color stories, Cable turned reformer, and in *The Silent South* (1885) he zealously advocated reforms in racial relations. The book made him so unpopular in the South that he moved to Massachusetts.

Like many other writers of local color fiction, Cable was a romantic realist and was inclined to play up the moral ending and the picturesque. But if his edification is sometimes a little forced, his exoticism is at least based on fact. He deserves to be remembered as the literary discoverer of romantic New Orleans and as the facile recorder of his discoveries.

Short Stories:
Old Creole Days (1879)
"Posson Jane" and Père Raphael (1909)
Novels:
The Grandissimes (1880)
Madame Delphine (1881)
Dr. Sevier (1885)
John March, Southerner (1894)
Essays:
The Silent South (1885)
The Negro Question (1890)

WILLA SIBERT CATHER 1873–1947

Willa Cather was born near Winchester, in the northern tip of Virginia, but from her ninth to her nineteenth year she was a Nebraskan, growing up in what was then a pioneer rural community, settled largely by Norwegian and Bohemian immigrants. After some tutoring at home she went to high school at Red Cloud and then to the University of Nebraska, where she was graduated in 1895. By that time she had acquired a deep interest in good music, an enthusiasm for the work of Henry James, and a desire to write, heightened by some experience with newspaper work and a few appearances in the college magazine.

Only gradually did she find her power as a writer. Her first published stories and poems appeared in 1900. She had then worked for five years on the Pittsburgh *Daily Leader*. Her first book, *April Twilights* (1903), a volume of poems, came out while she was teaching English in Allegheny High School. In 1906 she moved to New York City to work on *McClure's Magazine*, of which she was managing editor from 1908 until 1911. It seems likely that the most important event of Miss Cather's years as editor was her connection with Sarah Orne Jewett, who advised her late in 1908 to find time and quiet to perfect her work if she wished her gifts to mature. Following this advice, Miss Cather resigned her editorship to write. With the novels that soon followed, *My Ántonia* among them, her reputation as a writer was firmly established.

The secure position of Miss Cather among present-day American writers is the result of her allegiance to the belief that fiction is a form of art worth practicing with the utmost seriousness. The effects which she chiefly sought were in the realm of subtleties of character and situation. But she was, nevertheless, aware of the importance of setting and physical action. She stood for tradition and refinement of art in life and in fiction.

Novels:
O Pioneers! (1913)
The Song of the Lark (1915)
My Ántonia (1918)
One of Ours (1922)
The Professor's House (1925)
My Mortal Enemy (1926)
Death Comes for the Archbishop (1927)
Shadows on the Rock (1931)
Poetry:
April Twilights (1903)
Short Stories:
The Troll Garden (1905)
Youth and the Bright Medusa (1920)
Obscure Destinies (1932)
The Old Beauty and Others (1948)
Essays:
Not Under Forty (1936)

WILLIAM ELLERY CHANNING 1780–1842

In 1803 William Ellery Channing was ordained a minister of the Federal Street Church, Boston, where he was soon renowned for his concern with charity and his willingness to bring controversial subjects into his pulpit. As early as 1806 he was thinking of himself as a "liberal" Christian, and by 1819, with his *Unitarian Christianity*, he broke with the conservative factions of the Congregational Church to become the leader of the Unitarian Church. The humanistic attitudes which

Channing applied to religion were the beginning of a Christianity characteristically American in its special regard for individual and free thought.

The System of Exclusion and Denunciation in Religion Considered (1815)
Unitarian Christianity (1819)
"The Moral Argument Against Calvinism" (1820)
"Remarks on the Character and Writings of John Milton" (1826)
"The Importance and Means of a National Literature" (1830)

CHARLES CHAUNCY 1705–1787

For sixty years one of the ministers of the First Church of Boston, Charles Chauncy is remembered as one of the first to turn away from Calvinism for the more comfortable but less emotional ways of Unitarianism. His *Seasonable Thoughts on the State of Religion in New England* (1743) demonstrates his skepticism about the relationship of religious "experiences" to true piety. His fifty-odd published books are convincing evidence that no one in New England was his superior in the exercise of a clear and functional style.

Seasonable Thoughts on the State of Religion in New England (1743)
A Compleat View of Episcopacy (1771)

JOHN CHEEVER 1912–

John Cheever, born in Quincy, Massachusetts, left home at the age of seventeen after his expulsion from the Thayer Academy at South Braintree, Massachusetts. Since then, except for service in the army and teaching in the English Department of Barnard, his career has been devoted to his writing. A large number of his short stories have appeared in *The New Yorker*.

Cheever defends middle-class suburbia as the setting for many of his short stories by saying, "Life can be as good and rich there as anyplace else." Although set in Italy, even *Some People, Places, and Things That Will Not Appear in My Next Novel*, according to one critic, has as characters "the same bewildered suburbanites" that appear in his other works.

Short Stories:
The Way Some People Live (1943)
The Enormous Radio and Other Stories (1953)
The Housebreaker of Shady Hill and Other Stories (1959)
*Some People, Places, and Things That Will Not Appear
    in My Next Novel* (1961)
Novel:
The Wapshot Chronicle (1957)
The Wapshot Scandal (1964)

SAMUEL L. CLEMENS (Mark Twain) 1835–1910

Samuel Langhorne Clemens spent his boyhood years in Hannibal, Missouri, where he became a printer's apprentice. Having learned to set type, he wandered eastward as far as New York, picking up printing jobs in one city after another. Then, back in the Middle West in the 1850's, he learned the pilot's trade and spent some of his happiest years steering boats up and down the Mississippi. Later, he adopted the pseudonym "Mark Twain," an expression used by steamboatmen when testing the depth of the channel. The job of piloting lasted until the boom days of river trade were cut off by the Civil War. In 1861, after brief service in the Confederate Army, he went out to the Far West. There, he took some fliers in mining stock, did some prospecting, and finally got into journalism of the masculine humorous sort which flourished in the Far West.

The journalistic work, in Nevada and in California, launched him on his career as a humorist. Having invested some of his royalties from his first popular book in a Buffalo newspaper, Clemens was an editor for a time. He financed many inventions and get-rich schemes and eventually set up as a large-scale publisher of books—his own as well as those by other authors. In 1894, when the author-businessman was fifty-nine, some important financial investments proved unwise, his publishing house failed, and he faced financial ruin. Refusing to accept bankruptcy, he paid off his debts dollar for dollar, earning enough to do so by publishing and by making a lecture trip around the world.

After he had hit upon his mature technique, two methods—that of the old Southwestern humorists and that of the funnymen—were intermingled in most of his writings. Whenever in his fiction (for example *Huckleberry Finn*), his training as a professional humorist caused him to add buffoonery and burlesque to materials inhospitable to the broadest comedy, his writings tended to suffer from unevenness of tone. However, he had the happy ability of always finding the best word, and more than any other classic fictionist, he captured the American language in print. In addition, he had a genius for creating living, memorable characters.

Travel Narratives:
The Innocents Abroad (1869)
Roughing It (1872)
A Tramp Abroad (1880)
Following the Equator (1897)
Novels:
The Gilded Age (with Charles Dudley Warner, 1873)
The Adventures of Tom Sawyer (1876)
The Prince and the Pauper (1882)
The Adventures of Huckleberry Finn (1884)
A Connecticut Yankee in King Arthur's Court (1889)
Puddn'head Wilson (1894)
The Mysterious Stranger (1916)
Autobiography:
Life on the Mississippi (1883)
Autobiography (1924, 1940)

JAMES FENIMORE COOPER 1789–1851

James Fenimore Cooper was born in New Jersey and soon moved to the town which his father had laid out—Cooperstown, New York. He was brought up in a community in which the Coopers were by far the most important personages; his future was from the first defined as that of a landowner and estate manager. He had the education of a gentleman, first under a private tutor in Albany and then in Yale College, which expelled him in 1806 for too much pleasure-seeking. After spending three years in the United States Navy, he married Susan Augusta De Lancey, daughter of a wealthy family in Westchester County. Both he and his wife had money of their own, and there was more in prospect. Thus, in 1819 at the age of thirty, Cooper was a gentleman farmer and a small capitalist, with neither the ambition nor the necessity for authorship.

Seldom perhaps, has a novelist developed more casually. The tradition is that, reading aloud to his wife a story of English country life, he remarked that he could do as well himself and set out to do so. The result was the novel *Precaution* (1820), abounding with moral sentiment on marriage and picturing English society. It was published in 1820, and, although not especially successful, it led directly to *The Spy* (1821) which was enormously so. The course of Cooper's life was changed abruptly, and he began to produce a stream of books which, at the time of his death in 1851, consisted of thirty-three novels and numerous volumes of social comment, naval history, and travel.

Cooper's right to be called the first great American novelist can scarcely be challenged. The recognition of his greatness came as early as when his friend Bryant referred to him as the American Hesiod or Theocritus, a poet of the youth of a nation.

Essays:
The American Democrat (1838)
Novels:
Precaution (1820)
The Spy (1821)
The Pioneers (1823)
The Pilot (1823)
Lionel Lincoln (1825)
The Last of the Mohicans (1826)
The Prairie (1827)
The Bravo (1831)
The Heidenmauer (1832)
The Headsman (1833)
Home as Found (1838)
The Pathfinder (1840)
The Deerslayer (1841)
Satanstoe (1845)
The Chainbearer (1845)
The Redskins (1846)

CHARLES EGBERT CRADDOCK: see Mary Noailles Murfree

HART CRANE 1899–1932

Hart Crane was born in Garrettsville, Ohio, and later lived in Cleveland, where he attended a public high school for three years. He did not go to college but while still in his teens dedicated himself to a poetic career. For a livelihood, Crane did various jobs in his father's candy business, working as clerk in a candy store, traveling salesman, warehouse manager, and the like, but he later found less uncongenial employment as a writer for advertising agencies, first in Cleveland and then in New York. Like Sherwood Anderson, whom he admired, he gravitated to New York and its literary coteries. Here Crane profited by his associations with Gorham Munson, Waldo Frank, Allen Tate, Malcolm Cowley, and others. Otto Kahn, the philanthropist, gave him a thousand dollars (and offered more) so that he might have leisure for his poetry. His magnum opus, *The Bridge*, was published in 1930 and met with a mixed reception. Neurotically unhappy for a long while, Crane sought peace of mind, without success, in the Adirondacks, Europe, Cuba,

Mexico. En route to the United States from Mexico, April 27, 1932, he committed suicide by jumping from the deck of a steamship into the Caribbean Sea.

Crane's fame, it now appears, rests securely upon *The Bridge,* perhaps the most ambitious poem in English since *The Waste Land,* to which it is in some ways similar, though it is neither as well unified nor as firmly sustained as Eliot's masterpiece,

White Buildings (1926)
The Bridge (1930)
Collected Poems (1933)

STEPHEN CRANE 1871–1900

Stephen Crane was born in Newark, New Jersey, the son of a Methodist preacher. He spent a semester at Lafayette College, where he shocked his English professor by declaring that Tennyson's poetry was "swill"; and a semester at Syracuse University, where he played shortstop on the varsity nine. Believing earnestly that he must devote his life to "the business of writing," he began with journalism. His brief career as a newspaper writer gave him rich and varied opportunities for observation: in the New York Bowery, in Texas and Mexico, and—under war conditions—in Greece and in Cuba. After his marriage in 1897 he lived in England; one of his close friends there was Joseph Conrad. Crane died in the Black Forest, in Germany, where he had gone with the hope of improving his health.

As a poet, Crane is an interesting link between Emily Dickinson and the Imagists of the 1910's. As a writer of fiction, he is important both as an early naturalist and as an expert craftsman.

Novels:
Maggie: A Girl of the Streets (1893)
The Red Badge of Courage (1895)
Short Stories:
The Open Boat and Other Tales of Adventure (1898)
The Monster and Other Stories (1899)
Whilomville Stories (1900)
Poetry:
The Black Rider and Other Lines (1895)
War Is Kind and Other Lines (1899)

MICHEL GUILLAUME ST. JEAN DE CREVECOEUR 1735–1813

Michel Guillaume St. Jean de Crèvecoeur was born in France. Educated in a Jesuit school and in England, he sailed for Canada before he was twenty and there enlisted in the army. About 1759 Crèvecoeur drifted down through the English colonies and in 1764 applied for naturalization in New York. He married and for approximately fifteen years lived as a gentleman farmer in a well-established and prosperous rural community. Soon after his marriage, he appears to have begun setting down his impressions of the country; and by 1780 he was forced to leave America because his moderate opinions had made both Whigs and Tories suspicious of him. For a time he was a protégé of Madame d'Houdetot, whom Rousseau had loved. Partly through her influence, he was sent back to New York as consul-general, and for seven years he did his best to keep alive American friendship with France. The last twenty-three years of his life were spent in Europe.

Crèvecoeur wrote well, though unevenly. The fashion of his day compelled him to shape his best-known book into a series of letters, but within these he displayed a considerable command of three different forms: the prose essay, the short story, and the dramatic dialog.

Letters from an American Farmer (1782)
Sketches of Eighteenth Century America (1925)
Travels in Pennsylvania and New York, ed. P. E. Adams (1962)

DAVID CROCKETT 1786-1836

Although he was born and reared in a Tennessee frontier log cabin and had little formal education, David Crockett became a United States Congressman and a hero of the folk. His accomplishments had become legendary even before his heroic death in the Alamo in 1836. In 1834 he had published his autobiography, *A Narrative of the Life of David Crockett of West Tennessee*. This and others of his accounts did much to bring in the fireside yarn, with its authentic rendering of Western ways of living, thinking, talking, and narrating, as an eventual literary influence upon authors such as Harte and Clemens.

Narrative of the Life of David Crockett of West Tennessee (1834)
A Tour to the North and Down East (1835)

EDWARD ESTLIN CUMMINGS 1894-1962

E. E. Cummings, the son of a minister, was born and educated in Cambridge, Massachusetts; in 1915 and 1916 he received his B.A. and M.A. from Harvard. During World War I he served with the ambulance corps, and through the error of a military censor he spent some time in a French detention camp. His book, *The Enormous Room*, details his experiences there. After studying art for a time in Paris, he began to experiment with new techniques of writing such as unconventional typographical arrangements, oddities of spelling and punctuation, and the abolition of capital letters. Magazines such as *Vanity Fair, The Dial*, and others accepted his poems, and he published many individual volumes of poetry and novels.

Poetry:
Tulips & Chimneys (1923)
Collected Poems (1938)
Poems: 1923-1954 (1954)
One Hundred Selected Poems (1959)
Novel:
The Enormous Room (1922)

EMILY DICKINSON 1830-1886

Emily Dickinson was the daughter of lawyer Edward Dickinson of Amherst, Massachusetts, a rather stern Calvinist. Despite her repressive surroundings she was a vivacious, fun-loving girl and was well educated in the Amherst Academy and Mount Holyoke. In time, something happened to her which caused her to become a recluse in her house at Amherst, where she wrote much verse but refused to publish it during her lifetime. Books of her poems were published starting in 1890. These were greatly edited. Her complete works are now available in an excellent three-volume edition, *The Poems of Emily Dickinson*, edited by Thomas H. Johnson (1955). Johnson also has edited her delightful letters.

Beginning in the 1920's many critics have praised Miss Dickinson, along with Whitman, for pioneering in modern poetry. The use she made of imperfect rhyme, or eye-rhyme, and, in particular, her habit of packing her lines with cryptic meanings have endeared her to present-day readers. Her vivid imagination and her playful spirit also made her as fond of poetic conceits as had been John Donne, idol of the moderns.

The Poems of Emily Dickinson, ed. Thomas H. Johnson (3 vols., 1955)
The Letters of Emily Dickinson, ed. Thomas H. Johnson (3 vols., 1958)

MR. DOOLEY: see Finley Peter Dunne

JOHN DOS PASSOS 1896–
John Dos Passos' father was a New York lawyer, the son of a Portuguese immigrant; his mother's family lived in Maryland and Virginia. Born in Chicago, Dos Passos was (as he has put it) "carted around a good deal as a child" — to Mexico, England, Europe, Washington City, tidewater Virginia. He prepared for college at Choate School in Wallingford, Connecticut, and was graduated from Harvard, *cum laude*, in 1916. During World War I he served first with a French ambulance unit and later in the United States Medical Corps as a private. After the war, he went to various parts of Europe and America as a newspaper correspondent.

Dos Passos' trilogy, *U.S.A.*, is the most impressive "social" novel which has been written thus far in America. The style, which Kazin well calls "a hard, lean, mocking prose," is an efficient instrument for the portrayal of the modern machine age. The books which have followed *U.S.A.* indicate that Dos Passos has been moving steadily away from his earlier position at the extreme left. And the later Dos Passos is obviously less doctrinaire and mechanical, and more human and humanistic.

Three Soldiers (1921)
Manhattan Transfer (1925)
U.S.A. (1937)
Adventures of a Young Man (1939)
The Grand Design (1949)
Chosen Country (1951)
Midcentury (1961)

JACK DOWNING: see Seba Smith

THEODORE DREISER 1871–1945
The twelfth in a family of thirteen children, Theodore Dreiser was born in Terre Haute, Indiana, where his father, a German emigrant, was proprietor of a woolen mill. The burning of the mill, which was not insured, left the family in extreme poverty. Dreiser's formal schooling was received in an Indiana high school and at Indiana University, where he stayed only one year because he felt that the curriculum "did not concern ordinary life at all." More useful than college to Dreiser were various odd jobs in Chicago — washing dishes in a restaurant, shoveling coal in a railroad yard, working in a hardware factory, collecting bills for a furniture store. Valuable also to the future novelist were his experiences as a reporter on the Chicago *Globe* and on other newspapers in St. Louis, Cleveland, Pittsburgh, and New York. His newspaper career extended until about 1905. For a while he was

connected with certain "pulp" magazines, and from 1907 to 1910 he was editor of *The Delineator*. Jobs like these were necessary to pay expenses; his novels brought him little money for many years. In the meantime, he had married but did not find marriage to his liking and was divorced. In time he married actress Helen Patgas and lived in the California movie colony for three years before moving to New York State in 1924. After a visit to Russia in 1927 he became an enthusiastic supporter of socialism, but towards the end of his life he had developed a serious interest in oriental mysticism.

No other American novelist has documented his stories quite so carefully or has written a social record of American life so convincingly authentic. Though Dreiser's work is often dull and sometimes reveals the author's lack of a sense of humor, it is important as the first entirely "naturalistic" American fiction.

Novels:
Sister Carrie (1900)
Jennie Gerhardt (1911)
The Financier (1912)
The Titan (1914)
The "Genius" (1915)
An American Tragedy (1925)
The Bulwark (1946)
The Stoic (1947)
Short Stories:
Free and Other Stories (1918)
Chains (1927)
A Gallery of Women (1929)

FINLEY PETER DUNNE (Mr. Dooley) 1867–1936

In Chicago, which had been his birthplace, Finley Peter Dunne attended high school and worked his way up from office boy on a newspaper to a job as a reporter. When in 1892 he chanced to put a piece commenting on current affairs into the dialect of an Irish saloonkeeper, he hit upon a way of writing destined to make him famous. After some experiments and changes, the saloonkeeper became Martin Dooley, whose unlearned but vivid diction and common-sensible philosophy showed his relationship with the long line of horse-sense humorists admired by Americans. Dunne's essays do more than amusingly illuminate the times which produced them: because they are rich in commentary upon the human foibles of all periods, they have enduring merit.

Mr. Dooley in Peace and in War (1898)
Mr. Dooley in the Hearts of His Countrymen (1899)
Mr. Dooley's Philosophy (1900)
Mr. Dooley's Opinions (1901)
Observations of Mr. Dooley (1902)
Dissertations by Mr. Dooley (1906)
Mr. Dooley Says (1910)
New Dooley Book (1911)
Mr. Dooley on Making a Will (1919)

TIMOTHY DWIGHT 1752–1817

Timothy Dwight, a Yale graduate at seventeen, gave up teaching in 1777 to become an army chaplain, but family responsibilities forced him to leave the army early in 1779. For the next fifteen years he worked feverishly, first as farm manager, preacher, teacher, and legislator at Northampton, Massachusetts. Dwight then became pastor of the Congregational Church at Greenfield, Connecticut, in 1783, and finally in 1795 he was appointed President of Yale University. In his writing, Dwight was much like Cotton Mather for his defense of the *status quo*, his flashes of foresight, and the derivative quality of his mind.

Poetry:
The Conquest of Canaan (1785)
The Triumph of Infidelity (1788)
"Columbia, Columbia, to Glory Arise" (1793)
Greenfield Hill: A Poem in Seven Parts (1794)
Nonfiction:
The Nature, and Danger, of Infidel Philosophy (1798)
Theology: Explained and Defended (5 vols., 1818-1819)
Travels; in New-England and New-York (4 vols., 1821-1822)

RICHARD EBERHART 1904–

Richard Eberhart was born in Austin, Minnesota, and attended the University of Minnesota for one year. He then went to Dartmouth College, graduating in 1926. In 1929 he received a B.A. and in 1933 his M.A. from Cambridge. He taught in Massachusetts until the beginning of World War II, when he went into the Navy. In 1946 he began working for the Butcher Wax Company, and six years later he became a vice-president. In 1955 he became director of the Yaddo Corporation. From 1959 to 1961 Eberhart was consultant in poetry at the Library of Congress. He has also taught in a number of schools—the University of Washington, the University of Connecticut, Wheaton College, and Dartmouth College.

Eberhart's preoccupation with death in his early poetry yielded somewhat in the 1940's to a concern about the evils of war. His latest poetry, often concerned with the human predicament in the atomic age, covers a wide range of moods and subjects. The poet's uncluttered style gives simple directness to his work.

A Bravery of Earth (1930)
Reading the Spirit (1936)
Song and Idea (1942)
Poems New and Selected (1944)
Burr Oaks (1947)
Brotherhood of Men (1949)
Selected Poems (1951)
Undercliff: Poems (1946-1953) (1953)
Great Praises (1957)
Collected Poems, 1930-1960 (1960)

JONATHAN EDWARDS 1703–1758

Jonathan Edwards was born in East Windsor, Connecticut, where his father was minister. He received his early education at home and was graduated from Yale College before he was seventeen. He spent two additional years at Yale in the study of theology, and, after eight months of preaching in a Presbyterian church in New York City, he spent three more years as a tutor. Early in 1727 he joined his grandfather, the Reverend Solomon Stoddard, in the church at Northampton, Massachusetts, married, and became full minister at Stoddard's death in 1729.

As a clergyman Edwards developed an absorbing interest in what we would now call the psychology of religion. He welcomed the "awakenings" which came periodically in his church and eventually announced that he could not conscientiously admit to communion those persons who had made no public relation of religious experience. His congregation was unwilling to accept this return to the stricter ways of the first generation in New England, and in 1750 Edwards was dismissed. From 1751 until 1757 he was pastor at Stockbridge, Massachusetts, at that time an Indian mission village on the frontier. He then accepted a call to the presidency of the College of New Jersey (now Princeton University), where he died of smallpox three months after his installation. To many, Edwards is the greatest theologian that America has yet produced and unquestionably one of the most original minds in our country's history.

A Divine and Supernatural Light (1734)
A Faithful Narrative (1737)
Sinners in the Hands of an Angry God (1741)
Some Thoughts Concerning the Present Revival of Religion
     in New England (1742)
A Treatise Concerning Religious Affections (1746)
Freedom of the Will [short title] (1754)
Original Sin Defended [short title] (1758)
Two Dissertations, I. Concerning the End for Which God
     Created the World. II The Nature of True Virtue (1765)

EDWARD EGGLESTON 1837–1902

Edward Eggleston was born in Vevay, Indiana. He attended the public schools there but was prevented from going to college by ill health. Brought up a devout Methodist, he soon became a circuit rider, preaching at ten widely separated stations on a four weeks' circuit in southern Indiana. His health broke under the strain of such strenuous employment, and he spent some nine years in Minnesota as Bible agent and pastor of small churches. He gave up the ministry in 1866 and turned to writing for religious papers; some of his most famous stories first appeared in such papers. He made a reputation with The Hoosier Schoolmaster (1871).

After 1870 Eggleston lived in the East, in Brooklyn and New York, and at Joshua's Rock on Lake George. About 1890, or earlier, his interest shifted from fiction to history, and he projected too ambitiously a comprehensive account of the growth of American civilization, two volumes of which he completed. Eggleston, "the first of the Hoosiers," was an important influence in making the American novel popular and in turning it toward realism.

The Hoosier Schoolmaster (1871)
The Circuit Rider (1874)
The Graysons (1888)

THOMAS STEARNS ELIOT 1888–

Born in St. Louis, where his grandfather had founded Washington University and where his father was president of a local industry, T. S. Eliot attended Smith Academy in St. Louis and then Milton Academy in Massachusetts in preparation for entering Harvard in 1906. Influenced by Irving Babbitt and George Santayana, he chose philosophy as his main course of study. Although he studied in Europe and completed a doctoral dissertation on the philosophy of F. H. Bradley, he never returned to Harvard for formal acceptance of the degree. He has resided in England since 1914 and since 1927 has been a British subject.

After his marriage to Vivienne Haigh Haigh-Wood in 1915, Eliot taught and for a time worked at Lloyds Bank in London. He then turned to editorial work on such publications as *The Egoist* and *The Criterion*, and he is still a director of Faber and Faber, a British publishing firm. He returned to the United States in 1932-1933 to give a series of Charles Eliot Norton lectures at Harvard. In 1948, a year after his first wife died, he was awarded the British Order of Merit and the Nobel Prize for Literature. In January 1957 Eliot married Miss Valerie Fletcher who had been his private secretary.

Eliot's essays altered the current of literary criticism. Owing to his influence, the "metaphysical" became a mark of excellence, and English and American poets were reappraised in the light of this new standard. This metaphysical revolution also produced a style of criticism which is remarkable for its close analysis of the relation of structure and style to content. Because Eliot is preëminently a poet, he ultimately transcends the political and religious questions to which he sometimes turns his attention. Even the excellence of his literary theories must take second place to the excellence of his verse in which he has striven for, and achieved, the utmost in condensation.

Poetry:
Poems (1917, 1919, 1920)
The Waste Land (1922)
Ash-Wednesday (1930)
Four Quartets (1943)
Drama:
The Rock, A Pageant Play (1934)
Murder in the Cathedral (1935)
The Cocktail Party (1950)
The Confidential Clerk (1954)
The Elder Statesman (1958)
Criticism:
The Sacred Wood (1920)
For Lancelot Andrewes (1928)
The Use of Poetry and the Use of Criticism (1933)
The Three Voices of Poetry (1953)
The Frontiers of Criticism (1956)
On Poetry and Poets (1957)

RALPH WALDO EMERSON 1803-1882

Ralph Waldo Emerson was descended from nine successive generations of ministers. His father, who was minister of the First Church, Unitarian, in Boston, Ralph Waldo's birthplace, died when Emerson was eight years old, leaving a widow and four sons in difficult financial circumstances. Nevertheless, with the assistance of their Aunt Mary Moody Emerson, all four sons went through Harvard, Ralph Waldo graduating in 1821. He taught school for a while, attended the Harvard Divinity School, spent a winter in Florida for his health, and, in 1829, became pastor of the Second Church of Boston and married Miss Ellen Tucker. In 1831 his wife died. A year later he resigned his pastorate because of his unwillingness to administer the Lord's Supper.

In 1833 Emerson went abroad and visited Landor in Italy, Coleridge and Wordsworth in England, and (most important of all, because the meeting was the beginning of a lifelong friendship) Carlyle in Scotland. Upon his return to America, he bought a house and two acres of land in Concord, married Miss Lydia Jackson, and in 1836 published his first volume, *Nature*. Except among the Transcendentalists, it met with a mild reception; but the two challenging addresses which followed soon after, *The American Scholar* in 1837 and *The Divinity School Address* in 1838, made Emerson famous. From 1840 to 1842 he assisted Margaret Fuller in editing *The Dial* and from 1842 to 1844 was himself editor. He lectured extensively and successfully in England in 1847-1848. In the 1840's and 1850's Emerson's energies were rigorously tested by the ever-increasing demand for his time as a lecturer in New England, the middle Atlantic states, and the "Northwest."

Emerson kept aloof from the slavery controversy in the 1830's and 1840's, but later events drove him inexorably into the ranks of the radical abolitionists. In 1859 he took his stand publicly as champion of John Brown. From 1861 to 1865 he was caught in the general hysteria of war; "Emerson," Hawthorne said in 1861, "is breathing slaughter like the rest of us." On January 1, 1863, he read the "Boston Hymn" in the Boston Music Hall, and in April 1865 he objected in his journal that Grant's terms of surrender were "a little too easy."

In 1871 Emerson was beginning to show definite signs of decline. His writings were becoming less coherent, and his memory was slipping. In 1872, with part of a fund that his friends had collected for him, he made his last visit to Carlyle and, upon his return from Europe, settled into a quiet retirement. In 1882 he died of pneumonia and was buried, appropriately, near Thoreau.

Emerson's ability as a lecturer to convince his audience of the individual's personal worth qualifies him to be judged and appreciated not primarily as a metaphysical philosopher but as a moral teacher. His poetry, influenced as it was by seventeenth-century poets, has become increasingly appreciated.

Essays:
Nature (1836)
The American Scholar (1837)
The Divinity School Address (1838)
Essays, First Series (1841)
Essays, Second Series (1844)
Representative Men (1850)
English Traits (1856)
The Conduct of Life (1860)
Poetry:
Poems (1847)

WILLIAM FAULKNER 1897–1962

William Faulkner was born in New Albany, Mississippi, and lived for most of his life in the neighboring county seat, Oxford, where the University of Mississippi is situated. The Faulkner (or Falkner) family has long been prominent in politics, railroad building, and planting; one great-grandfather of William's was the author of a popular ante-bellum romance, *The White Rose of Memphis*. The Sartoris family, prominent in a number of Faulkner's novels, appears to be in part a projection of his own clan.

Early in World War I, Faulkner, just out of high school, ran off to Canada to join the British air force. He was sent to England for training and saw about one year of service in France before he was wounded in a crash. Back in Mississippi, he was for a time a student in the university; he then worked at such odd jobs as clerking in the college postal station and house-painting. Encouragement. for his writing apparently came from various friends, among them Phil Stone, an Oxford lawyer; Stark Young, then teaching at Amherst; and Sherwood Anderson, with whom he lived in New Orleans in 1922.

In 1929 he married Estelle Oldham and by that time had already decided on writing as his career. After 1936 he occasionally went to Hollywood to write for various motion pictures, and made some visits abroad for the State Department. However, in spite of these trips and occasional visits to New York, Faulkner spent much of his time in Oxford, Mississippi. Even after he became a writer in residence at the University of Virginia, he continued to return to Oxford until 1959 when he announced his intention to settle in Charlottesville, Virginia. He held an honorary post at the University until his death in 1962. He received among other awards the Pulitzer Prize for both *A Fable* (1954) and *The Town* (1957) and, in 1950, the Nobel Prize for Literature.

The fiction of William Faulkner has as many different planes of interest as that of any contemporary American writer. On one level much of it is sheer horror, a twentieth-century throwback to the Gothic romance. On another it is Hawthornesque in its exploration of the methods and effects of symbolism and allegory. On still another it is a vast and intricate legend of the disintegration of the Old South, epiclike in conception and not unworthy of comparison with James Joyce's portrayal of Dublin in *Ulysses*. To the student of technique it is notable for its bold experimentation with narrative point of view, while the reader with an eye for style finds it full of some of the lushest rhetoric of our time. All in all, Faulkner's stories are almost incredibly subtle. They make such great demands of their readers that the surprising thing is that they have been as popular as they have.

Novels:
Soldier's Pay (1926)
Mosquitoes (1927)
Sartoris (1929)
The Sound and the Fury (1929)
As I Lay Dying (1930)
Sanctuary (1931)
Light in August (1932)
Pylon (1935)
Absalom, Absalom! (1936)
The Wild Palms (1939)
The Hamlet (1940)
Intruder in the Dust (1948)
Requiem for a Nun (1951)
A Fable (1954)
The Town (1957)
The Mansion (1959)
The Reivers (1962)
Short Stories:
These 13 (1931)
Doctor Martino and Other Stories (1934)

The Unvanquished (1938)
Go Down, Moses (1942)
Knight's Gambit (1949)
Big Woods (1955)
Poetry:
The Marble Faun (1924)

LAWRENCE FERLINGHETTI 1919–

Lawrence Ferlinghetti was born in Yonkers, New York. It was in San Francisco, however, that he made his first mark in the world of letters as the owner of the City Lights Bookstore and as the publisher of City Lights Books. He is considered one of the key figures in the beginnings of the "beat" movement, not only because of his publications, but also because he encouraged poets to meet and exchange ideas in his bookstore. His own poetry, too, is a significant part of the "beat" movement.

Pictures of the Gone World (1955)
A Coney Island of the Mind (1958)
Her (1960)
Starting from San Francisco (1961)

F. SCOTT FITZGERALD 1896–1940

F. Scott Fitzgerald was born in St. Paul, Minnesota, and educated in the public schools of St. Paul, at the Newman School of Hackensack, New Jersey, and at Princeton University. In college he formed a friendship with Edmund Wilson and contributed poems and stories to the *Nassau Literary Magazine*. He left Princeton in 1917 to join the army, soon after the United States entered World War I. He was commissioned a lieutenant in the infantry but was not sent overseas. In 1920 he married Zelda Sayre of Montgomery, Alabama. That same year he published *This Side of Paradise*, a novel about the flaming youth of the postwar era, which made him famous. Thereafter, Fitzgerald devoted himself to the writing of prose fiction. He often lived abroad—in Paris, in Italy, and on the French Riviera. His last years were spent in Hollywood, where he died of a heart attack.

Fitzgerald is admired particularly for capturing the spirit of the 1920's—both the recklessness and the fear and cynicism that colored its gaiety. During the late 1940's and early 1950's there was a notable Fitzgerald revival to which many distinguished writers and critics contributed, and Fitzgerald achieved, suddenly, a critical importance. Most students are now inclined to agree with Arthur Mizner's judgment that "Fitzgerald's reputation as a serious novelist is secure."

Novels:
This Side of Paradise (1920)
The Beautiful and Damned (1922)
The Great Gatsby (1925)
Tender is the Night (1934)
The Last Tycoon (1941)
Short Stories:
Flappers and Philosophers (1920)
Tales of the Jazz Age (1922)
All the Sad Young Men (1926)
Taps at Reveille (1935)

BENJAMIN FRANKLIN 1706-1790

The details of Benjamin Franklin's early life are familiar through his autobiography. There he tells of his ancestry and birth in Boston, of his early apprenticeship to his printer brother, of the circumstances which led to his running off to Philadelphia when he was seventeen, of his disillusion there and in London concerning easy roads to wealth. In 1728 he founded his own printing firm, determined to make his fortune by hard work and thrift. Only men with financial security could afford to indulge themselves in the public service which he had in the back of his mind.

It took just twenty years for him to make enough money so that he could retire. He then turned first to science, long one of his enthusiasms, and within a few years was internationally famous for his *Experiments & Observations on Electricity*, first published in London in 1751. Already, however, he was busy with public projects and political affairs, notable among them the founding of the Library Company of Philadelphia (1731), the organization of the American Philosophical Society (1743), the proposal for the Academy of Philadelphia, later the University of Pennsylvania (1749), and his service as clerk of the colonial legislature (1736-1751).

There was scarcely a stage in the process of binding disparate colonies into a great nation wherein the calm counsel of Benjamin Franklin had no part. He was probably the first American to assert the principle of "no taxation without representation"; between 1757 and 1775 he was the chief representative of the colonial point of view in England; in 1775-1776 he was a key member of the Second Continental Congress, where he was one of the drafting committee for the Declaration of Independence; between 1777 and 1785 he was in France, where he was largely responsible for the alliance without which the Revolution could hardly have been successful and where he helped to negotiate the treaty of peace; and in 1787, back in Philadelphia, he ended his good works by acting as a balance wheel in the stormy Constitutional Convention.

In an age which tended to like ornate Latinate prose Franklin cultivated simplicity in style and structure. He felt that his literary purposes were utilitarian and did not think of himself as an author in the belletristic sense, although all his life he had a critical eye for style both in prose and in poetry.

"The Dogood Papers" (1721)
A Dissertation on Liberty and Necessity, Pleasure and Pain (1725)
Poor Richard's Almanac (1732-1764)
Plain Truth (1747)
Experiments and Observations on Electricity (1751; 2d ed., 1754; 4th ed., 1769)
Autobiography (first part written 1759; first published 1868)
The Interest of Great Britain Considered with Regard to Her Colonies (1760)
The Ephemera [in French] (1778)
Dialogue Between Franklin and the Gout [in French] (1780)

HAROLD FREDERIC 1856-1898

Harold Frederic was born in Utica, New York. When he was eighteen months old his father died, and his mother thereafter supported the family by operating a dairy. During his school days, Frederic helped her. Later he was successively an office boy, a retoucher of photographs, and a farm hand. At twenty he became a reporter, and at twenty-four an editor, for a Utica newspaper. From 1884 to the year of his death, he served as a London correspondent for the New York *Times*. It was while he was abroad that he wrote his best-known fictional works, alternating days on which he toiled over his novels with days devoted to journalism. Frederic's work anticipated the harsh, blunt realism characteristic of modern American literature, but he is unique in the elaborate efforts he made to write with a high degree of authenticity.

Seth's Brother's Wife (1887)
The Lawton Girl (1890)
The Copperhead (1893)
The Damnation of Theron Ware (1896)

MARY E. WILKINS FREEMAN 1852–1930

The most realistic of the New England local colorists, Mary E. Wilkins was born in Randolph, a village in eastern Massachusetts. She attended the schools of Randolph and of Brattleboro, Vermont, where her family lived for a while and her father kept a store, and she spent one year (1870-1871) at Mount Holyoke Female Seminary. After the death of her parents in 1883, she returned to her native village to live; the village and the country around it furnished the material for her early stories. After her marriage in 1902 to Dr. Charles M. Freeman of Metuchen, New Jersey, Mrs. Freeman attempted, with indifferent success, to enlarge the scope of her writing.

Despite a voluminous and varied output, her reputation and importance still rest upon the early stories of village and rural life in Massachusetts. Because the style of these stories is as spare and angular as the characters it is used to describe, Mrs. Freeman is, with justification, considered a realistic writer of New England.

A Humble Romance and Other Stories (1887)
A New England Nun and Other Stories (1891)

PHILIP FRENEAU 1752–1832

As a young man of sixteen, Philip Freneau entered Princeton, where he became a close friend of James Madison and H. H. Brackenridge and was graduated in 1771. He tried teaching and the study of theology, with no enthusiasm, and by 1775 he was in New York writing satires. The next year he went to the West Indies. In 1778 when he was returning to New Jersey, his ship was captured by the British, but he was permitted to land near his home and promptly enlisted in the militia. He became both a propagandist and a blockade runner for the cause of the Revolution. On one of his voyages in 1780 he was captured and held for six weeks on a prison ship.

The war over, Freneau turned again to the sea to make a living. In 1790, after six years of shipping, Freneau married and settled down to a literary career. In 1791 in Philadelphia he founded the *National Gazette* to provide a focal point for the opposition to the policies of Hamilton. But Freneau's enthusiasm for the French Revolution and Citizen Genêt lost him support and the *National Gazette* expired in 1793. During the last thirty-nine years of his life, Freneau was in almost constant financial difficulty. His literary ventures were of little assistance, and in 1803 he was forced once more to return to the sea. Between 1795 and 1815 five volumes of his poems were collected. Although he was obviously imitative in his forms and themes, he has historic interest as a precursor of Bryant, Emerson, Poe, Whittier, and Longfellow.

The Rising Glory of America (with H. H. Brackenridge, 1772)
The American Village (1772)
The British Prison-Ship (1781)
The Poems of Philip Freneau (1786)
*The Miscellaneous Works of Mr. Philip Freneau Containing His Essays
  and Additional Poems* (1788)

ROBERT FROST 1874-1963

Despite the fact that he was born in San Francisco, California, Robert Frost's forebears for nine generations had been New Englanders, and most of his life, from 1885 to his death, he lived in New England. Frost's father died in San Francisco when the boy was ten, and the widow went East to Lawrence, Massachusetts, with her children, to live with their grandfather. Frost attended school in Lawrence and did such good work that, at graduation, he was high-school valedictorian. In the autumn of 1892 Frost entered Dartmouth, but, finding college life unattractive, he shortly withdrew. During the next few years, he worked in a mill for a time, took a tramping trip through the South, did some teaching, some newspaper work, and married Elinor White, who in high school had been his only rival for class valedictorian. In 1897 he tried college again, this time Harvard, where he enjoyed the study of Latin, Greek, and philosophy. At the end of two years, however, he again left college and moved to a farm near Derry, New Hampshire, which had been given to him by his grandfather. Because farming proved rather unprofitable, Frost turned to teaching at nearby Pinkerton Academy (1905-1911) and then at New Hampshire State Normal (1911-1912).

Meanwhile, he had made a rather discouraging start as a poet. From early boyhood he had been an enthusiastic reader and writer of poetry. In his teens he had begun to publish a few of his poems in magazines. His poetry, however, did not seem very attractive to most buyers: in twenty years, he earned about two hundred dollars, in all, from his verses. In 1911, at thirty-six, he decided to sell his farm and to spend a few years in concentrated poetic work, to determine once and for all whether he could succeed in literature. Attracted by the relatively low cost of living in England, he went abroad with his family in 1912. By 1913 he managed to find a British publisher for his first book of verse, *A Boy's Will*. This, as well as his second book, *North of Boston* (1914), was very favorably received by English readers and critics.

When, in 1915, Frost returned to America, he learned that his two books, upon republication in this country, had won appreciation of a sort to make him rub his eyes. Regardless, he resumed his old vocations of farming—in New Hampshire and Vermont—and of teaching; but now he gave more time to composition. After 1915 he taught at Amherst College, the University of Michigan, the University of Vermont, and the Bread Loaf School of English at Middlebury College, and he also published numerous books of verse. Frost received the Pulitzer Prize for American Poetry four times: in 1924, 1931, 1937, and 1943. A careful study of his poetry will show that, for all his appearance of rustic simplicity, Frost has more of significance to say than many of his contemporaries among whom he holds a high position.

A Boy's Will (1913)
North of Boston (1914)
Mountain Interval (1916)

Selected Poems (1923, 1931, 1934)
New Hampshire (1923)
West-Running Brook (1928)
A Further Range (1936)
A Witness Tree (1942)
Come In (1943)
A Masque of Reason (1945)
Steeple Bush (1947)
A Masque of Mercy (1947)
The Road Not Taken (1951)
Hard Not to be King (1951)
In the Clearing (1962)

HAMLIN GARLAND 1860–1940

Born on a farm in Wisconsin, Hamlin Garland moved with his family to Iowa and then to South Dakota. As a boy he learned the endless routine of the dirt farmer but still found time for the world of books. At an early age, encouraged by his mother, he determined to make himself a teacher, yet he was twenty-four before he really broke with farming. He chose to study in Boston, and there he quickly educated himself in the theaters, in the homes of writers, actors, and artists, and most of all in the Boston Public Library. Gradually he found modest employment as a lecturer, teacher, and reviewer. In 1887, when he returned to South Dakota to visit his parents, he had acquired enough perspective to see that farm life was far from idyllic. When he returned to Boston he wrote the tales collected in *Main-Travelled Roads*. After 1916, when he moved to New York, Garland attained a new popularity by turning to autobiography. In 1922 *A Daughter of the Middle Border* won the Pulitzer Prize for Biography.

Garland was interested in many things, perhaps too many for his artistic salvation. To him, veritism was only one cause among many, and although he tried to present life truthfully he never had an irrepressible passion to say something important supremely well.

Short Stories:
Main-Travelled Roads (1891)
Novels:
Rose of Dutcher's Coolly (1895)
The Captain of the Gray-Horse Troop (1902)
Essays:
Crumbling Idols (1894)
Autobiography:
A Son of the Middle Border (1917)
A Daughter of the Middle Border (1921)

HENRY GEORGE 1839–1897

Henry George, born in Philadelphia, quit school by the time he was thirteen in order to make a living. From 1858 to 1880 he lived in San Francisco, where he worked at what he could find to support his wife and four children. While in New York organizing a wire service for the San Francisco *Herald*, he had first-hand experience of the power of monopolies when he saw his news service killed by the opposition of the Associated Press. He then decided to study and seek a cure for the economic injustices of his time. He wrote extensively, if not always accurately, on economics, and his ideas were soon discussed everywhere. After 1888 his plan known as the Single Tax was frequently an issue in municipal, state, and even national elections. Twice he ran for mayor of New York City, dying in the last days of his second campaign.

George's Single Tax has been dismissed by many economists as oversimplified or unworkable, and the left wing of today is likely to be scornful of his rejection of the Marxist interpretation of history. Yet George remains admired for his criticisms of the English classical economists, for his reaffirmation and extension of the theory of "natural rights," and for his basic moral strength.

Our Land and Land Policy, National and State (1871)
Progress and Poverty (1879)
Social Problems (1883)

ALLEN GINSBURG 1926-

Allen Ginsburg was born in Newark, New Jersey; he attended Columbia University, where in 1949 he received his B.A. The most significant poet of the "beat" generation, he has read his poetry not only in coffeehouses but in major universities both in the United States and in England. His poetry, though neither disciplined nor startlingly original in its statements, is significant as an accurate expression of a truly free imagination.

Howl (1956)
Kaddish (1961)
Empty Mirror (1961)
Reality Sandwiches (1963)

WILLIAM J. GRAYSON 1788-1863

William J. Grayson was a down-state South Carolinian, born in the Beaufort District. From Columbia College (later the University of South Carolina), where he was graduated in 1809, he proceeded to law and politics. He sat in the state legislature, served two terms in the national House of Representatives, and from 1841 until 1853 was Collector of the Port of Charleston. In the conservative literary circles of Charleston he had a leading place as a contributor to the newspapers and to such magazines as *DeBow's Review* and the *Southern Literary Messenger*. Unlike Calhoun he rejected secession as an instrument to obtain what the South wanted, and a letter to Governor Seabrook, published in 1850, helped halt a strong movement for separation. His Unionist sentiment, however, did not keep him from defending slavery, first in a series of essays published in the Charleston *Courier* and reprinted as *Letters to Curtius* (1851) and then in the poem for which he is best known today, *The Hireling and the Slave* (1854).

As a poet Grayson can scarcely merit much attention. His ideas, however, were those of a class and a time which the serious student, observing the South of the present day, cannot afford to ignore.

Poetry:
The Hireling and the Slave (1854)
Essays:
Letters to Curtius (1851)

ALEXANDER HAMILTON 1757-1804

Alexander Hamilton was born in the West Indies. At an early age he displayed an amazing talent for business and was sent to New York to finish his education. In 1774, when he was an undergraduate at King's College (now Columbia University), he joined the Whig opposition to the British and soon distinguished himself as a speaker and pamphleteer. In 1776 he served in the Continental Army and became Washington's aide-de-camp. Despite a temporary break with his commander he served brilliantly to the end of the war and thereafter was a nationally known lawyer and public servant. His most important contributions to government were his draft of the call for the Constitutional Convention, his success in obtaining the ratification of the new form of government by New York, his term as first secretary of the treasury in 1789-1795, and his influence as Washington's most trusted adviser. Hamilton's opposition to Aaron Burr, first in the Presidential election of 1800 and later in the contest of 1804 for the governorship of New York, resulted in the famous duel in which Hamilton was killed.

On political questions Hamilton was always well informed, and he wrote clearly and effectively for the audience to which he addressed himself. There are few better practitioners of argument in American literature.

*A Full Vindication of the Measures of the Congress from
    the Calumnies of Their Enemies* (1774)
The Farmer Refuted (1775)
The Federalist (with Jay and Madison, 1787-1788)

GEORGE WASHINGTON HARRIS 1814–1869

Though he spent most of his life in Knoxville, Tennessee, George Washington Harris was forced to leave that peaceful town to try his hand at various jobs in order to make a living. As a writer for the New York *Spirit of the Times*, he won fame as a writer of wildly comic stories couched in the quaint language of his Tennessee mountain character, Sut Lovingood, who used both great and little men as victims of his humor. A climatic figure in the development of the Southwestern humor much enjoyed by Mark Twain, G. W. Harris is particularly admired for his ability to capture in print the comic movement and the poetry of the oral tale.

Sut Lovingood Yarns (1867)

JOEL CHANDLER HARRIS 1848–1908

Joel Chandler Harris was born near Eatonton, Georgia. His mother, deserted by his father, took in sewing for a living. Between the ages of thirteen and seventeen (the Civil War years), Harris lived on the nearby plantation of Joseph Addison Turner and helped Turner print a weekly paper. At this time he got an education by working on the paper and by reading in Turner's excellent library; he also became intimately acquainted with the life of the Southern plantation and especially with the speech and folklore of the Negroes. After the war he worked for brief periods on newspapers in Macon, New Orleans, and Savannah. In 1876 he joined the staff of the Atlanta *Constitution*, and for twenty-four years, through editorials, book reviews, feature articles, and especially the Uncle Remus stories, he helped mightily to make the *Constitution* the most influential newspaper ever published in the South. Without esteeming his tales the less as comic masterpieces of their kind, or enjoying them the less for their unalloyed humor, one can be glad that these stories contributed to some reconciliation between the North and the South.

Short Stories:
Uncle Remus: His Songs and His Sayings (1880)
Nights with Uncle Remus (1883)
Mingo, and Other Sketches in Black and White (1884)
Uncle Remus and His Friends (1892)
Told by Uncle Remus (1905)
Novels:
Sister Jane (1896)
Gabriel Tolliver (1902)

BRET HARTE   1836–1902

Bret Harte was born in Albany, New York, and had a rather sketchy education. After his widowed mother moved the family to San Francisco, he joined them—in 1854—on the Pacific Coast. There he taught school, worked in the mines for a short time, served as a Wells Fargo Express messenger, and eventually became a printer. Developing his skill as a writer, he in time worked into various editorial jobs on some of the California magazines.

In 1868 he published "The Luck of Roaring Camp" in the newly founded *Overland Monthly*, of which he was editor. When the issue containing "The Luck" reached the East, the story was an immediate success, and other stories in the same vein augmented Harte's popularity. In 1871, with an impressive contract from the *Atlantic Monthly* in his pocket, Harte started East, leaving the Far West permanently. His journey across the continent was a triumphant progress, and he was hailed in the East as a new genius.

The part of his life which came after this journey was largely an anti-climax. A few more stories and some of his many poems were up to the early standard, but his work became repetitious and, in the end, not much more than the working out of a formula. In 1878 he went abroad on a consular appointment to Germany. From 1888 until his death in 1902 he lived in England.

Harte's great success is important in American literary history because of the impetus it gave to local color writing. The unconventional morality—for the time—of his fiction prepared the way for characterization and scenes in later fiction which increasingly departed from prudish standards.

Short Stories:
The Luck of Roaring Camp and Other Sketches (1870)
Tales of the Argonauts (1875)
Colonel Starbottle's Client (1892)
Novel:
Gabriel Conroy (1876)
Poetry:
The Lost Galleon (1867)
"Plain Language from Truthful James" (1870)

NATHANIEL HAWTHORNE   1804–1864

Although Hawthorne's seventeenth-century ancestors were important men in Massachusetts, the family declined in prominence during the century which followed. When Hawthorne's father died in 1808, he left a widow and three children in reduced circumstances.

In 1825 Hawthorne was graduated from Bowdoin College, where Longfellow was his classmate. After graduation he returned to his mother's house in Salem and lived there in comparative seclusion for twelve years. During those years he read and wrote but destroyed much of what he had written. After anonymous publication in magazines, his tales were first collected in *Twice-Told Tales*.

Soon after Hawthorne discontinued his life of solitude, he became, for about a year, a weigher and gauger in the Boston Custom House; for several months in 1841 he was at Brook Farm, the Utopian community headed by George Ripley. In 1842 he married Sophia Peabody, a follower of the Concord Transcendentalists.

Hawthorne returned to Salem in 1845, and in 1846 there appeared a second collection of his tales, *Mosses from an Old Manse*. This volume attracted few readers, so, because of his financial needs, in 1846 Hawthorne accepted an appointment as surveyor in the Salem Custom House. Inasmuch as he held the appointment as a loyal Democrat, he was dismissed in 1849, after three years' service, to make room for a Whig incumbent. The three years following his dismissal were his most productive: in 1850 *The Scarlet Letter* appeared; in 1851, *The House of the Seven Gables*; and in 1852, *The Blithedale Romance*. The House of the Seven Gables was written at Lenox, in the Berkshires, where Hawthorne met and became the close friend of Herman Melville.

From 1853 to 1857 Hawthorne was consul at Liverpool, having been appointed by his old college friend, Franklin Pierce, then President of the United States. Hawthorne returned in 1860 to "The Wayside" in Concord, which he had purchased a short time before going abroad. His last novel was *The Marble Faun* (1860). At his death he left many uncompleted works of fiction.

Of all the writers of the New England flowering, Hawthorne, justifiably, seems the most certain to endure. Many have noted that he reflects the New England spirit in his consciousness of sin and anticipates in his symbolism a now common manner of literary expression.

Short Stories:
Twice-Told Tales (1837; enlarged, 1842)
Mosses from an Old Manse (1846)
The Snow Image and Other Twice-Told Tales (1851)
Novels:
The Scarlet Letter (1850)
The House of the Seven Gables (1851)
The Blithedale Romance (1852)
The Marble Faun (1860)
Autobiography:
Our Old Home (1863)
The American Notebooks (1868, 1932)
The English Notebooks (1870, 1941)
Passages from the French and Italian Notebooks (1871)

ERNEST HEMINGWAY 1899–1961

Ernest Hemingway was born in Oak Park, Illinois. He went through high school, winning some fame in boxing and football, and then became a reporter on the Kansas City *Star*. During World War I, he served on the Italian front. In postwar days, as a newspaper correspondent, he was one of the expatriates who inhabited the Left Bank in Paris. There he began to write fiction and was "discovered" by the critics in the United States. He returned to his homeland to write, going abroad now and then for travel in Europe or for big game hunting in Africa. During the Spanish Revolution and World War II he was a correspondent abroad. After the war, he lived in Cuba until he was forced to leave because of the Castro revolution. After some traveling he settled in Idaho and, following hospitalization, died of a gun-shot wound — perhaps by his own hand.

Hemingway was influenced by Mark Twain's style, which, though like oral speech, was notable for its poetic overtones. Sherwood Anderson and Gertrude Stein, whom he knew in Paris, probably encouraged him to cultivate this apparently naïve colloquial style. From them, too, he may have received instruction in emphasizing basic emotions which led Oscar Cargill to classify him, as well as these two teachers of his, as "Primitivists." From Stephen Crane, by contrast, Hemingway perhaps learned something about handling symbolic or connotative details to give prose what he calls "a fourth or fifth dimension." As a result, in Hemingway's best narratives, there is a unique combination of strength — even at times brutality — with poetic subtlety and depth of sympathy which appeals to modern readers.

Drama:
The Fifth Column (1938)
Short Stories:
In Our Time (1924)
Men without Women (1927)
Novels:
The Sun Also Rises (1926)
A Farewell to Arms (1929)
To Have and Have Not (1937)
For Whom the Bell Tolls (1940)
Across the River and into the Trees (1950)
The Old Man and the Sea (1952)

OLIVER WENDELL HOLMES 1809–1894

The birth and rearing of Oliver Wendell Holmes were in the tradition of the Brahmin class to which he belonged. He was born in an old house which had historical associations with important battles of the Revolution. He was what he called "a man of family" — one "who inherits family traditions and the cumulative humanities of at least five generations." He was educated at a leading private school, at Harvard, and abroad. In his profession, medicine, he won honors first as a scholar and later (1847-1882) as a noted professor at Harvard. At the request of his friend, James Russell Lowell, then editor of the *Atlantic Monthly*, Holmes made a contribution to the new magazine. It took the form of a series of papers entitled *The Autocrat of the Breakfast-Table* which lasted from 1857 to 1858 and which brought fame not only to its author but to the magazine as well. In books like his *Autocrat*, rather than in novels such as *Elsie Venner*, Holmes excelled. And his verse, like his prose, is at its best when it is most informal.

Nonfiction:
The Autocrat of the Breakfast-Table (1858)
The Professor at the Breakfast-Table (1860)
"Mechanism in Thought and Morals" (1870)
The Poet at the Breakfast-Table (1872)
Poetry:
Poems (1836, 1852, 1862, 1865, 1877)

Before the Curfew and Other Poems (1888)
Novels:
Elsie Venner (1861)
The Guardian Angel (1867)
A Mortal Antipathy (1885)

WILLIAM DEAN HOWELLS 1837-1920

William Dean Howells was born at Martin's Ferry, Ohio. His father was a printer and journalist in several Ohio towns, and the boy learned early to help. He received little formal education, but he had a passion for languages and literature. From 1856 to 1861 Howells was a reporter and an editorial writer on the *Ohio State Journal* of Columbus. He wrote in 1860 a campaign biography of Lincoln and was rewarded by an appointment as consul at Venice. In the meantime, he had been trying his hand at poetry. When three of his poems appeared in the *Atlantic* in 1860, Howells paid his first visit to New England. James T. Fields, editor of the *Atlantic*, Lowell, and Holmes received him most cordially. Hawthorne, after talking with Howells, wrote on his card as an introduction to Emerson, "I find this young man worthy."

Howells was in Venice from 1861 to 1865. In 1862 he married Eleanor Mead, of Brattleboro, Vermont. When he returned to America, he was made an assistant editor of the *Atlantic* and settled in Cambridge. In 1872 he became editor-in-chief and continued in that position until 1881. Howells moved in 1888 to New York, where he lived—allowing for excursions back to New England and to Europe—the rest of his life. From 1900 on he wrote the "Easy Chair" department of *Harper's Monthly*, which brought him increasing influence and prestige. He received honorary degrees from Harvard, Yale, Columbia, and Oxford and for many years was president of the American Academy of Arts and Letters.

Howells was strong in the belief that realism in fiction should portray the typical rather than the exceptional and that the typical was comparatively decent. Consequently, Howells has been much criticized by Naturalists, Freudians, and Socialists. But he wrote well, and during the last two decades of the nineteenth century he was our chief recorder in prose fiction of the domestic life of middle-class America.

Autobiography:
Venetian Life (1866)
Literary Friends and Acquaintance (1900)
Criticism:
Modern Italian Poets (1887)
Criticism and Fiction (1891)
Novels:
Their Wedding Journey (1872)
A Modern Instance (1882)
The Rise of Silas Lapham (1885)
A Hazard of New Fortunes (1890)
A Traveler from Altruria (1894)

WILLIAM INGE 1913-

Born in Independence, Kansas, William Inge was educated in his own state and, upon receiving his M.A. in 1938, joined the staff of Stephens College for Women where he taught until 1943. He gave up teaching to become the drama-music critic for the St. Louis *Star-Times*, but in 1946 he returned to academic life and became an instructor in English at Washington University, to remain there until 1949. In 1944 he was much impressed with Tennessee Williams' *Glass Menagerie* and decided that he would attempt playwriting. His first play, *Farther Off from Heaven*, was produced in 1947 in the experimental theater run by the late Margo Jones in Dallas. Ten years later, this was rewritten as *The Dark at the Top of the Stairs*.

"The average play of the fifties," observes Gerald Weales, "concerns itself with the problems of adjustment, of acceptance." In achieving such adjustment, the characters are likely to solve important psychological problems. Because he fits this pattern, Inge is "probably the most representative playwright of the fifties."

Farther Off from Heaven (1947)
Come Back, Little Sheba (1949)
Picnic (1952)
Bus Stop (1955)
The Dark at the Top of the Stairs (1957)
A Loss of Roses (1959)
Splendor in the Grass (1961)
Natural Affection (1961)

WASHINGTON IRVING 1783–1859

Washington Irving was born in New York City, the eleventh and last son of Scotch-English parents. A delicate boy, he found his chief pleasures in light literature, the theater, art, travel, and, most particularly, good company. At nineteen, while reading law, he contributed a series of essays dealing largely with the theater to his brother Peter's newspaper, the *Morning Chronicle*, signing them in the eighteenth-century manner as "Jonathan Oldstyle." Between 1804 and 1806 he traveled in Europe, unconcerned about the political turmoil in Napoleon's empire, but much impressed with such new friends as Washington Allston, the painter.

Back in New York and admitted to the bar, he joined his brother and James Kirke Paulding in the *New Yorker*-like series, *Salmagundi*, which ran for twenty numbers in 1807-1808. A more extended burlesque, begun with Peter Irving, resulted in *A History of New York . . . By Diedrich Knickerbocker* (1809). In 1815 he went to Liverpool on business and found that family affairs there were in great disorder because of a brother's illness. Three years later the Irving firm was bankrupt, and his great decision—to make his living by authorship—was more or less forced upon him.

Various governmental appointments were urged upon him in his later years. He wisely refused offers of nominations to a seat in Congress, to the post of mayor of New York, to the secretaryship of the Navy. In 1841, however, he accepted the appointment of minister to Spain and was in Madrid from 1842 until 1845, when he resigned. Except for this period, much of his time after 1835 was spent in the rambling, stepped-gabled cottage at Sunnyside, near Tarrytown and Sleepy Hollow on the Hudson, where he died on November 28, 1859.

Irving's historical work exemplifies the antiquarian spirit which he shared with Scott and other romanticists, but he is most significant for bringing American fiction into the main stream of world literature. Though he owes much to many of his immediate predecessors and contemporaries, there is much in Irving that is his own.

Short Stories:
The Sketch Book (with many essays, 1819-1820)
Bracebridge Hall (1822)
Tales of a Traveller (1824)
The Alhambra (1832)
Nonfiction:
Salmagundi (with others, 1807-1808)
A History of New York . . . By Diedrich Knickerbocker (1809)
The Crayon Miscellany (1835)
Astoria (with nephew Pierre, 1836)
Adventures of Captain Bonneville, U.S.A. (1837)
Life of Oliver Goldsmith (1840)
Life of Washington (5 vols., 1855-1859)

HENRY JAMES 1843–1916

Born in New York City and for a number of years a resident of Boston, Cambridge, and Newport, Henry James eventually became an expatriate. In his early life, the frequent removals of his family from place to place prevented him from taking root anywhere. There were long and repeated visits to Europe—to England, Germany, France, Switzerland, Italy—and intermittent sojourns in America. By the time he had reached maturity, periodic migrations had become a habit—especially migrations to Europe.

After an important year in Paris (1875-1876), where he came under the influence, in varying degrees, of Turgenev, Maupassant, Flaubert, Daudet, and Zola, he began in England a residence which proved to be permanent. For some twenty years (1877-1897) he lived principally in London, and for almost another twenty years (1897-1916) he lived principally at Rye. During these years, however, he continued his frequent excursions to the Continent, and three or four times he revisited the United States. As early as 1880 he could report that he felt himself to be "a thoroughly naturalized Londoner." But it was not until 1915, when he was seventy-two, that James, apparently in protest against American isolationism during the early years of the first World War, became a British subject.

Despite the excellence of his large output of criticism and short fiction, James is important chiefly for his novels. He began as a writer of the international novel and even in his later work continued to employ international characters and comparisons. In his later work the center of his interest shifted increasingly to psychological processes and "method." James was perhaps the first novelist to recognize fully the complexities which may grow out of the relationship of one sensitive person to another, and to record them with fine discrimination and microscopic detail.

Novels:
Roderick Hudson (1876)
The American (1877)
Daisy Miller (1878)
The Portrait of a Lady (1881)
The Bostonians (1886)
The Tragic Muse (1890)
The Spoils of Poynton (1897)
What Maisie Knew (1897)

The Wings of the Dove (1902)
The Ambassadors (1903)
The Golden Bowl (1904)
Short Stories:
Terminations (1895)
Criticism:
Hawthorne (1879)
Partial Portraits (1888)
Notes on Novelists (1914)

RANDALL JARRELL 1914–

Born in Nashville, Tennessee, and a graduate of Vanderbilt University, Randall Jarrell has taught at various colleges and universities from 1937 until the present, with a four-year interruption for service in the Army Air Force. Jarrell's writings inspired by his service experiences established him as a poet. From 1956 to 1958 he was poetry consultant to the Library of Congress.

Jarrell's poetry is characteristically stark and violent. Although some critics feel that he often fails to justify the source of the emotions which he presents, his seeming lack of control may be justified as a demonstration of his scorn for polished art as opposed to sincere and immediate statement. He has written some perceptive criticism and one novel, *Pictures from an Institution* (1954).

Poetry:
Blood for a Stranger (1942)
Little Friend, Little Friend (1945)
Losses (1948)
The Seven-League Crutches (1951)
Selected Poems (1955)
The Woman at the Washington Zoo (1960)
Novel:
Pictures from an Institution (1954)

ROBINSON JEFFERS 1887–1962

Robinson Jeffers was born in Pittsburgh, the son of a classical scholar and a theologian. At the age of five he was reading Greek; at fifteen he had some mastery of Italian, French, and German, together with a love of mountains and of poetry. After a year at the University of Western Pennsylvania (now Pittsburgh), he entered Occidental College as a junior, and in 1905, aged eighteen, he took his B.A. Precocious, shy, but blessed with a rugged physique and a love for the outdoor life, he would probably have found any of the workaday vocations difficult. Graduate work in England gave way to preparation for medicine, medical school to a determination to write, although it was accompanied by courses in forestry, zoology, and law in the University of Washington. Finally, in 1912, he attained independence with a small income from the legacy of a distant relative, and late in the following year he was married, after many tribulations. A plan to live abroad was spoiled by the outbreak of war in Europe, and late in 1914 Jeffers and his wife settled at Carmel, California. There they lived until his death, and there Jeffers built a house with his own hands and found the materials for most of his distinctive poetry.

As the most blackly pessimistic of contemporary American poets, Jeffers has often been compared with Eugene O'Neill, and it is true that they share a temperamental melancholy which critics like to call Celtic, as well as a great debt to the themes and methods of Greek tragedy. Jeffers, however, is more clearly the product of an age in which the modern sciences have destroyed most of the basic assumptions of the past.

Flagons and Apples (1912)
Californians (1916)
Tamar and Other Poems (1924)
"Roan Stallion" (1925)
The Women at Point Sur (1927)
Cawdor, and Other Poems (1928)
Dear Judas, and Other Poems (1929)
Thurso's Landing, and Other Poems (1932)
Give Your Heart to the Hawks, and Other Poems (1933)
Solstice, and Other Poems (1935)
Such Counsels You Gave to Me, and Other Poems (1937)
Be Angry at the Sun (1941)
Medea (1946)

THOMAS JEFFERSON 1743–1826

Thomas Jefferson was born near Charlottesville, Virginia, the son of a planter who had married into the famous Randolph family. At fourteen he inherited nearly three thousand acres of land and a considerable number of slaves. He studied hard at William and Mary during 1760-1762. He then read law, was admitted to the bar in 1767, and succeeded in combining his profession with the management of large estates. On New Year's Day, 1772, he married Martha Wayles Skelton, an attractive widow with whom he was deeply in love.

Member of the Virginia House of Burgesses, 1769-1774; member of the Virginia Conventions of 1774 and 1775; Virginia delegate to the Second Continental Congress, 1775-1776; member of the legislature of the new state of Virginia, 1776-1779; governor of Virginia, 1779-1781; member of Congress under the Articles of Confederation, 1783-1784; American minister to France, 1784-1789; Secretary of State, 1790-1793; vice-president, 1797-1801; President of the United States, 1801-1809—the list by itself is a thumbnail sketch of the birth and youth of a new nation. Jefferson was in the forefront of most of the great political developments of his age.

One of the many paradoxes of his life is that Jefferson should be remembered for the studied sentences of his public papers, for he was inclined to distrust rhetoric and oratory. Behind the words of his great state papers, however, are both the maturing of a great people and a deep faith in the integrity of the common man.

Summary View of the Rights of British America (1774)
"Autobiography" [up to 1790] (completed 1821; published 1829)
First Inaugural Address (1801)
Second Inaugural Address (1805)

SARAH ORNE JEWETT 1849–1909

Sarah Orne Jewett was born in the village of South Berwick, in the southwest corner of Maine, just ten miles from the seacoast. Although she became cosmopolitan, traveling in Europe and spending a good deal of time with friends in Boston

(Annie Fields, William Dean Howells, Thomas Bailey Aldrich), South Berwick was her lifelong home, and she always returned there to write. Her formal schooling was irregular and fragmentary; her real education for writing came from riding and talking with her father, a country doctor, as he visited his many patients in the fishing villages and on the upland farms, and from reading in her father's library. Her first story appeared in the *Atlantic Monthly* in 1869, when she was only twenty. In 1877 she published *Deephaven*, a collection of stories and sketches about a Maine village, nominally Deephaven but really South Berwick. Miss Jewett wrote many such sketches and stories which appeared at frequent intervals in the *Atlantic* and were collected from time to time in book form. Though her work is not as great as Hawthorne's, her stories of New England are the best that have been written since Hawthorne. Her work is authentic literary art, and she adds to the New England spareness a needed delicate grace.

> *Deephaven* (1877)
> *Country By-Ways* (1881)
> *A White Heron and Other Stories* (1886)
> *A Native of Winby and Other Tales* (1893)
> *The Country of the Pointed Firs* (1896)

JAMES JONES 1921–

The prominent family into which James Jones was born in Robinson, Illinois, suffered severe financial reverses during the depression of the thirties. Jones nevertheless attended the University of Hawaii in 1942 and New York University in 1945. He did not become interested in serious writing, however, until he read some of Thomas Wolfe's works while serving in the army. Impressed by Wolfe's depictions, especially those of his family, Jones decided to try his hand at creating a novel. Although his first manuscript was rejected, his second attempt, *From Here to Eternity*, a rough and moving story of life at an American army base, was a best seller, won the National Book Award, and was made into a successful film in 1953. His later novels have been popular; the latest to appear, *The Thin Red Line*, has been praised as a rugged picture of army life.

> *From Here to Eternity* (1951)
> *Some Came Running* (1957)
> *The Pistol* (1959)
> *The Thin Red Line* (1962)

JOHN PENDLETON KENNEDY 1795–1870

The son of well-to-do and socially prominent parents in Baltimore, John Pendleton Kennedy received his formal education in a private preparatory school and at Baltimore College. He participated briefly in the War of 1812 at the Battle of Bladensburg, studied law in Baltimore, and was elected to the Maryland legislature. For three terms (1838-1844) he was a Whig member of Congress, where he staunchly advocated the benefits of internal improvements and of the protective tariff. He was appointed secretary of the Navy by President Fillmore and had an active part in organizing Commodore Perry's expedition to Japan in 1852. In the meantime, as a result of his marriage to the daughter of a wealthy manufacturer in Baltimore, he had become more and more closely identified with the business life of that city. He was a public-spirited citizen and the recipient of many offices and honors. His writings, like his public activities, were extremely varied. He wrote several political works and the biography of a friend, but he is remembered in literature for three fictional works, "unlike enough," says Parrington, "to have been written by different men": *Swallow Barn*, *Horse-Shoe Robinson*, and *Rob of the Bowl*.

Novels:
Swallow Barn (1832)
Horse-Shoe Robinson (1835)
Rob of the Bowl (1838)

Nonfiction:
Quodlibet: Containing Some Annals Thereof (1840)
A Defense of the Whigs (1843)
Memoirs of the Life of William Wirt (2 vols., 1849)
Letters of Mr. Paul Ambrose on the Great Rebellion in the United States (1865)

JACK KEROUAC 1922–

The "beat" or "hipster" movement had its origins in bohemianism but has adopted a metaphysical interest in Zen Buddhism. Jack Kerouac, born in Lowell, Massachusetts, and educated at Columbia University, is a leading writer in the group. He is interested in both aspects of the movement, as evidenced by the title of one of his books—*The Dharma Bums*. ("Dharma" is the Buddhist word for truth.) Kerouac, as R. W. B. Lewis remarks, has "returned to the ever-expanding spirit, at once visionary and sensual, of Walt Whitman," and one of his books derives its title from Whitman's "Song of the Open Road."

The "beat" movement, at first centered in San Francisco, has spread across the country. Kerouac has lived the wandering life he describes in his books and, with Gregory Corso and Allen Ginsburg, has helped bring attention to the "beat" phenomenon.

Novels:
The Town and the City (1950)
On the Road (1957)
The Dharma Bums (1958)
The Subterraneans (1958)
Doctor Sax (1959)
Tristessa (1960)
Big Sur (1962)
Visions of Gerard (1963)

Poetry:
Mexico City Blues (1959)

JOSEPH KIRKLAND 1830–1894

Joseph Kirkland was born in Geneva, New York, but in his early boyhood he moved westward to Michigan with his family. Although his formal education was confined to a few years, he received a great deal of informal education from his parents who were both schoolteachers. His mother was Caroline Kirkland, the author who, in the 1840's, wrote several books about life on the Michigan frontier. In 1843 he returned east with his family—to New York City; in 1847 he took a trip to England. Shortly afterwards he began a career in business, interrupted by a few years of service in the United States Army during the Civil War. He was a clerk in New York, an auditor, a coal-mine operator, a worker in an Internal Revenue office in

Illinois. At fifty, after study in night school, he was admitted to the bar, and he practiced law until his death in 1894. Kirkland is probably more significant historically than when judged by standards in literature: he was important as a trail blazer for the American realistic movement.

Zury: The Meanest Man in Spring County (1887)
The McVeys (1888)
The Captain of Company K (1891)

SARAH KEMBLE KNIGHT 1666–1727

The daughter of a Boston merchant, Sarah Kemble Knight was a woman of enterprise and intelligence. After her husband's death, she efficiently attended to the business of the estate. In addition, she kept a dame's school, which Benjamin Franklin is said to have attended, did a good deal of legal work, and managed a rather large household. She lived in Boston until 1713; then she moved to New London, Connecticut, where she lived until her death. She is remembered today for her *Journal* (October 1704-March 1705), which was a record of a trip through Rhode Island and Connecticut to New York and thence back to Boston. Madame Knight's sense of comedy plus her flair for observation gave her little book added importance as an early humorous depiction of the characters and manners of rural New England and New York.

Journal (written, 1704; published, 1825)

SIDNEY LANIER 1842–1881

Sidney Lanier was a Southerner, but he did not belong to the planter aristocracy. His background was urban and professional: his father was a lawyer, and the boy grew up in the little city of Macon, Georgia. When the Civil War broke out shortly after his graduation from Oglethorpe College, he enlisted as a Confederate soldier, and he served faithfully for the war's duration, spending the last five months in a federal prison.

Lanier wanted ardently to be a musician and a poet. Since there was little opportunity for the cultivation of music and poetry in the South during the reconstruction years, he sought a more favorable environment and found it in Baltimore. In that half-Northern, half-Southern city, in the 1870's, he played the flute with professional skill in the Peabody Symphony Orchestra. His studies at this time of Old and Middle English and of the Elizabethan period resulted in a series of lectures at Peabody Institute and in an appointment, in 1879, as lecturer on English literature at Johns Hopkins University. Before he was quite forty, death of tuberculosis cut short a career of promise.

Lanier's reputation as a poet does not stand nearly so high today as it did at the turn of the century. He has been found prudish and sentimental, vague and confused. Some Southern regionalists have found him too sophisticated and "modern." However, he has written many lines that are felicitous and true, and the musical aspects of his verse are yet to be properly appreciated.

Novel:
Tiger Lilies (1867)
Nonfiction:
The Science of English Verse (1880)
The English Novel (1883)
Shakespeare and His Forerunners (2 vols., 1902)

Poetry:
Poems of Sidney Lanier, ed. Mary Day Lanier (1884)

SINCLAIR LEWIS 1885-1951

Sinclair Lewis was born at Sauk Centre, in central Minnesota. His father was a physician; his mother died when he was only five. Small-town life was uncongenial to him. Yearning for the romance of the East, he spent six months at Oberlin to prepare himself for college entrance examinations and entered Yale with the class of 1907. There he earned much of his way by newspaper work, spent two summer vacations on the then traditional cattle-boat tour to Europe, and gained some reputation as a writer for the college literary magazines. Dropping out of college at the beginning of his senior year, he joined the group at Helicon Hall, the Socialist community established by Upton Sinclair at Englewood, New Jersey, with the profits from *The Jungle*. A brief stretch as janitor ended in illness. When he recovered he spent some months as a free-lance writer and editor in New York City and then returned to Yale to graduate in 1908. Seven years of odd literary jobs followed—reporting, editing, reading for publishers, writing advertising. Meanwhile he was writing fiction in his spare time.

About the time that his third book was published, Lewis at length found himself selling his short stories; he promptly gave up his job as advertising manager for the firm of George H. Doran to begin the untrammeled wandering of a free-lance writer. His success was almost immediate, although it was five years before he startled the literary world into heated debate on the merits of *Main Street* (1920). For *Arrowsmith* he was offered the Pulitzer Prize, which he dramatically refused; in 1930 he received the Nobel Prize, being the first American writer so honored. He died in Italy in 1951, and his body was returned for burial at Sauk Centre.

It is clear that the novels of Sinclair Lewis are the historical record of the crassness of an epoch. The United States between World Wars I and II had need of reformers, and in Lewis it had one of its most persistent, although by no means most virulent, gadflies. Life seemed so interesting to him that he seldom was discouraged about it, and he never plumbed the depths of pessimism as did Mark Twain.

Our Mr. Wrenn (1914)
The Job (1917)
Main Street (1920)
Babbitt (1922)
Arrowsmith (1925)
Elmer Gantry (1927)
The Man Who Knew Coolidge (1928)
Dodsworth (1929)
It Can't Happen Here (1935)
Gideon Planish (1943)
Cass Timberlaine (1945)
World So Wide (1951)

ABRAHAM LINCOLN 1809-1865

An autobiography which Abraham Lincoln wrote in 1859 tells the main details of his early life in his characteristic style. It reads, in part:

"I was born February 12, 1809, in Hardin County, Kentucky. My parents were both born in Virginia, of undistinguished families. . . .

"I was raised to farm work, which I continued till I was twenty-two. At twenty-one I came to Illinois, Macon County. Then I got to New Salem . . . where I remained a year as sort of clerk in a store. Then came The Black Hawk War; and I was elected a captain of volunteers, a success which gave me more pleasure than any I have had since. I went the campaign, was elected, ran for the legislature the same year (1832), and was beaten — the only time I ever have been beaten by the people. The next and three succeeding biennial elections I was elected to the legislature. . . . During this legislative period I had studied law, and removed to Springfield to practice it. In 1846 I was once elected to the lower House of Congress. Was not a candidate for reelection. From 1849 to 1854, both inclusive, practised law more assiduously than before. . . ."

Lincoln's account breaks off at the time of the repeal of the Missouri Compromise (1854), a political move which caused him to return to public life when the Republican Party was founded. In 1858 the Lincoln-Douglas debates on the subject of popular sovereignty, attracted nation-wide attention and led to Lincoln's becoming a dark-horse candidate for the Presidential nomination. He was nominated in 1860, subsequently elected, and began to serve in 1861 as the Civil War was starting. His wartime leadership was rewarded by his reëlection in 1864. About a month after his second inaugural, he was shot to death by John Wilkes Booth in a Washington theater. That Lincoln took great pains in his writing is evident in his most famous utterances — most of them masterpieces of American oratory.

The Collected Works of Abraham Lincoln, ed. R. P. Basler (9 vols., 1953)

VACHEL LINDSAY 1879-1931

Born and reared in Springfield, Illinois, Vachel Lindsay, from childhood, was a member of the intensely evangelical Disciples of Christ church and interested in oratory. After studying in Springfield and in Hiram College in Ohio, he lived in Chicago, attending the Art Institute (1900-1903) and working at various part-time jobs. He also studied at the New York School of Art (1904-1905). He went on tramping trips to various parts of the country, and he made still other tours as a lecturer for the Y.M.C.A. and the Anti-Saloon League. It was during a walking trip from Illinois to New Mexico in 1912 that he composed the poem "General William Booth Enters into Heaven," which won him his first national acclaim.

Shortly after this first success, Lindsay became a favorite of the lecture platform and traveled to every corner of the country. In the end he wearied of his appearances because he felt the theatrical quality of his reading obscured not only his message but also his lyric artistry. His later books of poetry, more lyrical in nature, did not succeed as had his earlier works. Always subject to occasional fits of melancholia, in his last years he gave way more and more frequently to a feeling of depression. He died by his own hand in 1931.

Better perhaps than any recent poet, Lindsay represented some of the important attitudes of the great Middle West — its agrarianism, its democracy, and its evangelism. His poems, in turn, reflect the man: not only his emotionalism and his religious and political convictions, but the robust humor and oratorical manner inherited from his rural background.

Autobiography:
Adventures While Preaching the Gospel of Beauty (1914)

Poetry:
General William Booth Enters into Heaven and Other Poems
  (1913)
The Congo and Other Poems (1914)
The Chinese Nightingale and Other Poems (1917)
The Golden Whales of California and Other Rhymes (1920)
Going-to-the-Sun (1923)
Going-to-the-Stars (1926)
The Candle in the Cabin (1926)
Every Soul Is a Circus (1929)

HENRY WADSWORTH LONGFELLOW   1807–1882

Henry Wadsworth Longfellow was born in Portland, Maine, and educated at Bowdoin and abroad. He taught modern languages at Bowdoin (1829-1835) and then, after a second trip abroad, at Harvard (1837-1857). Meanwhile his fame, which had begun to flourish when *Voices of the Night* was published, was augmented by such books as *Ballads and Other Poems* (1842) and *Evangeline* (1847). Carefully sheltered in childhood and early manhood, never worried by poverty, the poet lived most of his days in peaceful old Craigie House in Cambridge. Scholars had long thought of Longfellow's life as peaceful and placid, but a study by Lawrance Thompson has shown that Longfellow won such peacefulness only after a youth full of storm and struggle. His fight against odds to become an author, his desperate sorrow following the death of his first wife in 1835, and his torture of spirit during the seven-year courtship of his second wife, Frances Appleton, all left their imprint on his life and work. His works were always popular, and by the time he died, just a few weeks after his seventy-fifth birthday, he was clearly established as the most famous and loved poet of his day.

Critics who disapprove of a large share of Longfellow's verse do so because they feel that its thought is commonplace, its mood sentimental, and its form not well related to its substance. Such critics are likely to admit, however, that at his infrequent best, he wrote poetry which deserves to be treasured by even fastidious readers.

Poetry:
Voices of the Night (1839)
Ballads and Other Poems (1842)
Poems on Slavery (1842)
Poems (1845)
Evangeline (1847)
Hiawatha (1855)
The Courtship of Miles Standish (1858)
Tales of a Wayside Inn (1863)
Household Poems (1865)
Christus: A Mystery (1872)
Kéramos and Other Poems (1878)
Ultima Thule (1880)
In the Harbor (1882)
Fiction:
Outre-Mer (1833-1834)
Hyperion (1839)

JAMES RUSSELL LOWELL 1819-1891

Of Brahmin background and training, James Russell Lowell was graduated from Harvard in 1838, and in 1843 he began his first and very brief editorial venture with a journal called *The Pioneer*. After his marriage to Maria White in 1844 he lived in Philadelphia, where he wrote for several liberal periodicals, but within a year he went to Europe, where he spent fifteen months in study. Five years after the death of his first wife in 1853, he married Frances Dunlap. When Longfellow retired, Lowell took the distinguished chair which Longfellow had held at Harvard and served there from 1856 until 1877. He was not only a teacher, a critic, and a poet, but also editor of the *Atlantic Monthly* (1857-1861) and of the *North American Review* (1864-1872), a minister to Spain (1877-1880), and a minister to England (1880-1885).

The wide range of activity represented in Lowell's life is paralleled by the wide range in the writing of this most versatile of the Cambridge authors. In the years before his appointment at Harvard, Lowell, largely because of the influence of his first wife, became a leading writer in behalf of abolition. And in the field of belles-lettres, Lowell wrote both criticism and poetry. Six years after the death of his second wife, he died at "Elmwood," the house of his birth.

Lowell's early criticism was frankly subjective and impressionistic, but beginning with the 1850's it was much improved as he gradually became more systematic while still expressing his judgments in memorable terms. He did write some good poetry, although his versatility somewhat diffused his energies. He was at his poetic best, perhaps, in some of his nature poems and in some of his odes.

Essays:
Among My Books (first series, 1870; second series, 1876)
My Study Windows (1871)
Democracy (1884)
Poetry:
Biglow Papers (first series, 1848; second series, 1867)
A Fable for Critics (1848)
The Vision of Sir Launfal (1848)
"Ode Recited at the Harvard Commemoration" (1865)
The Cathedral (1869)

ROBERT LOWELL 1917-

A member of the famous Lowell family which included Amy Lowell and James Russell Lowell, Robert Lowell, born in Boston, was graduated *summa cum laude* from Kenyon College in 1940. He was an editorial assistant at Sheed and Ward until 1942; in 1943 he was jailed as a conscientious objector. He was awarded the Pulitzer Prize in 1947 for his *Lord Weary's Castle*, an apt reflection of his Roman Catholic convictions. That same year he received a Guggenheim fellowship and was appointed consultant in poetry for the Library of Congress. He has taught at Boston University, the State University of Iowa, and Kenyon College.

Robert Lowell is generally considered one of the most significant of modern American poets. The remarkable discipline which he exercises is revealed in the conciseness and the biting precision of his statements.

Poetry:
Land of Unlikeness (1944)
Lord Weary's Castle (1946)

The Mills of the Kavanaughs (1951)
Life Studies (with an autobiographical fragment, 1959)

CARSON McCULLERS   1917 –

Carson McCullers, born in Columbia, Georgia, often is compared with such diverse writers of the South as William Faulkner and Katherine Anne Porter — proof that she writes in a unique way. Expecting to have a career in music, she studied in the Juilliard School of Music and Columbia University. She broke off her schooling, took up writing, and at the precocious age of twenty-two published her first novel. Immediately she was recognized as an important new talent, and readers have eagerly awaited her relatively infrequent, subsequent works. Her second novel, *Reflections in a Golden Eye*, an account of a grotesque adventure into the underworld of the emotions, was ranked high among writings in the new Gothic school. Her third novel, *The Member of the Wedding*, charmingly and wistfully portrayed a Southern family, in particular the adolescent girl through whose eyes the events were seen. Critics abroad as well as in the United States have praised Mrs. McCullers' sense of construction and character, her feeling, her lucidity, and her poetic symbolism.

The Heart Is a Lonely Hunter (1940)
Reflections in a Golden Eye (1941)
The Member of the Wedding (1946)
The Ballad of the Sad Café (1951)
The Square Root of Wonderful (1958)
Clock Without Hands (1961)

ARCHIBALD MACLEISH   1892 –

Archibald MacLeish is a writer who has distinguished himself in the field of public service as well as that of literature. He was born and reared in Glencoe, Illinois. After graduating from Harvard Law School in 1920, he joined a law firm in Boston, and during three years there he found himself increasingly attracted to poetry. After deciding to become a writer, MacLeish went abroad with his family and for six years wrote poems and short stories. Returning to the United States in 1929 for financial reasons, he served on the editorial staff of the new business magazine *Fortune*, and his views on economics and politics achieved new dimensions. He came to believe that it was the responsibility of writers to take politics seriously, and he set an example himself in his writings and, subsequently, in his work in government offices. In 1939 he became Librarian of Congress and for two years worked on the reorganization of the library. During World War II, he helped establish the Office of Facts and Figures, which later became the Office of War Information. In 1944 he became Assistant Secretary of State and helped create in the American people an awareness of the importance of the United Nations. In 1946 Mr. MacLeish was in charge of the American delegation to the UNESCO organization conference in Paris.

Although creative work took second place during the time MacLeish worked for the government, when he resumed publishing after the war, his writings showed growth. He won the Pulitzer Prize three times — in 1933 for an epic poem *Conquistador;* in 1953 for *Collected Poems*, a volume of poetry written over a period of years from 1917 to 1952; and in 1958 for his play *J.B.* The modern adaptation of the story of Job in his play *J.B.* was produced in New York, across the country, and at the World's Fair in Brussels, winning widespread acclaim.

Poetry:
Tower of Ivory (1917)
The Happy Marriage (1924)
Streets in the Moon (1926)
The Pot of Earth (1928)
The Hamlet of A. MacLeish (1928)
Conquistador (1932)
Frescoes for Mr. Rockefeller's City (1933)
Public Speech (1936)
The Land of the Free (1938)
America Was Promises (1939)
Act Five and Other Poems (1948)
Collected Poems, 1917-1952 (1952)
Songs for Eve (1954)
Drama:
Nobodaddy (1926)
Panic (1935)
The Fall of the City (1937)
Air Raid (1938)
The Music Crept by Me upon the Waters (1953)
J.B. (1958)
Essays:
The Irresponsibles (1940)
The American Cause (1941)
A Time to Speak (1941)
A Time to Act (1943)
Poetry and Opinion (1950)
Freedom Is the Right to Choose (1951)

NORMAN MAILER 1923–

After graduating from Harvard in 1943, Norman Mailer spent two years in the army. His experience as a clerk and rifleman in the Pacific theater served as a background for a war novel which he wrote at the age of twenty-five, *The Naked and the Dead*. This was a best seller and was later made into a motion picture. He has since written several other novels, compiled an autobiographical collection of his early stories, newspaper pieces, and columns written for the *Village Voice* in *Advertisements for Myself*, and published a collection of poems, *Death for the Ladies*. More recently he has written monthly reviews and feature articles for *Esquire*. He has come to be known as a "hipster" or a proponent of the "beat" trend in literature.

Novels:
The Naked and the Dead (1948)
Barbary Shore (1951)
The Deer Park (1955)
The Man Who Studied Yoga (1956)
Poetry:
Death for the Ladies and Other Disasters (1962)
Autobiography:
Advertisements for Myself (1959)

BERNARD MALAMUD 1914–

Bernard Malamud was thirty-eight when he published his first book, *The Natural*, in 1952. This first work, which is about a home-run hitting baseball player, is in contrast with most of his writing which concerns the world of Jewish small businessmen—shopkeepers, tailors, and salesmen—who, in spite of grief, conscience, suffering, and heartaches, show their understanding of humanity because they have wisdom, humor, and compassion. Portrayed in a style which is simple and straightforward, the people he creates are both comic and pathetic.

Novels:
The Natural (1952)
The Assistant (1957)
A New Life (1961)
Short Stories:
The Magic Barrel (1958)
Idiots First (1963)

COTTON MATHER 1663–1728

Son of Reverend Increase Mather and grandson of John Mather, Cotton Mather received his B.A. from Harvard in 1678 when he was fourteen. Four years after taking his M.A. in 1681, also at Harvard, he was installed as his father's co-minister at the Old North Church in Boston. There he remained all his life, marrying three times, burying most of his fifteen children, preaching literally thousands of sermons, and writing untiringly. He published 444 separate items, and great quantities of material are still extant in manuscript. He wrote in an extensive variety of forms and cultivated and defended an elaborate, allusion-studded style.

The Wonders of the Invisible World (1693)
Magnalia Christi Americana (1702)
Essays to Do Good [Bonifacius] (1710)
The Christian Philosopher (1721)
Manuductio ad Ministerium (1726)

HERMAN MELVILLE 1819–1891

Herman Melville, born in New York City, moved with his family to Albany when he was eleven. Two years later his father died, leaving the family in debt. During the seven ensuing years the boy was occupied clerking and working on his uncle's farm at Pittsfield, Massachusetts. At the age of twenty he shipped as a sailor on a merchantman bound for Liverpool. Following his return he taught school in Albany and Pittsfield and tried his hand at writing.

The most decisive event of Melville's life came on January 3, 1841, when at the age of twenty-one he shipped from New Bedford on the *Acushnet*, a whaler, for the South Seas. Melville was gone three years and nine months. The exact details of his wanderings in the Pacific are in large measure still uncertain, but it is known that, after some eighteen months on the *Acushnet*, Melville deserted at the Marquesas Islands. After a month or two among the cannibals he escaped to Tahiti; further travels may have taken him to Japan. In 1843 he joined the crew of the frigate *United States* at Honolulu and remained with this ship until his arrival at Boston more than a year later.

The eight or nine years following his return from his voyage were Melville's great productive period when he poured forth a veritable torrent of books. From the summer of 1850 till the autumn of 1851, Melville and Hawthorne were near neighbors and frequent companions, the former residing at Pittsfield, the latter at Lenox. After Hawthorne left the Berkshires, however, their friendly intimacy was interrupted. In 1856, when Melville was on a recuperative journey to Italy and the Holy Land, the two men met again in England. From 1866 to 1885 Melville was Inspector of Customs in New York City. He was a prolific writer and at his death left several unpublished works, including the just completed *Billy Budd*.

Recent studies, like Richard Chase's, have found in Melville's writings a rich and inexhaustible mine of symbolic meanings. The conferences, lectures, library exhibits, and the like which marked in 1951 the centenary of the publication of *Moby Dick* testified to the current widespread recognition of Melville's importance.

Novels:
Typee (1846)
Omoo (1847)
Mardi (1849)
Redburn (1849)
White Jacket (1850)
Moby Dick (1851)
Pierre (1852)
Israel Potter (1855)
The Confidence Man (1857)
Billy Budd (1924)
Short Stories:
The Piazza Tales (1856)
Poetry:
Battle Pieces and Aspects of the War (1866)
Clarel (1876)

HENRY LOUIS MENCKEN 1880–1956

Henry Louis Mencken was born in Baltimore of German ancestry. His education at Baltimore Polytechnic was augmented by some correspondence-school work, but he never attended college. After becoming a reporter at nineteen, he plied his trade so successfully that within a couple of years he became an editor. In those two years he had launched into creative work to produce some short stories and a book of mediocre poetry, *Ventures in Verse*, which was to appear in 1903. He worked as a journalist on the Baltimore *Herald* (1903-1906) and intermittently on the Baltimore *Sun* papers (1906-1941). When a book by Mencken on George Bernard Shaw (1905) and another on the philosophy of Nietzche (1908) attracted attention beyond Baltimore, he became editor of a national magazine, *Smart Set* (1908-1914). His writings for this periodical and his syndicated weekly column for the *Evening Sun* won him a national following. In 1924, when the *American Mercury* was established, he became its editor, to serve until 1933. No one was much surprised when, with his retirement from the *Mercury*, Mencken began to write his reminiscences, for his influence was already on the wane. His followers, however, regarded him as a great emancipator, their leader in attacks upon old-fashioned conventions and values. The power and gusto of his style, inspired in part by his love for words, had much to do with his appeal.

Poetry:
Ventures in Verse (1903)

Nonfiction:
George Bernard Shaw—His Plays (1905)
The Philosophy of Friedrich Nietzsche (1908)
Prejudices (six series, 1919-1927)
The American Language (1919; revisions in 1921, 1923, 1936;
    supplements in 1945, 1948; condensation in 1963)
Treatise on the Gods (1930)
Autobiography:
Happy Days: 1880-1892 (1940)
Newspaper Days: 1899-1906 (1941)
Heathen Days: 1890-1936 (1943)

ARTHUR MILLER   1915–

After his graduation from high school in New York City, Arthur Miller worked for
two years in Manhattan. He began his literary career when, interested in writing,
he enrolled in the University of Michigan. Following his graduation in 1938 he returned to New York where he worked in the Federal Theatre Project. The theater
did not last long, however, and Miller had to turn to radio script writing. It was not
until 1947 that he achieved his first success in the legitimate theater with the
production of *All My Sons*. He has won the Pulitzer Prize for *Death of a Salesman*
and for *A View from the Bridge*.

Miller is seriously concerned with both the content and the form of his
drama. To him the moral statements in his dramas and the quality of the structure
of his plays are equally important. He has not only written in the classical Greek
tradition in *A View from the Bridge*, but he has also consciously gone against the
Greek tradition in *Death of a Salesman*, in which he seeks to demonstrate the
significance and worth of even a nonheroic protagonist.

The Man Who Had All the Luck (1944)
All My Sons (1947)
Death of a Salesman (1949)
The Crucible (1953)
A View from the Bridge (1955)
After the Fall (1963)

WILLIAM VAUGHN MOODY   1869–1910

William Vaughn Moody was born in Indiana, and as a boy he was fond of outdoor
exercise, music, painting, and study; his liking for all these stayed with him. In
1889 he entered Harvard, and although he worked his way through, he found time
for many contributions to the *Harvard Monthly*. Having satisfied the requirements
for graduation in three years, Moody spent his senior year in Europe. Before he
died, he returned to Europe five more times; like Howells and Henry James he
found the other side of the Atlantic a second home. In 1893, however, he returned
to Harvard for two years of graduate study and then taught at the University of
Chicago. There he spent his free time editing textbooks and traveling on vacations. In addition, there was always writing, which he was coming to regard as his
real profession. In 1902 he was enabled to give it his full time through the success
of a textbook, *A History of English Literature*, written in collaboration with his
friend Robert Morss Lovett. His production in the remaining years of his life was
not large, primarily because of the tumorous condition which caused his death.

Moody was on the whole, traditional in his forms, although not slavishly so. Frequently reminiscent of the later English Victorians, his verses nevertheless reveal a sensitive and observant individual whose bookishness did not obscure his fresh perceptions. Although he did not like the characteristics of the progressive era in which he lived, his humanism enabled him to evaluate his world with detachment and quiet penetration.

Poetry:
The Masque of Judgment (1900)
Poems (1901)
The Fire-Bringer (1904)
Drama:
The Great Divide (produced, 1906)
The Faith Healer (1909)
Textbook:
A History of English Literature (with Robert Morss Lovett, 1902)

MARIANNE MOORE 1887–

Marianne Moore, born in St. Louis, Missouri, was graduated from Bryn Mawr in 1909 and began publishing her poetry in the *Egoist*, edited by Richard Aldington and during the war by his wife "H.D." Her first associations, therefore, were with the Imagist group which stressed the importance of hard, clear, accurate images. Her first book of verse came out in 1920. She taught in the government Indian school in Carlisle, Pennsylvania, worked as an assistant at the New York Public Library, and was an editor of *The Dial* from 1925 to 1929. Her home for many years has been in Brooklyn.

Miss Moore's poetry has won many awards, among them the Pulitzer Prize, the Bollengen Prize in Poetry, and the National Book Award. She has created a very personal poetical style; her verse, elegant and brilliant, is rendered in exquisitely meticulous language. She has had a great influence upon younger poets.

Poetry:
Poems (1921)
Observations (1924)
Selected Poems (1935)
The Pangolin and Other Verse (1936)
What Are Years? (1941)
Nevertheless (1944)
Collected Poems (1951)
Like a Bulwark (1956)
O To Be a Dragon (1959)
Essays:
Predilections (1955)

MARY NOAILLES MURFREE (Charles Egbert Craddock) 1850–1922

Mary Noailles Murfree was born in middle Tennessee near the fine old town of Murfreesboro (named at the beginning of the century for her great-grandfather, a Revolutionary officer from North Carolina). Her father was a successful lawyer, an owner of plantations in the delta country, and an admirer of Scott and Dickens. Miss Murfree was educated in the traditional Southern manner at young ladies' finishing schools—at the Nashville Female Academy and at Chegary Institute in

Philadelphia. The Murfrees spent some fifteen summers at Beersheba Springs, a fashionable resort in the Cumberland Mountains; it was the country around Beersheba which furnished the materials for Miss Murfree's early stories, though she later visited, and utilized in her fiction, the wilder, more primitive Great Smokies, which lie to the east of the Cumberland range.

Miss Murfree's reputation rests chiefly on her earlier books, although she later wrote many volumes of mountain stories and of historical fiction dealing with the colonial Southwest and the Civil War, all under a pseudonym. Her work, like that of most of the writers of the local color school, seems much less important now than it did at the end of the last century.

In the Tennessee Mountains (1884)
The Prophet of the Great Smoky Mountains (1885)

FRANK NORRIS 1870–1902

Born in Chicago to well-to-do parents, Frank Norris moved with his family to San Francisco in 1884. Somehow, at the age of seventeen, he persuaded his family to allow him to study art in Paris. During his stay abroad, however, he changed his allegiance from the Atelier Julien to literature. Back in California as a student at the University of California (1890-1894), he discovered the appeal of the French naturalistic school led by Zola, and of Rudyard Kipling. His writings as a student at Harvard (1894-1895) showed this influence.

Gifted with a talent for friendship, Norris took great delight in becoming one of the Bohemian group in Paris and equal delight in becoming a friend of athletes, men-about-the-campus, and scholars in his college fraternity. At the same time he was very much a conscious literary artist, and his critical writings attest that he had thoroughly developed theories about technique. The career which came to an untimely end when Norris died in 1902 had been a promising one indeed. In his novels he foreshadowed some of the aspects of the writings of notable modern authors—the unflinching depiction of sordid detail of Faulkner, the brutality of Hemingway, and the poetic fervor of Wolfe.

McTeague (1899)
The Octopus (1901)
The Pit (1903)
Vandover and the Brute (1914)

O. HENRY: see William Sydney Porter

FLANNERY O'CONNER 1925–

Born in Savannah, Georgia, Flannery O'Conner was graduated from Georgia State College for Women in 1945 and then studied creative writing at the State University of Iowa, receiving the degree of Master of Fine Arts in 1947. Her first published work was a short story which appeared in *Accent* in 1946. Many of her later stories also appeared in "little magazines" such as the *Partisan Review*, the *Kenyon Review*, and the *Sewanee Review*.

The grotesque elements which often figure prominently in her novels and her short stories she justifies by claiming that they are useful for teaching or instructing. Her novel published in 1960 was strongly affected by her religious beliefs.

Novels:
Wise Blood (1952)
The Violent Bear It Away (1960)

Short Stories:
A Good Man Is Hard to Find (1955)

JOHN O'HARA 1905–

John O'Hara was born in Pottsville, Pennsylvania and graduated from Niagara Prep School in 1924. When his father's death prevented him from attending Yale University, he entered into a varied career as an engineer, boat steward, call boy, freight clerk, guard in an amusement park, steel worker, Hollywood press agent, private secretary, motion-picture writer, critic, and feature writer.

O'Hara's short stories and novels are noted for the accuracy with which they report the conversation, manners, and morals of a certain segment of American society — the Hollywood, country club, and hotel-bar sets. Edmund Wilson has called O'Hara the "outstanding master of *The New Yorker* short-story sketch."

Novels:
Appointment in Samarra (1934)
Butterfield 8 (1935)
Ten North Frederick (1955)
A Family Party (1956)
From the Terrace (1958)
Ourselves to Know (1960)
Elizabeth Appleton (1963)
Short Stories:
Files on Parade (1939)
Pal Joey [later a musical comedy, 1952] (1940)
Sermons and Soda-Water (1960)
Assembly (1961)
Hat on the Bed (1963)
Drama:
Five Plays (1961)
Essays:
Sweet and Sour (1954)

EUGENE O'NEILL 1888–1953

Son of a popular actor James O'Neill, Eugene O'Neill was born in New York City. The varied experiences of his youth included not only academic study (at Princeton, 1906-1907, and at Harvard, 1914-1915) but also two years at sea, a tour in vaudeville, and a turn at newspaper reporting. In 1912, forced into a year of convalescence because of tuberculosis, O'Neill's interest in drama grew as he spent much of his leisure time reading plays, especially those of the Greeks, Elizabethans, and moderns. He began his career as a dramatist in 1916 with his first significant one-act play, *Bound East for Cardiff*. His first full-length play, *Beyond the Horizon*, produced in 1920, won a Pulitzer Prize, the first of four he received. In his last years he suffered from Parkinson's disease and found it almost impossible to continue writing.

By common consent O'Neill is the greatest dramatist that America has produced. His plays are interesting both for their bold experimentation and their psychological insights. Although the degree to which he used Freudian psychology may prove injurious to his future reputation, there is no denying the originality and power of his best work.

Bound East for Cardiff (1916)
Beyond the Horizon (1920)
The Emperor Jones (1921)
Anna Christie (1922)
The Hairy Ape (1922)
Desire Under the Elms (1925)
The Great God Brown (1926)
Strange Interlude (1928)
Mourning Becomes Electra (1931)
Ah, Wilderness! (1933)
The Iceman Cometh (1946)
Moon for the Misbegotten (1952)
Long Day's Journey into Night (1956)
A Touch of the Poet (1957)

THOMAS PAINE   1737–1809

Thomas Paine was born in England, and leaving school at thirteen he searched fruitlessly for a quarter of a century before he found an agreeable occupation. At thirty-seven, penniless and unknown, Paine met Benjamin Franklin, who gave him a letter of introduction to use when he went to America later that year. After a serious illness, he readied himself for a new profession by a series of contributions to the *Pennsylvania Magazine*. With the publication of *Common Sense* in January 1776, his career as a propagandist of genius was begun. His contributions to the Revolution included pamphlets, service in the Continental Army, and various kinds of work for the Continental Congress.

In April 1787 Paine sailed for France and became a supporter of the French Revolution. However, as an honorary citizen and member of the National Convention, he opposed the execution of Louis XVI; and by December 1793, he was imprisoned as a foreigner. *The Age of Reason*, his last "offering" to mankind, so shocked people that many were willing to burn Paine at the stake. After his return to America in 1802 he was shot at, insulted, and humiliated even on his deathbed.

No man of his time was better able to express, simply and clearly, the views which effected vast changes in the political, social, and religious constitution of Western civilization. The force, directness, and variety of his appeals to reason and emotion made him the foremost propagandist-agitator of his time.

Common Sense (1776)
The American Crisis (1776-1783)
The Rights of Man (Part I, 1791; Part II, 1792)
The Age of Reason (Part I, 1794; Part II, 1795)

EDGAR ALLAN POE   1809–1849

The son of a wandering theatrical family, Edgar Allan Poe was orphaned at two and became the ward of the John Allan family of Richmond, Virginia. Never legally adopted, he could not live quite the normal life of a son in a well-to-do family. Although in his early years both Mr. and Mrs. Allan did what they could to spoil him, friction grew between him and his foster father until he was withdrawn from the University of Virginia after less than a year of attendance. There followed a period of service in the army (1827-1829), an unhappy brief career at West Point (1830-1831), and a final break with Allan (1832).

Before the break Poe had published three books of poetry, none very success-ful financially. Driven to try to make a living with his pen, he began writing tales. A sign that he had some success was that one of them, "The MS. Found in a Bottle," won a one-hundred-dollar prize in 1833. Befriended by one of the contest judges, John Pendleton Kennedy, he began a career as editor, serving on the staff of the *Southern Literary Messenger* (1835-1837), *Burton's Gentleman's Maga-zine* (1839), *Graham's Magazine* (1841-1842), and other periodicals. Other tales won repute for him, and he was an alert and canny editor; but his poverty, his fiery temper, and his instability worked against his success. His pay as an editor was usually small, less than sixteen dollars a week, for instance, for his very successful work as editor of *Graham's*. Even in 1845, after he had won wide popularity, a collection of his verse, *The Raven and Other Poems*, and a volume of stories, *Tales of the Grotesque and Arabesque*, did not have financial success.

Although Poe was not at all times the brooding, gloomy person tradition has painted, his life was on the whole an unhappy one. In 1831 he found a home with Mrs. Maria Clemm, mother of Poe's cousin, Virginia—a home in which, although members of the family were devoted to one another, poverty and sickness made life hard. In 1835 he married thirteen-year old Virginia, a fragile child who suffered from a devastating illness destined to end her life when she was twenty-six. He died in mysterious circumstances, in Baltimore, October 7, 1849.

Poe was outstanding as a critic, a fiction writer, and a poet. His discussions of contemporary writers and his treatises on poetry and fiction won him a place as the greatest critic of his day. Employing the principle of the single effect, he wrote masterful horror stories and invented the detective story as a genre. His musical poems, often creating strange and mysterious worlds, were highly influential on French poets, who in turn did much to shape modern English and American poetry.

Poetry:
Tamerlane and Other Poems (1827)
Al Aaraaf, Tamerlane, and Minor Poems (1829)
Poems (second edition, 1831)
The Raven and Other Poems (1845)
Short Stories:
"The MS. Found in a Bottle" (1833)
"The Fall of the House of Usher" (1839)
Tales of the Grotesque and Arabesque (1840)
"The Murders in the Rue Morgue" (1841)
"The Masque of the Red Death" (1842)
Tales (1845)
"The Cask of Amantillado" (1846)
The Narrative of Arthur Gordon Pym (1838)
Essays:
"Review of *Twice-Told Tales*" [revision in "Tale Writing," 1847] (1842)
"The Philosophy of Composition" (1846)
Eureka: A Prose Poem (1848)
"The Poetic Principle" (1850)

KATHERINE ANNE PORTER   1894–

Katherine Anne Porter was born in Indian Creek, Texas, the great-great-great-granddaughter of Daniel Boone, and spent her early life in Texas and Louisiana.

She was educated in various convent schools of the South. She married in 1933 and was soon divorced; in 1938 she married Albert Russel Erskine, Jr., and they were divorced in 1942. Miss Porter has lived in various parts of the world: in the South, in New York City, in Europe, in Mexico. Using details from her experiences, she has therefore employed a variety of backgrounds in her fiction. She was awarded a Guggenheim Fellowship for creative writing in 1931 and again in 1938. In 1944 she was Fellow of Regional American Literature in the Library of Congress, and in 1958-1959 she was writer in residence at the University of Virginia. Although *Ship of Fools* is her major novel, she has written primarily short stories and novelettes.

Throughout her career Miss Porter has worked scrupulously and painstakingly, refusing to print anything until completely satisfied with it. Her devotion to her craft has been richly rewarded, for, although she has published comparatively little, she has achieved high distinction in the art of fiction.

Novel:
Ship of Fools (1962)
Short Stories:
Flowering Judas and Other Stories (1930, 1935)
Pale Horse, Pale Rider (1939)
The Leaning Tower and Other Stories (1944)

WILLIAM SYDNEY PORTER (O. Henry) 1862–1910

William Sydney Porter was born in Greensboro, North Carolina. After clerking in a drug store, he went to Texas, where he lived on a ranch and later became a bank teller. Accused of embezzlement, he fled to Central America only to return because of his wife's illness and (after trial and conviction) to serve a term of three years (1897-1900) in the federal penitentiary at Columbus, Ohio. While in the penitentiary he began to write short stories for the magazines under the pen name of "O. Henry." The last ten years of his life were spent in New York producing many stories which proved to be enormously popular all over the United States.

O. Henry's stories arc not great literature. They rely for their interest chiefly upon ingenuity of plot, and in style they are marked by a journalistic smartness. His work, however, has a social significance in that it describes aspects of New York which previous writers had missed.

Cabbages and Kings (1904)
The Four Million (1906)
The Voice of the City (1908)
Rolling Stones (1912)

KENNETH REXROTH 1905–

Kenneth Rexroth was born in South Bend, Indiana. Since he did not finish high school, it was mostly by means of self-education that he learned enough Latin, Greek, Chinese, and Japanese to translate poems from these languages into English. In the 1920's he made his home in San Francisco, where he was a columnist for the San Francisco *Examiner*, and where he co-founded the San Francisco Poetry Center.

As a leader of the "beatnik" movement, Mr. Rexroth has taken a stand against rich capitalists, the dull middle class, and academic critics, holding that these form part of "the social lie." He rejected this movement when, in his opinion, "the new bohemianism" became more a fad than a true rebellion. His poetry suffers sometimes from being a little vague and very vehement, but he represents the "beat" movement at its best.

Poetry:
In What Hour (1940)
The Phoenix and the Tortoise (1944)
The Signature of All Things (1949)
The Art of Worldly Wisdom (1949)
The Dragon and the Unicorn (1952)
In Defense of the Earth (1957)
Essays:
The Bird in the Bush (1959)

EDWIN ARLINGTON ROBINSON 1869–1935

Edwin Arlington Robinson was born in the village of Head Tide, Maine, and spent his youth in nearby Gardiner, the "Tilbury Town" of his poems. After finishing the high-school course in Gardiner, he entered Harvard, but he left after two years, returning to Gardiner to devote himself to the writing of poetry. In 1897 he moved to New York, where he lived for the rest of his life, except for summers spent, after 1911, at the MacDowell Colony near Peterborough, New Hampshire. He went to Europe once, but never traveled in the United States beyond New England and New York City. Unmarried, shy, and with little money, he lived quietly and inexpensively. In his lifetime he published over twenty volumes of poetry and was awarded the Pulitzer Prize three times.

Although Robinson writes in the New England tradition, the Puritan accent in his poetry is neither strong nor triumphant. His poetry is, in fact, modern in temper and reflects the New England tradition in its decay. His poetry is also modern in its diction, even though it is written in nineteenth-century forms.

The Children of the Night (1897)
Captain Craig (1902)
The Town Down the River (1910)
The Man Against the Sky (1916)
Merlin (1917)
Lancelot (1920)
Collected Poems (1921)
The Man Who Died Twice (1924)
Dionysus in Doubt (1925)
Tristram (1927)
Matthias at the Door (1931)

THEODORE ROETHKE 1908–1963

A native of Michigan, Theodore Roethke attended the University of Michigan, received his B.A. in 1929, and then attended the University's law school for a year. From 1930 to 1931 he studied at Harvard. In 1931 he took the position of instructor in English at Lafayette College. After receiving his Master's degree in 1936, he became an instructor of English at Pennsylvania State University and later taught at various other colleges. In 1954 he was awarded the Pulitzer Prize for his *The Waking*.

Roethke is much admired by critics of poetry. His poetry is sometimes logical and witty, sometimes purely evocative. His more lyric poems are both powerful and original.

Open House (1941)
The Lost Son (1949)
Praise to the End! (1951)
The Waking: Poems 1933-1953 (1953)
Words for the Wind (1958)
I Am! Says the Lamb (1961)

JEROME DAVID SALINGER 1919–

J. D. Salinger has been one of the most talked about but also one of the most retiring of contemporary authors. He has taken care to keep his private life out of view of reporters and photographers. He was born in New York City and went to school in that area. During World War II he served in France. He published his first story at the age of twenty-one and has since published frequently in *The New Yorker* and other magazines. Although his works are few in contrast to those by other well-known authors, they have been the subject of numerous critical and scholarly articles. Salinger's works deal in many instances with the world of sensitive children and adolescents who see through the "phony" exterior of the adults in the world around them.

Novel:
Catcher in the Rye (1951)
Short Stories:
Nine Stories (1953)
Franny and Zooey (1961)
Raise High the Roof Beam, Carpenters; and
    Seymour: an Introduction (1962)

CARL SANDBURG 1878–

Born in Galesburg, Illinois, Carl Sandburg left school at thirteen to drive a milk-wagon; later he was a porter and then a worker in a brickyard. He traveled a good deal (mostly on the underside of boxcars), stopping off to work here and there. During his enlistment for the Spanish-American War, he was persuaded by an alumnus that he ought to go to Lombard College at Galesburg. After working his way through Lombard, he became a traveling salesman of stereopticon slides, and he was engaged in this work when, in 1904, his first book, a little pamphlet called *In Reckless Ecstasy*, was published. A few years later Sandburg went to Milwaukee, working as labor reporter on Socialist Victor Berger's Milwaukee *Leader*. In 1908 he married Lillian Steichen, who, like him, was interested in the fortunes of laborers. In 1912 he and his wife drifted to Chicago, where he worked for several publications, notably the *Daily News*.

When *Poetry* was started in Chicago, Sandburg was one of its early contributors; and in 1916 his first book of poems to be put out by a nationally known publisher appeared. In fitting recognition of his talent, Sandburg was awarded the Pulitzer Prize for Poetry in 1950.

Meanwhile, Sandburg developed an interest in folklore. His great collection of ballads, gathered during his wide travels, was presented on many platforms and eventually published in 1927. Folklore also figured importantly when he turned to history and wrote his moving biography of an earlier midwesterner, Abraham Lincoln.

The poetry, ballad collection, and biography are all of a piece. They spring from Sandburg's desire to voice the thoughts and feelings he learned from the common people. His poetry is expressive of his times in both its form and its subject matter. It is free verse of the sort that was becoming fashionable when he started to write. He writes in the American vernacular, the richness of which was being discovered in his youth. He, like others, was bewildered by the shift from the agrarian way of living to industrialization and was resentful of the abuses that accompanied the shift. But, he, like others, found his hope and belief in the common man.

Poetry:
In Reckless Ecstasy (1904)
Chicago Poems (1916)
Cornhuskers (1918)
Smoke and Steel (1920)
Slabs of the Sunburnt West (1922)
Good Morning, America (1928)
The People, Yes (1936)
Complete Poems (1950)
Collected Poems (1951)
Harvest Poems, 1910-1960 (1960)
Songs:
The American Songbag (1927)
Nonfiction:
Abraham Lincoln: The Prairie Years (2 vols., 1926)
Abraham·Lincoln: The War Years (4 vols., 1939)
Novel:
Remembrance Rock (1948)
Autobiography:
Always the Young Strangers (1953)

DELMORE SCHWARTZ 1913–

Brooklyn-born Delmore Schwartz, teacher, editor, and critic, began writing poetry as a college student. In 1956 he took the position of poetry editor and occasional movie reviewer for *The New Republic*. He served on the staff of the *Partisan Review*, from 1943 to 1946 as editor, and from 1947 to 1955 as associate editor. He has lectured at New York University, Kenyon School of English, Harvard, Princeton, the University of Chicago, and Indiana University.

Schwartz' critical work is admired for its independent position, its soundness, and its depth of thought. His poetry and fiction are characterized by an ironic tone and a richly textured style.

Poetry:
In Dreams Begin Responsibilities (1938)
Shenandoah (1941)
Genesis (1943)
Vaudeville for a Princess (1950)
Summer Knowledge (1959)

Short Stories:
The World Is a Wedding (1948)

SAMUEL SEWALL 1652-1730

For nearly sixty years following his graduation from Harvard in 1671, Samuel Sewall was active in business and politics. For a period (1681-1684) he managed the colony's printing press; he spent a year in England (1688-1689), engaged in private business and assisting Increase Mather in his unsuccessful efforts to bring about the restoration of the colony's charter. He was captain, in 1701, of the Ancient and Honorable Artillery Company; and from 1718 to 1728 he was Chief Justice of the Superior Court of Massachusetts. Sewall was the only one of the three judges of the Salem witch trials ever to admit publicly that the court had been guilty of a grave error. But perhaps more worthy of note is his remarkably concise and suggestive *Diary* (1674-1729) which affords a rich and vivid picture of life in colonial Boston.

Autobiography:
Diary (1674-1729; published, 1878-1882)
Nonfiction:
The Selling of Joseph (1700)

KARL JAY SHAPIRO 1913-

Karl Shapiro was born in Baltimore, Maryland, the son of a Jewish father and a Catholic mother. A year at the University of Virginia, perhaps a shade more committed than most American colleges to the ancient cult of the "gentleman," was obviously painful. Shapiro was publishing poetry at twenty-one, and a slim collection, *Poems*, appeared in 1935. Between 1936 and 1940 he was a student at Johns Hopkins University. There he evidently read to good purpose, for his later verses reveal an acquaintance with a wide range of subjects and poetic devices. Selective Service caught him in 1941, and at the time Evelyn Katz, his fiancée, saw *Person, Place, and Thing* through the press in 1942, he was on active duty "somewhere in the Pacific." His postwar work has included a year as poetry consultant at the Library of Congress, teaching at Hopkins and at Nebraska and, 1950-1955, editing *Poetry, A Magazine of Verse*. He is presently editor of *The Prairie Schooner*.

Shapiro's *V-Letter and Other Poems* (1944) won the Pulitzer Prize for him at thirty-one. It, with his other work, is among the best records thus far available of what the war has done to his generation. Some critics have complained of a certain superficial cleverness in Shapiro's work, but the lasting impression is of an honest and intelligent man probing the great questions of life.

Poetry:
Poems (1935)
Person, Place, and Thing (1942)
V-Letter and Other Poems (1944)
Essay on Rime (1945)
Trial of a Poet and Other Poems (1947)
Poems of a Jew (1958)
Essays:
Bibliography of Modern Prosody (1948)
In Defense of Ignorance (1960)

HENRY WHEELER SHAW (Josh Billings) 1818-1885

Henry Wheeler Shaw was born in Lanesboro, Massachusetts. He prepared for college at Lenox Academy and then attended Hamilton College for about two years before he was expelled for a prank. At seventeen he migrated to the West. He was, at various times, a farmer, a coal operator, and a proprietor of an Ohio River steamboat before he returned to the East and settled down to be a real estate operator and an auctioneer in Poughkeepsie, New York. In the late 1850's, when some of his comic writings for newspapers were widely reprinted, he got off to a start as a successful funnyman. He moved to New York City and remained there the rest of his life.

Josh Billings, Shaw's creation, was famous not for stories but for essays or single sentences packed with amusingly phrased common sense. His kinship with Poor Richard was obvious, but his cacography showed that his writing was also related to that of such a contemporary as Artemus Ward.

Josh Billings, His Sayings (1865)
Josh Billings on Ice and Other Things (1868)
Josh Billings' Farmer's Allminax (1869-1879)

IRWIN SHAW 1913–

Irwin Shaw, novelist and short-story writer, was born in New York City, attended Brooklyn College, and was graduated in 1934. While in college he wrote a column for the student magazine and plays for the dramatic society. After graduation he wrote magazine fiction, dramas, serials for the radio, and then went to Hollywood to write screen plays. During World War II he served as a private in the United States Army Signal Corps in North Africa, the Middle East, Britain, France, and Germany. Out of this experience came *The Young Lions*, one of the most popular and highly regarded of the war novels. This was followed by short stories and novels on other aspects of the American scene.

Novels:
The Young Lions (1948)
The Troubled Air (1950)
Lucy Crown (1956)
Two Weeks in Another Town (1960)
Short Stories:
Sailor Off the Bremen (1940)
Welcome to the City (1942)
Act of Faith (1946)
Mixed Company (1950)
Drama:
Bury the Dead (1936)
Siege (1937)
The Gentle People (1939)
Retreat to Pleasure (1940)
Sons and Soldiers (1943)
The Assassin (1945)

WILLIAM GILMORE SIMMS 1806-1870

Though born in the most aristocratic of Southern cities, Charleston, South Carolina, William Gilmore Simms did not belong to the aristocracy. The death of his mother and his father's removal to Mississippi left the boy to the care of an impoverished grandmother. His schooling was irregular; for a time, he was apprenticed to a druggist. At the age of eighteen he visited his father in Mississippi, where he saw the mixed life of the frontier. After his return to Charleston, he first experimented in poetry and journalism and then turned to the writing of fiction, his first novel appearing in 1833. Two years later he achieved a popular success with *The Yemassee*. For a good while his works were more favorably received in the North than in his native city, where an eighteenth-century classical taste in literature persisted longer than almost anywhere else. By marriage in 1836 he connected himself with the planter aristocracy and acquired the country estate, midway between Charleston and Augusta, known as "The Woodlands." Here Simms wrote his books and entertained his friends.

In the 1850's he became the leader of a group of younger writers in Charleston, which included the poets Paul Hamilton Hayne and Henry Timrod; he was instrumental, together with the other members of the group, in founding the distinguished though short-lived *Russell's Magazine* (1857-1860). In the 1850's, also, he became an active opponent of abolitionism and contributed to the Southern manifesto, *The Pro-Slavery Argument* (Charleston, 1853). The Northern invasion of South Carolina inflicted severe personal hardships on Simms, among them, the burning of his house and the loss of a fine library.

Simms has often been regarded as a lesser Cooper, but this is an uncritical view because Simms' materials and methods were his own. Parrington compares Simms with the early English novelists, Henry Fielding and Tobias Smollett, and notes the element of the picaresque as particularly distinguishing his work from Cooper's.

> *Martin Faber* (1833)
> *Guy Rivers* (1834)
> *The Yemassee* (1835)
> *The Partisan* (1835)
> *Mellichampe* (1836)
> *Richard Hurdis* (1838)
> *The Border Beagles* (1840)
> *Katherine Walton* (1851)
> *Woodcraft* (1854)
> *The Forayers* (1855)

UPTON SINCLAIR 1878-

Upton Sinclair was born in Baltimore but brought up in New York, where he was graduated from the College of the City of New York in 1898. By then he was already earning his own living by selling stories and jokes. His first serious novel was published in 1901, shortly before he became active as a Socialist. The League for Industrial Democracy (formerly the Intercollegiate Socialist Society) and the American Civil Liberties Union are largely of his creation. Three times he has run for Congress and three times for the governorship of California. In *I, Governor of California and How I Ended Poverty* (1933) and other pamphlets he set forth his platform, EPIC (End Poverty in California). This program found wide public support in the early days of the New Deal, and he was very nearly elected. With eruptions of fascism and communism in Europe, Sinclair turned his attention to these phenomena.

Sinclair has always written with amazing fluency and a consequent unevenness. As a propagandist, akin in spirit to Thomas Paine, he has been found radical and unsound by conservatives; and extreme left-wing thinkers have condemned him for not adhering to the Marxist line. But of his earnestness and sincerity there is no longer much question. He is master of the literary method of "exposure," best shown in *The Jungle* (1906).

Novels:
The Jungle (1906)
King Coal (1917)
Oil! (1927)
Boston (1928)
The Wet Parade (1931)
Dragon's Teeth (1942)
It Happened to Didymus (1958)
Affectionately, Eve (1961)
Nonfiction:
The Brass Check (1919)
The Goose-Step (1923)
I, Governor of California and How I Ended Poverty (1933)
Autobiography:
American Outpost (1932)

JOHN SMITH 1579–1631

John Smith, known today mostly because of his lively travel accounts, in 1606 led the expedition which was to result in the first permanent British colony on this continent, and in 1614 he explored New England thoroughly from the Penobscot River to Cape Cod.

A True Relation (1608)
Map of Virginia (1612)
A Description of New England (1616)
The Generall Historie of Virginia, New England, and the Summer Isles (1624)

SEBA SMITH (Jack Downing) 1792–1868

Seba Smith was born in Buckfield, Maine, and lived in Buckfield and other Down East towns until he was twenty-three. He left school to work at odd jobs but eventually completed his education when, at twenty-six, he was graduated with honors from Bowdoin College. After some traveling he returned to Maine where he became assistant editor of the *Eastern Argus*. In 1829 he began his own newspaper, the Portland *Courier*, for which Smith invented the humorous character Jack Downing to say his say about contemporary politics. Jack was the first in the long line of common-sensible figures which included influential comic oracles such as Hosea Biglow, Josh Billings, Mark Twain, Mr. Dooley, and Will Rogers.

The Life and Writings of Major Jack Downing of Downingville (1833)
My Thirty Years Out of the Senate (1859)

WILLIAM DEWITT SNODGRASS 1926–

William DeWitt Snodgrass was reared in Beaver Falls, Pennsylvania. He attended Geneva College in 1943, but his education was interrupted by two years of service in the Navy. In 1946 he returned to Geneva College, where he received his B.A.

in 1947. At the State University of Iowa, where he studied under Robert Lowell, he received his M.A. in 1951 and his M.F.A. in 1953. He taught at Cornell University, the University of Rochester, and in 1959 became assistant professor of English at Wayne State University. In 1960 he won the Pulitzer Prize for his poems, *Heart's Needle*.

Though autobiographical in tone and nonacademic in spirit, the poetry of W. D. Snodgrass is polished and traditional in form. His undisguised concern with himself, the individual, is one of the unique and pleasing features of his poetry.

Heart's Needle (1959)

LINCOLN STEFFENS 1866–1936

Lincoln Steffens, a Californian whose father was indulgent up to a point, was graduated from the university of his native state in 1889. He spent three years in study in Europe, and while there he married a fellow American but neglected to inform his family of the fact. This caused him to lose his father's favor and financial assistance, but on his own he found a place, not too easily, on the New York *Evening Post* and was soon extraordinarily successful. By the investment of a small legacy from one of his Leipzig classmates he obtained financial freedom which enabled him to pursue with few restrictions the task he set himself—an understanding of the ethical implications of social and political processes.

Considered the founder of the school of "muckrakers," Steffens, in his explorations of corruption in government and business, came to believe that one could not lay all the blame for these abuses on "evil" individuals. He saw bribery and bossism, crime and organized vice as connected parts of a vast "System" for which citizens themselves, through their indifference and selfishness, were responsible.

Nonfiction:
The Shame of the Cities (1904)
The Struggle for Self-Government (1906)
Autobiography:
Autobiography (1931)

JOHN STEINBECK 1902–

John Steinbeck, born at Salinas, California, grew up in a rich but strike-tormented valley where he learned at first hand about the life of the agricultural and factory workers. From 1919 through 1925 he attended Stanford University, taking the courses that attracted him without worrying about degree requirements and dropping out now and then to work as a common laborer. Already determined to be a writer, he contributed to the university magazines. After leaving Stanford, he worked briefly as a reporter in New York City. Illness caused him to return to California, where he became a caretaker on a mountain estate. His first published book, *Cup of Gold*, said to be the fourth that he wrote, appeared in 1929. Steinbeck's popularity began with *Tortilla Flat* (1935), rejected by nine publishers before it was accepted by Covici. In 1940 he received the Pulitzer Prize for *Grapes of Wrath*, and in 1962 he was awarded the Nobel Prize for Literature.

Steinbeck has been called a primitivist, and it is true that he tends to glorify rudimentary folk. Yet, as Frederick Ives Carpenter has pointed out, he combines several of the great skeins of American thought: Emerson's mystical monism, Whitman's sense of democracy, and a pragmatic belief in effective action. Though aware of human failure, Steinbeck still creates in his characters a zest in living which is perhaps more essential for survival than an understanding of life.

Novels:
Cup of Gold (1929)
To a God Unknown (1933)
In Dubious Battle (1936)
Of Mice and Men (1937)
The Grapes of Wrath (1939)
The Moon is Down (1942)
The Wayward Bus (1947)
The Pearl (1948)
East of Eden (1952)
Winter of Our Discontent (1961)

Short Stories:
The Pastures of Heaven (1932)
Tortilla Flat (1935)
Cannery Row (1945)
Sweet Thursday (1954)

Autobiography:
Travels with Charley (1962)

Nonfiction:
The Sea of Cortez (1941)

WALLACE STEVENS 1879–1955

Wallace Stevens was born in Reading, Pennsylvania. His mother was of Pennsylvania descent and his father, a lawyer, of Dutch ancestry. After attending Harvard and New York Law School, Stevens entered law practice in New York City, and it was during his years as a lawyer that he began to publish poems in the newly founded *Poetry* and the more avant-garde New York magazine, *Others*. In 1916 he moved to Hartford to work for an insurance company, continuing his writing of poetry but not publishing his first volume, *Harmonium*, until 1923. In 1931 he published a revised version of this first book, adding a few new poems. Stevens' period of greatest productivity, however, did not begin until after 1934, when he became vice-president of the insurance company by which he was employed.

Stevens' matter and manner, divorced as they frequently were from the mundane, had relevance to one of his major concerns—loss of belief and direction from man's life. Though he did not go unappreciated during his early years as a poet, it was not until the 1930's and 1940's that his originality, his artistry, and his insights won for him a large audience and a place as a leading American poet.

Harmonium (1923; revised, 1931)
Ideas of Order (1935)
Owl's Clover (1936)
The Man with the Blue Guitar and Other Poems (1937)
Parts of a World (1942)
Notes Toward a Supreme Fiction (1942)
Transport to Summer (1947)
Three Academic Pieces (1947)

HARRIET BEECHER STOWE 1811–1896

Litchfield, Connecticut was the birthplace of Harriet Beecher. Her father was a

New England Calvinist, and one of her brothers the famous pulpit orator, Henry Ward Beecher. At fourteen, after an education in private religious schools, she became a teacher. Seven years later her family moved to Cincinnati, where Harriet taught in a seminary for a time. At twenty-four, she married Calvin Stowe, a member of the faculty, and in 1850 the Stowe family moved East.

From childhood, Mrs. Stowe escaped some of the grimness of her surroundings by imagining interesting adventures for herself. This imagination was of service to her when, in Cincinnati, she composed stories to be read to a literary club. The sale of some of these stories later brought important additions to the meager income of Professor Stowe. Somehow, while caring for her large family, Mrs. Stowe still found time to write numerous stories and sketches. Less sensational, but probably of more lasting value than her novels, were her works dealing with life in prewar New England, important contributions to the local color movement.

Novels:
Uncle Tom's Cabin (1852)
Dred (1856)
The Minister's Wooing (1859)
The Pearl of Orr's Island (1862)
Oldtown Folks (1869)
Poganuc People (1878)
Short Stories:
Sam Lawson's Oldtown Fireside Stories (1872)

WILLIAM STYRON 1925–

Although he has lived in the North for many years, William Styron, born in Newport News, Virginia, was reared in the South and regards himself as a Southerner. After graduating from Duke University, where he majored in English and was considered the "campus esthete," he worked for a few unhappy months as an associate editor in a publishing house. His first novel, *Lie Down in Darkness*, won him the Prix de Rome of the American Academy of Arts and Letters. It was the product of a short-story writing course at the New School for Social Research in New York City in which his teacher, Hiram Hayden, urged him to write a novel. Employing stream-of-consciousness he here recounts the downfall of a Southern middle-class family. The critics praised the book highly, comparing the young writer with Faulkner, Wolfe, and Joyce. Although Styron's later two books (*The Long March* and *Set This House on Fire*) perhaps do not live up to the promise of his first work, they have found many admirers.

Lie Down in Darkness (1951)
The Long March (1952)
Set This House on Fire (1960)

ALLEN TATE 1899–

Allen Tate, a distinguished member of the Nashville group headed by John Crowe Ransom, was born in Kentucky. He attended Vanderbilt, where he was graduated in 1922. Although engaged almost continuously in writing, he has found time for other employments: in the 1930's he was a member at different times of the English departments of Southwestern University at Memphis, the North Carolina Woman's College at Greensboro, and Princeton; in 1942-1944, he held the chair of poetry in the Library of Congress. Later, he taught at New York University. In 1951 he joined the English faculty of the University of Minnesota.

Tate and his Nashville associates are "reactionary" in the better sense of the word. They have sought to recover certain values of the past: the Southern cultural tradition, the religious point of view, and an intellectual fiber best exemplified in the poets of seventeenth-century England. The writings of this group have had wide influence on present literary criticism.

Poetry:
Poems: 1922-1947 (1948)
Essays:
Reactionary Essays on Poetry and Ideas (1936)
"Narcissus as Narcissus" (1938)
Reason in Madness (1941)

EDWARD TAYLOR c. 1645-1729

Very few biographical facts concerning Edward Taylor are known. He was born in Coventry, England. In 1668, at the age of twenty-two or twenty-three, he left England, presumably for liberty of conscience, and came to Boston, where he was cordially received by Increase Mather. He was admitted to Harvard College and was graduated in the Class of 1671. A lifelong friendship with Samuel Sewall, of the same class, dates from his college years. Following his graduation, Taylor became pastor of the church at Westfield, Massachusetts. He lived quietly at Westfield during the remaining fifty-eight years of his life, serving the community for that long period both as minister and as physician. Twice married, he had seven children by his first wife and six by his second. Taylor's poetry takes rank not only as the best poetry written in America before the nineteenth century but also as one of the classics of New England literature.

The Poems of Edward Taylor, ed. Donald E. Stanford (1960)

WILLIAM TAPPAN THOMPSON 1812-1882

William Tappan Thompson was born in Ohio and orphaned at fourteen. With background experience as a printer's devil, as a political executive in Tallahassee, Florida, and in newspaper, magazine, and printing work in Augusta, he became an editor of a weekly newspaper, *The Southern Miscellany*, published in Madison, Georgia, in 1842. It was in this newspaper that Thompson introduced the naïve but sensible Major Jones, the Georgian imitation of Seba Smith's Jack Downing. The letters of Major Jones, with their accurate use of the vernacular speech of Georgia, were clearly related to the humor based on the oral tale, so popular in the Southwest at the time.

Major Jones's Courtship (1843)
The Chronicles of Pineville (1845)
Major Jones's Sketches of Travel (1848)

HENRY DAVID THOREAU 1817-1862

Henry David Thoreau, born in Concord, Massachusetts, was graduated without distinction from Harvard College in 1837. After graduation he assisted his brother John for a while in teaching a private school. He also helped his father manufacture lead pencils in the 1840's; but he gave up pencil making because of a desire for fresh experiences. In 1839 he and John went on a famous journey, the literary record of which, *A Week on the Concord and Merrimack Rivers*, appeared ten years later.

Thoreau was a frequent contributor to *The Dial* from 1840 to 1844. In 1841, and again in 1847-1848, he was a member of Emerson's household, doing odd jobs. In 1838 Thoreau had delivered before the Concord Lyceum his first lecture and continued lecturing for many years. However, he was not very successful as a lecturer — much less successful and less popular than Emerson.

In 1845 Thoreau began his famous residence at Walden Pond. Two years later he left Walden, not from a sense of failure or disappointment but because of a desire to explore new modes of living. In 1846, during his residence at Walden, Thoreau was arrested because of his refusal to pay the poll tax and spent a night in the Concord jail. The reason for his rebellion was his opposition to Negro slavery and the movement to increase slave territory in the Southwest. He helped at least one fugitive slave to evade the Boston police and escape into Canada. Along with Emerson, he gave active support to John Brown. When the selectmen of the village refused to sanction a memorial service to Brown, Thoreau rang the bell of the town hall himself.

Thoreau had traveled a good deal in many places. His excursions to the Maine Woods, Cape Cod, Monadnock, and the White Mountains furnished material for much writing which appeared in part in magazines during Thoreau's lifetime and which was collected after his death. In 1856 he visited Whitman in New York, and in 1861 he traveled as far west as Minnesota, but his health was already failing. He died of tuberculosis in Concord in 1862 just before he reached his forty-fifth birthday.

Only in comparatively recent times has Thoreau attained his present high reputation. The growth of his fame has no doubt been owed not only to a recognition of his fine literary qualities but also to various special appeals which his works make to modern readers. His lessons in simplicity and economy have appealed to those who are harassed by the complexity and expense of modern life.

Essays:
"Civil Disobedience" (1849)
"Plea for John Brown" (1860)
Autobiography:
A Week on the Concord and Merrimack Rivers (1849)
Journal [The Journals] (1837-1861; published, 1906)
Walden; or Life in the Woods (1854)
The Maine Woods (1864)
Cape Cod (1865)

JAMES GROVER THURBER 1894-1961

James Grover Thurber was born in Columbus, Ohio, where he attended grade school, then high school, and finally Ohio State University. When World War I began, Thurber quit the university without completing his work for the B.A. degree. Unable to enlist because an accident in boyhood had blinded him in one eye and because the sight of his other eye had deteriorated, Thurber became a code clerk in the State Department in Paris and served until 1920. He next became a journalist, first on the Columbus *Dispatch*, then on the Chicago *Tribune* in Paris, then on the New York *Evening Post*. In 1926 he began selling to *The New Yorker*, and in 1927 he became a member of its staff. He served briefly as managing editor but resigned to devote a larger share of his time to writing. Since 1926 Thurber's drawings and writings have been featured by the magazine.

Thurber's humor, though whimsical, is far from sentimental. The unique outlook on which it is based may be one reason why many feel that Thurber is the greatest of modern American humorists. Certainly his clear style and versatility have also contributed to the admiration he has won.

Short Stories and Sketches:
Is Sex Necessary? (with E. B. White, 1929)
The Owl in the Attic (1931)
The Seal in the Bedroom (1932)
The Middle-Aged Man on the Flying Trapeze (1935)
Let Your Mind Alone (1937)
Fables for Our Times (1940)
The White Deer (1945)
The Beast in Me and Other Animals (1948)
The Thirteen Clocks (1950)
Further Fables for Our Times (1956)
Alarms and Diversions (1957)
Wonderful O (1957)
Drama:
The Male Animal (with Elliott Nugent, 1940)
Autobiography:
My Life and Hard Times (1933)
The Thurber Album (1952)
The Years with Ross (1959)

HENRY TIMROD 1828–1867

Henry Timrod attended the Coates School in Charleston, South Carolina—his birthplace—and studied for a year and a half at the University of Georgia. After trying the law, he turned to tutoring in planters' families. Later he was a contributor to *Russell's Magazine* (1857-1860), a journal of literary promise published in Charleston and edited by his friend Paul Hamilton Hayne. In 1861 Timrod enlisted in the Confederate army, but because of ill health he was able to serve less than a year. Undertaking the work of a war correspondent, he observed at close range the battle of Shiloh. In 1864 he edited a newspaper in Columbia, South Carolina; this position ended abruptly when Columbia was taken by Sherman's army. The three last years of his life were a losing struggle against poverty and disease. His poems were collected, with a memoir, by Paul Hamilton Hayne in 1873. Timrod's early verses were imitative of Wordsworth. The war called forth his latent originality and inspired his best poems in which he achieved a distinctive fusion of romantic and classical elements.

Poems of Henry Timrod, ed. P. H. Hayne (1873)

MARK TWAIN: see Samuel L. Clemens

ROYALL TYLER 1757–1826

After his graduation from Harvard in 1776, Boston-born Royall Tyler studied law and in 1780 was admitted to the bar. He practiced in Maine and later in Massachusetts. He took an active part in the suppression of Shays' Rebellion in the latter part of 1786, and in March of the following year he visited New York on a mission related to that uprising. There he saw his first play and within three weeks was himself a successful playwright. In 1791 he left Boston to settle in Vermont, where he lived the rest of his life. He was Chief Justice of the Supreme Court of Vermont from 1807 until 1813 and in 1811-1814 was professor of jurisprudence in the university of that state. .

In his nationalism, his Federalistic political views, his pursuit of literature as an avocation, and his easy mastery of the dominant literary types of his day, Tyler was akin in spirit to the Connecticut Wits. He is now known almost exclusively as the author of *The Contrast*, the first comedy by an American to achieve production by a professional theatrical company.

Drama:
The Contrast (produced 1787)
Novels:
The Algerine Captive (1797)
The Yankey in London (1809)

JOHN UPDIKE 1932–

John Updike, one of the youngest of the new novelists, was born in Skillington, Pennsylvania, served as an editor of the Harvard *Lampoon*, and was graduated from Harvard in 1954. He spent a year at the Ruskin School of Fine Arts in Oxford, and on his return to the United States he joined the staff of *The New Yorker*. Seven of his works have been published—collections of poetry and short stories as well as three highly acclaimed novels (*The Poorhouse Fair*, *Rabbit, Run*, and *The Centaur*). He is still a frequent contributor of poems and stories to *The New Yorker*. Updike has been praised for his sensitivity to the "dislocations of modern life" and for his stylistic virtuosity.

Poetry:
The Carpentered Hen (1958)
Telephone Poles and Other Poems (1963)
Short Stories:
The Same Door (1959)
Pigeon Feathers (1962)
Novels:
The Poorhouse Fair (1959)
Rabbit, Run (1960)
The Centaur (1963)

ARTEMUS WARD: see Charles Farrar Browne

ROBERT PENN WARREN 1905–

Robert Penn Warren was born in Guthrie, Kentucky, and took his B.A. at Vanderbilt (in the class of 1925), his M.A. at the University of California, and his B.Litt. at Oxford. He has taught at Vanderbilt, Louisiana State University, the University of Minnesota, and at Yale, first as Professor of Dramatic Composition and since 1961 as Professor of English. At Vanderbilt he was a member—along with John Crowe Ransom, Donald Davidson, Allen Tate, and others—of the now famous group of poets known as "Fugitives." At Louisiana State University, he was co-editor (with Cleanth Brooks) of the influential and important *Southern*

Review (1935-1942) and co-author (also with Brooks) of a revolutionary textbook, *Understanding Poetry* (1938).

Though Warren is certainly an admirer of Faulkner, and though his fiction doubtless resembles Faulkner's in some ways, he is no mere disciple. He possesses certain advantages conveyed by a more academic and more cosmopolitan experience. He is in a sense, therefore, less provincial than Faulkner, but his truest work, like Faulkner's, is at once Southern in its origins and universal in its meanings.

Poetry:
Thirty-Six Poems (1936)
Brother to Dragons (1953)
Promises (1957)
Criticism:
Rime of the Ancient Mariner by S. T. Coleridge (1946)
Selected Essays (1958)
Novels:
Night Rider (1939)
At Heaven's Gate (1943)
All the King's Men (1946)
World Enough and Time (1950)
Band of Angels (1955)
The Cave (1959)
Wilderness (1961)
Short Stories:
The Circus in the Attic and Other Stories (1947)

EUDORA WELTY 1909–

A native of Jackson, Mississippi, Eudora Welty still makes her home in the town in which she was born. Although she remained close to home by attending the Mississippi State College for Women, she left the state to study at the University of Wisconsin and Columbia, and she worked at various writing and publicity jobs before she began to write seriously about the small-town Mississippi life so familiar to her. Her novels and short stories have won many awards.

Characteristic of Miss Welty's work is the accurate reproduction of colloquial speech for comic effect and the creation of characters whose personalities are a grotesque and at times symbolic combination of the ordinary and the eccentric.

Novels:
The Robber Bridegroom (1942)
Delta Wedding (1946)
The Ponder Heart (1954)
Short Stories:
A Curtain of Green (1941)
The Wide Net (1943)
The Golden Apples (1949)
The Bride of the Innesfallen (1955)

WALT WHITMAN 1819–1892

The son of a carpenter, Whitman was born on Long Island and spent his early life there, in Brooklyn, and in New York. He attended the public schools of

Brooklyn, read omnivorously, and listened to Elias Hicks, a Quaker preacher. Other early experiences included participating in a debating society, working in printing offices, and teaching country schools on Long Island and "boarding round." In the 1840's he was connected with various newspapers, including the Brooklyn *Daily Eagle*, which he edited in 1846-1847. His knowledge of American life was further enlarged in 1848 by a leisurely journey down the Ohio and Mississippi to New Orleans, a stay of two or three months in that city, and the return journey by way of Chicago and the Great Lakes. Upon his return to Brooklyn, he resumed journalistic work and assisted his father in building houses.

Whitman was not a soldier in the Civil War, but he was none the less one of the war's real heroes. He served indefatigably as a volunteer nurse in the Washington hospitals, distributing knickknacks among the soldiers, writing letters home, radiating cheerfulness and the will to live. He also visited the camp hospitals of the Army of the Potomac in Virginia. His hitherto magnificent health suffered under the strain and exposure. In the summer of 1864 he was ill with "hospital malaria," from the effects of which he never fully recovered. In 1873 he had a paralytic stroke, and he continued a partial invalid during the remaining nineteen years of his life.

Whitman's poetry was original and revolutionary and indisputably American. He broke with the conventions and traditions of English verse. He employed free rhythms, which are comparable with those of the Old Testament. There have been, and still are, sharp differences of opinion as to the absolute merit of his work as poetry. Intellectual critics object to his emotionalism and vagueness; formal critics to his lack of close structure; academic critics to his apotheosis of the uncultivated. But there can be no question of his power and influence.

Poetry:
Leaves of Grass (1855; revisions, 1856, 1860, 1867, 1871,
    1876, 1881-1882, 1889, 1891-1892)
Drum-Taps (1865)
Sequel to Drum-Taps (1865-1866)
Essays:
Democratic Vistas (1871)
Autobiography:
Specimen Days and Collect (1882)

JOHN GREENLEAF WHITTIER 1807-1892

Born on a farm near Haverhill, Massachusetts, educated in country schools, long a worker on his father's farm and at the cobbler's bench, John Greenleaf Whittier saw things through the eyes of a common man, and his words were drawn from nature rather than art. From Robert Burns, his first and most important model, he learned a simple style of versifying which pleased ordinary readers. A member of a religious sect which had contributed many great opponents of the slave system, Whittier followed the promptings of his Quaker Inner Light to work zealously for reform.

He was mostly self-educated and was an energetic man in spite of his poor health. For several decades Whittier devoted a large share of his energy to the antislavery cause. He was successful in practical politics, winning his own election to the Massachusetts legislature in 1835, acting as a lobbyist at the State House, and giving assistance to political leaders who were helpful to abolitionism. As a pamphleteer, as a poet, and as an editor of various periodicals, notably of the *National Era* (1845-1860), he attacked slavery ferociously.

After the war Whittier turned to a field of work in which he had already shown proficiency—the portrayal of the rural New England life which he knew so well. It was as a local colorist that he did his most distinguished work. In these poetic writings he followed the tradition represented before his birth by the poet of Scottish rural life, Robert Burns, and carried on in the work of Robert Frost.

Poetry:
Legends of New England (1831)
Mogg Megone (1836)
Poems Written During the Progress of the Abolition
   Question . . . (1837)
Lays of My Home and Other Poems (1843)
Voices of Freedom (1846)
Songs of Labor and Other Poems (1850)
Home Ballads, Poems, and Lyrics (1860)
In War Time and Other Poems (1863)
Snow-Bound (1866)
The Tent on the Beach and Other Poems (1867)
Among the Hills and Other Poems (1869)
Ballads of New England (1870)
At Sundown (1890)

Novel:
Leaves from Margaret Smith's Journal (1849)

RICHARD WILBUR 1921 –

After graduating from Amherst College in 1942, Richard Wilbur went to Harvard University, where he received his M.A. in 1947. From 1950 he was Assistant Professor of English at Harvard; in 1954 he became Associate Professor at Wellesley; and in 1957 Professor at Wesleyan University. In 1957 he received the Pulitzer Prize for Poetry for his *Things of This World*. He has translated some Molière, Guillén, and Quasimodo.

Though Wilbur is fundamentally an intellectual poet, his sophistication has not cut him off from an understanding of things beyond his immediate world. His poetry is always disciplined and often light in spirit, but his concern about the problem of atomic power has brought to his poetry very serious moments.

The Beautiful Changes (1947)
Ceremony and Other Poems (1951)
Things of This World (1956)
Poems 1943-1956 (1957)
Advice to a Prophet (1961)

ROGER WILLIAMS 1603?–1683

Roger Williams, a Puritan and the first vigorous proponent of the separation of church and state, was originally a student of divinity in the Anglican Church, but, unable to tolerate the measures of Charles I, he eventually sailed for Massachusetts. Because of his independent thinking in religious matters and his defense of the rights of the Indians, he was forced to leave Massachusetts for what is now Rhode Island, where he set up the independent government of the Providence

Plantation. Williams has an honored place in American history as the first vehement supporter, both in his actions and in his writings, of the principle of freedom of thought.

A Key into the Language of America (1643)
The Bloudy Tenent of Persecution for the Cause of Conscience (1644)
George Fox Digg'd out of His Burrowes (1676)

TENNESSEE WILLIAMS 1914–

Born in Mississippi, Tennessee Williams received part of his higher education in that state. However, he took his B.A. degree at the State University of Iowa in 1938. Even as a boy he was fond of reading and interested in writing, but not until 1940 did his writing ability gain recognition when he won a thousand-dollar fellowship to write a play. The outcome of his efforts was *Battle of Angels*, which, though itself unsuccessful, was later rewritten as *Orpheus Descending* (1957). Success came in 1945 with the production of *The Glass Menagerie*. He later won Pulitzer Prizes for both *A Streetcar Named Desire* and *Cat on a Hot Tin Roof*.

Williams' plays are characterized by their concern with the psychologically sick who often express themselves in violent actions. The significance of these plays, however, is based on their expression of the lack of love among men. His *Night of the Iguana* is the fullest statement of his philosophy.

Drama:
Battle of Angels [Orpheus Descending, 1957] (1940)
The Glass Menagerie (1945)
A Streetcar Named Desire (1947)
Summer and Smoke (1948)
The Rose Tattoo (1951)
Camino Real (1953)
Cat on a Hot Tin Roof (1955)
Suddenly, Last Summer (1958)
Sweet Bird of Youth (1959)
Period of Adjustment (1960)
The Night of the Iguana (1961)
Novel:
The Roman Spring of Mrs. Stone (1950)

WILLIAM CARLOS WILLIAMS 1883–1963

William Carlos Williams was born in Rutherford, New Jersey. After graduating from the University of Pennsylvania he continued into the medical school and received his M.D. in 1906. Following his internship and a year in Leipzig studying pediatrics, he set up practice in Rutherford, where he remained throughout his entire medical career. The year 1909 not only marked Williams' return to his home town; it was also the year that he published *Poems*, the first of many works that include poetry, fiction, plays, and translations.

Some have criticized Williams for his imagistic tendencies, but it is these tendencies which have contributed to his tight, clear style. Though Williams is a precise writer, he is by no means a traditionalist. His poetry, unrhymed, eccentric in meter, is, in fact, representative of the works of those poets who adopted free verse as the means of achieving the feeling of American speech. The quality of his attention to the simple descriptive statement won for him enthusiastic followers who in the 1930's organized into a group called the Objectivists.

Poetry:
Poems (1909)
The Collected Later Poems of William Carlos Williams (1950)
The Collected Earlier Poems of William Carlos Williams (1951)
The Desert Music (1954)
Journey to Love (1955)
Sappho (1957)
Autobiography:
The Autobiography of William Carlos Williams (1951)

JOHN WINTHROP 1588-1649

John Winthrop, lawyer and author of his *Journal* or *The History of New England* (1630-1649), was the first governor of the Massachusetts Bay Colony and was eight times reëlected. A devout Puritan, he shared his wealth with others and spent much of his time promoting the good of the colony. Though now he is read chiefly in his *Journal*, his series of letters to his third wife, Margaret, is worthy of note as perhaps the finest picture of a happy Puritan marriage in our literature.

"A Modell of Christian Charity" (1630)
The History of New England [*Journal*] (1630-1649)

JOHN WISE 1652-1725

John Wise, Harvard graduate and Congregational minister, became involved in politics in 1687, when Governor Edmund Andros ordered the Massachusetts towns to appoint commissioners to collect taxes levied by the governor and council. The town of Chebacco, with Wise as one of the leaders, refused. Wise was charged with sedition, jailed in Boston, fined, suspended from the ministry, and forced to post a bond for good behavior. In 1688, however, Edmund Andros was chased out of New England. Wise became the champion of democratic, local control in church and, by implication, in state. His *Vindication* was the first colonial book to discuss "natural rights" and to show faith in the adequacy of man's reason in the construction of good government. It was, consequently, widely read during the Revolution.

Wise has been described by Moses Coit Tyler as "the most powerful and brilliant prose-writer produced in this country during the colonial time," and by Vernon Louis Parrington as "the keenest mind and the most trenchant pen of his generation of New Englanders."

The Churches Quarrel Espoused (1710)
A Vindication of the Government of New-England Churches (1717)

THOMAS WOLFE 1900-1938

Thomas Wolfe was born and brought up in Asheville, North Carolina, which is situated high in the Smokies and is described with remarkable completeness in his *Look Homeward, Angel*. After graduating from the University of North Carolina, Wolfe studied at Harvard, taught at New York University, and traveled in England and France. On his visits to Europe he was able to concentrate on his writing. While still at the height of his career he became ill with pneumonia and died.

Wolfe was a great romantic genius with all the vitality, the exuberance, the undisciplined ardor which the name implies. He was Wordsworth's "creature moving about in worlds not realized." His closest affinities were with Coleridge, whom he often quoted, and with Whitman, whom he obviously emulated. His prose at its best has a lyrical exultation; at its worst, it is so unpruned as to verge on the bombastic. But more eloquently than any other writer since Whitman, Wolfe restated the American dream: the right of every man "to live, to work, to be himself, to become whatever thing his manhood and his vision can combine to make him."

Look Homeward, Angel (1929)
Of Time and the River (1935)
The Web and the Rock (1939)
You Can't Go Home Again (1940)

JOHN WOOLMAN 1720–1772

John Woolman was born on a farm on Rancocas Creek, midway between Burlington and Mount Holly, New Jersey. There he lived until he was twenty, learning to love the Quaker way of life in his family, the village school, and the weekly Meeting. He then went into a shop in Mount Holly, five miles away, and in his spare time learned the tailor's trade. Soon he felt the call to visit other Meetings, as was the custom of those Friends who wished to become ministers and elders in a sect which had no professional clergy. His tact, his literary skill, and, most of all, his unimpeachable sincerity made him successful in Quaker politics and action, and he was chiefly responsible for consolidating Quaker sentiment for the emancipation of Negro slaves. His inclination to help arouse the English Quakers to the importance of this cause sent him to England in 1772. He arrived in London in June, visited Friends there and in the neighborhood, and then, wishing to go to the North, chose characteristically to walk rather than have any part in the oppression of postboys and horses. He got as far as York, where he died of smallpox.

The sweet reasonableness of Woolman's writings and the apparent carelessness in their organization clothe a keen and penetrating intellect, stored with the rich wisdom of the Bible and of personal experience, and directed by convictions which are often revolutionary.

Some Considerations on the Keeping of Negroes (Part I, 1754; Part II, 1762)
A Plea for the Poor (1837)
The Journal (published, 1774)

HERMAN WOUK 1915–

Herman Wouk, a native of New York City, was graduated from Columbia University with honors in 1934. He worked for a number of years as writer for various radio comedians and assisted the comedian Fred Allen in writing weekly radio scripts. During World War II, he served for three years as an executive officer aboard a destroyer minesweeper in the Pacific. His Pulitzer-Prize winning novel, *The Caine Mutiny* (1951), draws upon his wartime experiences. *Marjorie Morningstar* was praised as a fine account of a young woman of the Jewish middle class.

Novels:
Aurora Dawn (1947)
The City Boy (1948)
The Caine Mutiny (1951)
Marjorie Morningstar (1955)
Drama:
The Traitor (1949)
Nature's Way (1958)
Autobiography:
This Is My God (1959)

61, 107, 129, 324; and science, 18, 52; and treatises, 26, 58, 59

Frederic, Harold, 185, 288

Free verse: and Stephen Crane, 172; and Lanier, 172; and Masters, 229; in modern poetry, 229, 231; and Whitman, 142, 229

Freeman, Mary E. Wilkins, 151, 180, 289

Freneau, Philip, 8, 45, 47, 52, 54, 55, 60, 270, 289; and romanticism, 56, 57, 61

Frontier, The, 4, 94, 134, 181, 192, 226; after the Civil War, 159-162; in drama, 135, 136; and humor, 161, 178; in literature, 159-162; see also The West and Westward expansion

Frost, Robert, 206, 224, 225, 290, 336; and diction, 232-233; and humor, 226-227; theory of prosody, 229-230, 232

Fuller, Margaret, 75, 76, 285

Garland, Hamlin, 151, 291; and realism, 185-186; and social criticism, 156

George, Henry, 156, 268, 291

Ginsberg, Allen, 236, 292, 303

Gothic influence, 63; and Faulkner, 201; and Hawthorne, 81, 102, 103; and Poe, 92, 101

Grayson, William J., 129, 130, 292; and European tradition, 139; and slavery, 124, 128

Green, Paul, 218

Hamilton, Alexander, 13, 43, 44, 46, 47-48, 50, 55, 59, 292

Hariot, Thomas, 5, 7, 9, 18, 23

Harris, George Washington, 161, 179, 180, 293

Harris, Joel Chandler, 151, 152, 175, 180, 293

Harte, Bret, 151, 177, 180-181, 279, 294

Hawthorne, Nathaniel, 72, 78, 80, 82, 203, 240, 285, 286, 294, 297, 302; and Calvinism, 76, 77, 86, 93, 102; and the Civil War, 122, 198; and European tradition, 103, 162; and the Gothic influence, 81, 102, 103; and literature, 76, 77, 81, 102-104; and Melville, 89, 90, 91, 104, 105, 311

Heller, Joseph, 249

Hellman, Lillian, 221

Hemingway, Ernest, 188, 203, 205, 216, 238, 267, 295, 315; and detail, 241; and plot patterns, 244; and psychology, 245, 246; and war, 199, 247, 249

Herne, James A., 191

Hersey, John, 248

Higginson, Francis, 6, 24

Histories, 22, 27-28, 58; and Henry Adams, 163-164

Holmes, Oliver Wendell, 79, 106, 296, 297; and essays, 97-98; and European tradition, 97-98, 108, 109; and poetry, 109-110, 111, 112, 171; and science, 76, 88, 97

Hopkinson, Francis, 46, 47, 60

Howells, William Dean, 157, 158, 162, 176, 203, 297, 302, 313; and Hawthorne, 82; and realism, 184-186

Humor, 95, 97, 128; in the American Renaissance, 106-107; of Clemens, 155, 181-183; in folk songs, 176, 177; and the frontier, 161, 178; in local color, 152; in modern fiction, 177-180, 249, 250; and realism, 183; of Robinson, 226-227; serious, in poetry, 225-228

Hutchinson, Anne, 12, 13

Imagery: and Dickinson, 173, 174; and T. S. Eliot, 228; and Hawthorne, 103-104; and Lanier, 172; and Melville, 104

Imagination: in drama, 218; logic of, in poetry, 227-228

Imperialism, 169-171

Indians, 4, 7, 8, 9, 18, 23, 50, 94; in literature, 33, 135, 137

Individual, The, 204-205, 208, 250

Industrial Revolution, in America, 79-81

Industrialism: 1914 to the present, 201; in the American Renaissance, 73, 79-81, 94; after the Civil War, 152-153; during the Civil War, 120, 124; in colonial literature, 8; criticism of, 156-158; in the new republic, 44, 45, 49, 50

Inge, William, 221-222, 297

Irving, Washington, 45, 48, 49, 50, 53, 58, 61, 65, 180, 298; and European tradition, 54, 162; and romanticism, 56, 57, 105

Jackson, Andrew, 42, 43, 48, 77, 78, 79, 94

James, Henry, 188-190, 274, 299; and European tradition, 163, 313; and psychology, 189-190, 245; and realism, 189; and social criticism, 157-158

James, William, 168-169, 171, 189

Jarrell, Randall, 236, 249, 300

Jeffers, Robinson, 202, 205, 226, 231, 233, 300

Jefferson, Thomas, 3, 7, 13, 43, 47-48, 49, 52, 53, 55, 58, 59, 63, 83, 129, 301

Jewett, Sarah Orne, 151, 180, 274, 301

Jones, James, 248, 302

Kaufman, George, 218, 219, 221

Kennedy, John Pendelton, 93, 94, 95, 105, 123, 302, 318

Kerouac, Jack, 250, 303

Slavery, 4, 12, 44, 213; in the American Renaissance, 73, 91, 94; and the Civil War, 84-86, 120-122; in literature, 90, 122-124, 125-127, 137, 138, 151; and religion, 123, 124, 125, 128

Smith, John, 5, 7, 8, 9, 15, 18, 23, 27, 326

Smith, Seba (Jack Downing), 106, 107, 177, 180, 227, 325, 330

Snodgrass, William DeWitt, 236, 326

Social criticism: after the Civil War, 154-159; in drama, 220-221, 223; and muckrakers, 156-158; after World War I, 199-202

South, The, 84, 95, 149; and the Civil War, 120-122, 140, 149-150; and literature, 91, 108, 125, 249; in local color, 151-152; religion and politics of, 93-94

Spirituals, 174

Steffens, Lincoln, 156-157, 171, 327

Steinbeck, John, 188, 203, 206, 238, 242, 244, 245, 247, 327; and psychology, 245; and social criticism, 202, 210

Stevens, Wallace, 227, 228, 229, 231, 234, 235, 328

Stowe, Harriet Beecher, 123, 158, 265, 328; and local color, 180, 181; and slavery, 123

Stream-of-consciousness, 243, 246

Styron, William, 249, 329

Superstition, 17-18

Symbolism: of Henry Adams, 164; and allegory in Hawthorne, 102-103; and allegory in Melville, 90, 104-105; of Stephen Crane, 187; and detail, 240; in drama, 190, 192, 219, 220; of Faulkner, 201; of Hemingway, 241-242; of Inge, 222; of Moody, 192; of Norris, 187; of Thoreau, 99

Tate, Allen, 231, 234, 235, 249, 277, 329, 333; and literary criticism, 224, 237

Taylor, Edward, 21, 31, 173, 330

Theater; see Drama

Thompson, William Tappan (Major Jones), 128-129, 130, 161, 179, 182, 330

Thoreau, Henry David, 49, 80, 83, 91, 98-99, 129, 330; and Emerson, 76, 99, 100; and European tradition, 99, 113, 162; and poetry, 112-114, 142; Puritan influence on, 77; and science, 76, 88, 99; and slavery, 85, 86, 121; and Transcendentalism, 76, 112, 113

Thorpe, Thomas Bangs, 178, 179, 182

Thurber, James Grover, 271, 331

Timrod, Henry, 125, 126, 139, 140, 325, 332

Tracts and treatises, 26, 46, 58-59

Transcendentalism, 72, 88, 164; and Dickinson, 166; and Emerson, 75, 100, 112, 126, 166; and Thoreau, 76, 99; and Unitarianism, 52, 75; and Whitman, 126, 165

Turner, Frederick Jackson, 82, 160

Twain, Mark: see Clemens, Samuel L.

Tyler, Royall, 45, 47, 62, 64, 192, 332

Uncle Remus: see Harris, Joel Chandler

Unitarianism, 13, 51, 73, 76; and Calvinism, 73; and Quakerism, 74; and Transcendentalism, 52, 75

Universalism, 52

Updike, John, 250, 252, 333

Utopianism, 16, 76, 108, 158, 200

Ward, Artemus; see Browne, Charles Farrar

Warren, Robert Penn, 236, 237, 243, 249, 333

Washington, George, 13, 43, 47, 50, 52, 59

Webster, Daniel, 123; and oratory, 130-133, 135, 140; and slavery, 124

Welty, Eudora, 249, 334

West, The, 45, 53, 81-84, 91, 153; and democracy, 77, 78; and dialect poetry, 177; and humor, 161, 177-178, 227; in literature, 82, 108; and music, 81, 83, 107

Westward expansion, 44, 50, 81, 159, 160, 162

Whitman, Walt, 12, 94, 95, 125-127, 140-143, 154, 162, 165, 172, 206, 225, 229, 280, 303, 327, 334, 338; and diction, 142-143, 232, 233; and Emerson, 126, 140, 141, 165; and the frontier, 159-160; and reunion, 149-150; and slavery, 121, 140; and Transcendentalism, 126, 165

Whittier, John Greenleaf, 79, 82, 126, 180, 289, 335; and poetry, 112, 123, 125, 139, 171, 176; and slavery, 84, 123, 125, 139

Wigglesworth, Michael, 29, 60, 73

Wilbur, Richard, 236, 336

Wilder, Thornton, 219

Williams, Roger, 7, 13, 17, 25, 26, 336

Williams, Tennessee, 221, 223, 266, 298, 337

Williams, William Carlos, 236, 337

Wilson, Edmund, 245-246, 287, 316

Wilson, Woodrow, 48, 199, 208, 212

Winthrop, John, 10, 16, 21, 27, 28, 270, 338

Wise, John, 17, 26, 338

Wolfe, Thomas, 205, 206, 238, 242, 243, 244, 247, 302, 315, 329, 338

Wood, William, 6, 24

Woolman, John, 12, 26, 29, 49, 51, 59-60, 339

World War I, 152, 159, 192, 208, 238; stories of, 198-199, 249

World War II, 152, 208, 209, 244; novels of, 247-249

Wouk, Herman, 248, 339

Yarnspinning, 177-179